Eastern Galactic Civilization

----- Unifying Religion, Philosophy and Science

John Chang

Here is a poem as evidence:

Chinese divine culture, the laws of the universe; break through the Stellar system, Galactic civilization.

No need to go into the mountains, no need to believe in religion; have the opportunity to read this book, the epiphany of the grand road.

Pyramid faith, Egypt and Maya; Australian red monoliths, brilliant light.

Freedom and democracy, the constitutions of Europe and America; the future of the world, hopefully greater.

Publishing:

Jul, 2024 1st edit Chinese ISBN 978-1-7635480-2-2
Jan,2025 1st edit English ISBN 978-1-7635480-7-7

Universal publishing

ISBN: 978-1-7635480-7-7

Author：John Chang (Hai Zhitao)

About the author:

John Chang (Hai Zhitao), born in 1961 in Beijing, P.R.China, is a member of the Australian Society of Authors.

On September 11, 2001, he was enlightened by the laws of the universe as a result of fishing in a rainstorm and the rain hitting the water surface.

In November 2003, he published his frist book 《Universal Law》; in January 2007, he completed the second book 《Golden Classic》; in 2008, he edited 《Chinese Systems Philosophy》 and 《Oriental Systems Literature》, with nearly 600 participating writers; in September 2013, he completed 《Great Ultimate Theory》; in October 2015, he wrote 《Crop Circle》; in April 2018, he finished 《World Systems Science》; in 2024, he completed 《Memoirs of Beijing No.51 Middle School》 and 《Eastern Galactic Civilization》.

At the same time, he successively founded the “Universal Law Association”; “Universal Publishing" ; “Universal Law Super University”; “Universal Law Art Painting house”, and vigorously disseminated the Universal Law in the world.

Reference website: http://www.universal-law68.com

One. Preface

In ancient times, there were three most famous Chinese cultural classics: discussions on unification, systems, and prophecies. They are:

1) 《I Ching》 (Book of Changes), edited and perfected by King Wen of the Zhou Dynasty. (Exploration of Eastern Religions)

2) 《Tao Te Ching》 , written by the scholar Laozi during the Spring and Autumn and Warring States periods. (Exploration of Eastern Philosophy).

3) 《Tui Bei Tu》 , written by the Tang Dynasty ministers Yuan Tiangang and Li Chunfeng. (Science of mind discussion in the East)

As a more in-depth comparison, analysis, summary, and expansion of the above three books, this book collects, organizes, and edits a large number of articles from past years. It is a summary of all thought works, showcasing the beginnings of Eastern innovative thinking, new culture, new civilization, and a new renaissance. It continues the concept of the unification of Chinese civilization, unifying religious beliefs, philosophical ideas, and scientific culture.

This book serves as a textbook for the Universal Law Academy, written for future generations in the hope that they can understand it.

Academic Thought Battle Fleet of the Galactic Civilization:

1) Early layout book: 《Memories of Beijing No. 51 Middle School》 (Black-colored book)

2) Mid-game strategy books: 《Crop Circle》, 《Golden Classic》, 《Universal Law》, 《Great Ultimate Theory》, 《Chinese Systems Philosophy》, 《Oriental Systems Literature》, 《World Systems Science》 (Seven-colored books)

3) Late endgame book: 《Eastern Galactic Civilization: Unifying Religion, Philosophy, and Science》 (White-colored book)

Practical Publishing Fleet of the Stellar System Civilization:

1) Ancient books: All Kinds of Books on Worshiping Crooked and Cultic Masters and False Gods and Religions.
2) Middle age books: All kinds of feudal dictatorship books that glorify the long-lived emperor.
3) Modern books: All kinds of single-subject weapons practical examination tool books.

This is a collection of Eastern Sinology studies that spreads belief in the Pyramid Civilization, or Atlantis Civilization, and attempts to unify all current Religions, Philosophy, and Science.

But in this world controlled by the Church of Stellar Civilization, it will inevitably cause controversy. Thanks to Australia's tolerance, this real-life continent of Atlantis carries the world's highest thoughts and wisdom.

Prophecy No. 67 of the 3rd Age of Nostradamus:

"A new sect of Philosophers,

Despising death, gold, honors and riches.
Will not be bordering upon the German mountains:
To follow them they will have power and crowds."

From left: Gong William, Luo Shan, Hai Zhitao

Commentary by Writer Yu Xiurong:

Mr.John Chang (海之涛 Hai Zhi Tao) is a man who contemplates with his eyes raised to the sky; he should be considered an advanced thinker among humans.

In the distant past, people often looked up at the sky and pondered, which led to the creation of primitive religions and their development into various modern religions. However, as productivity has advanced, humans have increasingly looked down at the ground, driven by more material interests.

Thus, modern human thought can be categorized into three aspects:

1) Human to Human: This is known as practical social science.

2) Human to Earth: This is known as practical natural science.

3) Human to Heaven: This should be what you refer to as the laws of the universe.

The first two are thoughts from the primary stage of human development. The last one, however, represents the advanced stage of human thought. Modern human thinking has not yet moved beyond the realms of human and earthly concerns. Only a very few who transcend these concerns engage in advanced human thought: the universal laws!

I wish you greater success!

By Mr. Xiurong, Yu (余岫榮)

Author of《Citizen Enlightenment》

(December 12, 2020)

Commentary by Writer Liang Xiaohui:

After reading Mr.John chang (海之涛 Hai Zhi Tao)'s 《Universal Law》, I am struck by its philosophical depth, standing at a vantage point that overlooks all others. In this book, Mr.John explains the universe, civilization, life, natural science, and social science through the theories of points, lines, and circles. He believes that while points, lines, and circles may seem simple, their philosophical implications are profound. They represent the highest laws of the universe, covering a vast range from the microcosm to the macrocosm. “Points” represent the origin and essence of things, “Lines” represent the path of development, and “Circles” symbolize the cycle and completeness of things.

Even more impressive are the prophecies within the book. The first edition of this book was published in November 2003, and I read the sixth edition from 2006. On page 226, the book predicts: "Around 2009 will be a turning point; P.R.China will enter a period of decline until 2039, possibly because the current system cannot adapt to social development, leading to intensified social conflicts." Reflecting on the past few years, it seems that Mr.John's prediction has come true.

Overall, Mr.John's 《Universal Law》 is ambitious in its simplicity. It is a work of profound philosophy and foresight. Not only does it provide a new understanding of the universe and civilization, but it also offers deep insights into the future. This is a masterpiece that has expanded my thinking.

By Ms. Xiaohui, Liang (梁晓晖)

Author of 《Midnight Dialogue – Once Upon a Time in Hakka Meixian》

(June 3, 2024)

In the back row, the author is the first from the left, Yaqing is the second from the left, Li Dongsheng (Secretary-General of Shihua) is the fourth from the left, and Yanzi is the fifth from the left.

Front row: Xue zhiyuan, second from left, Gao Juying, third from left, Zhou Changli, sixth from left.

(The writers from World Chinese writers Association)

Table of Contents

Four. Unifying Science

Finally: Jinsheng's daughter

Back row: Jinsheng, Hai Zhitao, Luo Shan, Luo Dingxian, XXX.

Front row: Sai Shenxian, Liu Haiou, Ya Qing, Laura, Li Mingyan, Wu Runyang **(Writers from Sydney, Australia)**

Two. Unifying Religion

Chapter Summary:

The classic work on the unification of civilization, 《Tao Te Ching》 , was written by the independent scholar Laozi during the Spring and Autumn period:

"There is a thing, formed in chaos, Born before Heaven and Earth. Silent and void, It stands alone and does not change, Goes round and does not weary, It can be the mother of Heaven and Earth. I do not know its name, but I call it Tao, And I name it as great. Great means passing away; Passing away means going far; Going far means returning. Therefore, Tao is great, Heaven is great, Earth is great, and man is also great. There are four greats in the domain, and man is one of them. Man models himself on Earth, Earth models itself on Heaven, Heaven models itself on Tao, Tao models itself on Nature."

Pioneers of Civilization Unification were individual thinkers:

1) Satellite System Civilization: Pioneer of civilization unification – Mr.Aristotle

2) Planetary System Civilization: Pioneer of civilization unification – Mr.Ptolemy

3) Stellar System Civilization: Pioneer of civilization unification – Mr.Copernicus

4) Galactic System Civilization: ?

Oppressive Groups and Parties:

The pioneers of civilization unification were independent and transcendent individual thinkers. The opposition mainly comes from domestic or large surrounding groups of religious believers. Although Mr.Jesus, Mr.Buddha, Mr.Muhammad, and Mr.Marx were ordinary people with simple thoughts and prophecies, the churches and parties they founded, along with all the subsequent derivative sects, most of them have turned into cults and mental illnesses, have been oppressors of civilization at various stages. To maintain the authority and so-called divinity of their founders, their followers control propaganda, build ruthless armies, and slaughter awakened thought propagators, like Mr.Galileo and Mr.Bruno, and this continues to this day.

In this world, everyone is unique. Some are good at sports, some are good at philosophy, and some are good at art.

A1. The Universe Establishes the "Universal Law" According to Its Form

Abstract: The universe has no other form but the "Explosion form". To create celestial bodies, animals, and plants, it must follow the ".", "1", "0" rules, also known as the "Universal Law".

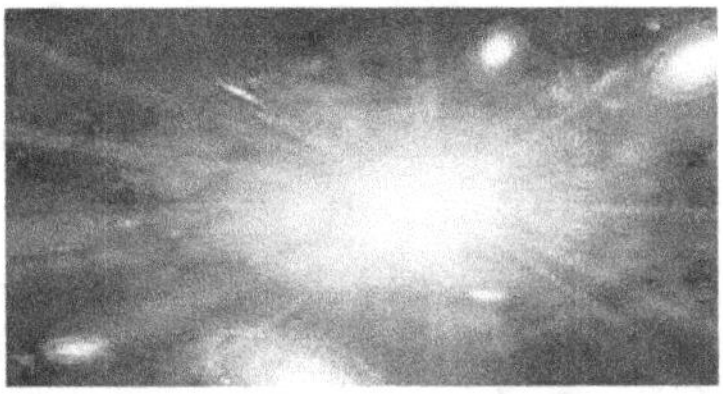

Fig. A1-1 The Big Bang

To date, no field of science, philosophy, or religion has provided an explanation of how God created planets, animals, and plants. Specifically, science has only the theory of "Universal gravitation", philosophy has no explanation, and religion offers only the concept of "Truth and goodness".

Without explanations, deceit prevails. Universities engage in plagiarism for titles, churches exploit the worship of their leaders for profit, and governments engage in ideological worship. If the government deceives, it won't oversee other deceptions in society, inevitably leading to counterfeit goods in healthcare, education, and daily necessities.

Scientists often attack religious believers as mentally unstable for kneeling to pray to Allah, God, and religious leaders or being scammed by strange religious leaders. Religious believers, in turn, attack scientists as pragmatists. The greatest pragmatism is serving the state by developing weapons to threaten the world. Philosophers are currently seen as sophists, blending ancient scholars' thoughts into "Chicken soup for the soul" and forcing it on the world.

Globally, governments fund various universities' educational budgets and students' tuition, amounting to hundreds of billions of dollars annually. Governments, businesses, and individuals also fund so-called religious charities, reaching trillions of dollars annually, much of which evades taxes and partly ends up in the pockets of cultists and funds terrorists.

If we had a theory that could convince scientists, philosophers, and religious leaders, wouldn't it save much of the educational funding? And if religions were unified, wouldn't it save much charitable funding and prevent wars? Wouldn't we see a peaceful era with the Sun and Moon shining brightly, and all falsehoods (Referring to various governmental, religious, and academic deceptions) subdued?

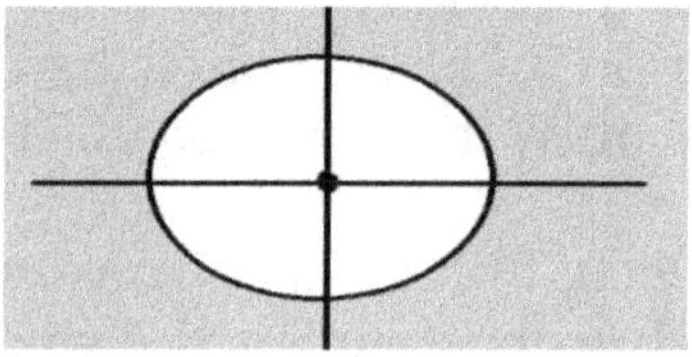

Fig. A1-2 ".","1","0" or "Point","Line","Circle" form

Now, I will present such a theory. Why is ".", "1", "0" or the "Universe's own 'explosion'" form the "Universal Law"?

When the universe exploded from a point, didn't its form resemble ".", "1", "0" (See photo) Fig. A1-2.

The Bible says: "God created man in his own image". In reality, the universe has only one form, the explosion form. It created a law according to this form, the Universal Law, and then created animals, plants, and celestial bodies according to this law, including humans. This corresponds to the prophecy in the Old Testament, which is wonderful. Thus, religious people have no argument against the concept of the "Universal Law".

On the other hand, the ".", "1", "0" theory is a form, not a formula or theory. Using this form to explain any material change is called "Metaphysics". The Chinese translation "Metaphysics" is derived from the 《I Ching • Xi Ci Shang Zhuan》 (《易经•系辞上传》): "What is above form is called the Tao, what is below form is called a tool". We believe that using form to explain all knowledge is the highest form of knowledge. In this respect, philosophers also accept our theory.

For scientists, when the universe exploded, its explosive matter broke through the calm space-time, causing space-time ripples. Space-time is essentially the medium ether, which can bend. Although the Michelson-Morley experiment proved there is no "Ether", the bending of space-time suggests that space-time is the "Ether".

Fig. A1-3 Water Drop

It's like a stone thrown into calm water, causing ripples; water is the medium. But space-time ether is a vacuum, not affecting light experiments.

Why is this so? Because time and space are energy, the ripples demonstrate the law the universe must follow. This law is the ".", "1", "0" rule, the Universal Law.

Furthermore, Mr.Einstein's theory of relativity derives the "Mass-energy equation", which presents the "." form; Mr.Newton's theory of universal gravitation presents the "0" form; and Mr.Maxwell's equations present the "1" form. The three major physical theories follow the ".", "1", "0" theory, meaning scientists also accept our theory.

From these arguments, we can say that the ".", "1", "0" theory convinces religious, philosophical, and scientific communities, unifying all natural science, philosophical, and religious theories. The mystery of how the universe created celestial bodies, animals, and plants is partially revealed.

In summary, the universe has no other form but the "Explosion form". To create celestial bodies, animals, and plants, it must follow the ".", "1", "0" rules, also known as the "Universal Law". The resulting civilization is called "Galactic Civilization" (Completed around year 2012, corresponding to the Mayan prophecy). Previous civilizations are collectively referred to as "Stellar System Civilization".

(Written in May 2017)

A2. All Humanity Believes in the Universal Law

Abstract: Sperm (Possessing "." and "1" characteristics) explores the Universal Law by merging with an egg (Possessing "." and "0" characteristics). Only through this union can' the three characteristics (".", "1" and "0") be realized. Every person born is the unconscious union both a sperm and an egg that understands the Universal Law, becoming a follower of the "Universal Law Galactic Civilization".

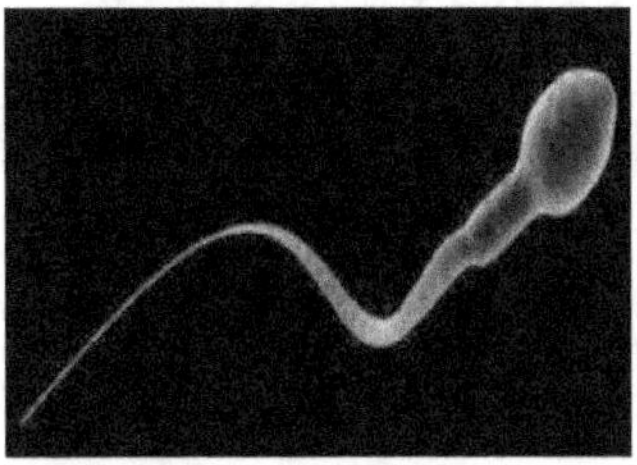

Fig. A2-1 Sperm

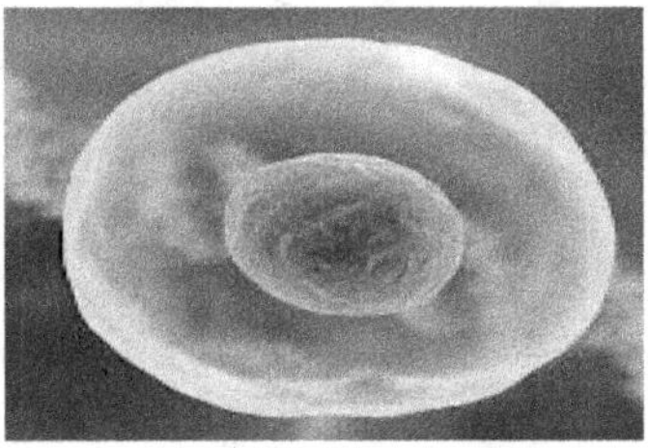

Fig. A2-2 Egg

Billions of sperm (Possessing "." and "1" characteristics) are exploring the Universal Law by merging with an egg (Possessing "." and "0" characteristics). Only through this union can the three characteristics (".", "1" and "0") be realized. Most sperm die during this exploration, but one succeeds, resulting in fertilization and becoming a human.

Each person born is the unconscious union both a sperm and an egg that understands the Universal Law, making him or her a follower of the Universal Law Galactic Civilization. Once born and conscious, and speaking, they enter the Stellar Civilization environment, forgetting the Galactic Civilization's Universal Law and getting deceived into various Stellar Civilization religions. When they believe in other religions instead of the Universal Law, their wisdom degrades. Seduced by the guise of truth and goodness, they are driven out of Eden (The Galactic Civilization), leading to mutual wars among Stellar Civilization religious believers, as described in the Old Testament.

If "Truth and goodness" were genuinely good, why wouldn't God allow belief in them? Because God knows these priests, pastors, and false monks exploit "Truth and goodness" to attract followers, collect money, commit wrongdoings, and kill.

The Galaxy can be seen with powerful telescopes and high wisdom, you are unconsciously feeling and being controlled . The Stellar System is visible and tangible, such as the Sun, having the most significant influence to you, just like family and close friends. Thus, lower Stellar Civilization religions have the greatest impact on people.

Accepting the Universal Law or Galactic Civilization is like using a powerful telescope to see a larger space. Understanding that from the moment of fertilization, you are a follower of the Universal Law Galactic Civilization, along with all living beings (Including animals and plants). After birth, influenced by the practical Stellar Civilization religions like Christianity, Buddhism, or Islam, but our book can helps you remember that you are already a follower of the Universal Law Galactic Civilization, fertilized, enlightened, baptized, and wise from the moment of sperm-egg union. Regardless of your post-birth faith, this understanding brings you back to Eden, the Galactic Civilization, under God's protection, preventing the slaughter of innocents.

The religion you believe in determines your level of wisdom. For example, if a monkey believes it can live by picking fruit in the trees for millions of years, it cannot easily adapt to farming for survival. Similarly, telling billions of long-term religious believers to follow the Galactic Civilization and avoid wars is also challenging.

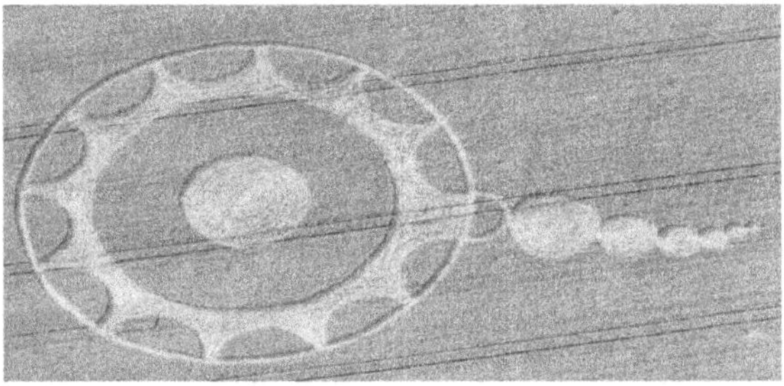

Fig. A2-3 Crop Circle Illustrating the Sperm and Egg Fertilization Process

In the womb, no priest or master guides the sperm to fertilize the egg; it independently explores and succeeds. All sperm become human through their arduous efforts, understanding the Universal Law. Likewise, knowledge taught by teachers or priests is outdated and copied, not original. The same applies to all plants, animals, and celestial bodies ----- they explore. Understanding this means transcending teachers, masters, and religious leaders, and not worshipping anyone. Independent exploration and transcendence embody belief in the Universal Law.

Lower Stellar Civilization religions revolve around people and followers, teaching some truth and goodness, then leading to degeneration. They emphasize worshipping leaders, masters, or priests, using various methods to deceive and suppress thoughts. They never teach transcendence.

Over the past 5,000 years, lower Stellar Civilization religions spread historical events and emotional benevolence, falsely worshipping Gods under names like

God and Allah. For primitive, slave, and feudal societies, this stabilized society. However, through worship, these religions competed for followers and territories, causing wars and creating refugees, taking many believers' lives.

Early polytheistic worship with chieftains, and then centralized in temples, monasteries, churches, etc., funded by numerous followers. Later, worship included local deities, emperors, and even cult leaders, focusing on people and names, offering emotional charity for marriages, births, and deaths.

These Stellar Civilization religions only brought stability to small regions, causing conflicts when spreading further. As their leaders were often illiterate and recorded by disciples, worshipping low-level Gods led to conflicts and wars.

Crop circle revelations indicate that the Universal Law Civilization will unify all Stellar Civilization religions. However, due to their long history and large following, this unification won't come through war but through integration into the Galactic Civilization.

The Universal Law Civilization won't use surgical removal like Western medicine, but holistic treatment like traditional Chinese medicine. As a unified Galactic Civilization, it focuses on spiritual healing without harming anyone, destroying temples, monasteries, or churches, while retaining the lower emotional charity of Stellar Civilization. Names will be adjusted, e.g., "Universal Law Stellar Buddhism"; "Universal Law Stellar Christianity", etc. Their temples and churches will become centers for spreading the unified wisdom of the Galactic Civilization, also propagating the primary emotional charity of Stellar Civilization. True unification will be achieved without the historical religious wars, much like the coexistence of oviparous and viviparous species.

Currently, Stellar Civilization religions resemble the chaotic Mayan civilization before European arrival, with constant wars. Although some religions are mild, they are primitive and ignorant, worshipping idols and false Gods, torn apart by barbaric religions in the name of Allah. The Universal Law Civilization's arrival on Earth will unify lower Stellar Civilization religions into the higher Galactic Civilization without the destruction seen in historical European-Mayan encounters.

Summary:

1. Galactic Civilization

- Main Buildings for Universal Law Galactic Civilization: Pyramids in Australia, Egypt, and Mexico (Key global locations)
- Main Educational Centers: Crop circles and public schools worldwide (Key global locations)
- Technological Testing Sites: Universities, research institutes, and laboratories worldwide (Major global cities)

2. Stellar Civilization

- Secondary Buildings for Universal Law Stellar Civilization: All Buddhist temples, Christian churches, and other lower faith buildings globally (Widely distributed among the populace)
- Secondary Educational Centers: Various religious schools and training centers globally (Widely distributed among the populace)
- Technological Testing Sites: Various practical technology schools (Widely distributed in cities)

3. Main Differences between Galactic and Stellar Civilizations

- Galactic Civilization: Belief shared by all celestial bodies, animals, plants, and humans, without leaders, emperors, or false Gods, spreading the Universal Law, including unified natural, social, and life sciences.
- Stellar Civilization: Belief held only by humans, worshipping leaders, emperors, and false Gods, gathering followers, power, and money, spreading human history or virtues like benevolence, righteousness, propriety, wisdom, and trust.

Fig. A2-4 Evidence of Extraterrestrial Civilizations, showing the four major Western Stellar Civilization religions with the most followers ------ Christianity (Cross); Islam (Crescent); Buddhism (Circle), and Communism (Star) ----- all unified under the "Eastern Universal Law Galactic Civilization". In reality, the kingdom of God appears in different eras, bringing missions and strength to different nations.

(Original work from June 2016)

A3. On Faith and Civilization

Abstract: Wrong beliefs mislead people, distort history, and result in countless deaths. Faith is the greatest issue and spiritual support on this planet. Without resolving this issue, even the most advanced society and science will be destroyed. Unifying these lower Stellar Civilization religions is an inevitable choice for the future.

Having faith is better than having none, but having wrong faith is worse than having none. Wrong faith leads to killings, wars, and disasters, as countless historical facts have shown.

True Faith:

- It does not rely on books written by religious leaders or followers' records of their words.
- It does not believe in leaders claiming to be Gods, sons of Gods, or messengers.
- It does not idolize these people or anyone.
- It observes natural phenomena, such as animals, plants, and celestial bodies.
- It believes in eternal, undeniable things.

Wrong Faith:

- It is based on books written by religious leaders and their nonsense.
- It relies on followers' records of leaders' words.
- It follows the political environment of the time.
- It follows religious leaders who oppose government corruption or advocate for national interests.

- It incites public opinion for revolution or power.

Wrong faith misleads people, distorts history, and causes countless deaths. Faith is the greatest issue and spiritual support on this planet. Without resolving this issue, even the most advanced society and science will be destroyed. For example, Muslims using one plane knocked down America's most advanced Trade Center. The most advanced democratic system can be also destroyed by corruption, money, and revolutionary killings.

Thousands of years ago, civilizations emphasized morality, and religions stressed goodness, but despite this emphasis, they still slaughtered. Followers worshipped leaders ignorantly while preaching morality. Many leaders claimed they could make followers wisdom, yet their writings and recorded words lacked wisdom. How could they make followers wise?

Many followers blindly worship idols of leaders, believing only in one leader and one religion, excluding others. How can they gain wisdom? After thousands of years, true wisdom and rational civilization have arrived, unifying all so-called moral emotional religions, worshipping no leader, philosophy, or science.

Examples of Wrong Faiths:

- Christianity and Catholicism worship leaders exaggerated as sons of God, heavenly kings, and virgin-born deities.
- Buddhism worships leaders who could not write or say anything meaningful, with followers making baseless claims and collecting money.

- Islam worships a leader who was illiterate, exaggerated by followers as a messenger, and continues to massacre infidels.

- Nazi worship glorified Hitler, who was nominated for the Peace Prize and became a national hero, leading to wars and genocides.

- Modern worship gathers public support with anti-corruption, anti-revolution, and truth and goodness slogans, establishing larger church organizations. Refugees and the uneducated are the main forces, with leaders claiming divinity and master status.

Examples from history include:

- Zhang Jiao of the Yellow Turban Rebellion in the late Han Dynasty, using Daoist truth and goodness to oppose the emperor.

- Hong Xiuquan in the Qing Dynasty, using Christian benevolence to oppose the Qing emperor.

- Mao zedong during the Republic of China, using European Marxist revolution to oppose the government.

- Li hongzhi in the Republic of China, using Indian Buddhist law wheel (Falun) to oppose communism.

Almost all these low-level Stellar Civilization religions have been used by peasant uprising armies and ignorant churches to oppose society and the "Fake righteous emperors", also promoted by Eunuchs and party newspapers.

True Faith and Civilization:

- We promote natural laws to show the world, truly developing Chinese civilization, benevolence, righteousness, propriety, wisdom, and faith, unifying religion, philosophy, and science.

- Extraterrestrial Galactic Civilization reveals that all religions of the Solar System civilization will be unified.
- Christian and Buddhist leaders also predicted the end of their religions, to be unified by the Galactic or Chinese Eastern Civilization.
- Communism has suffered a major blow since the Soviet Union's collapse, with only a few countries struggling. The Gods still punish them with pollution, water hazards, and food poisoning. Soon, this faith will be suppressed and eradicated worldwide.
- Islam is on the decline, massacring civilians and oppressing women. Many countries are legislating against public oppression of women and restricting Islamic schools and buildings. Soon, this faith will be banned globally.

The Future we will see that Eastern or Chinese civilization will once again demonstrate its great vitality, unifying the world not by force but by culture and civilization. The Universal Law, the common faith of all humanity, will continue to grow worldwide, becoming the future direction of Solar System civilization.

(Written in Sep. 2016)

A4. Nostradamus' Prophecy on Eastern Civilization

Abstract: Under the dark rule of the church, Copernicus independently unveiled the "Stellar Civilization", creating five hundred years of Western scientific and technological civilization. To this day, it continues to expand powerfully. But once the lid on the revival of Eastern civilization is lifted, do you know what will happen?

----

1. Introduction

Nostradamus (Latin name, December 14, 1503 - July 2, 1566), originally named Michel de Nostredame (French name), was a French Jewish prophet proficient in Hebrew and Greek. He wrote his famous collection of prophecies, known as 《Les Propheties》 or 《The Centuries》 in quatrains format, first published in 1555. Over time, many researchers have found that many historical events were accurately predicted in these short poems, with a correctness rate of over 95%. Most of his prophecies have come true over the past five hundred years.

2. Nostradamus' Prophecies about Eastern Civilization

Although there have been many controversies about Nostradamus' prophecies over the years, with some attributing them to coincidence, others claiming they are forced interpretations, and some even reaching the level of worship, this is quite normal. This is because the thoughts of prophets are not something that ordinary people can understand. If you try to explain them with common sense, it certainly won't work. It's like a Qigong master who can strike people from a distance. If you ask modern physicists to explain it, they will say it violates the laws of physics. Even if you knock down all the experts from a distance, they can't explain it because no law can account for such low-probability events. Not everyone has this ability.

The same goes for famous prophets throughout history. Over thousands of years, billions and billions of people have lived on Earth, but there have only been a few dozen true prophets, with only a handful being top-tier. The numbers are too small to produce universal laws. But don't worry, in the near future, people will understand. It's like some people only see things in their home; others can see the Earth; some have already seen the solar system, and more have seen galaxies.

Here we present a few of his prophecies about Eastern civilization, which astonishingly predict the emergence of a "Galactic Civilization based on Universal Law", Which poem is it? Look here:

Fig. A4-1 Nostradamus

Century VII, Quatrain 14:

"He will come to expose the false topography,
the urns of the tombs will be opened.
Sect and holy philosophy to thrive,
black for white and the new for the old."

This poem predicts the arrival of the "Galactic Civilization based on Universal Law", mainly concerning religion and philosophy. Why do we say this? From the line "Sect and holy philosophy to thrive", it becomes apparent.

Additionally, what are the "Water urns of historic significance" in the poem? Doesn't this resemble the related Chinese prophecy, where Mr.Liu Bowen (刘伯温) mentioned "Old water" in his 《Burning Book》, referring to the longevity water in the ancient urn, signifying those who spread sects and holy philosophy.

Nostradamus' prophecies not only align with the《Book of Revelation》 in the Bible, but also match many ancient and modern Chinese prophecies.

The following two poems predict the future, where after the completion of the "Galactic Civilization based on Universal Law", Eastern civilization becomes exceptionally powerful, impacting Western civilization and involving religion.

Century X, Quatrain 65:

"O vast Rome, thy ruin approaches,
Not of thy walls, of thy blood and substance:
The one harsh in letters will make a very horrible notch,
Pointed steel driven into all up to the hilt."

Century XVII, Quatrain 9:
"The learned enemy army
Sways back and forth to the right and left,
Huge camps, plague,
Ambushed and defeated, Pyrenees,
Venice, Alps, not their things,
Near rivers, ancient tombs discovered."

Previously, these prophecies seemed unlikely, suggesting the East would invade the West in the future. However, after the arrival of the divine Eastern culture and the "Galactic Civilization based on Universal Law", these predictions become very possible.

"O vast Rome, thy ruin approaches", implies the end of Christian civilization or the "Stellar Civilization" represented by Rome, corresponding to the prophecy of the last Pope in Rome.

They swept across Europe, reaching the heart of the "Stellar Civilization" (Brought by Copernicus), which is the cradle of the European Renaissance ----- Rome. This signifies the triumph of the "Oriental Renaissance" over the "Western Renaissance", and the "Galactic Civilization" over the "Stellar Civilization".

Could it be that a future Eastern army will aggressively attack? Does this mean the armies representing Christianity and Islam will have collapsed by then? Otherwise, how could a currently weak Eastern army, unable to defeat even its neighboring small countries, so easily reach Rome? And who led this force?

"The one harsh in letters" is that the Eastern pictographic script? Deeply engraved on the golden dome of the Vatican ---- how amusing! Although theoretically possible now, in terms of actual warfare and an Eastern offensive reaching Rome, it's hard to say.

3. Summary

Let's analyze the future situation. In Copernicus' time, under the oppressive rule of the church, everyone was afraid. Yet, he independently uncovered the "Stellar Civilization", creating five centuries of Western scientific and technological civilization, which continues to expand powerfully. What immense strength!

In contrast, the East, under the combined suppression of imperial power and religious authority for thousands of years, has seen countless deaths in constant resistance. But once the lid on the revival of Eastern civilization is lifted, do you know what will happen?

Because Europe has been pressed under a volcano for only a few hundred years, while the East has been under one for thousands of years. The future revival of Eastern civilization, once it erupts, will unleash a powerful stream of Eastern cultural energy that will sweep across the universe. As prophesied by the original teachings of Buddhism with the "Turning of the Dharma Wheel"; the Christian "Rainbow Covenant"; the Mayan "Seven-Color Warriors"; Laozi's Daoist prophecy of the "Beginning of Heaven and Earth and the Mother of All Things", and others, an Eastern civilization will be created that will last a thousand years. This civilization will bring forth ten super masters from the East, combining "Technology and life" and "Life and wisdom", far surpassing the "Stellar Civilization" brought about by Western civilization.

Civilization will inevitably lead to the strength of the nation. By then, the Eastern civilization will command the world, incorporating the entire wisdom of humanity into the "Galactic Civilization", or directly joining the "Galactic Civilization" family. This will not only be a form of science and technology but also a combination of wisdom and soul energy ----- a blend of religion, philosophy, and science. The five major religious systems of the West, Eastern and Western philosophical systems, and all current university science and technology will be unified under Eastern civilization, an energy so vast, unparalleled in history.

Why will the East surpass the West in the future? Because the West's few hundred years of democracy have been too successful, they have developed ideological burdens and dare not make breakthroughs. In the next 500 years, no masters will emerge from the West, just as the East, under thousands of years of feudalism, has not seen a master since Copernicus introduced the "Stellar Civilization".

However, since around year 2012, the East created the "Galactic Civilization based on Universal Law", leading to a significant shift in the overall mindset of Easterners in the future. The rulers of China may no longer follow Western ideologies and dogmas, having newfound confidence and awakening.

In the future, we can once again see that the Western "Phonetic script civilization" (Used by most countries worldwide) can only reach the "Stellar Civilization", while the Eastern "Pictographic script civilization" (Used by Chinese, Egyptian, and Mayan civilizations) can directly achieve the entire "Galactic Civilization". This exactly confirms the prophecies of both ancient and modern times.

Aristotle brought the "Satellite System Civilization"; Ptolemy brought the "Planetary System Civilization"; Copernicus brought the "Stellar Civilization"; and now, in year 2012, the "Galactic Civilization" has been created. The Chinese Han (汉) civilization in the East has already occupied the high ground of world civilization. Without any warfare, it unified global religion, philosophy, and science, directly influencing the thoughts and civilizations of the next 500 years, while awaiting and welcoming the arrival of the "Cosmic Civilization". The course of human history is already very clear.

(Written in April 2019)

References:

1. Nostradamus: 《The Centuries》

A5. Jesus Christ as the Passover Sacrifice and the Galactic Civilization Sacrifice

Abstract: Reflecting on how today's world civilization has reached a new turning point, where global thoughts are in great turmoil. What is the reason behind this? For Western civilization, it is particularly challenging. If they abandon the belief that Jesus is God and Christianity, they essentially give up their traditions and history. However, if they continue to accept Jesus as God, it means they will continue to battle against Islam, which stemmed from Christianity, or maintain the Stellar civilization while rejecting the Galactic civilization. Jesus now becomes the focus again, being the Passover sacrifice who was believed to have been resurrected, but now becomes the sacrifice for the Galactic civilization.

There is a story: In ancient times, before going to war, people would pull out a sheep as a sacrifice. Other sheep would envy the chosen one, wondering why it was selected. They would speculate, "Why was it chosen and not us? Could it be different from us? Surely, the chosen sheep must be extraordinary, perhaps even a son of humans!"

The sheep destined for sacrifice would cry out desperately, "I entrust my life to humans! Don't kill me, don't abandon me!" But no matter how it cried and prayed for mercy, humans were indifferent. A single cut, and it became a pre-war sacrifice.

From then on, this sacrificed sheep became an idol among its companions. They revered it as a human's son and spread their worship, claiming it now sits at the right hand of humans, becoming one of them.

The flock would pray to humans for all their needs, believing it was effective. Some sheep even avoided slaughter and died a natural death. Clever sheep then realized they could help others pray and worship humans, thus securing food for themselves as a reward.

Every week, the flock would gather, singing and dancing, worshiping the sacrificed sheep as a human. They firmly believed it was the son of humans, destined to rise again.

Similarly, our wisdom level, seen by extraterrestrials, is akin to that of cats and dogs.

Jesus was a sacrifice killed during the Passover by highly intelligent aliens (Christians call them God or Jehovah).

Why choose this timing for his death? Because extraterrestrial beings had already grasped the historical progression of Earth's humanity, aligning this event with a future breakthrough in the Galactic civilization.

After the establishment of Christianity, numerous derivative churches emerged. Throughout history, they were often cruel, combining church and state, fabricating lies, and suppressing dissent. Priests or pastors frequently judged and killed the innocent in God's name, with church doctrines becoming law. Philosophers like Mr.Bruno were killed this way, and Mr.Galileo and Mr.Copernicus were also judged during the so-called Dark Ages.

Thus, extraterrestrial beings conveyed messages through spiritual transmission, inspiring Muhammad to establish Islam, orchestrating the birth of Islam. Muslims named the extraterrestrial being who enlightened them "Allah".

The purpose of this extraterrestrial named "Allah" was to curb the atrocities of Christians and maintain global peace and stability. Consequently, countless wars ensued between Christians and Muslims. Christians, after numerous wars, reflections, and enlightenment, eventually led to the Italian Renaissance and later democratic constitutionalism.

Unexpectedly, Muslims became even more bloodthirsty, frequently killing in the name of "Allah," mirroring the early deeds of Christians, resulting in countless innocent deaths.

Western civilization, through the Renaissance, developed materialism, idealism, metaphysics, and atheism, spreading globally, opposing Christianity and Islam. However, have they truly liberated humanity? It's another lie. If they are truly advanced, why restrict publishing and media?

We acknowledge that Western civilization, through centuries of thought and enlightenment, and painful lessons, began developing science and technology from around the 16th century, now very mature. Currently, global education systems primarily derive from the West, with top talents advancing a unified scientific and technological system. Their most successful humanistic development is freedom, democracy, and the rule of law, limiting the powers of the church and emperors.

Chinese divine culture, the Universal law, and Galactic civilization have birthed the "Great Ultimate Theory", an innovative educational theory system from the East, different from Western religious, philosophical, and scientific theories. It doesn't develop churches, incite masses, propagate lies, or amass wealth and power. With just paper and pen, it unifies all Religions, Philosophies, and Sciences.

This is the extraterrestrial civilization depicted in Crop circles, and the ancient prophecies of Eastern civilization unifying the globe without weapons, killing, or destroying temples, and without making fame or virtue, illuminating China.

Once we understand the historical trajectory of Earth's civilization, we enter the crossroads of Stellar and Galactic civilizations. What is the greatest resistance to human civilization's evolution now? Here is another story.

A fly and a swift were good friends. One day, the swift said to the fly, "You should evolve quickly, see how high and far we fly!"

The fly disdainfully replied, "With your breeding capabilities, you can't even produce a few nests a year. Look at us flies, we produce billions of offspring annually!"

The swift responded, "I can eat thousands of your offspring in one meal."

The fly insisted, "Even if you eat freely, you can't finish us off!"

The fly rejected the swift's suggestion to let it evolve into a swift, preferring to remain a fly.

In the dialogue between the swift and the fly, can you tell which has the advantage in evolution? Observing the biological world, such situations are common. Not all species follow a path of higher evolution; some go in the opposite direction, while most maintain their status quo.

Thus, in the biological world, different levels exist, from lower to higher. These levels are evidence of species refusing higher evolution in their evolutionary history.

Similarly, human civilization is divided into different nations and races. Some nation's people are very intelligent, always leading world civilization; others are intellectually weak, driven by advanced civilizations and nations, some even coerced by gunfire. This is the result of not following the path of civilization.

In reality, human beings, like all biological entities, react to civilization breakthroughs similarly. For instance, modern Western civilization broke through around 400 - 500 years ago, initially facing rejection and resistance when entering Eastern countries, hence the Boxer Rebellion. The West proved their strength through wars, forcing Eastern thought to change. Consequently, Japan quickly accepted Western civilization and grew strong, while China was awakened by force, slowly adapting and catching up.

Even now, many Chinese still do not embrace modern Western civilization. Having just abandoned the Qing era, then nostalgically recall Mao's era, they always want to maintain the old times. America and the West continue to force the Chinese government and people to change their mindset through international political and economic actions. In resistance and reluctance, the Chinese government covertly supports conservative nationalists in vandalizing McDonald's and KFC.

Returning to the present, modern Western civilization has influenced the world for about 400 - 500 years, affecting almost all countries and regions, although a few still reject and resist. Scientifically and technologically, most have accepted its impact on daily life. However, Western civilization faces significant obstacles in religion, history, and culture due to its short and light history, impeding large-scale cultural renewal, especially against Islamic and Chinese civilizations.

Around year 2003, the Universal law and Galactic civilization emerged from the East, particularly China, viewed as a true counterattack against modern Western civilization. This time, it allied with Egyptian and Mayan civilizations, three hieroglyphic civilizations nearly engulfed by Western civilization and deemed as outdated. For instance, Egyptian civilization was subsumed by Islamic civilization, Mayan civilization was wiped out by Christian civilization, and Chinese civilization was almost destroyed as the "Four Olds".

The Universal law and Galactic civilization aim to theoretically and technically surpass Western civilization, proposing that immediate cessation of worshiping early Stellar civilization idols (Like God, Allah, doctrines, Buddha, and various religious leaders and emperors) is necessary. This signifies the end of stellar civilization, much like the swift's suggestion to the fly. Western civilization might be troubled, perhaps responding like the fly, boasting of billions of believers annually.

Regardless of Western reactions and rejections, similar to early Eastern responses to Western civilization, we will soon witness an Eastern Renaissance, unifying global religious, philosophical, and scientific systems. Technology will rapidly advance, sweeping through armies and weapons worldwide. However, Eastern theoretical systems may not break into the Western mind through war, as Westerners have a higher acceptance level compared to Qing-era Easterners. Easterners will likely adopt peaceful methods, presenting choices similar to natural species evolution.

Like many natural species during major transitions, some reject evolution and maintain their status quo. For instance, some egg-laying species refuse live birth, monkeys refuse to become apes, and some apes remain in Africa, refusing to explore Eurasia, becoming conservative apes.

History shows that only a minority of people or nations lead global civilization with immense courage and determination, followed by the majority, with some refusing, marking each civilization evolution.

If some follow, and others refuse, it may indicate imperfect theory or incomplete explanation, leading to misunderstanding, or other reasons causing future human division. Those rejecting "Galactic civilization" will be "Stellar sapiens"; those embracing it will be "Galactic sapiens", akin to human history's divided nations and races.

"Stellar sapiens" will continue to worship deities, doctrines, and emperors, knowing only power and money, blocking civilization-advancing information, and ultimately degenerating and perishing, like the Peking Man and Mountain Cave Man, or historically extinct ethnicities (Like the Khitans).

Those who accept the universal laws and the Galactic Civilization (Ancient prophets referred to this as "No King, No Emperor, Setting the Universe") or call "Galactic Sapiens" will become a new human species or group. If they do not encounter strong resistance from "Stellar Sapiens", they will prevail in the competition, usually peacefully and without wars, unlike the barbaric times of killing and temple destruction, and will unify the globe.

Some remote areas, due to information blockades, will continue to maintain the status of Stellar Civilization, much like present-day Africa. (The African continent is at least tens of thousands of years behind the Eurasian continent in terms of civilization and has already rejected multiple rounds of evolutionary progress.)

This is the history of human evolution or biological evolution, natural selection, and survival of the fittest. However, Darwin's theory of evolution has its conditions: some species can continue to survive without evolving, as long as there are no threats from external civilizations, like the humans in Africa.

Eastern civilization, mainly Chinese civilization, will become the protagonist in the revival of future civilization. A new Oriental Renaissance will be beneficial to the development of global civilization, as it injects new blood and is expected to receive global blessings and welcome.

The religion, philosophy, and science developed by Western civilization, which caused a history of killing, will be reassessed and judged. For example, are these religions beneficial or harmful to future humanity? Has the developed philosophy caused harm to society? Has scientific technology, developed on a large scale into weapons (Organized by governments), endangered human survival?

Ultimately, it will be suggested that all Western churches and their derivative churches be ended. This is merely a suggestion, not coercion. Believers can continue to choose their faith without being harmed. However, if governments step in to stop the construction of any more churches and temples, and simultaneously close Christian and Islamic churches, as well as Buddhist temples, the effect would be better. The current Pope in Rome will become the last Pope, as prophesied by historical prophets. All heavenly dreams (Galactic Civilization) will soon be realized!

The prophecies of the Bible will also come true. Alien civilizations (God) will surpass Eastern civilization (赤县 Red China), striking at the root of Western churches (All churches), that is, the firstborn. The universal laws of China, Egypt, and the Mayan pyramid civilizations will be resurrected, forming a Galactic Civilization.

The Western religious system will, of course, not admit defeat. They will continue to lie and deceive the world, saying that without these religions, society will be unstable, and human morality will decline. In reality, it is quite the opposite. Eastern Confucians have long said, "Human nature is inherently good". Without these churches preaching, human nature is inherently good. Sheep are born gentle and do not eat animals. Humans are not born to make weapons and kill. The world is full of Western religions and cults, and governments develop a large number of weapons to protect themselves. Without these religions and doctrines, there would naturally be fewer wars and no need to develop new weapons.

The continuous decline of human morality is precisely because of the emergence of these false Western churches and cults, which fabricate lies, suppress voices of justice, and spread false truths, false ideologies, and false morality, creating different forms of worship such as religious attire, headscarves (Or bald heads), and pseudo-church food to divide people.

Perhaps most people do not understand why this is currently a turning point. How did we suddenly rise from "Stellar Civilization" to "Galactic Civilization"? Yes, all developments progress steadily, and when they reach a critical point, they suddenly break through and soar. You cannot predict it, just like the stock market, where you cannot know when it will suddenly rise.

Is this Universal law and Galactic Civilization theoretical system the best? Is there something better? So far, we have not seen anything better, but the breakthrough point has arrived. In the foreseeable future, this will be the first time that Eastern civilization, after enduring hardships for hundreds of years, will comprehensively surpass Western civilization, from religion and philosophy to science. From ancient to modern prophecies, and Heavenly, Earthly, and alien civilizations are all cooperating with this surpassing, truly giving a feeling of "The Sun and Moon shining together."

The next wave of civilization breakthrough will be towards "Universal Civilization", but we do not know when or in what way or theoretical system, because it is too far in the future. We can only make a small prediction: the form of "Cosmic Civilization" will be explosive, likely a civilization system expanding throughout the universe, no longer the "No King, No Emperor, Setting the Universe" black hole-style Galactic Civilization system. (Stellar Civilization is "With kings, Gods, and worship," a solar system).

After thousands of years, from "Galactic Civilization" to "Cosmic Civilization", people of that time will, like modern people, have long been accustomed to these things and will need someone to break the "Galactic Civilization" theoretical system again. However, this is a good phenomenon because knowledge has progressed, just like Copernicus' theoretical system (Which started the Stellar Civilization with the Sun as the center) broke Ptolemy's theoretical system (Planetary system with the Earth as the center).

Today's world civilization has entered a new turning point, causing global ideological chaos. The reason lies here. It is quite difficult for Western civilization too; they need to give up the worship of Jesus as God and Christianity, just like the Qing people had to cut off their queues, which means partially giving up their traditions and history. But continuing to accept Jesus as God also means they will continue to battle Islam or maintain the Stellar Civilization while rejecting Galactic Civilization.

Jesus has once again become a focus. He is the Passover sacrifice, felt to have been resurrected, but has once again become the sacrifice of Galactic Civilization.

(January 2019)

References:

1. The Bible

A6. Galactic pyramid and atlantean civilizations

Abstract: Stellar system civilizations worship false Gods, idols, and emperors; and research also tends to be discrete individuals, such as mathematics, physics, chemistry, economics, and politics. Galactic civilizations, on the other hand, do not worship any of these, and research is conducted on all disciplines as a whole.

Stellar system civilizations are mostly practical and detail-oriented, worshipping materialism, money, and power. In the use of writing, they favor the universal phonetic script. Galactic civilizations focus on spirituality, abstraction and metaphysics, and use an abstract hieroglyphic script.

The emergence of Galactic civilization is beyond the Stellar civilization, but also by the Stellar civilization of the obstruction and resistance, the great difference between them, the history of the war and competition is often seen. For example, countries that used hieroglyphics in ancient times, such as the Egyptian and Mayan civilizations, were basically eaten up by countries that used pinyin writing, leaving only the Chinese civilization behind. The emergence of the Galactic civilization allowed the hieroglyphic civilization to flourish, and finally the spiritual realm completely unified the globe.

---

1. Introduction

In the past few days, I took advantage of the long vacation around New Year's Day to go to the northern part of Sydney alone. It is said that the Egyptian pyramids and hieroglyphics were found. Driving several hundred kilometers along the highway surrounded by mountains, searching and looking around, enjoying the rocks and blue water along the way, although I did not find anything, I relived the spiritual exploration of the ancient mankind, and gained a deeper understanding of the Australian customs and culture.

2. Origin of Pyramid Beliefs

Although it is not known from what inspiration the ancient human pyramid beliefs were built, or directly from Alien civilizations, the inspiration for our current “Universal laws” came from the heavy rain from above, the process of raindrops landing in the sea, from the expansion of water droplets, from the waves of the sea.

Fig. A6-1 Water droplets

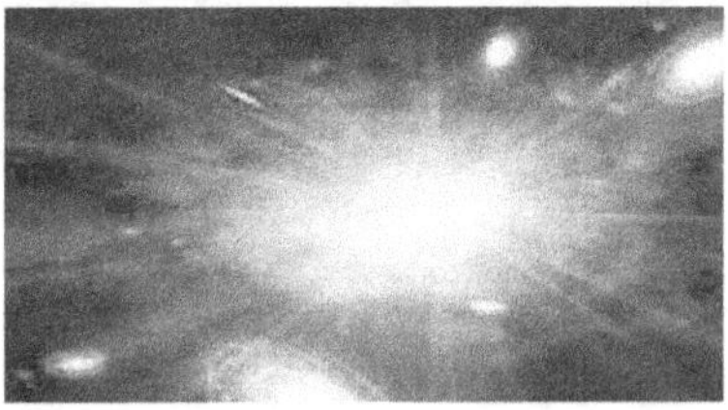

Fig. A6-2 The Big Bang

From the form of the mother of heaven and Earth and the beginning of all things. Evolving into the metaphysical form of philosophy "." , "1" and "0" patterns, and flat geometric patterns.

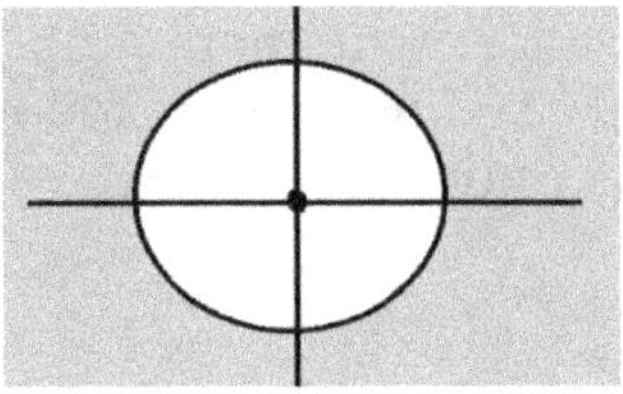

Fig. A6-3 "." , "1", and "0".

The further evolution of the three-dimensional, or pyramidal, form is the origin of the Pyramid beliefs of the Galactic civilizations that we have today as the laws of the universe.

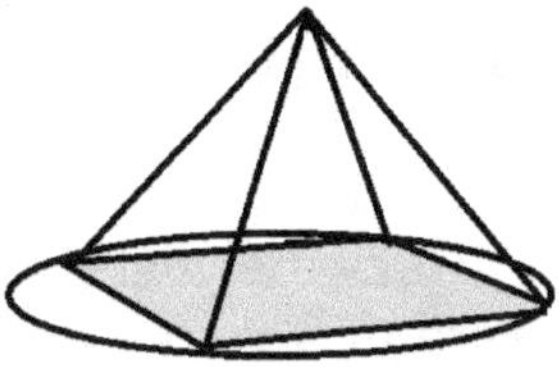

Fig. A6-4 Pyramid Form

If the ancient mankind also got the pyramid belief from such inspiration, or is the masterpiece of the Alien civilization as the Alien experts say, then we can only rejoice! Because we have understood the Galactic civilization and have begun to agree with the thoughts of the Alien civilization, i.e., to assimilate the Galactic civilization, which once again confirms the prophets of various countries from ancient times to the present day who predicted that the Chinese hieroglyphic civilization would unify the globe.

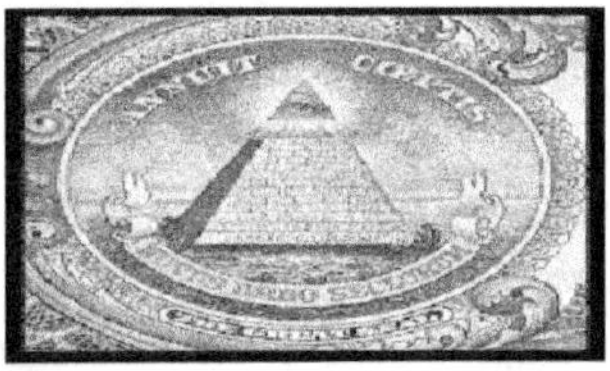

Fig. A6-5 Patterns on a Dollar

Let's go back to ancient Egypt for a moment and look for traces of their archaeological findings. The following pictures are of murals in the tombs of the pharaohs.

Fig. A6-6 Frescoes in the Tomb of the Pharaohs in Egypt.

This mural depicts a pharaoh from the 14th century B.C., an ancient Egyptian pharaoh who promoted monotheism. The only God he worshipped was Aten ---- the Sun, which is the Sun, and impersonal. He also positioned himself profoundly; the best pharaohs should not be fierce men, but androgynous, the father of all beings and the mother of all.

The Sun God, with no human images. The animals, people and plants, all worshipped the Sun God, and the ancient civilizations of Egypt worshipped the Sun, not the vanities and leader of modern religions.

Look at these Stellar system civilizations of today, the largest state-sponsored churches around the globe, what did have people worshiping?

Do you think these believers are not ashamed? Their intelligence and beliefs are far inferior to those of the ancient Egyptians thousands of years ago, billions of people? It's now the 21st century, and they are still kneeling on their knees? What words can I use to describe this? If you're not fighting with each other, who is?

Fig. A6-7 Idols Worshipped Today

Fig. A6-8 Worshipping believers

Why do these people worship? According to the believers, some of the dogmas in the church or some of the prophecies spoken by the bishops still have some truth in them and seem to be the language of God. For example, the Bible prophecies, "Man was created by God in His image", but these believers have been kneeling and worshipping for thousands of years, understand these biblical prophecies? None of them can understand or explain.

Only when the Galactic civilization of universal law arrives can these prophecies be truly understood and interpreted, and the religious leader is no more than a prophet, whose words, deeds, and sermons are no different from those of modern man. Look at what the image of God looks like, and what the image of created man looks like.

The form of the Big Bang, which we have shown above, assuming that this is the form of God, is also the form of the Tao, the mother of heaven and Earth and the beginning of all things, as prophesied by the Taoist master Lao Tzu.

What is its biological response? It is this starfish form, which is in an explosive state.

Fig. A6-9 Starfish Form

Notice this, as the starfish evolves further and one of its branching legs becomes the head of the breach, it becomes the circular turtle form. We have already talked about this idea of circular breakthroughs; when the cycle has been going on for a round, it has to break through, and the location of the breakthrough point is the head. Only the idea of the head can break through; no position on the body can break through.

Fig. A6-10 Round Turtle Pattern

When the Round Turtle evolves further and climbs up the bank, it lengthens its body in order to climb faster, and this is the reptile.

When the reptile stood up, it became an upright animal, which is the ancestor of the ape, which in turn became our modern man. Imagine the old Christian prophecy, aren't we made in the form of God? It corresponds exactly to biblical prophecy. So believers don't even understand it and they all go and worship these so-called Gods and words of God.

Of course there are many other prophecies in the Bible, including many prophecies of the Patriarchs of Islam and Buddhism, and the large number of believers formed in the later period of time do not have the ability to do this, so they just have to worship and memorize the prophecies that their Patriarchs speak. And these prophecies can be understood only when the Galactic civilization of universal laws arrives and is being discovered one by one corresponding to the present theoretical system.

But many of today's practical scientists, who do not understand prophecy (Of course, some Western scientists are believers), who deny the a priori nature of the supernatural, who do not understand that we have now reached the age of life and intelligence, whose microscopes have a very short lens and see only molecules and atomic segments, and who speak of materialism and practicality, and who study the details of the refinement of matter. For example, in a forest, they only study the leaves that fall from the trees to the ground, and study the different forms and variations of various leaves, without seeing the overall structure of the forest. So they deny the existence of prophecy and the things of life and intelligence. Further, they also deny that man was created in the form of God. The theory of evolution they have established is mechanical and does not incorporate life and intelligence, so they will not understand that all breakthroughs are created by Spirit and only afterward accomplished with matter. This is just as philosophy leads breakthrough discoveries before science comes to continue the building, as has been the case throughout the ages, for example, Copernicus used philosophy to prophesy the Sun-centered theory, which later led to scientific arguments and discoveries.

Scientific research is actually a continuation of the spirit of philosophy, not a professional salary and promotion of material steps, money can not buy the spirit, for example, you give those soccer players more money, they can not win, because they simply do not have the spirit of scoring. The Chinese women's volleyball team didn't have much salary back then, so why did they win five consecutive championships, it is not money. The Red Army was millet plus rifles, climbed snowy mountains and ate tree barks can defeat eight million well-armed Mr. Jiang jie Shi national army! You now give them a few million more people and modern airplanes and tanks, they can't beat the weak countries around them. Can scientists do experiments? Just can't study what that spirit is!

3. The spread of civilization

Look at the ancient ancestors, they rely on such a spirit of exploration, 10,000 people in two years to complete the construction of the pyramids, of course, you can not imagine how they built with boulders, in the conditions at that time, they use what tools? Just by whatever scientists of today calculate the number of workers who built it, 200,000 people can only finish a pyramid in a hundred years; if you only calculate the material and money, and the high price of salary that those academicians want, of course, it can't be finished in a few hundred years, but have you calculated the role of the spirit?

When you have mastered the most powerful faith in the world, when you have mastered the top wisdom and civilization in the world, the powerful force that comes from the potential of the heart can climb the snowy mountains, cross the grasslands, cross the vast ocean, cross the infinite deserts, and cross the continents of Asia, America, and

Australia, and build a lots of huge pyramids in a triangular area without money.

They were showing the peoples of the time and the future that what they had discovered was the most powerful Galactic universal law pyramid civilization that squashed the religious beliefs and engineering techniques of all the peoples of the globe at the time. You people of the future are powerful, so come on!

The difficulty of the engineering and the simplicity of the tools did not matter to these ancestors who had powerful beliefs, and this is the power of the spirit. If you look at the structure and architecture of the pyramids, and the geometric math and physics included, it is difficult for modern science and technology to reach.

Human civilization is usually on a 10,000 year cycle, starting with primitive writing and bows and arrows, and it took 5,000 years to develop to today's level, and with each push like the current civilization, there are Satellite system civilizations, Planetary system civilizations, Stellar system civilizations, Galactic system civilizations, and Cosmic system civilizations.

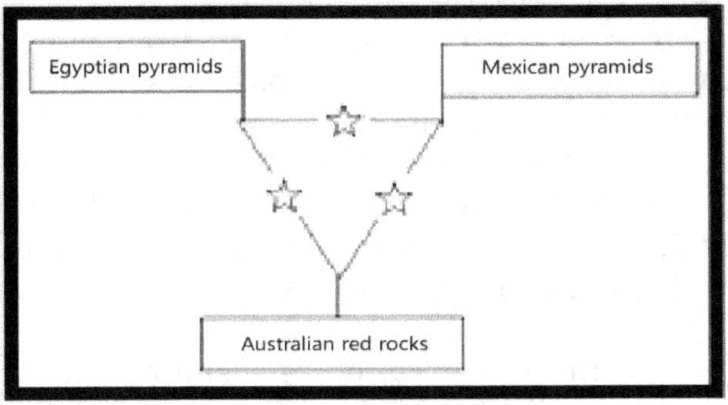

Fig. A6-11 The Magic Triangle

Judging from the pyramid buildings left behind in the ancient times, they have also reached the Galactic universal law pyramid civilization stage. However, due to interference from unknown reasons, the civilization was interrupted and what was left behind were fragments.

Ancient era development of the Universal law pyramid civilization, reached this stage, it is estimated that the modern contradiction and the existence of the Pyramid civilization of the time like the era, also can not be reconciled with the system of those backward countries at that time, can not be balanced with the religious beliefs of those peoples, and then continued to war, and ultimately is a lose-lose situation.

According to current documentary fragments and legends, the ancient Greek philosopher Plato recorded in his book 《Dialogues》 that Atlantis, also translated as the Atlantic Island, the Great Western continent, the ancient continent with a high level of civilization according to legend, which was destroyed by the Great Flood around 10,000 years B.C..

Plato hints: "Around nine thousand years before Thoreau, across the Pillars of Hercules (The Strait of Gibraltar), there was a very large island, from which you could go to the other islands, and across those islands was a whole piece of land surrounded by the ocean, which was the kingdom of 'Atlantis'. At that time Atlantis was about to start a great war with Athens, but unexpectedly Atlantis was suddenly hit by Earthquakes and floods, and in less than a day and a night, it became hard for Greek ships to reach".

Atlantis represents the Pyramid civilization and Athens at the time represented the backward religious forces. In recent times countries have searched for the geographic location of Atlantis, with an archaeological team claiming in

2011 that the location of Atlantis was under a mudflat in southern Spain, and in 2013 undersea pyramids suspected to be the remains of Atlantis were found in the waters west of Portugal.

In recent years, pyramid-like mountains or Egyptian-like hieroglyphics have also been found in Australia, with further archaeology and excavation underway.

From the above text fragments can be seen, the Universal law pyramid civilization has been expanding to the globe, but also with the then relatively low civilization and the national ethnicity of the country to fight, and still a long war. But natural undersea sinking and great floods killed key pyramid innovators in the natural disasters of Atlantis, and the Universal law Pyramid civilization beliefs disappeared, and the rest of the civilization was beaten into a primitive state. After that, no one understood Pyramid civilization for thousands of years, so naturally no one would build pyramids again.

This is just like today's advanced democracies, Europe and the United States, in the process of advancing democracy globally, conquering all the backward countries and nations around the globe. Are they acting as policemen, spending a lot of money and sacrificing many innocent soldiers in order to plunder the property of backward countries?

The advancement of civilization by human beings is a process, when you discover an advanced civilization idea, you must find ways to advance it globally, and it is totally free of money and free of charge, and you will not plunder anything from the backward countries at all, for example, when China was just opening up, Europe, America and the West all provided China with a great deal of economic assistance to help your economic development and advancement.

Just like the Alien civilization puts out all kinds of crop circle on the Earth, they spend a lot of money to come here, risking to be dissected by the lower civilization, totally gratuitous to spread the civilization, and did not rob this planet of any resources, they also don't look down on this planet of any minerals.

But most of the lower civilizations were stupid and ignorant, usually thinking in terms of profit, who would do it without profit? What is even more ignorant is that instead of transforming with the advanced civilizations, they fight against the spread of civilization. The rulers of most backward countries think that they are bullied by advanced countries only because their military is not good, and they must first develop military weapons to fight against the advanced countries.

What the spreading civilization is most afraid of is that the backward countries' civilization is not working, but they develop their military vigorously, and their military surpasses the surrounding countries, such as Nazi Germany, then they have to engage in a global life and death duel. Probably the first few times of the spread of the ancient civilization, all appeared this situation, so all destroyed.

4. Mayan prophecy

Mayan pyramids, is another area of the spread of the Pyramid civilization, corresponding to the Egyptian pyramids, in the global civilization of the strategic location, there are also a large number of text fragments. It is currently believed that the Pyramid civilization chose to occupy only three key points around the globe in order to avoid a major clash with all the backward civilizations around the globe, unlike other lower religions that build temples everywhere, reach out to the people, and attract the masses of believers to donate and worship.

According to Mayan prophecies, our planet is already in the so-called Fifth Solar Era, and so far the planet has passed through four solar epochs, and at the end of each of these epochs, a shocking destruction took place.

The first solar age was Matlactilart, which ended in destruction by a flood, said to be Noah's flood.

The second solar era was Ehecatl, which was blown to pieces by the “Wind Gods”.

The third solar period was Tleyquiyahuillo, which was on the road to destruction because of a rain of fire.

The fourth solar age was Tzontlilic, which was destroyed by an Earthquake caused by the rains of fire.

According to Mayan legend, from the first to the end of the fourth solar age, the Earth was plunged into unprecedented chaos and ended in a tragedy so terrible that the Earth must have warned of its demise.

The Mayans said, “The Earth is not owned by man, but man belongs to the Earth”. They developed grandiose numbers, astronomical in the view of current science, which are not used even in modern times. Among the Mayan calendars, there is a calendar called the “Chokin Calendar”, which is based on a year of 260 days, and strangely enough, there is not a single planet in the solar system that applies this calendar.

According to this calendar, the approximate position of this planet should be between Venus and Earth. The symbols in the “Chokin Calendar”, which express the core of the Milky Way as described by the Mayans, are very similar to the Tai Chi Yin-Yang diagram. Some Mayan scholars believe that the “Drekking Calendar” is a record of the “Milky Way Season”. According to the Drekking Calendar, the Earth is in the “Fifth solar era”, which is the last “Solar era". During this period of the Galactic Season, the solar system is undergoing a "Great Cycle" that lasts 5125 years, from 3113 BC to December 21, 2012 AD.

Most Mayan prophecies are chronological records, declaring an end at the "Fifth Solar Age". Therefore, the Mayan prophecies that the Earth will be renewed at this time and move into a new era are not apocalyptic.

During this "Great Cycle", the Earth and the Solar System are passing through a beam of galactic rays from the galactic core, which has a cross-sectional diameter of 5125 Earth years. In other words, it will take the Earth 5125 years to pass through this ray. The Mayans divided this "Great Cycle" into 13 phases, each of which is documented in great detail, and each of the 13 phases is divided into 20 evolutionary periods, each lasting 20 years. The calendar cycle is very similar to the Chinese "Heavenly Stems" and "Earthly Branches", and the calendar is cyclical, not linear as in the Western Era, with no end in sight.

When the stars of the solar system through the beam of galactic rays after the "Big cycle", there will be a fundamental change, the Mayans called "Assimilation of the Milky Way". From the Mayan prophecy of the "Great Cycle", from 1992 to 2012 this 20 years, the Earth has entered the "Great Cycle" final phase of the last period.

The Mayans believed that this was a very important period before the "Assimilation of the Milky Way" and called it the "Earth renewal period". After the "Earth Renewal Period", the Earth will step out of the galactic rays and enter a new phase of "Assimilation into the Milky Way Galaxy", as explained in Wikipedia and Baidu Encyclopedia.

The above is the explanation from Wikipedia and Baidu's Encyclopedia.

5. Summary

Once again, the Mayan prophecy of the fifth solar era has ended, that is, in the year 2012 or so now. Previously, the prophecy said that it was the end of the world, but it has been found that in terms of natural disasters on Earth, nothing has happened, but in terms of knowledge, society and humanities, the "Stellar civilization" has come to an end, and after that it has entered into a new epoch, a new phase of "Assimilation of the Galaxy". The new phase of "Assimilation of the Galaxy".

The Mayan prophecy of "Assimilation of the Milky Way" is too imaginative, and the Chinese Divine Culture, the Galactic Civilization Theory System of Universal Laws, which we completed around 2012, is "Assimilating the Milky Way". You can't help but admit that the Mayan godfather and prophet who told the prophecy is probably also the son of God, and has countless believers and worship like today, from the time of the founding and their prophecies, all one by one corresponds to the present day, which can't help but say that it is a providence or coincidence.

(Article original, picture online, write in January 2020)

A7. The "Rainbow Warrior" in the Maya Civilization Prophecy

Abstract: "Rainbow Warriors" from all nations, cultures, regions, and countries spread light across the world. The concept of "Rainbow Warriors" aligns with the idea of the Seven Colored Books.

In Mayan culture, people generally know the Mayan prophecy, the Mayan calendar, and the crystal skull, but few people mention or notice the legend of the "Rainbow Warrior." This is precisely the essence and ending part of the Mayan prophecy, which is very similar to our current human destiny at stake!

"The Mystery of the Crystal Skull" finally mentioned the emergence of the "Rainbow Warrior" and the changes in the world. Please take a closer look at this description. We think this paragraph is a description of the new and old changes in the world today, and it also predicts the changing trend of the world after 2012.

Here are a few excerpts:

We don't have to be separated, because we are one, we advance together regardless of skin colour, class, or belief, and are united like the seven colours of the rainbow. All mankind is brothers and sisters. We must respect the Earth we live on, and respect all life in the universe. If humans make the right choice, the indigenous people will lead the world into a new era of harmony with nature.

At the end of this cycle and the beginning of the next cycle, ancient knowledge will return to the world, and people with special talents will be born among people. At this time, people with special psychic abilities will appear in human beings.

This is a period of alternating between the new and the old. Although the new era is bound to come, it is still unknown in what form and whether it is beneficial to the survival of mankind.

Those who pursue spiritual attainments have become “Rainbow Warriors”, they take up the task of educating others. Although catastrophe is inevitable, these people are full of spiritual hope. Through their efforts, the disaster will be reduced, if not entirely avoided. At least the consequences will be alleviated. From all nations, all cultures, all regions, and all countries of the “Rainbow Warrior”, to the rest of the world, spreading light and spreading the concept that humanity should live in harmony with other creatures on Earth.

They inherited the spirit of the ancestors, and they have the brilliance of wisdom in their minds and the power of love in their hearts. They will not harm any life. They love every creature and this crazy world. They educate people to rebuild the balance between heaven and Earth.

“Rainbow Warriors” can wait until they are reunited with the angels before returning to their world because they want mankind on Earth to regain a feeling of love, and spread this love again to the entire planet. Moreover, God also wants to create a miracle in the world.

They finally predicted that at this critical moment, the Atlanteans and other humans living on Earth would continue to ride on flying objects and pay attention to every major action and possible change of humans. This is the rainbow warrior who saved the Earth Goddess, and the spacecraft of the alien civilization came to us, composing a pattern similar to the crop circle. **(Written on April 2017)**

References: 1. Coris Marton (UK): 《The Mystery of the Crystal Skull》

A8. The "Rainbow" New Covenant Prophesied in the Bible

Abstract: The rainbow predicted by the "Bible", that is, the colourful golden book.

---

1. Introduction

The God uses the rainbow to make a covenant with mankind, and will no longer destroy the world with floods.

2. Bible Prophecy

Genesis 9 : 13 - 17

9:13. I do set my bow in the cloud, and it shall be for a token of a covenant between me and the earth.

9:14. And it shall come to pass, when I bring a cloud over the earth, that the bow shall be seen in the cloud.

9:15 And I will remember my covenant, which is between me and you and every living creature of all flesh; and the waters shall no more become a flood to destroy all flesh.

9:16. And the bow shall be in the cloud; and I will look upon it, that I may remember the everlasting covenant between God and every living creature of all flesh that is upon the earth.

9:17. And God said unto Noah, This is the token of the covenant, which I have established between me and all flesh that is upon the earth.

3. Galactic civilization and Pyramid belief

Explanation: Seven golden books are like a light, divided into red, orange, yellow, green, cyan, blue, purple, with colourful. Light is the fastest spreading in the universe. This colourful golden books just like the light of the seven wisdoms, and spreading to the entire universe.

From top to bottom, the Seven Books are getting closer and closer to the masses of the Stellar civilization, complex and practical; from bottom to top, they are getting closer and closer to the wisdom, simplicity and abstraction of the universe.

At the top is a "Sky eye", looking at sentient beings. There is such a picture in the crop circle, as well as the Egyptian civilization, and the current seven books of our civilization are also available, indicating that we have approached and understood the last wave of ancient civilizations.

1) God: Celestial Eye

2) Cosmic Civilization Book:

Like this universe, it is characterized by graphics and symbols, corresponding to a "Green" golden book.

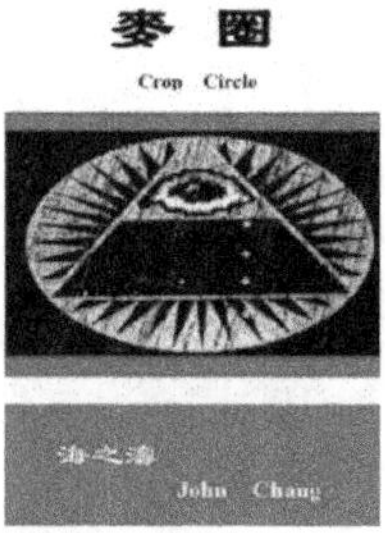

Fig. A8-1 The Alien's work Explained by John Chang

《Crop Circle》 (Published in 2015).

3) Galactic Civilization Book:

For example, the Milky Way galaxy is characterized by the unity and interweaving of all disciplines, corresponding to the three main golden books. The colour is "Yellow, blue, red".

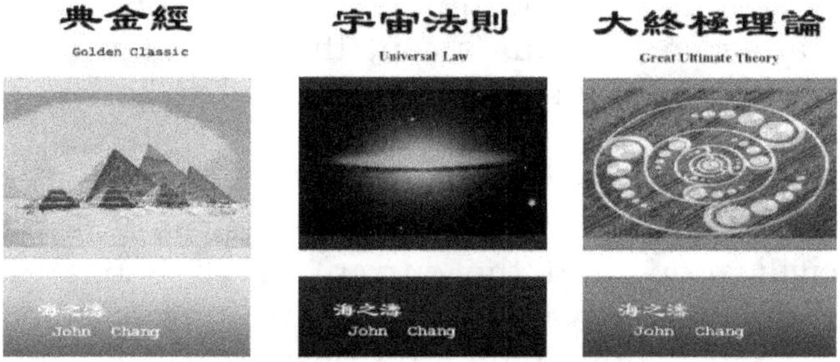

Fig. A8-2 John Chang's Works

《Golden Classic》 (Published in 2007);
《Universal law》 (Published in 2003);
《Great Ultimate Theory》 (Published in 2013),

4) Stellar civilization books:

Like the solar system, the characteristics are individual subjects, such as mathematics, physics, chemistry, history, geography, politics, and economics, etc., each author writes some points, and not related to each other, the corresponding colour is "Cyan, orange and purple".

Fig. A8-3　John Chang's Edited Works

《Chinese Systems Philosophy》 (Published in 2008);
《Oriental Systems literature》 (Published in 2010);
《World Systems Science》 (Published in 2018),

(Year 2017)

Three. Unifying Philosophy

Chapter Summary:

The institutional unification of the classic book 《I Ching》 is said to have roots in ancient times with Fuxi (伏羲), who observed the symbols of heaven and Earth. In the middle ages, King Wen of Zhou (周文王) interpreted the principles of the 《I Ching》. After then, Confucius and his disciples annotated the 《I Ching》, which eventually became known as the 《Yi Zhuan》. The fusion of the original text and commentary ultimately resulted in the creation of the 《Zhou Yi》 (周易).

The 《Tuan》 (彖) commentary states: "Great indeed is the origin of Qian, from which all things derive their beginnings. It governs the heavens, with clouds moving and rain falling, giving shape to all forms. The great cycle of light and darkness completes itself, with the six positions of the hexagrams unfolding in their time. It rides upon the six dragons to regulate the heavens. The way of Qian transforms, correcting all natures and destinies. By preserving and uniting the great harmony, it ensures continued prosperity. It brings forth all beings, and all nations find peace under its influence."

Pioneers of Institutional Unification:

The pioneers who established unified systems were all rulers:

- In the era of Primitive abdication systems, the institutional unifier was the Yellow Emperor.
- During the Slave enclave system, the institutional unifier was King Wen of Zhou.

- In the era of the Feudal county system, the institutional unifier was Qin Shi Huang.
- Under the Democratic parliamentary system, the institutional unifier was George Washington.
- Unified Republican System?

Opposition from Groups and Parties:

The pioneers of new systems were all outstanding and exceptional rulers who led their nations to establish new systems. The primary opposition to these new systems came from the domestic aristocratic interest groups and the surrounding backward regions governed by Primitive, Slave-based, or Feudal autocracies. Additionally, advanced rulers were hindered by the corruption and ignorance of their times, as well as by the masses and followers who were brainwashed through propaganda, violence, slaughter, and wars. This opposition has manifested in various forms, such as the book burnings and persecution of scholars caused by internal conservative forces, and the evil Axis powers that obstructed the progress of democracy in modern times — obstacles that persist even today.

B1. Universal Law

Abstract: What is the highest law of the universe? It was said that the ".", "1", "o" as a kind of symbol and graphic, represents the highest law of the universe. They seem to be simple, but profound philosophy, if translated into their national language, written in Chinese or "Point", "Line" and "Circle", which is not a law of the universe, because the language of States changed their graphic and symbol shape, but also are given to different interpretations.

Fig. B1-1 Tree rings

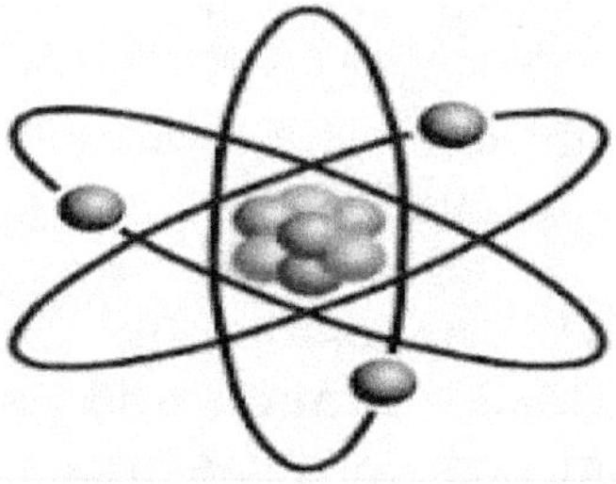

Fig. B1-2 Atom

What is the highest universal law? It was said that the ".", "1", "o" as a kind of symbol and graphic, represents the highest law of the universe. They seem to be simple, but profound philosophy, if translated into their national language, written in Chinese or "Point", "Line" and "Circle", which is not a law of the universe, because the language of states changed their graphic and symbol shape, but also are given to different interpretations.

Therefore, the characters can be exercised for their pronunciation, but not represent their significance.

"." called "Point", and represents a real substance and truth, a kind of force and power control center. It is the source of all things, is the only unique and rule status. Defined as energy gathered into a point or aggregated energy.

"1" called "Line", represents an exploration, enterprise and competition. It also represents a top-down development process, such as the human society. "Emperor-minister; Father-son"; the celestial body center of the universe, Galaxies, Stars and Planets; science is exploration, science is "1". Defined as the energy to break through the boundary or breakthrough energy.

"O" is "Circle", represent a hierarchy and orderly, a stable could not go beyond the boundaries. Defined as the energy or stabilization energy required to establish various stability boundaries.

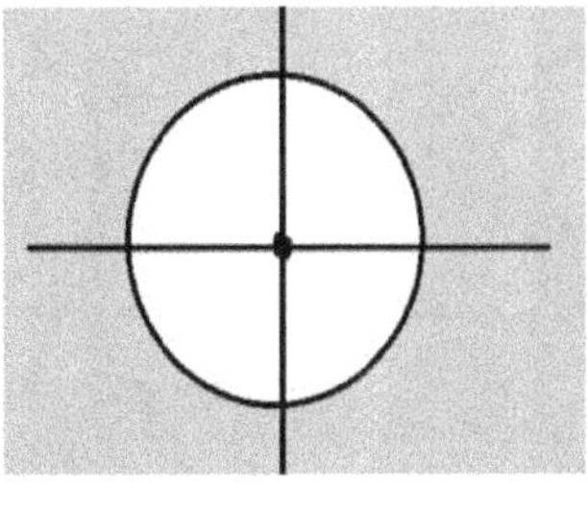

Fig. B1-3 The ".", "1", "o" called the "Point", "Line" and "Circle"

Most of the current religious talk stability and stressed that such limits, including their often said that the ethics regulations, and "Virtue and morality". These regulations are "O" (Circle) without the wall, to break through these regulations and crimes, will be input to "O" with the wall of prison.

If humanity according to these regulations and creed do, the nations of the world, society and the family will be stable and beautiful. But because there is no emphasis on "1" (Line), that is, scientific progress and exploration, we can only practice in the mountains, and wait for death, said the religious tenets of these regulations and the rules do not fully reflect the universal law.

(Published at 11/2003)

Reference:

1. John Chang: 《Universal Law》 (2003), Ch.1, Universal Publishing, Australia.

B2. "Metaphysics" Unifies Nature

Abstract: All the forms of matter and living beings follow the explosion form of the universe, or the universal law. We did not use any formulas or theories, but only the philosophical "Metaphysics" to complete the great unity from the Galaxy to the Quark. This is the highest state of philosophy.

The forms of all matter and living things follow the explosion form of the universe, or the laws of the universe, such as the form of galaxies; the form of stellar systems; the form of natural objects; the form of plants; the form of lower animals; the form of Sperm and Eggs of higher animals; The morphology of viruses and bacteria; the morphology of the nervous system; the morphology of cells, etc...

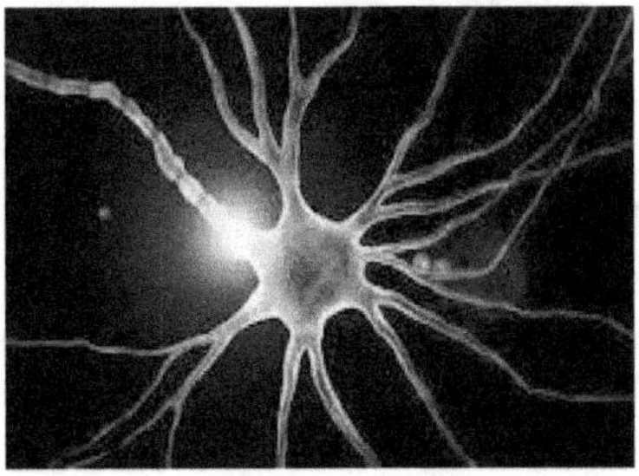

Nervous system morphology

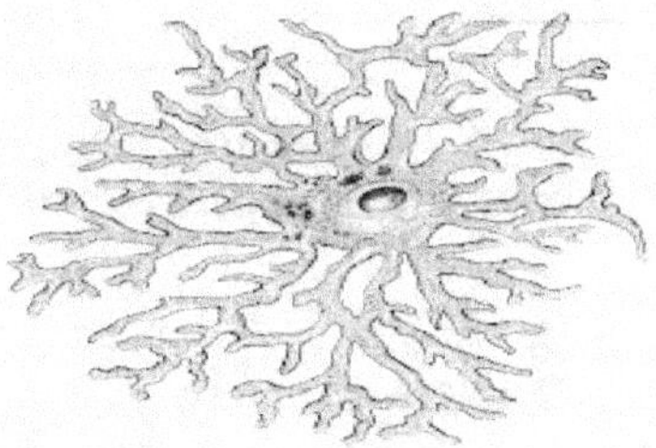

Cell morphology

Galaxy Form

Sunflower Form

Sea clam morphology

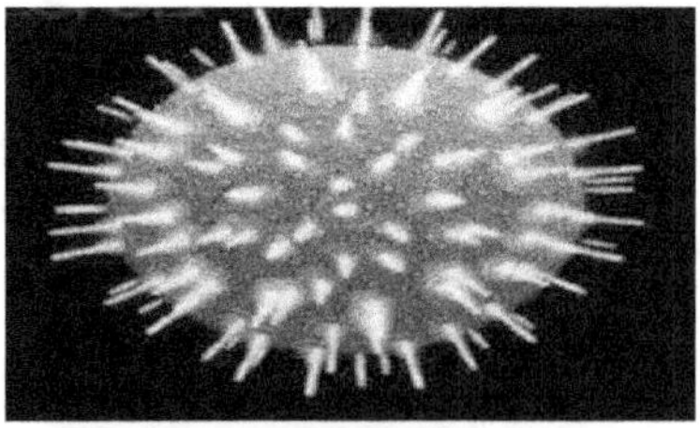

Virus morphology

Starfish morphology

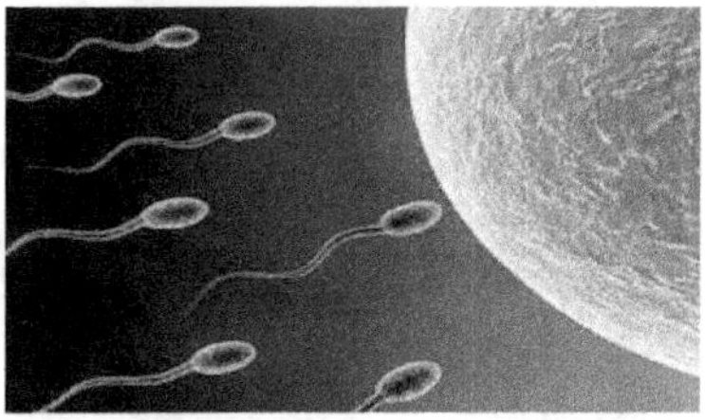

Sperm and egg morphology

Fig. B2-1 All matter in nature obeys the universal law (Online picture)

In other words, we did not use any formulas or theories, but only used philosophical "Metaphysics" to complete the great unification from the Galaxy to the Quark. This is the highest state of philosophy, not spiritual chicken soup.

The above examples can also be said to be the so-called theology, which all follow the explosive form of the universe (Or the form of God). Religionists or priests use these tricks to establish churches and dojos. Some leaders simply call themselves Gods or "Masters" or engage in "Truth and goodness" statements to confuse good people and use them to solicit money. They made some decorative headscarves and clothing, or bald their heads to maintain the church's brand. If anyone opposed it, they would wage war.

Scientists tried to explain them. For example, Mr.Newton spent the rest of his life explaining them, but was unsuccessful. Mr.Einstein also spent a whole life trying to unify all the theories, but he was also unsuccessful. It was not a matter of Gravitational theory and Quantum theory, but a question of whether stones and animals could be unified.

Because they are going in the wrong direction, they all want to use dead things or formulas to complete. In fact, it is not a question of formulas, but a question of philosophy.

(Written in June 2017)

B3. The Great Tao is Simple: ".", "1", "0"

Abstract: Taking advantage of the New Year's holiday in January 2019, I went to the Blue Mountains west of Sydney, Australia, where birds and flowers, beautiful mountains and green waters, forests and grasses, and the Three Sisters peaks, like three small pyramids, are really wonderful for Gods to practice. At night, I look up into the deep space, the stars are shining, my imagination is flashing, and I actually feel the energy from outer space, and write several articles in one breath. What year is this year? Are all historical predictions coming true?

Fig. B3-1 Three Sisters, Blue Mountains, Sydney

I think that Professor Zhang Shousheng (张首晟) passed away recently. He had such a few words before his death. If you summarize all the knowledge of mankind, what would you write? He gave these answers:

1. The three fundamental constants of nature
2. Everything is made of atoms
3. Euclidean geometry axioms
4. Natural selection, survival of the fittest

5. All men are born equal
6. Let freedom the wind blows
7. A pen is better than a sword
8. An invisible hand
9. The great way is simple

Let's analyze his answers.

The first, "The three fundamental constants of nature", is actually the simplest description of the basis of physics.

The second, "Everything is made of atoms", is the simplest basis for describing chemistry.

The third, "Euclidean Geometry Axiom", is the simplest foundation of all mathematics.

The fourth, "Natural selection, survival of the fittest", describes the evolution of biology to the simplest.

The fifth, "Everyone is born equal", is the simplest description of the institutional laws of political science.

The sixth, "Let the wind of freedom blow", is the simplest description of free trade in economics.

The above six items are basically a simple summary of all the subjects we have learned from elementary school to university for so many years. After finishing college courses and entering society and work, the above six items can be included in the following three items.

"A pen is better than a sword" is correct in terms of society, work, writing and creativity.

In the past, Napoleon, Hitler, and the Emperor of Japan all wanted to use force to unify the world, but the result was a disastrous defeat. Even if rulers like Alexander and Genghis Khan have unified most of the Earth by force, what is the final result? Everyone knows that they all fell apart in a short time. Therefore, unification by force cannot last long. Only theories and civilizations created with pen can unify the world for a long time.

The "Invisible hand" is correct in terms of social development and historical predictions.

We know that in the long river of history, many nations and countries once existed, but they all died out afterwards. We also know that many ancient Chinese and foreign prophecies are telling future generations that you must follow the laws of nature. If you don't, you will perish, including any country and nation, no matter how powerful you were at that time. Similarly, in economics and the stock market, no matter how rich and wealth you are, there is an invisible hand operating. If you violate the market, even if you have money, you will lose. This is the invisible hand.

The last item is "The great way is simple", which is also the most critical.

But where is simple? How far is simple? What is the best simple? Many prophets and scholars have been exploring since ancient times.

For example, the previous Professor Zhang Shousheng, from the perspective of science, he stated the simplest aspects of each major, such as mathematics, physics, chemistry, biology, politics, and economics, but where is the simplicity of all the overall natural sciences, social sciences and life sciences? He could not say. But for a professional scientist (He is not a philosopher), it is already very good.

What is it that Western theologians have made the most simple? It is the creation of God, everything is pushed to the creation of God, that is the work of God and Allah, we don't need to explore. This is similar to the various Gods and creations worshipped by all other ethnic groups in the world, such as Pangu's creation of heaven and Earth, which is totally incomprehensible nonsense.

What is the great simplicity given by the highest philosopher in modern times in the west countries? It's "Materialism, idealism, and metaphysics". By the way,

"Marxism" also seems somewhat vague, yet it somehow appears to be related.

And what is the simple way that the highest scientist in the west countries is looking for? It is to unify the four field theories, but it has not yet reached it at all.

Let's take a look at what is the great simplicity that Lao Tzu (Li Er) said thousands of years ago? Lao Tzu, in the first chapter of the 《Tao Te Ching》, writes:

"The Tao that can be spoken is not the eternal Tao; the name that can be named is not the eternal name. The nameless is the origin of Heaven and Earth; the named is the mother of all things."

Lao Tzu continues in Chapter 25:

"There was something formless and perfect before the universe was born. Silent, vast, standing alone, unchanging, it is ever-present and in motion. It can be regarded as the mother of the universe. I do not know its name, so I call it Tao. If forced to give it a name, I would call it 'Great'. Great means flowing, flowing means far-reaching, and far-reaching means returning. Therefore, the Tao is great, Heaven is great, Earth is great, and humanity is great. Within the universe, there are four great things, and humanity is one of them. Humanity follows the Earth, the Earth follows Heaven, Heaven follows the Tao, and the Tao follows what is natural."

Note that the essence of Lao Tzu's 《Tao Te Ching》 is in the first few sentences of Chapter 1 and the explanation of Chapter 25, but he did not say the "Tao" either. What is it, where is best simple? He just gave descriptions and predictions.

Look here, does he predict and describe our theoretical system of the universal law and Galaxy civilization today:

Could this image of the Big Bang be the very image of the "Origin of Heaven and Earth and the mother of all things"? Is it not the "Something formed in chaos, born before Heaven and Earth; silent, vast, standing alone, unchanging, ever-moving, and capable of being the mother of Heaven and Earth"? Laozi's words may seem complex, but they still offer a prophecy and description of the ultimate simplicity of the Tao.

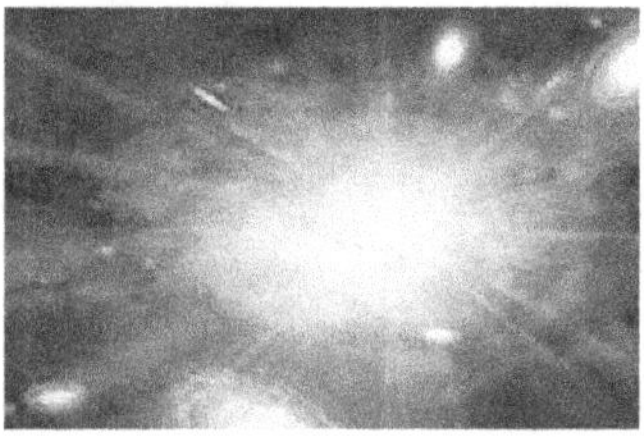

Fig. B3-2 Big Bang Image

Lao Tzu further elaborates in Chapter 42 of the 《Tao Te Ching》:

"The Tao gave birth to One; One gave birth to Two; Two gave birth to Three; Three gave birth to all things. All things carry yin and embrace yang, achieving harmony through the blending of energies."

Notice what he predicts here: what happens after the origin of Heaven and Earth, as the Big Bang unfolds.

Fig. B3-3 The shape of a droplet is shown

One wave follows another, continuously expanding outward ------ this is "The Tao gave birth to One; One gave birth to Two; Two gave birth to Three." The rolling motion up and down signifies "Carrying yin and embracing yang," while maintaining a balance in the center represents "Achieving harmony through the blending of energies."

Through all these descriptions and prophecies, Lao Tzu seeks to understand what the Tao is, what ultimate simplicity is. He not only wants to grasp the Tao's simplicity but also to derive from it everything that occurs in the natural world and society.

You can't just say that “Atom” is the simplicity of everything, but it can only deduce that it is the simplicity of “Matter”.

In the 《Tao De Jing》, Lao Tzu is indeed attentively deducing in a comprehensive way, but his most important central description is still too complicated and too long, not to be simple. Therefore, few people have understood Lao Tzu since ancient times, and many articles have been compiled and misinterpreted, including a large number of his Taoist disciples and disciples.

Only when the Chinese culture with the universal law come, we can truly understand Lao Tzu’s prophecies, and can truly complete the “Great Way to Simple”, that is, “Mysterious and Mysterious, the Gate of All Wonders”; or “Invisible Hand”, no need any weapon, as long as a pen, unifies the world, which is called “A pen is better than a sword”.

Of course, we also sincerely admire Lao Tzu today. The person who can describe the “Best way to simple” most clearly, most meticulously and closest to “The universal law and the Galaxy civilization” is the top Eastern philosopher Li Er, the ancestor of Li.

Through the above analysis, we can say with certainty that metaphysics ".", "1" and "o" are the way to simplicity that transcends everything. This has led to a series unite of studies on natural science, social science and life science.

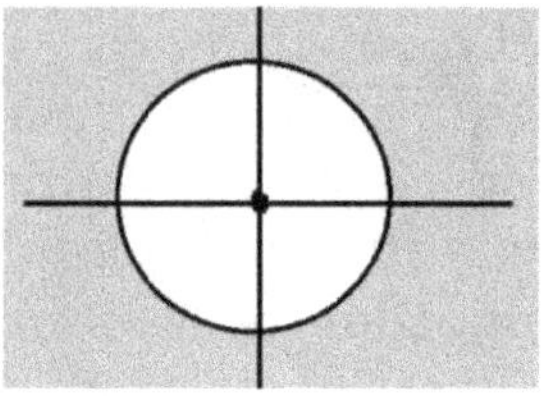

Fig. B3-4 ".", "1" , "o" plan

To put it simply and straight forwardly, whoever has mastered the universal's best way simplicity, will master the highest philosophy; and unified all disciplines, including Religion, Philosophy, and Science; and touched the breakthroughs of Galactic civilization and future civilization.

(January 1, 2019 wrote)

References: 1. Lao Tzu : 《Tao De Jing》

B4. On the Great Learning and the Doctrine of the Mean

Abstract: A true university does not concern itself with ornate buildings, beautiful campuses, or bustling crowds of students. Instead, it is defined by the breakthroughs in knowledge, the innovation in scholarship, and the establishment of an entire civilization. Without profound knowledge, there is no university; with it, even a vast wheat field can become a university. Profound knowledge is something that everyone, people of all ages, and those who have left the school campus, can learn.

Fig. B4-1 Confucius

The great Chinese philosopher Confucius said, "The way of the Great Learning lies in manifesting clear virtue, loving the people, and reaching the ultimate goodness." This means that the purpose of the university is to promote righteousness, to encourage people to abandon the old and embrace the new, and to help them achieve the most perfect state.

Confucius wrote 《The Great Learning》, and its essence lies in these few opening sentences, similar to Laozi's 《Tao Te Ching》. However, judging from the subsequent chapters, Confucius's thinking does not extend as broadly as Laozi's. Laozi's concept of the "Tao" in the first chapter is extended to almost every natural and social domain in subsequent chapters, while Confucius's later discussions mostly revolve around self-cultivation, family governance, and ruling a nation.

Even so, Confucius still identified the key to what a true university is — namely, abandoning the old and embracing the new, constantly improving, and reaching the highest level of wisdom. In essence, a university is about profound knowledge.

Profound knowledge must be broad, innovative, and groundbreaking. For example, Copernicus pioneered the great knowledge of the "Stellar Civilization" — the heliocentric theory — which sparked a scientific revolution that has lasted for nearly 500 years. Much of the knowledge taught in today's global schools originates from the 500 years following Copernicus.

In other words, the era of Copernicus established many university campuses and elevated numerous ordinary schools to university status. This era also gave rise to many great masters, such as Newton and Einstein, who all centered their work around the great knowledge of the "Stellar Civilization" created by Copernicus.

A true university does not concern itself with ornate buildings, beautiful campuses, or large crowds of students. Instead, it is defined by the breakthroughs in knowledge, the innovation in scholarship, and the establishment of an entire civilization. Without profound knowledge, there is no university; with it, even a vast, empty wheat field can become a university. Profound knowledge is something that everyone, people of all ages, and those who have left school, can learn — not just the young people in school uniforms on campus.

What is the academic spirit of Harvard University, a leading institution in the world? Since 1843, the Harvard University Board of Governors has adopted the university spirit of "Being a friend to Plato, a friend to Aristotle, but above all, a friend to truth."

But what is the university spirit in North Korea and Iran? It is to praise Kim Jong-un and Allah. Humanities teachers write about the greatness of the Kim family and Allah's rule; science professors research weapons and nuclear arms for maintaining stability. Can this be called a university?

In the West, any education controlled by priests, imams, or monks cannot be called a university; it can only be called a school. Western governments stipulate that students who graduate from these religious schools are essentially at a middle school level, and their teachers are also at a high school level. This is because such schools cannot innovate, cannot abandon the old and embrace the new, cannot criticize the doctrines and founders from thousands of years ago, and cannot surpass these founders because their founders are considered divine. Therefore, religious schools typically only teach doctrine, theology, or practical subjects like language, literature, and nursing.

Let's turn our attention back to Chinese universities, which are all following a certain Western dogma — "Maxist ideology." Any innovation is suppressed, and publication is strictly controlled. No thoughts are allowed to surpass this Western ideology, which is considered a universal truth, revered as "Great, glorious, and correct."

So, what is this "Ideology"? We know that the highest philosophical thoughts in modern Western history over the past few centuries are Metaphysics, Idealism, and Materialism. Almost all Western philosophy intertwines around these three core concepts, forming what is known as dialectics. This philosophical system was created by many top Western philosophers over the millennia, such as Aristotle, who studied metaphysics. It wasn't the work of a single person. We've also discussed how the dialectical combination of these three concepts partially reflects the principles of Cosmic law and Galactic civilization.

According to the principles outlined in the book The 《Universal Law》, metaphysics represents ".", while materialism and idealism represent "1" and "0". The relationship between these three concepts reflects the dialectical relationships of universal laws.

However, it is astonishing that Marxism insists on only one of these concepts, materialism, while opposing the other two — idealism and metaphysics — or heavily criticizing them. This represents a deviation from philosophy, which, in the context of ancient Chinese philosophy, means not following the Doctrine of the Mean.

In reality, the highest state of materialism is pragmatism. And what is the most practical? Naturally, it's power and money. As ancient feudal emperors often said, "Political power grows out of the barrel of a gun," and "Money can make the devil turn the millstone."

《The Doctrine of the Mean》, another work by Confucius, emphasizes its core principles right in the first chapter: "The Mean is the great foundation of the world; harmony is its universal path. When the Mean and harmony are realized, Heaven and Earth find their proper place, and all things are nurtured."

This means that "The Mean" represents the greatest foundation of all things in the world, and "Harmony" is the universal path shared by people throughout history. When "The Mean" and "Harmony" are achieved, Heaven and Earth attain their rightful positions, and all things can flourish.

In other words, ancient Chinese philosophers adhered to the principle of maintaining the Mean, while Western modern philosophers tend to follow extremes. This highlights the difference between Eastern and Western philosophers. Many people in China revere Western extreme philosophers as their spiritual ancestors and regard their so-called "Ideologies" as sacred texts, when in fact, they are forsaking what is near for what is far, abandoning the root for the branch.

To revitalize Chinese national thought, we must follow the example of Western governments by banning all forms of poison, including both material and ideological, from entering China. We must not allow any dogmatic teachings into our schools. Any student who graduates from religious or dogmatic philosophical schools should be considered to have only a middle school education, and their professors should be regarded as high school level. Only by doing so can we establish high-quality universities, attract high-level professors and students, and ultimately revive the wisdom and civilization of the Chinese nation.

History has proven that after a great fall comes a great rise, and after the darkness of night comes the dawn. The darkest period of Europe's Middle Ages, spanning 500 years, paved the way for the Renaissance and the creation of the "Stellar Civilization". Similarly, China's thousands of years of feudal darkness are the precursor to the revival of Chinese civilization and the birth of the "Galactic Civilization".

Therefore, a university is not just a physical entity; it is a spirit and soul, a reflection of a nation's cultural spirit. It cannot be bought with money. Just like in football, no matter how much money you have, you cannot buy the spirit of the players. With a strong national cultural spirit, you can inspire awe across the world without spending a penny!

The educational system of the Eastern Laws of the Universe and Galactic Civilization has already been established. China, Egypt, and the Maya, the three ancient civilizations, have united to integrate the entire theoretical system of the current "Stellar Civilization", encompassing all religious, philosophical, and scientific knowledge from both East and West. The future direction of research has been set.

Thus, a university is synonymous with "Great knowledge" and the advancement of civilization. Only with "Great knowledge" can a university campus be formed, attracting a large number of excellent teachers and students. This is how we can break the cycles of history and elevate civilization to a higher level.

(Written in April 2019)

References:

1. Confucius: 《The Great Learning》 and 《The Doctrine of the Mean》

B5. On Human Social Systems

Abstract: Economists often divide the development of human society into six stages: Primitive society, Slave society, Feudal society, Capitalist society, Socialist society, and Communist society. However, this paper argues that socialist and communist societies are more like utopian fantasies rather than actual social systems. Capitalism also cannot be considered a social system because it merely represents a free market economy and free enterprise economy. Capitalist activity has existed since primitive society, beginning with barter exchanges, and will continue until the end of human society.

Human society can be divided into political and economic aspects. Politically, it can be categorized into five stages: Primitive society, Slave society, Feudal society, Democratic society, and Unified society. These five stages form a complete cyclical process, similar to the life cycle of a person or the cyclical patterns of celestial bodies.

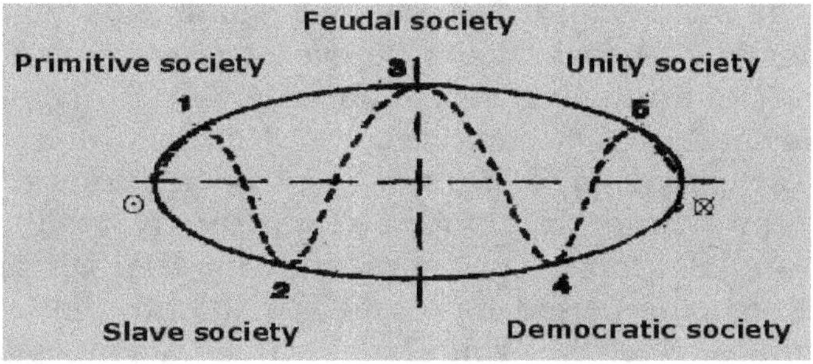

Fig. B5-1 The political and social system

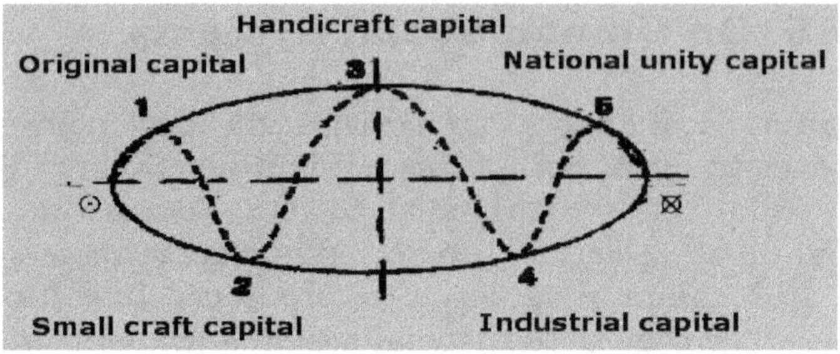

Fig. B5-2 The capital activity system

From an economic perspective, corresponding to the political systems are: Primitive capital, Small-scale handicraft capital, Handicraft capital, Industrial capital, and State unified capital. This also forms a complete cyclical process. Politics and economics influence each other and often conflict, but social and economic scholars have mistakenly conflated them, leading to incorrect classifications of social systems. For example, upon observing large-scale industrial activities by capitalists, they declare it a Capitalist society, which then gives rise to theoretical debates about Socialist and Communist societies. These theoretical debates have further escalated into class struggles in some countries, causing significant political and economic upheaval globally over the past century, resulting in the untimely death of millions.

Feudalism declined after five cycles. Taking China as an example, the early Han, Tang, and Song dynasties represent the first, third, and fifth waves of prosperity, while the Northern and Southern Dynasties and the Five Dynasties and Ten Kingdoms period represent the second and fourth waves of chaos. After the Song Dynasty, feudalism began its decline.

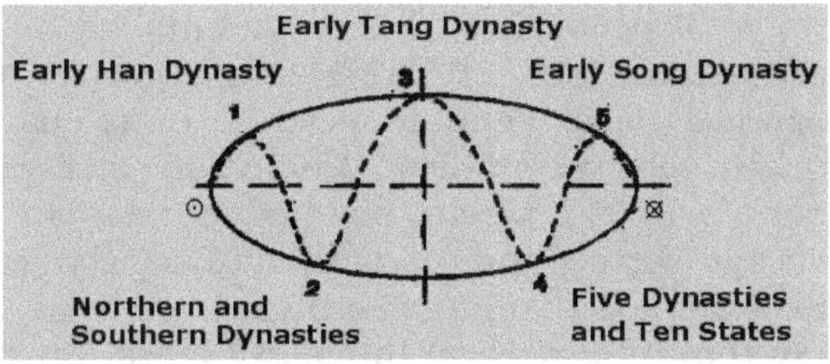

Fig. B5-3 The five-wave cycle of feudalism

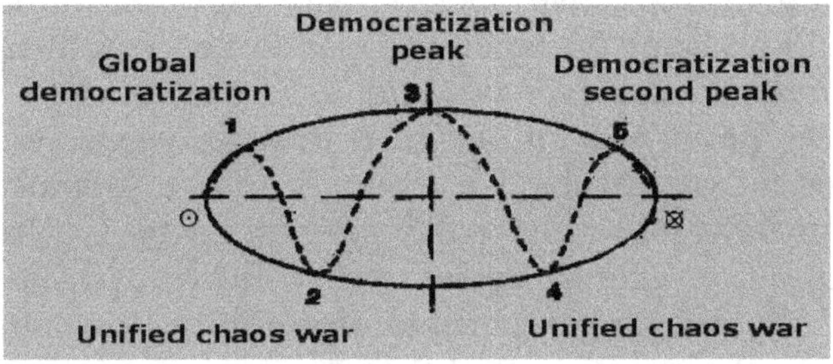

Fig. B5-4 The five-wave cycle of democracy

It is speculated that in the future, all countries will democratize, reaching a first peak, followed by three and five more peaks of democracy, with two major wars in between — likely religious wars and wars for unification —spanning several hundred years. After several hundred or even a thousand years of democracy, society will enter a unified system. What is a unified system? Simply put, it is the unification of religious thought, scientific culture, and nation-states.

The five political systems — Primitive society, Slave society, Feudal society, Democratic society, and Unified society — are analogous to the stages of a person's life: Childhood, Adolescence, Youth, Middle age, and Old age. Childhood corresponds to Primitive society, where people run around naked, knowing nothing. Adolescence corresponds to a Slave society, where parents shout and scold, and sometimes lead children around with ropes. Youth corresponds to a Feudal society, where parents arrange marriages, jobs, or studies. Middle age corresponds to a Democratic society, where one gains freedom and autonomy. Old age corresponds to a Unified society, where one enjoys the happiness of a large family.

We can say that after several thousand years, Primitive society went through several hundred years of turmoil before evolving into a Slave society. After several thousand more years, Slave society experienced another few hundred years of upheaval and evolved into a Feudal society. The Feudal society persisted for a few thousand years, with a similar period of unrest before evolving into a Democratic society. Eventually, society will progress into a Unified society. This is a grand cycle, with shorter periods of turbulence ("1") and longer periods of stability ("0"), similar to the laws of human evolution. Each time society transitions from turmoil to stability, it takes a step forward, which is the fundamental truth of the laws of the universe.

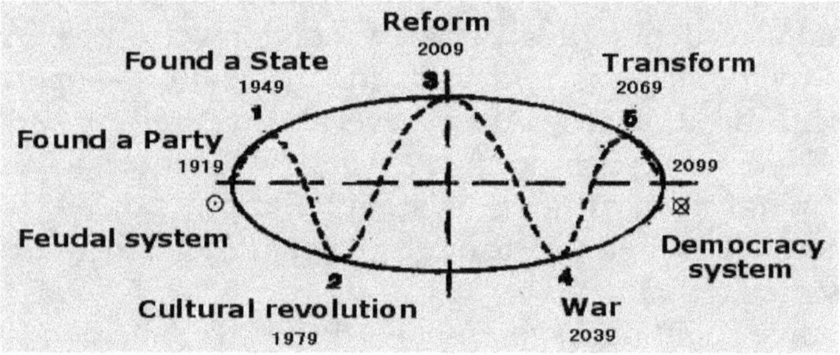

Fig. B5-5 Transition from Feudalism to Democracy

This figure represents the transitional period in China as it moved from the end of the Qing Dynasty's Feudal system to a Democratic society, with each cycle lasting approximately 30 years, plus or minus five years. The establishment of the Communist Party in 1919 and the founding of the People's Republic of China 30 years later represent the upward phase of progress. From 1949 onwards, the country experienced a period of chaos, signaling a downward phase of regression. The end of the Cultural Revolution in 1979 marked the beginning of another phase of reform and progress. Around 2009, a turning point was expected, with China entering a downward phase until 2039, due to the current system's inability to adapt to social development and increasing contradictions. If China can transition to a democratic system, it may avoid this 30-year downturn.

Extraterrestrial civilizations are also aware of this. They have created a series of Crop circles in the fields of England to demonstrate this phenomenon — an absolute marvel!

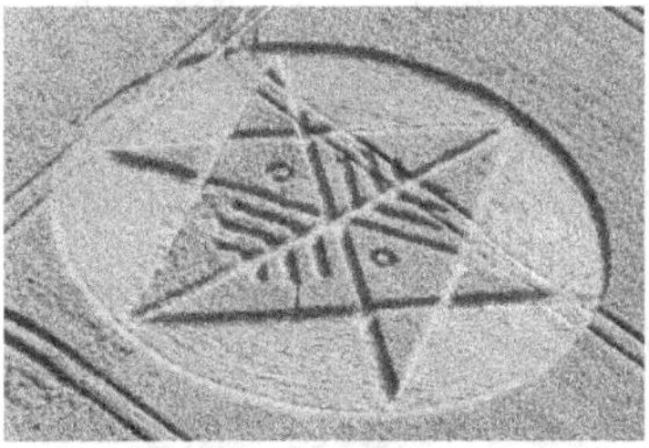

Fig. B5-6 Aug. 22, 2014, Ackling Dyke, nr Sixpenny Handley, Dorset, UK. Crop circle, describing politics, fighting with bows and arrows, Primitive society.

Fig. B5-7 Jul.5,2009, Silbury Hill, nr Avebury, Wiltshire, UK. Crop circle depicting politics, chieftain's feather makeup, and Slavery society.

Fig. B5-8 Jul 23, 2012, Longwood Warren, nr Winchester, Hampshire, UK. The crop circle depicts political science, the crown monarchy, and Feudalism.

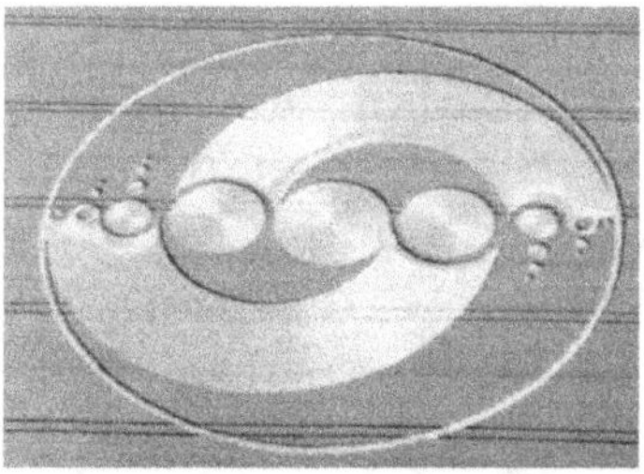

Fig. B5-9 Jul. 28, 2002, in Avebury, Wiltshire, UK. The crop circle describes political science, two parties competing for power, the separation of powers, and the Democratic system.

Fig. B5-10 Aug. 3, 2008, in Yatesbury, Wiltshire, UK. The crop circle describes political science, the law is a diamond, the universal laws are the hardest, Unified system.

(Written in 2016, images available online)

References:

1. John Chang: 《Universal Law》 (2003), selected chapters 9 and 18,
2. 《Crop Circle》 (2015), published by Universal Publishing.

B6. On Money and Power

Abstract: At present, the main pyramid worship sites of "Galactic civilization" have been established, such as Egypt, Mexico and Australia, and have been widely spread since tens of thousands of years ago.

And those "Stellar civilizations" have many main worship sites, such as Christian, Islamic and Buddhist churches and temples, etc. They spent a lot of money to build these many low-level primitive things. I just hope they can continue to spread some kindness and stop violence and war. The believers are all ignorant and stupid, but like some corrupt and barbaric churches, I believe they will soon die out in the near future.

My friend said to me: "Some people say that the more money, the greater the power, the better. You spend so much time writing books without seeking power and making money. Why?"

I said: "The concept of human beings is not measured by money and power. Yes, you said that the richest people in the world are rich people, but have they been rich for three generations? Within a few generations, the money will be spent out by the children and grandchildren."

My friend said: "If these rich people donate money to the church or building churches and temples, will the role of money be magnified, and finally spread to the world?"

I said, "It depends on whether the things they donated money to build are meaningful? There are many rich people who have done this. There were a lot of mud tires and idols within the temples or churches, but they all only brought war."

My friend said, "How are you going to do that?"

I said: “Originally, I thought, if I had money, I would build a few Pyramids in a triangle, such as one in Egypt, one in Mexico, and one in Australia. I didn’t expect that wealthy people (Or the government) built them for me tens of thousands of years ago. The three Pyramids in Egypt; the three groups of pyramids in Mexico, and the pyramids in Australia (Big red rock). I didn't use hundreds of thousands of Egyptian labourers to build these pyramids without spending a penny or organizational manpower. These are the most precious antiques, and do you say it is not magic?"

The friend said: “Only state can funded to build these Pyramids, and the world's richest man can not do them!"

I said: “Yes, and between Egypt and Mexico, there is the Chinese 《I Ching》 and gossip civilization; between Egypt and Australia, these is Indus Valley civilization; between Mexico and Australia, these is Easter Island civilization. I also want to build a civilization to spread the laws of the universe, but I didn’t spend anything, nor did I look for believers or publish pujas to incite the crowd. It’s all done there. It’s a miracle! I imagined giving these memorials to the locals to manage them. They also have military police to protect these memorials and always spread the laws of the universe, and the longer the time, the higher the value of the antiques."

My friend disagrees: "Those are the property of other people's countries, of course they are protected by the military and police?"

I said, "You don’t know. If you don’t know the purpose of these things, how they are yours, it’s like you gave a computer to a monkey, but it doesn’t know how to use and what to do. It’s its property, but it is only for safekeeping. These pyramids are placed in these countries, but they don’t know why they are placed there and what their function is. They only take care of them, and they charge for guarding fees and entrance fees."

Fig. B6-1 Big Red Rock, Australia

Fig. B6-2 Mayan Pyramids in South. America

Fig. B6-3 Egyptian Pyramids

The friend said to me, "The church cheated on money. Many churches have demonstrated their doctrine and power, and many dictators in the world have great power in control of the country's resources! What do you think?"

I said, "No matter how high the churches are built, also pointless; no matter they have big powers, not high as the law of the universe!"

The friend said: "How do you explain? "

I said: "These dictators, though it seems there is a lot of power in their country, bravado for blessing and oppressing the people, they must be governed by the UN's international law (That is the law of Stellar civilizations). Like the former Iraqi President Saddam, although he has power, as long as he does not abide by the regulations of the United Nations, and the United States will organize some army overthrown him. That's it! The United Nations' international law (ie. the law of Stellar civilizations) is higher than the law compiled by these dictators, but it must follow the laws of the universe. If they don't, all countries in the world will war and fall behind. So the highest law and power is the universal law. Look at the centre of the Galaxy, it doesn't care how the Sun turns, but the solar system will never turn out of its palm."

My friend said, "What about the global university education?"

I said, "The global universities should be the laboratory on the laws of the universe. The scientists are verifying the laws of the universe. Although there are millions of papers every year, most of them understand and explain the universal law, mainly single subjects, which are a supplement to the overall laws of the universe."

My friend said: "What about religion for the whole world?"

I said: "Although the universal law have unified them, it is not easy to completely give up worshiping false Gods and people in a short time for them. The main reason is that the church needs to incite and make money.

At present, 'Galactic civilization' or the main pyramid belief sites have been established, such as in Egypt, Mexico and Australia, and they have been widely spread since tens of thousands of years ago.

Fig. B6-4 Church

And those low-level 'Stellar civilizations' mainly worship in many places, such as Christianity, Islam, and Buddhist churches and temples. They have spent a lot of money to build these many low-level and primitive things, and only hope that they will continue to spread some kindness, stop violence and war. Believers are ignorant, but barbaric churches like Communist and Islam believe that they will soon die out in the near future. "

(Edited on Oct 8, 2016)

B7. On Systems - Unified System, Republic System, and Unified Republic System

Abstract: Although there are currently over 130 countries globally that claim to be "Republics", according to the "Galactic Civilization Theory of Universal Laws", none of these countries can be considered true republics based on their political nature. The concepts of the "Unified System", "Republic System", or a combined "Unified Republic System" represent the governmental structure of "Galactic Civilization", akin to the United Nations system of the Solar System. Only when each country's political system mirrors that of the United Nations can it truly be called a republic. From galaxies to individual stars, from the United Nations of the Solar System to each country, all would adopt a "Republic" system, which is the envisioned future governance model.

Fig. B7-1 United Nations General Assembly

1. Introduction

The issue of a nation's governance system is the most significant problem in human society. It determines the progress or backwardness of a country and its people and also the loss of countless lives and resources. We have already discussed that human society has passed through three major governance systems: "Primitive Demise System, Slave Enclave System, and Feudal County System". We are now approaching the next two: "Democratic Parliamentary System and Unified Republic System", completing the five major governance systems.

2. Social Governance Systems

1) Feudal System and Democratic System

In ancient times, emperors used a series of feudal theories to govern the people, with the emperor as the supreme authority. Laws applied downward, with the elite exempt from punishment, which maintained relative social stability. They were very successful over thousands of years, despite numerous wars and deaths, and many countries have not easily changed these systems. Some countries still maintain symbolic monarchies, such as the United Kingdom, Japan, and Thailand.

In modern times, a new type of permanent and absolute ruler has emerged, not called an emperor (As the old emperors have long been ousted), but rather a variant of the emperor — a dictator with lifelong tenure, often appointed by their predecessor or through family inheritance, as seen with Nazi Germany or North Korea. Sometimes, these dictators possess great abilities and are genuinely supported by the people of their era and class. However, in the end, they often cause the greatest harm to their country and people.

The feudal system is akin to asexual reproduction in a family lineage, while the democratic system is more like sexual reproduction. The modern democratic system evolved from the feudal system, following the path of biological evolution with slow but transformative changes. The United States, a relatively young nation, almost bypassed the feudal stage and directly became a democracy.

The democratic system requires judicial independence, the nationalization of the military, and independent administrative operations, known as the separation of powers. Judicial independence ensures oversight of the highest leaders; nationalized military forces prevent the formation of party armies; and independent administrative operations prevent the state from becoming a party-state.

The competition between two parties serves to optimize and oversee future leaders, avoiding the pitfalls of inbreeding. However, the competition between two parties can also cause internal conflicts, which often weaken economic development, as resources are spent on internal party disputes. It is similar to a family, where much energy is spent resolving internal marital conflicts.

2) Unified Republic System

The "Unified Republic System" is a governing system that follows the "Democratic Parliamentary System" and represents another evolutionary breakthrough in human society's political structure. Currently, there is no direct biological comparison for this system since biological evolution on Earth has only reached the stage of sexual reproduction. In practical terms, the governing system operates similarly to the current United Nations. Each country holds two-party elections to elect a president, but once in the United Nations, the UN chairman is no longer elected by two-party systems but is instead chosen on a rotating basis. This is the essence of the "Unified Republic System."

In reality, the management model of the "Galactic Civilization" family is also similar to the United Nations of Earth's solar system, following a "Unified Republic" management model, which is the envisioned "Unified Republic System" of the future.

Let's first examine the current definition of "Republic". According to encyclopedias, a republic is a form of government where the head of state is not a monarch but an official elected by the people under the law. Countries that implement a republic system are usually called "Republics". There are currently 135 countries in the world with "Republic" in their official names.

Frankly, this definition of a "Republic" is quite confused. If the ruler is elected by the people and chosen according to the law, rather than being privately appointed from above, it should be considered a "Democracy". Countries with such a system should be called "Democratic nations". Conversely, if the ruler is appointed by divine right or monarchy, that system is feudalism, and the country should be called a "Feudal nation".

The aforementioned definition of a "Republic" seems similar to that of a "Democracy". If the definition of a "Republic" is that all ethnic groups "Coexist peacefully" within a "Country", it would be somewhat accurate, but this does not reflect the nature of the political system.

According to the "Galactic Civilization Theory of Universal Laws", while more than 130 countries globally claim to be republics, none of them truly qualify as such when considering the nature of their political systems. Most of these nations' leaders have adopted practices that mislead both their citizens and the world, elevating their own rule under a guise of progressiveness.

For example, nations where multiple parties or more than two parties elect the head of state under the law — most Western countries — should be collectively referred to as "Democratic nations". Therefore, the United States should be called "The Democratic Nation of America". In contrast, nations where the ruler is appointed by their predecessor, regardless of any changes in title or appearance, are essentially dictatorships or monarchies. North Korea, for instance, where the supreme leader is not democratically elected but rather designated by the previous president, should be internationally recognized as "The Feudal Nation of North Korea."

In summary, the international community should categorize and name countries based on their actual political systems, rather than accepting the labels those countries self-proclaim. These categories might include five levels, reflecting a range of governance systems. For instance, "The United Arab Emirates" accurately reflects its nature as a federation of sheikhdoms, acknowledging its origins in primitive or slave-based Islamic worship systems characterized by practices such as polygamy and the arbitrary treatment of women. Similarly, "The Kingdom of Jordan" should be referred to as "The Feudal Nation of Jordan."

Looking at the development of political systems globally, most African nations lean towards "Primitive Systems"; Middle Eastern countries towards "Slave Systems"; Asian countries towards "Feudal Systems", and European and American countries towards "Democratic Systems". However, none have reached the level of a "Republic", that is, a "Unified Republic System".

So, what exactly is a "Republic"? The governance structure of the United Nations exemplifies a "Unified Republic System". The principle behind it is that a republican state operates through rotating leadership rather than election by multiple parties or a single party, nor is the leader chosen entirely by individual votes.

What is the definition of a "Unified Republic System"? It is a governance system that, building upon the democratic principles of multiparty systems and the separation of powers (Judicial independence, nationalized military, and independent administrative operations), adopts a unified republic administrative management system. This system is similar to the current United Nations or a super-large council and Prime Minister (or Secretary of State) administrative model, where leadership rotates, somewhat akin to a large corporate board of directors and management structure.

The "Unified Republic System" follows the "Democratic Parliamentary System" and represents a further evolution and breakthrough in human society's governance structures. The practical implementation is similar to the current United Nations: each country holds two-party elections to elect a president, but once within the United Nations, the UN chairman is no longer elected by the same process. Instead, the position is filled on a rotational basis, which is the hallmark of the "Unified Republic System".

3) Galactic Civilization's "Unified Republic System"

In the family of the "Galactic Civilization", there are trillions of star systems (Some with one planetary system, others with several). Only a few of these star systems meet the criteria to be considered members of the "Galactic Civilization" (The criteria for membership in the "Galactic Civilization" will be discussed later), while the majority are members of the "Stellar Civilization" or "Planetary Civilization", and many are not anything at all.

Within those star systems that have reached the standards required for membership in the "Galactic Civilization", their organizational structure resembles the current United Nations. There are 8 permanent member star systems and 21 non-permanent member star systems (This is hypothetical, based on the number of star systems that have reached civilization standards within the Galaxy; currently, the "Solar System Civilization" does not meet the criteria for a Galactic civilization). The chairman rotates, and the Secretary-General is elected by the council.

The 8 permanent member star systems of the "Galactic Civilization" are the strongest within the civilization (Similar to the 5 permanent members of the United Nations on Earth). The 21 non-permanent member star systems are the second strongest, while the rest are general members.

This political structure is referred to as the "Unified Republic System" because it would be impossible for the center of the Galaxy to hold elections involving all star systems or to have competition between two major political parties. In essence, the "Unified Republic System" of the Galactic Civilization operates without political parties, and the highest governance is based on a rotational leadership.

4) The Expected "Republican System" of the Solar System Civilization

If the Solar System civilization wants to join the "Galactic Civilization" and become a member of it, then every country within the Solar System must adhere to the "Republican System" of the Galactic Civilization.

What does this mean? It means that from the United Nations on Earth to every country, they must adopt a "Republican System" rather than a "Democratic System" or a "Feudal System".

Let's take an example. If China wants to become a "Republican System" or a true "Republic," the political reform trial could be as follows: China currently has 23 provinces, 5 autonomous regions (which have never really been autonomous), and 4 municipalities directly under the central government (which often conflict with provincial administration, wasting management resources). It is suggested to cancel autonomous regions and turn them into provinces, merge smaller provinces into larger ones, finally forming 24 large provinces. The 5 economically strongest provinces could become permanent members, such as Guangdong, Fujian, Jiangsu, Zhejiang, and Shandong; the next 5 strongest provinces could become non-permanent members, and the rest would be regular members. If a province's economy improves in the future, it could first become a non-permanent member, and adjustments could be made accordingly. If a non-permanent member province performs exceptionally well, it could become a permanent member, but the number of permanent members would be kept at 5, and non-permanent members would also be 5.

The President of the country would be held by the provincial governors, who would rotate, but the 5 permanent member provinces would have veto power, and the 5 non-permanent member provinces would have voting rights. The presidency would rotate every six months, completing a cycle every 12 years, giving each governor a chance to serve as president, similar to the United Nations and the Galactic Civilization.

Provincial governors would have equal status, and no one would have long-term control over the highest authority in the Party, the government, and the military, which is very risky for the country. A leader who wants to go to war would face almost no opposition; one who wants to sell off national territories and squander money abroad would do so without anyone daring to speak up, because everyone is under his control, at his mercy.

The Secretary-General, equivalent to the Prime Minister, would be nominated by the Council of 24 Provincial Governors and handle national affairs. The 5 permanent member governors would have veto power. The Secretary-General's term would be three or five years, longer than that of the President (Under the Unified republican system, the tenure of the highest national leader should not be too long, provincial governors can have longer terms, and the prime minister managing the administration can have a longer term). In principle, managing the country would be like managing a super-large company. Provincial governors would be equivalent to the board of directors, the President would be the Chairman of the Board, and the Prime Minister (or Secretary-General) would be equivalent to the manager, with the law independent of the company, overseeing it.

Currently, each country has two sets of teams: party and administration. As long as there is a separation of powers under the "Democratic System" — i.e., the independence of law, administration, and the military — two parties are not necessary. A one-party system like Singapore's is feasible, or even no parties at all. The country would no longer need party competition and elections but would instead elect directly into the administration.

In short, the President and Prime Minister would check and balance each other, the Prime Minister would be supervised by the Provincial Governors' Council, and the highest national leader, while having the greatest power, would serve in a rotating role with no real administrative authority. If corruption occurred, it would be easily detected.

Furthermore, the election and selection of provincial governors would actually start from the county level, with each province divided into 24 counties. The 5 strongest economically would be called "Permanent Member Counties", and the next 5 strongest would be "Non-Permanent Member Counties". The Chairman of the County Council would become the provincial governor, rotating every six months, completing a 12-year cycle. Permanent and non-permanent member county governors would have voting and veto rights. You could think of the Provincial Governors' Council as analogous to the House of Representatives in the West, and the County Council as analogous to the Senate.

In counties, where the government is closest to the people, the county governors would be directly elected by the people, with the county governor's council chairing. This would allow for selection and examination, competition, and elimination. Corruption and bribery would be difficult to hide, even if someone became president. The other provincial governors would be watching, so the highest leader's time in office would be short, and he would only have one opportunity. This system prevents power from becoming concentrated. Even if corruption occurred, the next president would easily uncover it since they would be from a different province, preventing the formation of a corrupt group from top to bottom. Everyone with ambition would have an opportunity.

In the current situation in China, many government agencies have overlapping and redundant functions. For example, the Ministry of Supervision, the Central Commission for Discipline Inspection, and the courts could all be merged into one. The National People's Congress and the Chinese People's Political Consultative Conference have become clubs for businessmen and celebrities and could be abolished entirely. With no more political parties, a large number of party organizations and institutions would no longer be necessary. Eliminating bloated sections and reducing the heavy taxes and cumbersome finances would allow taxes to be returned to the people. This is a very simple national reform and would be the future "Galactic Civilization" system.

In other words, China doesn't necessarily need to follow the Western "Democratic System" path; it could directly leap to the "Unified Republican System" of the Galactic Civilization. Just like the United States, it bypassed the "Feudal System" of emperors and went directly to a "Democratic System".

I believe that China's future leaders will have the courage and wisdom to make this leap. It has been prophesied that Chinese civilization will unify the globe. By adopting the new system of the "Galactic Civilization" based on universal laws, China would become the power — from its economy to its political system, from its theory to its technology. It would surpass the Western countries' "Democratic System", and only then could it truly be called the "Republic of China", the first true "Republic" system in the world and the most advanced political system of our time.

When all the countries around the world are stunned and start following China's "Unified Republican System", that's when Chinese civilization will lead the globe. In political systems, it will have met the basic membership standards of the "Galactic Civilization".

Simply put, the above system design is akin to projecting the "Galactic Civilization" system downwards. We could consider the current United Nations as the Galactic Civilization's family; each province within a country is equivalent to the United Nations; and each county within a country is equivalent to a province. Multi-party elections could be conducted at the county level, making the situation very clear.

In theory, this "Unified Republican" political system is designed according to the "Heavenly Stems" and "Earthly Branches" as depicted in the Chinese 《I Ching》 system. For example, the "Heavenly Stems" consist of 10 positions, i.e., permanent and non-permanent members arranged spatially, while the "Earthly Branches" consist of 24 provincial governors, each serving as president for six months, completing a 12-year cycle, arranged temporally.

One point to emphasize is that under the "Primitive System", "Slave System", and "Feudal System", the chief or emperor typically holds office for life; under the "Democratic System", the president typically serves from two to eight years; under the "Republican System", the chairperson serves from six months to a year. As systems evolve, the tenure of the highest leader continually shortens because the legal framework of society has become more complete. Continuous changes in decisions by an emperor are no longer necessary; even without an emperor, the social management system of the entire country will still function properly.

In other words, a president of a country holding long-term, independent power is extremely risky, which is why countries under the primitive, slave, and feudal systems often engage in wars. The cases in modern times are too many. For example, the former president of Iraq continuously waged wars; North Korea's leadership's long-term unchanging governance has led to poverty among its people; the former president of the Philippines indulged in corruption , because of long-term rule and leadership, leading them to believe they had become a God. They continuously drained the country, slaughtered their own people and foreigners, and waged wars. The reason why there are so many wars and killings in modern countries is mainly due to the long-term governance of the ruler, turning into a dictatorship.

Therefore, in modern society, governance that exceeds eight years should be regarded as feudal and dictatorial, even if a country initially started as a democratic one. If a president's term exceeds eight years, it can be considered a transition to a Feudal system.

3. Religious Worship System

1) Worship system

In the "Stellar system civilization", if the majority of people are controlled by a certain dictatorial emperor, it is called "Behavioral control". Although the body and residence are controlled by the ruler of the country, people say that the brain is one's own, you can't control it, can you? But the reality is that you can, and that is various religions. If people worship a certain religious leader, or a certain God that the leader speaks of, it is called "Thought control".

Why don't the rulers of the country shut down those places of worship when they know exactly what these religions are? It is because these places do control the less intelligent people and give them comfort in their minds. Rulers and religious leaders have used each other to form a huge system of secularism since ancient times. That is to say, more than 7 billion people's dwellings are now controlled by the rulers of the state, while about 6 billion people's minds are controlled by various religions. Whether you shout "God", "Allah", or "Long live the Emperor", it is all the same.

At present, most of the countries in the world are religious countries, whether you are a Christian, or an Islamic, or a Buddhist, or any other form of religion, as long as there is a religious dogma, the country belongs to the "Stellar system civilization".

There are many other forms of religion, including belief in God, belief in Godlessness, belief in human beings, and belief in clay idol, which are called by different names, but are essentially the same. Most people in the West believe in theism; while most people in the East are said to have no faith, but actually believe in atheism. Whether one believes in a God or in no God, as long as there is an organization with members, charges, and dogmas, it is called a religion.

2) Criteria for a "Galactic Civilization"

The main goal of entering the "Galactic civilization" is to abolish the mechanism of the emperor and the mechanism of religious masters, and to establish the mechanism of "Republican unity", which is also the independence of the three powers, i.e., the independence of the executive, the judiciary and the army. According to the theoretical system of universal laws, i.e. "." , "1", "0" law, the administration is "."; Judicial is "0"; Military is "1".

Simply put, the criteria for entering the "Galactic civilization" and becoming a basic member is that in the administration and state management, there are no emperors and parties; in the belief system, there is no worship, there is no so-called God, Allah, Buddha and so on. Therefore, if you look at the universe, how many "Stellar civilizations" can enter the "Galactic civilization"?

With the current status quo of the solar system civilization, can only be regarded as a "Stellar civilization", can not enter the "Galactic civilization" family, because you can not even meet the most basic membership requirements, not to mention entering the executive director of the Galactic system.

Although the current Western national ruling system, such as the democratic political system, is more advanced than many disguised feudalisms in the East, its ideological system, such as religious beliefs, is still relatively primitive and backward, which is why there are a large number of wars of religious beliefs and believer shootings.

Previously, there was no theoretical system that could touch or break the old theories and mechanisms of these Western religions, but around 2012, the theoretical system of the "Galactic Civilization of Universal Laws" has been established, which has caused a major theoretical crisis in the current global domination system, as well as in the major religions' ideological systems, that is to say, their set of deceptions has begun to fall.

Although the current Western church believers are very calm, thinking that they have a long history and a large number of people, they have killed too many people from history to the present, and their sins are deep. The prophecies of the ancient people of the East and West have already said that most of the various Western churches, in the future, will be swept into history by Eastern civilization.

Although the ruling classes of the world's countries claim that their countries are advanced "Republics", none of them have yet reached it, and are waiting to be upgraded, as mentioned above, in order to reach it.

4. Summary

What we have emphasized above is the Galactic Civilization's concept of "No king, no emperor, and stable world". After decades of propaganda and promotion, the Chinese government has done a good job in the concept of "No God", which has finally eliminated the ignorance and worship of most of the people, and limited the development of the Western false God religions in China, but the biggest problem in China is that it has not eliminated the "King", i.e., the feudal dictatorship and bureaucratic system.

Fig. B7-2 Black hole of the Galaxy

Fig. B7-3 Crowd of worshippers

The West, on the other hand, after centuries of development, has mainly eliminated the "King", i.e., the feudal authoritarian system, but has retained ignorance and the worship of the "Gods", which are actually their godmothers. Note that the overall system in the West is not much more advanced than that in the East, i.e., the governments of the East and the West have did half right.

So as soon as the governments of the East eliminate the "King", i.e., the feudal bureaucracy, then the East immediately enters the "Galactic civilization", as we have discussed above.

(May 2019 Original, Image from the Internet)

B8. Galactic Civilization Festival = Passover + Chi Xian Festival + Easter

Abstract: Why establish a Galactic Civilization? Because the current human belief system is no longer able to support the development of modern human society, just like we currently have hardware that supports WINDOW 10, but you still use WINDOW 2 software to run. We are already in the 21st century, but most of the people (Billions of people) are still kneeling and worshiping the illiterate people of thousands of years ago, and their sermons!

Passover is a Jewish holiday that commemorates that when God want to kill all firstborn creatures in Egypt, it killed only the eldest sons of the Egyptians and passed the eldest sons of the Israelis.

It is written in Chapter 12 of the Book of Exodus in the Old Testament that when the Israelites were in Egypt, they were subjected to hard labour by the Egyptians. The Lord invited Mr. Moses to tell the people to take out the lamb according to their family and kill as Passover lamb. Take a handful of hyssop and dip it in the blood from the basin, and hit the lintel and the left and right door frames. None of you can leave your door until morning.

God killed the Egyptians and crossed the Israeli houses which was with blood on the door lintel or on the left and right door frames, so saved the Israelites. As a result, Mr. Moses led the Israelites to leave Egypt, free from slavery, and head to the beautiful land of Canaan promised by the Lord. Passover is a sacrifice to God.

Easter (Latin: Pascha), also known as the Lord's Resurrection Day, was an important Christian holiday. Before the crucifixion of Jesus in Christianity, the Last

Supper was the Passover dinner with the disciples. According to the Jewish definition of a day, it started at sunset and ended at sunset on the second day. Jesus died that year on the day of Passover (Thursday sunset to Friday sunset) . This holiday is to commemorate the resurrection of Jesus Christ on the third day after the crucifixion in 30/33 A.D. It is the peak of Christian faith and is therefore regarded by Christians as a symbol of rebirth and hope.

Most churches believe that Jesus was killed on Friday (The day before the Sabbath), so their "Passover" memorial, must be held on the Friday of Holy Week, called Holy Friday. Jesus was resurrected on Sunday, and Easter will be held at the same time as the Passover. Due to some historical changes, it is impossible for the annual Passover to happen on Friday, so the Easter day of most churches does not coincide with the Jewish holiday.

"Chi xian" (赤县 Red County) Festival: also called the Chinese Festival, to commemorate the great ideas of Chinese civilization. These ideas includes from 《He Tu》, 《Luo Shu》, 《The Book of Changes》, 《Tao De Jing》, ..., to the seven colourful golden books (Unification of religion, philosophy and Science), all the ideological essence of the five thousand years, can also be referred to as Chinese education for short. Why do explain this? This is to pave the way for the Trinity of the Galaxy Civilization Festival.

"Chi xian" (赤县 Red County) and "Shen zhou" (神州 Divine Land), were commonly known as "China". According to legend, the land ruled by the ancient Chinese tribe leader Mr. Huang di was called "Shen zhou"; the land ruled by Mr. Yan di was called "Chi xian".

《Records of the Grand Historian - Biography of Mencius and Xun Qing》: "China is called the Divine Land of the Red County."

《Comprehensive Discussion of Ancient and Modern Times》: "Five thousand li southeast of Kunlun is called the Divine Land. In this land, there is a place called the Homeland of Harmonious Broth, covering three thousand li. It is the region of the Five Sacred Mountains, the residence of emperors, and the birthplace of sages."

《Chronicles of the Primordial Sage》: "In ancient times, in the Divine Land, the Tao of Immortality was used to educate the world. From the Three Sovereigns to the Five Emperors, all who practiced it became immortals."

《Taiqing Elixir of Gold and Jade Scripture》: "In ancient times, the sages regarded China as the Divine Land. They aligned the Nine Provinces with the Eight Trigrams, with the Pole Star above and the earth's core below. Therefore, the Nine Provinces exist here".

"Hua xia" (华夏) was also called "China". For thousands of years, the Han nationality has formed a splendid Chinese culture on the basis of Jin, Yan, Qin, Qi, Wu, Yue, Chu and other countries, and also formed great Chinese culture which is with the ethnic minority compatriots who lived and multiplied in this "Shen zhou" land.

The seven colourful golden books started to write at the religious massacre on September 11, 2001, and ended at Easter in 2018, which lasted 17 years. The average main books were completed in about year 2012. Based on Eastern and Western civilizations, combined with the ancient civilizations of China, Egypt, and Maya, the Stellar civilization (Solar system) was put to an end and the Milky Way civilization was established. In order to celebrate this great historical process, we established the Galaxy Civilization Festival.

The Galaxy Civilization Festival = Passover + Chinese (Red county) Festival + Easter, the Trinity, which confirms the prophecies of the Old Testament of the Bible.

The biblical prophecy was that after passing the red place, Chi Xian (Or red county, or China), all firstborn of other religions will be killed, or terminated only the source of these churches, that was not the believers, and then a new civilization was resurrected.

The 《Old Testament》 of the Bible was originally mostly prophecies of the future, a bit like a 《Tui Bei Tu》 (Chinese prophecy Book), which metaphors many stories about history and the future, so it is called "Covenant", which is an agreement with God in the future. People in the church today, like pastors and priests, do not understand at all. Therefore, ordinary churches do not talk about the 《Old Testament》, only the so-called 《New Testament》. The 《New Testament》 was relatively simple. It is just the Biography of the Master and the Acts of the Apostles, as well as their preaching stories, but it was not an agreement with God or a book of future prophecies at all.

Modern churches use people to preach by deceptive methods, that is, they mainly boast that the leader was a God, and allow believers to worship and defraud money. This has led to a large number of cults. Because most cults believe that if you use worship to cheat money, we can also cheat, and the number of cheaters is larger and wider, which brings a lot of wars and deaths.

Because the Passover and Easter are so close in history, it seems that someone specially arranged it, because God had to let Jesus die on Passover, so when Jesus died, he shouted "My God, why did you abandon me!" It's not abandoning, it's arranged. Only when you die, you will be resurrected three days later. It is also the trinity of Passover, Chinese Festival and Easter, which is the Galaxy Civilization Festival come. How meaningful and far-reaching is this!

This is from the so-called theological aspect, in fact, it is prophecy. Many prophecies in ancient and modern times, both at home and abroad, revolve around the 7 colourful golden books, that is, the Galactic civilization. I didn't know before. Others told me that I took a closer look and thought about it. It was really like this, and the ancients predicted it very accurately, including time, place, and characters, as if they have seen today's things at hundreds of years ago. Not only did the prophets have Chinese people, but even foreigners from far away in Europe saw today's scene. It's incredible to be able to predict what happened in China. This phenomenon of time and space travel may be the direction of future research.

From the aspect of natural science morphology, the shape of the Galaxy system is different from the shape of the Star system, gathering all the stars and then surpassing them. The star system can not surpass, just gathers planets and circulates. Therefore, the Galactic civilization is different from the Stellar civilization, which has the double meaning of transcendence and resurrection.

The "Transcendence" of Galactic civilization means to surpass all current religions and their derivative religions, because they are full of blood and violence; or full of money and power struggles. Furthermore, It also goes beyond modern religion, philosophy and science.

The "Resurrection" of the Galactic civilization means that the ancient civilizations of China, Egypt and Maya are all activated, that is, the pyramid civilization is revealed.

Why establish a Galactic civilization? Because the current human belief system can no longer support the development of modern human society, just as we currently have hardware that supports WINDOW 10, but you still use WINDOW 2 software to run it. We have reached the 21st century, but most people are still kneeling down and worshipping the illiterate thousands of years ago, and their preaching, isn't it weird! Another example is a Muslim woman who was persecuted by Muslim men. She wears a Muslim veil when she goes to receive the award. She does not hate this religion, only Muslim men. Isn't this ridiculous? In fact, these Muslim men are also victims of these religions!

So we must update the software, that is, we need a stronger belief system to support modern civilization in the 21st century. Only in this way can our planet have permanent peace.

Although there were some philosophical systems in ancient times, such as Confucianism and Taoism, or some philosophical thought systems, such as materialism, idealism, metaphysics and atheism, appeared in the early times, but most of these systems revolved around the social and humanistic realm and were full of errors, unable to support the current scientific theoretical system and modern civilization, so a more powerful theoretical system is needed. This is that we currently establish of the Universal law and Galaxy civilization.

Regarding the universal law civilization content that supports the modern civilization systems, our book and the previous introduction articles have covered it. I will not repeat it here. We will only talk about the time of the "Galaxy Civilization Festival".

The time of the Galaxy Civilization Festival includes the Passover, Chinese (Red County) Festival and Easter. It has the characteristics of a "Trinity Festival", which means that it is across the red place (“Chi xian” or China), and then God was resurrected and reached the galactic civilization.

This is a three-day consecutive holiday, a day of global celebration. The three festivals are also the longest holidays of the year, and they are global and do not belong to one ethnic group or one church. I believe it will appear in the future.

This three-day all-in-one festival combines the civilizations of the East and the West, namely Judaism, Chinese religion and Christianity, the ideological essence of the three major ethnic groups, corresponding to the culture passed on by Gods. The "Gods" we are talking about may be highly intelligent aliens, just as cats and dogs treat us as Gods. They are obviously looking at us in another dimension, and then controlling our thoughts. They know everything, including the future of our planet. These were also prophesied by the strange books hundreds of years ago, as well as the prophecies of civilizations such as Egypt and Maya. They seemed to know everything we did.

In the future, during these three-day long holidays each year, a large number of people will come to the Great Red Rock Pyramid in Australia; the Egyptian Pyramid; and the Mayan Pyramid for ceremonies, showing the Galaxy Civilization that was born around year 2012.

(First edited on Nov.23, 2018)

B9. On Chinese Civilization

Abstract: Broadly speaking, the Chinese civilization arose in the land of China and were created and developed by Chinese people. Maybe some Chinese persons went abroad for different reasons, but their background are Chinese civilization, written in Chinese, not a dogma or civilization created by Westerners and spread to China.

Many people ask me what is the Chinese civilization, and what are its representatives? Such as some of the Western religions that exist in China have been spread in China for thousands of years, and some have been integrated into the Chinese civilization, and some are in absolute dominance in China. Do these Western religions and dogmas belong to Chinese civilization?

I said no, they cannot represent Chinese civilization. Even though their some have been completely assimilated by Chinese civilization, they still cannot represent Chinese civilization. Take Buddhism for example, they have built a large number of clay sculpture in China, worshipped idols and made money. They have been assimilated by Chinese civilization, but they do not belong to Chinese civilization.

So what can represent Chinese civilization? Broadly speaking, Chinese civilization was born in this land of China, and it was created and carried forward by the Chinese. Maybe this Chinese went abroad for different reasons, but his background is Chinese civilization, writing in Chinese, not the dogma and civilization created by Westerners and spread to China.

What is the difference between Western religion and Eastern religion? Western religion was more accumulates wealth and power, worships idols and kills more than

Eastern religion. As we can see from history, countless world wars have come from the West, such as Europe and the Middle East, and there are almost no world wars extending from the East. There is an exception for the Mongols fighter from the East to the West, but the Mongols have no civilization. They are a nomadic steppe people. They have no fixed homeland and cannot be counted as Eastern civilization.

But the West is not. They have ancient Greek and Roman civilizations, but they are still like to kill. Thousands of years of war have made them believe in weapons even more, believing that weapons can unify the world. Therefore, the chief scientists of all countries in the Western world are now weapons experts, and they are also the largest industry supported by the government.

Someone asked whether Confucianism represent Chinese civilization? I said no. Confucianism is only a part of Chinese civilization and cannot represent Chinese civilization. Although the ruling classes in the past have vigorously praised Confucianism, and some have even spent a lot of money to promote it to the world, but Confucianism only helps the ruler to rule or make the people ignorant, and it is of little importance in Chinese civilization.

We will now show what Chinese civilization includes. Simply put, Chinese civilization has existed in China for more than 5,000 years, starting from the mythologies emperor Yan and Huang period.

1) Chinese characters: According to legend, they were mainly created by Mr. Cang jie and Emperor Huang (The mythologies emperor Yan and Huang period), but the most likely fact is that there were some characters before, but Mr. Cang jie and Emperor Huang combined the Chinese characters into a whole system and created many new texts have been added.

2) Number Image Theory: 《He Tu》(河图) and 《Luo Shu》（洛书）(Xia and Shang Dynasties), according to legend, are Mr. Fu xi gossip and Hong Fan nine categories, and there is "Mr. Fu xi king the world, the dragon and horse go out of the river, and then the text draws gossip, and call 《He Tu》", "The book came out from Luo, and was called 《Luo Shu》 and carried by the turtle, listed on the back, there are number to nine, Mr. Yu （禹）put it as ranked, with nine categories, often Tao is in order" legend. Due to the uncertain time, we tentatively they create and develop the number and image theory and works in the Xia and Shang dynasties.

3) The theory of hexagrams: 《The Book of Changes》(Zhou Dynasty), according to legend, was formed by King Wen of the Zhou Dynasty, with creation of 64 hexagrams. This book uses a set of symbol systems to describe the simplicity, change, and difficulty of the state. It expresses the philosophy of Chinese classical culture on cosmology. Its central idea is to interpret the inherent characteristics and laws of natural operation, interpret the alternation of Yin and Yang, and describe everything in the world. 《The Book of Changes》 was originally used for divination, and later influenced philosophy, religion, politics, economy, medicine, astronomy, arithmetic, literature, music, art, military, and martial arts etc. throughout China.

4) Moral theory: 《Tao De Jing》 (Spring and Autumn period), a philosophical work of Mr. Lao Tzu (Li Er), is an important source of Taoist philosophy. It takes the philosophical "Morality" as the keynote, discusses the ways of self-cultivation, governance, military use, and health preservation, and also discusses politics etc. It has profound cultural meanings and is acclaimed as the king of the ten thousand scriptures.

5) Confucian theory: 《The Great Learning》, 《Doctrine of the Mean》, 《Mencius》 (Spring and Autumn and Warring States Period). The authors were Confucius and Mencius. Confucianism is also known as Confucius and Mencius thoughts. The Zhou Dynasty ritual and music tradition, with benevolence, forgiveness, sincerity, filial piety, etc. as the core values, emphasizes the moral cultivation of gentlemen, emphasizes the complementarity of benevolence and etiquette, emphasizes the five ethics and family ethics, advocates civilization and benevolent governance, despise punish, criticizes tyranny, and strives rebuild the order of etiquette and music, change customs, protect the country and the people, and be to fit in with the world and the spirit of humanism.

A large part of Confucianism is a practical part of sociology, so the rulers prefer and strongly admire it. After the Spring and Autumn and the Warring States Period, Chinese philosophy almost stopped moving, only revising these Confucianism until the advent of Western philosophy, which was related to the suppression and abolition of other Chinese academic thoughts and the cult of Confucianism by the Chinese rulers.

6) Historiography: 《Historical Records》 and 《Three Kingdoms》 (Han and Jin Dynasties). The peak and masterpieces of historiography are from the Han Dynasty to the Jin Dynasty. The representative figures are Mr. Sima Qian and Mr. Chen Shou. Although there have been some historians in the past dynasties, none of the works can surpass Mr. Sima Qian in the Han Dynasty. Mr. Sima Qian was study of heaven and people relationship, through the changes of the past and the present, and become own doctrine, had a profound impact on the development of later historiography and literature.

The method of narrating history in the chronology style pioneered by 《Historical Records》 was passed down by the "Official History" of the subsequent dynasties. 《Historical Records》 was also an excellent literary work, and Mr. Lu Xun called it "The swan song of the historian, the 《 li Sao》 without rhyme".

7) Poem: 《Tang Poems》 (Tang Dynasty), the main authors, Mr. Li Bai, Mr. Du Fu, Mr. Bai Juyi, etc. Since the 《Book of Songs》 , 《Chu Ci》 , 《Han Fu》 , and 《Yue fu》 , China has always had the tradition of verse. The 《Book of Songs》 mostly uses four characters as a sentence, and the number of characters 《Yue fu》 in the Han Dynasty has changed. The development of the Wei and Jin Dynasty, Southern and Northern Dynasties has an unfixed number of characters, and there are also five, six or seven characters, but the number of sentences is not limited. In addition to inheriting the genre of ancient poem, Sui and Tang Dynasties also developed modern poetry with a neat and beautiful melody, which had more stringent requirements for rhyming, flatness and other metrical rhythms. Tang poem developed a variety of themes, expressed personal emotions, reflected social reality, and had a profound artistic conception, reaching a very high level of art. After the Tang Dynasty, no one can surpass 《Tang Poems》 , including the so-called great poets of the subsequent dynasties.

8) Poetry: 《Song Poetry》 (Song Dynasty), the main author, Mr. Su Shi, Mr. Xin Qiji, Mrs. Li Qingzhao, etc. Song Poetry was a new style of poetry relative to ancient style poetry. The sentences are long and short, which is easy to sing. Because it is the lyrics with music, it is also called "Music Poetry", the song movement, long and short sentences, poems with music, etc., marking the highest achievement of Song Dynasty literature. Song Poetry began in the Liang Dynasty, formed in the Tang Dynasty and flourished in the Song Dynasty. In ancient Chinese literature, there is a fragrant and gorgeous artistic conception, which competes with Tang poem and lays the foundation for the formation of Opera in Yuan Dynasty. After the Song Dynasty, no one surpassed 《Song Poetry》 .

9) Opera: 《Dou E's Injustice》 (Yuan Dynasty), the main author, Mr. Guan Hanqing. Opera in Yuan Dynasty, also known as long and short sentences, is a form of literature and art that prevailed in the Yuan Dynasty, including medley play and scattered music. The medley play in Song dynasty is a kind of performance characterized by comical humour, and it developed into opera form in Yuan dynasty. Each screenplay was mainly divided in quarters, with additional wedges at the beginning or between the quarters. It was the popular in the metropolis (Now Beijing) area. There were also medley play in the Ming and Qing dynasties, but each screenplay was not limited in four parts. The scattered music was popular in the Yuan, Ming and Qing dynasties. Its content was mainly lyric, and there were two types: Small plays and pantomime. Opera in Yuan Dynasty should be the source of all modern operas, such as Peking opera.

10) Novels: 《Romance of Three Kingdoms》, 《Water Margin》, 《Dream of Red Mansions》, 《Journey to the West》 (Ming and Qing Dynasties), the main authors are Mr. Luo Guanzhong, Mr. Shi Naian, Mr. Cao Xueqin, Mr. Wu Chengen, etc. They are at the same level as Western novelists, such as Mr. Shakespeare. Compared with other literary styles, novels have a large capacity, can show the characters' personalities and fate in detail, show intricate contradictions and conflicts, and can also provide an overall and broad social life environment in which the characters live.

11) Prose: Masterpiece 《Republic of China Prose》 (Republic of China), such as articles like "Remember Mr. Liu Hezhen" (Mr. Lu Xun); "My Mother" (Mr. Hu Shi); "One on the Way" (Mr. Yu Dafu), etc. The prose material is very wide and free, not restricted by time and space, and expressive methods are eclectic. It can narrate the development of events, describe the image of characters, express emotions, and make comments. The author can also freely adjust and change according to the content needs. But from the perspective of the prose, no matter how extensive the content and how flexible the expression method is, the theme of the expression must be clear and concentrated.

The above 11 items are the development and inheritance of Chinese civilization, and each dynasty and every generation has independent innovation and transcendence.

Talking about the present, after the Republic of China, that was, from 1949 to the present, almost nothing has been created to surpass the previous ones. Poetry is not better than Tang and Song dynasties, novels are not better than Ming and Qing dynasties, and prose is not better than the Republic of China. Looking at these things published today, the literature strongly supported by the state and the government at the financial level is mainly inherited from the former Soviet Union's peasant revolution novels, but the content and quality are far inferior to the former Soviet Union's novels 《And Quiet Flows the Don》 (Russian: Тихий Дон) and 《How The Steel Was Tempered》 (Russian: Как закалялась сталь) and so on, just say that they copied the form of Soviet peasant novels.

Mr. Jin Yong's martial arts novels are a breakthrough. Although he also inherited the framework of the novels of 《Three Swordsman and Five Righteousness》 in the Ming and Qing Dynasties, he was the only author who surpassed the series of martial arts novels in the Ming and Qing Dynasties. Except for Mr. Jin Yong's martial arts series of novels, no one in other themes can surpass the Ming and Qing dynasties. No matter how these contemporary so-called masters write, no one in fantasy novels surpasses 《Journey to the West》; no one in historical novels surpasses 《Romance of Three Kingdoms》 (Although there are also a large number of messy historical novels, emperor biography, etc.); no historical novels about peasant revolutions surpassed 《Water Margin》; in terms of feudal families, no one surpassed 《Dream of Red Mansions》.

Although the purses of these so-called writer masters are bulging, what are they writing about? Are they all blushing! Most of them are chicken soup for the soul, kneeling and licking with tears, not to mention novels without depth and breadth, but like short stories or prose, and how many people can beyond the period of the Republic of China.

Look at the awards given to Chinese writers by the Western societies. Whether they are literary awards or film awards, they are all peasants' "Hillbilly awards". In their eyes, the Chinese civilization is at this level, and the state supports so-called "Excellent works" are just sorghum consciousness and ignorance, inability to innovate, and worship power and money.

Could it be that Chinese civilization is such a negative energy, low level and junk goods? In fact, it is not. There are many reasons for this. It's mainly about publishing control at the national level. You can't write about other aspects. Only peasant themes and war dramas do not affect the rule before you can be approved the publication. There are also authors, who write only those low-level and praised things can make money and even become officials.

The ancients unlike today, they don't use these works for food, and they don't need your approval to publish. Among the 11 innovations of the ancients listed above, none of them were approved and funded by the government, and none of them praised the emperor and the government. They were the author's natural innovation. Almost all were oppressed and controlled by the imperial court at the beginning, and then become a part of Chinese civilization which can not be surpassed today.

As for the scholars of the imperial Academy supported by the imperial court, such as the Champion, runner up and third place etc., their works did not know what they have, and they were probably all bad products, and they have not made any contribution to Chinese civilization!

In addition, if Chinese civilization is just these 11 things listed above, and can you say that they can unify the world? Of course can not. Why do Western prophets say that Chinese civilization will unify the world? Don't they know that there are only these culture and civilization in Chinese history?

Westerners are so self-confident that they look down on Eastern civilization at all and deliberately suppress it, calling it non-mainstream culture and peasant culture. They already have strong science and technology. They can declare to the outside world that Western civilization will unify the world. Why on the contrary say that Chinese civilization will unify the world?

This is the innate will of heaven, and there is something that appears in all Chinese and foreign prophets, that is, "Chinese civilization will unify the world" and the theoretical system that must be "Deterrence and Convince"!

"Deterrence" means something that makes them fearful and frightens them. "Convince" means to be convinced by mouth or sincerely admire. This is something that the first-class scholars in the West can't achieve! In addition, there is no other way to the bad religions they have created, and they often have religious wars and dead people, which is also a headache!

12) Unified theory: the seven colourful golden book that appeared in the 21st century, a rainbow, that is, the light of wisdom, to be precise, it is the culture of Chinese civilization, the universal law, and the civilization of the Galaxy. Around year 2012, the Star civilization was ended and the Galaxy civilization was established.

The titles of the seven rainbow golden books are 《Crop Circle》, 《Golden Classic》, 《Universal Law》, 《Great Ultimate Theory》, 《Chinese Systems Philosophy》, 《Oriental Systems Literature》 and 《World Systems Science》, writing began on September 11, 2001, the 9.11 religious massacre, and finally between Passover and Easter in 2018. The entire theoretical system unifies all Eastern and Western civilizations, including all Eastern and Western religions, philosophies and science.

The previous Eastern civilization only involved the sociology part, and these seven rainbow golden books almost covered the natural sciences, social sciences and life sciences, and combined them into a unified whole. It unifies all Western and Eastern civilization without using weapons and wars. This corresponds to the entry of foreign, the expansion of Chinese civilization to the world, and the civilization defeats barbarism and ignorance in this way (The civilization is thought and knowledge, the barbarism is weapons and slaughter), if you dare to enter the circle of Chinese civilization, we dare to eat and assimilate you, and expand the circle of civilization to the extreme.

The Chinese civilization established in these 12 parts are complete, and they are all written under hardships, such as the King Wen of the Zhou Dynasty, who was imprisoned in Mai li to write 《The Book of Changes》; Mr. Lao Zi was seclusion for 《Tao Te Ching》; Confucius was trapped in Chen and Cai to make 《Chun Qiu》; Mr. Sima Qian was castrated to write 《Historical Records》; the writers of 《Tang poem》 and 《Song poetry》 were displaced; the official career and family of the writers of novels in Ming and Qing Dynasty were broken. It is such individual who supports the entire Chinese civilization, which shows the perseverance of the Chinese nation.

The 12 parts also correspond to the 12 "Earthly Branches" of the Chinese 《The Book of Changes》, (The "Heavenly Stems" are a number from 1 to 10), which constitutes the centre of Chinese civilization, and corresponds to the predictions of Chinese and foreign prophets from ancient times to the present. The Chinese civilization will unify the world was completed basically.

Western civilization wants to surpass the above 12 items of Chinese civilization. I am afraid that it cannot be accomplished by a single country or a nation. Even if all countries and nations in the world unite, whether they can surpass this spiritually transmitted culture, the universal laws and the Galaxy civilization are all question? We can wait and see.

Note.

1） The mythologies emperor Yan and Huang period: 3000 B.C - 2100 B.C

2） Xia and Shang dynasties: 2100 B.C - 1100 B.C

3） Zhou Dynasty: 1100 B.C - 256 B.C

4） Spring and Autumn period: 770 B.C - 476 B.C

5） Warring States Period: 475 B.C - 221 B.C

6） Han and Jin Dynasties: 202 B.C - 420 A.D

7） Tang Dynasty: 618 A.D - 907 A.D

8) Song Dynasty: 960 A.D - 1279 A.D

9) Yuan Dynasty: 1271 A.D - 1368 A.D

10) Ming and Qing Dynasties: 1368 A.D - 1911 A.D

11) Republic of China: 1912 A.D - 1949 A.D

(First Edited on Nov.23, 2018)

B10. The Way of God and the Rod of God

Abstract: The 《Book of Revelation》 in the Bible points out the battle between the Western "Stellar Civilization's" beastly weapons and the Eastern "Galactic Civilization's" lamb-like philosophy. The lamb's philosophy will ultimately triumph over the beast's weapons because it follows the "Way of God"! However, the mere presence of the universal law, the "Way of God," is not enough. There must also be a "Rod of God," a force that awakens and shakes the ruling system, establishing fairness in human society.

The mission and revolution created by heroes or nobility follow the "Way of God" from top to bottom. This entails reforms through stages such as "Primitive demise system; Slave enclave system; Feudal county system; Democratic parliamentary system and Unified republican system."

The mission and revolution created by the working class, peasants, and slaves follow the "Rod of God" from bottom to top, which means revolting against tyranny. The "Rod" strikes corrupt emperors, churches, landlords, and capitalists, maintaining societal stability.

1. Introduction

The "Way of God" has been developed in the East since ancient times, such as the 《I Ching》 created by King Wen of Zhou; the Taoist, Confucian, and Legalist principles of "Freedom, democracy, and rule of law," which have been followed for millennia. In the West, philosophers like Aristotle introduced materialism, idealism, and metaphysics, which have guided scientific revolutions.

In contemporary times, it is represented by the universal law and the theoretical system of the "Galactic Civilization" within China's divine cultural heritage. Prophecies from various civilizations, both ancient and modern, have already foretold the realization of the "Way of God". Examples include:

- "Taoism": Predicted as "The beginning of heaven and Earth, the mother of all things".
- "Chinese script prophecy": Represented as "Ding" (鼎) (Tripod).
- "Buddhism": Foretold as "The turning of the Dharma wheel, bloodless conquest, sweeping across the universe".
- "Christianity": Foretold as the "Rainbow Covenant".
- "Mayan prophecy": Represented as the "Warriors of the Rainbow".
- "Egyptian prophecy": Seen in the "Eye of the Pyramid".
- "Judaism": Foretold in the "Passover and Easter", representing the Galactic Civilization surpassing the Stellar Civilization.
- "Islam": Foretold as "Seeking knowledge, even if it is as far as China".

All of these are manifestations of the "Way of God", fulfilled through various religious and philosophical systems across different times and cultures.

2. Social and Historical Background

Historically, as early as the Spring and Autumn and Warring States periods, and continuing through the Han and Tang dynasties, China held a unique and prestigious position in global civilization. Despite facing powerful military entities like the Xiongnu in the north, the smaller neighboring nations were more focused on learning Chinese culture rather than heavily developing their own military forces. At that time, China's economy accounted for one-third of the world's total. Even up to the Ming Dynasty, China maintained its position as a global leader in comprehensive national strength, but it refrained from large-scale military expansion or waging wars abroad. For example, during conflicts with the Xiongnu, China mostly adopted a defensive stance, and the seven voyages of Zheng He were aimed at trade and building friendships rather than conquest.

In contrast, after Copernicus ushered in the "Stellar Civilization" in the West, European science and technology advanced beyond that of Eastern nations. Using these advancements, the West developed weapons from Chinese gunpowder technology and proceeded to conquer vast parts of the world, including China itself, forcing their goods and culture upon the Chinese. At the time, China was under the corrupt rule of the Qing Dynasty, whose thought and culture had regressed significantly. The Chinese people were symbolically oppressed, even forced to wear queues, which represented a "Binding of the mind". The Qing government relied on dictatorship and forced people, both domestically and abroad, to kneel in submission. This repression led China into a state of physical and spiritual weakness, earning it the nickname "Sick Man of East Asia", a condition similar to that imposed during Mongol rule.

Western observers, witnessing China's decline into the "Sick Man of East Asia", could not believe that such a country was capable of producing advanced thought. They appropriated original Chinese philosophies — such as Taoism, Confucianism, Legalism, Yin-Yang theory, and concepts of wealth redistribution — and repackaged them under new names like "Freedom, democracy, rule of law, dialectics, and communism". These ideas were then reintroduced into China. In addition to philosophy, the West's weapons and gunpowder technology, initially derived from the East, were also turned back against China.

In the 19th century, the Qing Dynasty's policy of isolation was shattered by the Western systems of free democracy and constitutional monarchy, leaving China bewildered and unprepared. The result was a series of invasions and humiliations, including the Opium Wars and the intervention of the Eight-Nation Alliance, along with the rise of imperialist Japan, which, supported by Western culture, exploited China for resources and territory. Faced with the superior military technology and ideological invasion from the West, the Qing government capitulated entirely, ceding land and paying reparations.

During the Republican period, the Soviet Union's Comintern used its ideology to launch yet another ideological invasion, targeting Chinese intellectuals at universities like Peking University and Tsinghua University. Western church systems were also introduced, alongside financial support to develop organizations and political parties. These groups organized large-scale domestic uprisings and peasant wars, seizing wealth from capitalists and the wealthy elite.

Many scholars from Peking University and Tsinghua University, unaware of the true nature of Marxism, mistakenly believed that Marx's teachings were original and absolute truths. As a result, they enthusiastically spread his ideas. At the time, the impoverished and weakened Chinese population, already suffering from the knowledge blockade imposed by the Qing Dynasty, were largely illiterate and struggled to meet basic needs. Even intellectuals were trapped in the "Sick Man of East Asia" mindset, unable to discern the truth from the falsehoods in

Marxist-Leninist ideology. To this day, Marxism remains a form of intellectual bondage, a new "Queue" that hinders the development of the Chinese people.

3. Future Development Scenario

Despite the rise of early Western civilizations like Christianity and Islam, which led to the extinction of ancient civilizations like Egypt and the Maya, China, as an Eastern civilization grounded in pictographic writing, miraculously survived. Throughout history, China's survival against the relentless onslaught of Western European civilization seemed precarious. In more recent times, China was ravaged by Marxism-Leninism, with events like the Cultural Revolution fundamentally undermining traditional Chinese culture. This movement can be seen as a “Western Marxist culture” revolution against “Chinese culture”, even attempting to replace Chinese characters with Western phonetic scripts, much like the early Islamic efforts in Egypt, which effectively erased Egyptian civilization. However, as an original "Galactic civilization", China has proven its resilience, and time has shown its cultural endurance.

"Eastern Chinese civilization" and "Western European civilization" represent two distinct types of civilizations — one abstract, one realistic. These can be termed "0" and "1" civilizations or "Yellow" and "White" civilizations. Millions of years ago, "Black" primates drove both the Yellow and White civilizations out of Africa. Over time, the "Yellow" and "White" civilizations evolved rapidly, enduring hardship and adversity, developing writing systems and complex cultures, while "Black" primates remained largely unchanged for millions of years, lacking writing and civilization. Over the course of tens of thousands of years, the Yellow and White races gradually evolved into modern humans, eventually forming Eastern and Western camps. It is impossible to declare one side superior or inferior, as each has experienced cycles of ascendancy and decline. For instance, a thousand years ago, Chinese civilization was leading in philosophy and societal structures, while today European civilization leads in science and technology.

After years of deep reflection on failures and lessons from war, particularly with the innovation of the "Galactic Civilization" theory in 2012, the Chinese people began to realize that the Western "Stellar civilization" pales in comparison to the "Eastern divine culture" and the "Galactic Civilization" based on universal laws.

The Western Islamic prophet Muhammad once predicted: "The ink of a scholar is more sacred than the blood of a martyr", and "Knowledge, even if it is in China, must be sought". This highlights that civilization and knowledge are forged from the blood of war and that Muslims are urged to pursue learning, resist blind obedience, and seek true knowledge from Chinese civilization.

The current "Western European civilization" or "Stellar civilization", its core values, like freedom, democracy, and the rule of law, are derived from ancient Chinese philosophies of Taoism, Confucianism, and Legalism. However, these ideas were renamed and rebranded for the West. Because west never fully grasped the essence of these concepts, its freedom has led to widespread gun violence, and its democracy has turned into mob rule. Yet, these ideals have been promoted worldwide, attracting a vast following. Ironically, most people globally are unaware that they are embracing ancient Chinese ideas, much like the nations surrounding China in ancient times followed Chinese culture. Today, following Western thought is, in reality, following Chinese philosophical development.

Conversely, in China itself, the public is often unaware of which ideas are truly ancient Chinese in origin. For instance, Tang Dynasty culture spread to Japan and became Japanese culture; Song Dynasty culture spread to Korea, becoming Korean culture; Ming Dynasty culture influenced Vietnam; and Republican-era culture shaped Taiwan. These regions have preserved essential aspects of Chinese culture, forming the "Sinosphere". However, mainland China has retained only a small portion of Han Dynasty culture and refers to itself as "Han Chinese". Modern Chinese society, whether elite or grassroots, largely follows Western Marxist peasant culture, celebrating red songs and training "Red youth" to oppose the West. This has led to anti-American sentiment and internet censorship. Yet, most Chinese citizens are unaware that by opposing Western "Freedom, democracy, and rule of law," they are actually opposing their own ancient Chinese cultural values — those of Taoism, Confucianism, and Legalism.

In recent years, with the spread of "Eastern divine culture" and the "Galactic Civilization" theory based on universal laws, this cultural misunderstanding has slowly been revealed.

Today, it appears that the competition between East and West is an economic rivalry. However, at a deeper level, it is a battle between Eastern and Western civilizations, a conflict between the "Eastern Chinese civilization" and the "Western European civilization". Chinese government officials and ordinary citizens are gradually awakening to this realization.

Regardless of the outcome of the competition, the Western “Stellar civilization” has already caused many disasters for mankind, including the historical massacres of various religions, the massacre of hard-working landowners and capitalists by the Communist Church, the weapons and land wars, and the accident of the Ukrainian nuclear power plant, which led to the complete disintegration of the former Soviet Union.

The “Stellar civilization” dominated by the Western civilization has also entered the final stage, and the Eastern “Galactic civilization” will rise, which is currently the first wave of the theoretical start, i.e., the stage when the lion has just awakened, and its theoretical system has already unified the whole world. If the Eastern civilization can develop to the 5th wave in the future, then the whole world will be unified in the Eastern “Galactic Civilization”!

Without a single war, the East will theoretically and technologically unify the world. Western nuclear weapons will become obsolete without ever being used, and even extraterrestrial civilizations recognize Chinese civilization through crop circles.

The current "Galactic Civilization" theory will decide the victor between Eastern and Western civilizations. The 《Book of Revelation》 prophesizes that the beast weapons (Nuclear weapons) of the Western "Stellar civilization" will battle the lamb theory (Galactic Civilization theory) of the Eastern "Galactic Civilization", and the lamb theory will triumph because it follows the "Divine Way".

"Easter" represents resurrection, while "Passover" symbolizes transcendence. Together, they predict the transcendence of the East over the West, with the "Galactic Civilization" surpassing the "Stellar civilization", as ordained by the divine plan.

No matter the outcome, 2020 — a year marked by significant historical shifts — will correspond to a major turning point for the "Galactic Civilization", destined to sweep away the dark forces of the "Stellar civilization", just as history has long foretold. The Chinese people, descendants of Yan and Huang, have never accepted their fate passively, as evidenced by the ancient tales of Hou Yi shooting down the Suns and Gong Gong ramming the Buzhou Mountain.

4. The Rod of God

The "Rod of God" refers to the instrument that upholds the "Way of God". When a nation's rulers become corrupt and tyrannical, the people or foreign invaders will rise to overthrow them. When a country needs to develop, it naturally requires the support of government policies to ensure progress and stability, such as promoting the original Chinese values of "Freedom, democracy, and the rule of law", thus enabling the return of positive energy and morality.

The "Rod of God" is both a tool for the lower classes to push the upper echelons of government toward reform and progress, and a legal weapon for the ruling government to manage the nation. The government must punish corrupt officials and eradicate societal corruption, guiding the people rather than falling prey to foreign ideologies and lies.

In ancient times, Chinese emperors, no matter how lacking in culture or philosophical insight, still used the wisdom of China's top philosophers — such as Laozi and Confucius — to assert their authority over neighboring nations and suppress domestic intellectual elites. However, contemporary Chinese rulers face a much more difficult situation. Despite their confidence in new ideas and theories, they rely on Western Marxist-Leninist philosophical deception to suppress China's intellectuals and cultural elites.

Historically, China's neighboring countries like Japan, Korea, and Vietnam were part of the Sinosphere, inheriting and emulating the cultural and philosophical systems of the

Tang, Song, and Ming dynasties. They revered Eastern civilization and its doctrines of Taoism, Confucianism, and Legalism (i.e., Freedom, democracy, and the rule of law). But today, China has become a cultural vassal of the Soviet Union, much like how the Egyptian pyramid civilization was destroyed by Islam. Now, China serves as a proxy for Western Marxism-Leninism, parading as its staunchest defender. Do neighboring nations not see this?

Naturally, they do, and as a result, they hold contemporary China in contempt. Despite China's advancements in nuclear weapons, space stations, and high-speed rail, these countries still label China as the "New sick man of East Asia". Countries like Korea and Japan stand shoulder to shoulder with the West in challenging China, while nations like Vietnam and India press even more aggressively against China, leaving it surrounded by adversaries — including Hong Kong, Macau, and Taiwan, which now serve as chess pieces encircling their "Motherland".

Faced with such circumstances, the Chinese government has been forced, under the advice of corrupt officials, to buy the loyalty of distant "Friends" from impoverished and corrupt regimes in Africa, Europe, and the Middle East (Such as Albania and Iran). These governments accept huge bribes in the form of kickbacks, but they are isolated islands themselves, surrounded by Western influence and barely able to survive. They beg China for money while their officials siphon off corrupt gains.

Ironically, it was Western sanctions that forced China to reform during the 1970s and 1980s, restoring landlords and capitalists to their positions, opening markets to the West, and seeking economic assistance. Eventually, the West approved of China's reforms and helped ease its economic struggles by ending its isolation. Yet now, despite its slight GDP growth, China shows little gratitude, instead opposing Western civilization and supporting the autocratic regimes under Western sanctions. Huawei, for instance, supported Iran's dictatorship and was consequently sanctioned by the United States, leading to China's growing confrontation with the entire Western world.

When the Chinese government surveys the global landscape, it sees that all backward, authoritarian regimes have become isolated. Some have already been overthrown, such as Iraq and Libya, and the former Soviet Union has long since dissolved. The remaining few are all surrounded by Western modern civilization, like North Korea, with its isolated militarism. Where are their allies? Even the last emperor of the Ming dynasty would lament from his grave, "Our Ming Dynasty was so economically powerful, yet why did we still fall?"

History may repeat itself. Empress Dowager Cixi found herself in a similar situation when she declared war on all the world's great powers because China was surrounded by enemies. In such a desperate position, what choice did she have but to declare war? Now, some may call for a one-nation military challenge against the entire Western world, but can you win? During the First Sino-Japanese War, the Beiyang Fleet was not inferior in strength to the Japanese navy, yet it was utterly defeated. Western strategists are simply waiting for such a move: for China to declare war on the world, so they can defeat it just like the Qing dynasty, weaken it through war, and force it to cede territory and pay reparations.

5. The Future of China

Does the Chinese government still have opportunities ahead? Certainly, it does, and it's not too late to act now. China must adopt both the "Way of God" and the "Rod of God". The "Way of God" refers to a unified republican system, while the "Rod of God" signifies further systemic reforms. I've discussed specific reforms in earlier writings, so I won't repeat them here. Suffice it to say, China must discard the remnants of Marxist-Leninist ideology that it copied from the Soviet Union — just as Deng Xiaoping wisely followed the Western path of market openness, rejecting Soviet orthodoxy with his famous question, "Is the Soviet moon really rounder?"

Additionally, China should demand explanations from Western societies for their historical invasions, such as the Opium Wars, the Eight-Nation Alliance, and Japan's invasion of China. These nations should issue formal apologies for the suffering inflicted upon the Chinese people.

By taking this approach, China could strategically sever ties with Marxist-Leninist ideologies, distance itself from authoritarian regimes that are surrounded by Western powers, and escape the isolation that these alliances bring. Furthermore, by drawing attention to the historical invasions and the resultant death and destruction suffered by its people, China would likely garner global sympathy. Claiming continued status as a developing country would also facilitate support from Western nations in both economic and technological spheres.

Once China sheds its dependence on Marxist-Leninist thought, it must not only revive its ancient ideals of "Freedom, democracy, and the rule of law", but also establish a new, more powerful intellectual framework rooted in Chinese civilization. Otherwise, it risks remaining the “Sick man of East Asia” in terms of thought, even if economically and militarily strong. Russia's strength, for example, doesn’t solely come from its weapons; it draws from its own cultural heritage, embodied in figures like Tolstoy, Pushkin, and Mendeleev. Without these cultural and intellectual pillars, Russia would be no different from Canada — a large nation with no cultural soul.

Imagine a future Chinese leader standing before the global community and declaring:

"There are only two written and civilizational systems in the world: the 'Galactic Civilization', which uses hieroglyphic systems, including Chinese, Egyptian, and Mayan civilizations; and the 'Stellar Civilization', which uses phonetic scripts, currently employed by the West and most nations globally. Since Egypt and Maya have perished, China alone bears the responsibility of preserving and advancing this unique system and civilization. True strength comes not from weapons or wealth but from thought and culture — this is the 'Way of God'".

Such a speech would resonate deeply with the Chinese people, uniting them with a renewed sense of pride and purpose. It would showcase China’s wisdom, channeling positive energy and faith in its cultural heritage. It would also compel neighboring nations to return to the fold of Chinese civilization, no longer daring to challenge its cultural supremacy. At the same time, it would demonstrate China’s capacity, as a single nation, to balance and counter the influence of Western civilization on a global scale.

This is the vision of a strong China — a nation not merely defined by its economic and military might, but by its philosophical and cultural leadership in the world.

6. The Creation and Promotion of Civilization

The "Way of God" has already been completed, establishing a unified theoretical framework for the world. However, the "Rod of God" represents the specific strategies and policies needed to implement this vision, guided by the "Way of God". This is a responsibility that must be fulfilled from the top down, primarily by China's highest leaders. These leaders, who enjoy the greatest honors, privileges, and support from the people, must make meaningful contributions to the future welfare of the nation and its civilization.

However, after observing global leaders for some time, I've noticed that most leaders and their cabinets focus on the well-being of their own people. They create favorable conditions for their intellectual elites and seek to improve the economic welfare of their populations. But the Chinese leadership seems to be an exception. Instead of prioritizing the Chinese people, they often focus on foreign rulers and impoverished foreign populations. For example, they monitor the U.S. government through Chinese media, provide aid to corrupt and impoverished nations, and use Marxist-Leninist theories to suppress China's own intellectual elites while censoring thought-provoking books and information.

Even more bizarrely, the Chinese government limits its people's access to knowledge by blocking educational websites and building a firewall to isolate its citizens from global discourse. At the same time, Chinese officials spend enormous sums on foreign dictatorships to improve the quality of life for oppressive rulers such as North Korea's Kim Jong-un, Cambodia's Pol Pot, or Iran's leadership — rather than helping their own people. These dictators live in luxury, buying high-end products to maintain control over their populations, while the Chinese government wastes its people's hard-earned money supporting these regimes. Ironically, this only causes resentment among the people of North Korea, Iran, and Cambodia, who see China as backing their oppressors, thus alienating China from neighboring nations.

Moreover, China brings in uneducated individuals from Africa, some carrying diseases like HIV/AIDS, to receive basic education in China, spreading illness and causing harm to the Chinese population. Meanwhile, education opportunities for Chinese citizens remain inadequate, and the gap between the rich and the poor widens. The increasing divide in wealth and education fuels dissatisfaction, with the undereducated becoming more susceptible to extreme nationalist rhetoric. Intellectual debates are stifled, creating a population dominated by fanatic supporters of outdated ideologies, including professors from prestigious universities like Peking and Tsinghua, who promote anti-American rhetoric. This situation exacerbates poverty among farmers, many of whom cannot afford to send their children to school and have no access to pensions — conditions that historically spark uprisings.

China's leaders must reflect deeply and develop a concrete strategy — the "Rod of God" — for governing this vast Eastern nation. If a leader of the caliber of King Wen of Zhou were to emerge, someone capable of authoring a text as transformative as the 《I Ching》," it would be a once-in-a-millennium event. If today's leaders are too busy or lack the intellectual capacity to draft such a strategy, they could delegate the task to their many secretaries. If that proves insufficient, they could use their authority to compel the nation's think tanks — comprised of China's most elite intellectuals, paid for by the state — to devise this system.

However, if even these intellectuals have been so thoroughly brainwashed and suppressed that they are unable to develop a robust theoretical framework, then China risks relying once again on outdated Western Marxist theories. In that case, China's leadership should at least adopt the modern Western political framework, as Japan and South Korea have done, embracing the highest stage of Western civilization: the democratic and free system of the United States.

The greatest fear is that China's leadership will mimic the medieval European Church, which stifled thought for so long that it couldn't break free from its outdated doctrines. This led to the persecution of new ideas, exemplified by the trials of Galileo and Copernicus, and the burning of thinkers like Giordano Bruno, who advocated for emerging "Stellar civilizations". Will history repeat itself in the East?

7. Historical Judgment

For thousands of years, it was rulers like King Wen of Zhou, who developed the 《I Ching》 and embodied the "Way of God", that truly held the highest spiritual and intellectual authority in Chinese civilization. Philosophers like Laozi and Confucius, despite not holding political power, became the spiritual leaders of Chinese thought. Laozi said, "Governing a large state is like cooking a small fish", while Confucius emphasized respecting virtues and eliminating corrupt governance to maintain order. Without their philosophical contributions, China might have succumbed to other dominant religions such as Buddhism or Islam. Thus, adhering to the "Way of God" is what makes one the true leader of Chinese civilization.

In contrast, the emperors throughout China's dynasties were often mere administrators of their time. The most capable among them used the "Rod of God", enforcing laws to punish corrupt officials and maintain social stability. However, many rulers indulged in luxury, ruling over vast harems while neglecting statecraft, and some were even killed before they could establish their reign. Few had the strategic vision or a comprehensive theoretical framework for governance.

If ordinary rulers governed China using the 《I Ching》 of King Wen or the free and democratic ideas of Laozi and Confucius, the Chinese people and neighboring nations would have accepted them. But ruling China with Mongol swords, Qing Dynasty queues, or Western Marxist-Leninist ideologies — how can that be sustainable?

Mr. Lu Xun, through his writings, captured the absurdity of such leadership, embodied by figures like Ah Q. These leaders proclaim, "We will never follow the West, the Chinese people have stood up!" But their feet remain firmly planted on Western Marxist ideologies. Their followers, including uninformed representatives like Mrs.Shen Jilan, and professors from universities' Marxism research centers, sing praises of the "New communist clothes" handed down from the Soviet emperor. Mrs.Shen Jilan, a rural representative who voted in favor 66 times in her lifetime, never proposed any policy suggestions but received frequent praise from top Party leaders. She once privately remarked, "The leaders love me for always raising my hand in support. I will never oppose any decision. They shouldn't allow the internet or criticism; the <People's Daily> should be the only newspaper." Is this the national policy of a confident China?

It's easy to sing the praises of the leadership, and many choose that path with no risk — some even become representatives or officials for it. But history will judge these leaders, no matter how surrounded they are by flattering sycophants and officials. Future historians will provide a fair evaluation of every leader — not now, but in time. Hopefully, China's future leaders will be wise and alert to these truths.

Currently, China's situation is extremely precarious. Since 2020, there has been a comprehensive ideological confrontation between China and the U.S., essentially a conflict between parliamentary democracy and a form of feudal church-like governance. This clash has already extended into the economic sphere, and if mishandled, it could lead to full-scale war. The West will not wait for China to fully surpass the U.S. in technological dominance.

If, however, the Chinese government were to adopt the "Way of God", based on "Divinely transmitted Chinese culture and the universal laws of the galaxy", it would be a wise and straightforward decision. This would symbolize China's awakening, prompting neighboring nations and Western countries alike to seek out and learn from Eastern wisdom.

8. Conclusion

Throughout Chinese history, feudal rulers have often lacked strategic foresight, stubbornly clinging to outdated systems — insisting on slavery during feudalism and clinging to feudalism in times of democracy. As Laozi observed long ago, China's rulers often remained mired in ignorance. Seeing this, Laozi gave up on China, riding his green ox westward, symbolizing his departure from a country he no longer wanted to engage with.

Yet, the modern American prophet Edgar Cayce held a different view, showing great confidence in China's future. He famously predicted, "China, by slowly growing, will preserve itself... One day she will awaken, cut off her queue, and start thinking and acting... Yes, this seems distant for humans, but for God, it is quick. Soon, China will awaken!" Cayce's mention of cutting the "Queue" doesn't refer to the Qing Dynasty's physical hairstyle but to the mental constraints shackling the Chinese people. His prophecy about China being the "Cradle for Christianity" points to the new "Covenant of the Rainbow", symbolizing the "Way of God".

Similarly, the Western seer Nostradamus foretold that Chinese civilization would witness the rise of a true philosophy, proclaiming that a "Sacred philosophy will flourish" — this aligns with the "Way of God".

Even financial magnate Jim Rogers has predicted that "The 19th century belonged to Britain, the 20th century to America, and the 21st century will belong to China".

However, for China to realize such a future, it must innovate its theories and philosophies. The 21st century cannot belong to China without intellectual and theoretical breakthroughs. America's power doesn't rest solely on its weapons but on the "Stellar civilization" of European enlightenment, its social institutions, talent, and scientific and technological foundations.

(Original academic exploration, July 2021, written on "Blue Mountain Poetry House.")

B11. On "Equalizing Rich and Poor" and "Communism"

Abstract: "Communism" was originally called "Equalizing Rich and Poor", first proposed by the leaders of the Northern Song Dynasty uprising, Wang Xiaobo and Li Shun. Marxism-Leninism in the West copied this ancient Chinese concept and simply changed its name, much like how "Big brother phone" became "Mobile phone". Why do many Chinese people prefer the term "Communism"? Because it is, in fact, an original Chinese concept.

China has another original philosophical idea that was copied by Marxism-Leninism, called "Yin-Yang". They renamed it "Dialectics". These Western imitators, leveraging the Industrial Revolution, repackaged old ideas in new bottles, gave them new names, and deceived their way into China.

Currently, China's achievements in weaponry are mostly based on Western technology, but the concepts "Communism" mentioned are Western imitations of Chinese ideas.

----

1. Introduction

Inequality between nations leads to war, as seen in the early invasions of Han China by the Mongols and the Manchus. Social inequality within a country also leads to war, as evidenced by the peasant uprisings throughout history. Inequality between people, or the disparity between rich and poor, leads to revolution, known as "Equalizing Rich and Poor" or "Communism".

2. Inequality Between Nations

There are many reasons for inequality between nations, including the wisdom of the people, the leadership style, and economic and cultural factors. Regardless, there is always imbalance, such as in import and export trade. However, emperors of the Celestial Empire (China) often considered themselves culturally superior, viewing neighboring tribes as uncivilized, and thus adopted appeasement policies. Due to economic imbalances between nations, leaders anticipated friction and wars. The traditional approach was to marry off daughters to foreign kings, treating these kings as sons-in-law. This allowed them to distribute a portion of the nation's wealth to foreign kings-in-law, helping them escape poverty, a strategy that can be called "One Belt, Many Roads" (A play on China's "One Belt, One Road" initiative). This appeased these nations, who then supported the Celestial Empire, implementing a system of "One Nation, Many Systems" where criticism and attacks on China were avoided.

Throughout history, Chinese feudal rulers enjoyed spending money on foreign nations. It's unclear whether they were isolated from the world or simply out of touch with reality (Perhaps their propaganda departments shielded them from external civilizations, controlling domestic thought, but also blinding the leaders' judgment). Or maybe they sought to address international economic inequalities. Despite the poverty, backward education, and healthcare in China, emperors continued to give out aid, reducing debts, and providing poverty relief to neighboring poor countries, as long as these countries remained peaceful, allowing the emperors to suppress domestic unrest. "Stability abroad before dealing with internal issues".

During the Song Dynasty, Chinese emperors gave substantial amounts of money to neighboring Liao, Jin, and Mongol nations, preferring to give money rather than wage war, thinking, "By helping you develop and civilize, you should be grateful". However, foreign nations didn't see it that way; they viewed China's actions as a sign of internal political corruption, and believed its officials were merely fattening themselves by exploiting the people. When the time was ripe, they would attack and seize these resources.

In the Ming Dynasty, China also gave money to the Manchus. Like the Song Dynasty, this resulted in the Manchus attacking China once they thought the time was right. During Mao's era, China was extremely poor, and many people starved to death, but Mao still sent aid to neighboring countries, even extending assistance to Tanzania in Africa and Albania in Europe.

China's so-called "Foreign friendliness" was perceived by foreign nations as either a sign that China needed something or that China looked down on them. It was like a wealthy man throwing a chicken bone to a beggar by the roadside. The wealthy man looked down upon the beggar, while the beggar did not feel grateful but instead harbored hatred. Given the chance, the beggar would pounce on the wealthy man, kill him, and take all his money.

Nations like Vietnam and North Korea, no matter how much aid China gives them, will never feel gratitude. Once given the chance, they will turn and attack China, as Vietnam did by launching attacks along China's borders in the 1970s. Thus, China's greatest threat does not come from the wealthy and civilized West but from the poor nations surrounding it. The distant West can only exert pressure from afar, leaving neighboring countries to encircle China. (The national policies of the Warring States Period and the Han and Tang dynasties were to "Ally with distant nations and attack close neighbors", establishing diplomatic relations with faraway states while dealing with nearby threats, thereby intimidating distant nations.)

The ruling dynasties attempted to balance the international economy by spending money abroad, but they did not win the recognition of neighboring countries. So, what do these countries recognize? They recognize your civilization, technology, and culture. For example, Japan and Korea were deeply drawn to China's culture, especially that of the Tang and Song dynasties. They admired Chinese civilization to the extent that they even adopted Chinese characters. Without waging war, they were already part of China's cultural and diplomatic sphere.

However, if a government suppresses its own Eastern civilization and culture using Western "Marxist culture", blocks criticism, censors the internet, and spreads propaganda, it will not gain friends no matter how much money it spends on neighboring nations.

Let me share a story: An Australian friend of mine came from Cambodia. In their village, hundreds of people were killed by the Khmer Rouge, almost every family was affected. Although China provided billions in aid to the Cambodian government, very little reached the common people, as corruption squandered it all. This did nothing to win the hearts of the Cambodian people. In their village, they erected a statue of Marx and Lenin at the entrance. Any villager passing by could spit or curse at it. The statue's face and the surrounding area were covered in yellow phlegm and urine. Every time this villager passed by, he would spit at and curse the statue. Hearing this made me feel terrible. How could the leaders of a country that governs one-quarter of the world's population worship Marxism-Leninism from a small Western country and be spat upon by the global population, even by uneducated Cambodian villagers?

This makes me think of China's ancient ancestors: Qin Shi Huang, Han Wu Di, and the emperors of the Tang and Song dynasties, who wielded their wisdom of Confucianism and Taoism, benefiting surrounding nations and earning their admiration of Chinese civilization. How could they bear to see this?

3. Domestic Inequality

The money the emperor distributes isn't his own — it's collected through heavy taxes on the hardworking population. This naturally places immense pressure on the people. Chinese citizens not only have to support the domestic bureaucracy but also fund corrupt officials and their mistresses in distant Africa and Europe. Despite their hard labor, most people still struggle to feed themselves, clothe themselves properly, or afford housing. Education and healthcare are lacking, and the majority of farmers work their entire lives without a pension. Meanwhile, government officials collude with business elites, dominating local areas, which naturally fuels resentment among the populace.

Although the government continues to strengthen its police force, emphasize stability, and promote positive messaging and harmony, when the time is right, the people's pent-up anger will inevitably turn into public protests and movements. They will rally around anti-corruption campaigns and even raise the banner of overthrowing the corrupt officials, potentially leading to peasant uprisings.

When the people are pushed to the point of revolt, the emperor typically sends troops to suppress them. At that moment, the deciding factor is who holds more power. If the government forces are stronger, the uprisings will be crushed and labeled as riots and disorder. But if the people's forces are stronger, the emperor's army will struggle to cope.

At this point, foreign enemies aren't idle — they are constantly watching China's internal unrest, waiting for the right opportunity. They are thinking, "How can the few scraps the wealthy gave me ever satisfy my hunger?" Once they observe that the government forces and the people are evenly matched in battle, they will suddenly strike, like a starving tiger pouncing on the fat meat they have long coveted.

The humiliation of being thrown a scrap of bone, combined with the thrill of robbing a rich man, and the vast economic and cultural differences will transform their anger into a powerful army, completely overturning the entire regime.

While the empire's forces are engaged in a delicate balance with the peasant army, the sudden emergence of violent foreign invaders will instantly tip the scales, and the dynasty will collapse in an instant. The emperor cannot comprehend why, after treating these foreign nations as sons-in-law and concubines, and providing them with so much aid, they repay him with betrayal.

This was the case with the Mongol and Manchu armies, both of which were small, marginalized tribes that had received considerable aid from the Chinese empire. How did they turn into such fierce and savage forces?

Even if you send vast amounts of aid to countries around the world today, including Africa and Europe, they still believe you are a backward, impoverished Communist nation without a proper system or legal framework, full of corrupt officials who siphon off aid money. They think your aid is merely a way for officials to earn kickbacks. For instance, when donations are sent to African nations through the Red Cross to build schools, it's often just an excuse for corruption. Do you think these nations don't see this?

Of course, if you give a few tens of thousands of dollars to corrupt African officials, they will call you "Grandfather" and support your policies. But if you offer the Australian defense minister a free trip to China, he will refuse outright — that's the difference in systems. China is one country, so how can it justify having two or even three systems? A well-functioning system earns the respect and unity of people worldwide, while a corrupt system causes even Hong Kong, Macau, and Taiwan — areas that are supposed to be part of China — to want to split away and demand a separate system.

Within the feudal system, major local officials rise through favors from higher-ups, or through directly funneling money from provincial banks and private enterprises. These officials dominate their regions, ensuring their superiors feel secure while they exploit the local populace. High-ranking officials control the region's financial resources, stamp approvals, and engage in corruption, with most of them being mediocrities who bought their positions. When foreign enemies arrive, these officials naturally deceive their superiors and prioritize their own safety.

The corruption of local officials is largely unchecked unless their superiors investigate them. Take, for example, a provincial party secretary who remarked from prison, "I thought I was safe. I was the top official of my region, and I was always the one investigating others. I kept showing loyalty to my superiors, and they trusted me. But I never expected that a sudden change in leadership would result in my downfall. My mistake was aligning myself with the wrong faction".

This is why corrupt officials hope for lifetime appointments for their superiors, so they are never replaced. They pledge absolute loyalty and oppose financial transparency because as long as their superiors stay in power, their corruption will go unchallenged.

When a regime is overrun with corrupt officials and traitors, corruption dominates governance, and competent individuals are sidelined (Nowadays, even high-achieving students are sometimes replaced by others due to connections.) These competent individuals eventually turn to foreign powers for support or rise up in rebellion, ostensibly to eliminating "The king's sidekicks." This explains the frequent lament: why are there so many traitors in Chinese history? But those who were influenced by powerful overseas civilizations lament the domestic feudal system and its abundance of corrupt officials, ignorant citizens, and propagandists.

From those who led the Jin and Mongol forces to attack the Song Dynasty, to those who helped the Qing defeat the Ming, or those who supported the Eight-Nation Alliance against the Qing, and those who worked with Japan to attack the Republic of China, all were Chinese individuals of notable talent and reputation. Figures like Zhang Bangchang, Wu Sangui, and Wang Jingwei are infamous examples. Why were they willing to be traitors and lead foreign forces against their own state?

The answer lies in the fact that China's truly talented and knowledgeable individuals were not in the imperial court. They were oppressed by imperial authority and a government full of mediocrities, unable to rise. Meanwhile, the mediocrities are good at currying favor, pledging loyalty with both hands and feet. Incompetent and unqualified, they resemble the bureaucrats managing Wuhan's virus outbreak — amateurs overseeing professionals. Similarly, the delegates attending the annual meetings are mere loyalists, raising their hands in agreement and offering no substantial policy suggestions because they fear losing their privileges — free meals and stays in luxury hotels.

In such a system, any policy, no matter how wrong, can pass, even the restoration of imperial rule. Take, for example, former Secretary Bo Xilai, who slapped Mayor Wang Lijun, showing how this system operates — it's full of house slaves. Provincial party secretaries express their loyalty to the central government, but why not to the people? It's because their power comes from the central leadership, not the people. In contrast, officials during the Qing Dynasty were more honest, calling themselves "Officials of the imperial court" rather than lying and claiming to be "Servants of the people."

Take the cases of Xu Caihou and Guo Boxiong, who dominated the military. Could you get promoted without bribery? Those who could bribe their way to the top were corrupt mediocrities. When enemies come knocking, these bribers will be unwilling to fight — they are now high-ranking officials. Meanwhile, competent individuals capable of leading in battle are suppressed, like Yue Fei and Yuan Chonghuan. Even if they are later given key roles, they end up betrayed by corrupt officials. Many talented individuals, crushed by corruption, turn to the enemy and help foreign forces attack the government and the incompetent officials. This explains why there have been so many "Traitors" in history.

Consider the former governor and party secretary of Hubei Province: who knows how much they embezzled or how much they paid to reach their positions. Even in the face of a deadly virus, they suppressed and imprisoned doctors while reporting to their superiors. They clearly wanted to avoid responsibility and shift blame upwards.

Among China's scientists, the truly talented are often suppressed, such as Ms.Tu Youyou, a "Three-no" scientist (No degree, no academic title, no affiliation). The publication of journals and magazines is monopolized by corrupt academicians. Only flattering content, such as praising the wives of academicians, is allowed to be published. Even when foreign experts recognized Ms.Tu Youyou with an award, these fake academicians attempted to sue her for not getting approval from the higher-ups.

In 1900, during the Boxer Rebellion, the Eight-Nation Alliance demanded compensation from the corrupt Qing government. The Qing court was forced to sign the Boxer Protocol on September 7, 1901, in Beijing. The Qing's representative angrily rebuked the Chinese interpreter working for the foreign powers, saying, "Why are you always speaking on behalf of foreigners? Aren't you Chinese?" The interpreter spat on the face of the Qing representative, retorting, "It's because corrupt officials like you have blocked my path, and that's why I am like this!"

In 2020, as the pandemic raged, nations worldwide demanded compensation from the Chinese government, still believing that, as in the Republic of China era, all the nation's wealth was controlled by a few large families. To them, demanding compensation was the same as asking these families to pay up ------- it had nothing to do with the Chinese people. It's no wonder they think this way, as the Chinese government didn't seek any input from the people or the National People's Congress before casually handing over tens of billions to the corrupt World Health Organization. That money represents the blood, sweat, and tears of the Chinese people.

4. Inequality Between People

The biggest inequalities between people are the wealth gap, the rural-urban gap, and the educational gap. Most impoverished people tend to be ignorant, and they can be easily stirred up emotionally, blindly believing in ideas like Marxism-Leninism's radicalism, the spiritual opium of the poor, robbing the rich to help the poor, wealth redistribution, and communism.

Theories advocating rebellion from the bottom to overthrow rulers are highly appealing to the lower-class, ignorant poor. In a closed-off, impoverished, and illiterate China, such ideas had a strong influence. The result was the deaths of tens of thousands of ordinary citizens and large-scale social upheaval. Eventually, the leaders of peasant revolutions became lifetime rulers (Though they no longer called themselves emperors), and after two or three generations, landlords and capitalists re-emerged, many having joined the revolutionary party, becoming part of the government, the National People's Congress, or the Chinese People's Political Consultative Conference. However, the workers and peasants who fought in the revolution ended up losing their jobs, becoming the new poor, and the system ultimately turned back into a feudal cycle.

Eliminating the gap between people is essentially about redistributing wealth and implementing communism — an idea first proposed over a thousand years ago by the Northern Song peasant rebellion leaders Wang Xiaobo and Li Shun.

Why do the Chinese people like and resonate so much with this concept? Because communism's roots are in China; a thousand years ago, China's peasant leaders were already calling for wealth redistribution, or what was then called

"Equalizing wealth". It's similar to how the modern "Mobile phone" used to be called the "Big brother phone".

Chinese peasants have long formed "Equal wealth" parties to fight against feudal dynasties. Figures like Zhu Yuanzhang were old party members, and in the end, the results of the peasant uprisings were often usurped by them, turning them into feudal emperors. Isn't that exactly what happened?

Marx and Lenin, these Western copycats, borrowed from the momentum of the Western industrial revolution's weaponry, changed the name, and packaged the old idea into a new theory. They even had the audacity to come to China and spread their ideology and form a party. Yet the true origin of this "Party" is in China, and the real founder of communism is Wang Xiaobo and Li Shun.

By this logic, when new party members swear their oaths, they should be standing in front of statues of Wang Xiaobo and Li Shun, raising their fists, and swearing to the original founders: "Today, we voluntarily join the 'Equal Wealth Party,' which was later copied by Western imperialists and renamed the 'Communist Party'. We will tread on the blood of our ancestors and forebears, dedicating our lives to the cause of equal wealth, to overthrowing all landlords, capitalists, and feudal emperors..."

"Arise, peasants suffering from hunger and cold... Are emperors and kings born noble?... Peasant rebellion is justified... The leader is here; there will be no taxes..."

Why should members of the "Equal Wealth Party" salute the Western Marxist-Leninist copycats? Isn't that backward? These Western plagiarists should be bowing and saluting Wang Xiaobo and Li Shun! The true ancestors of communism are in China.

5. Conclusion

It must be acknowledged that modern technology mainly originates from the West. No matter how the current false academicians and fake PhDs in the Chinese Academy of Sciences boast about their research, how they manufacture advanced weapons, or claim to be meritorious experts and professors who are worth ten divisions, all of this is based on technology borrowed from the West.

However, in the fields of social sciences and philosophy, many ideas later developed in the West are influenced by Chinese civilization. For example, Marxist dialectics is essentially a copy of China's "Yin and yang" philosophy, just under a different name. Western Marxist-Leninist political systems also borrowed and rebranded certain governing concepts. For instance, they replaced the title of "Emperor" with "Leader for life" and changed "Imperial officials" to "Servants of the people". Although these names sound modern and appealing, the essence remains unchanged.

Most so-called contemporary Chinese scholars, under the control and suppression of the national propaganda machine, are left only producing feel-good platitudes, without any opportunity to truly express themselves.

The Nobel Committee has sharp insight. They recognized the work of Ms.Tu Youyou, a "Three-no" scientist (No academic title, no doctoral degree, and no experience working overseas), as a genuine Chinese invention. Meanwhile, the majority of China's current academicians and so-called experts are merely copying Western technology. The only thing Westerners copied from China is communism.

(Jun. 2020, academic research)

B12. On the Proletarian Revolution Theory

Abstract: Western society has always been eager to explore various theoretical models, some of which have been quite controversial. One such example is the theory of proletarian revolution, which advocates for the dispossessed workers and peasants to overthrow and kill the landowners and capitalists, seizing their property. But is this theory, proposed over a century ago, still relevant today? Should it still hang as a symbol of struggle?

----

1. Western Revolutionary Theories

Let's start with a story: Once there was a farmer who was destitute — no house, no land, no money — and well into his years, still unable to marry. He worked as a long-term laborer on a landlord's estate. One day, he thought, "Why don't I just kill the landlord? I could take his house, his land, and his wife."

However, the landlord was wealthy and had many guards and retainers, making it impossible to strike. So, the farmer began to rally his equally impoverished coworkers: "Whoever helps take over the landlord's estate will get land, a house, and a wife." His fellow workers, motivated by the promise of wealth, banded together, seized weapons, and killed the landlord. Soon, they were in the throes of a revolution, busy dividing up land and property.

But some farmers had even greater ambitions, thinking, "If we can kill the emperor, why can't I become the emperor? The emperor has even more land and riches!" Thus was born the rallying cry: "Are emperors born by divine right?" Hearing this, the masses grabbed their tools and weapons.

Yet, the emperor had even more resources and hired larger armies. And thus began a peasant war.

During the late Ming Dynasty, when Li Zicheng led a rebellion, he raised the famous slogan, "When the Dashing King arrives, no taxes will be collected." His promise was simple: If I become the emperor, farmers will no longer pay taxes, and everyone will have land and food. This revolutionary spirit, using food and land as incentives, drew tens of thousands of poor farmers to pick up their tools and revolt. However, after taking Beijing, Li Zicheng realized that if farmers didn't pay taxes, he wouldn't have any revenue. So he reversed his stance, planning to reclaim land and reinstitute taxes. Unsurprisingly, this killed the revolutionary spirit, leading to his eventual defeat.

This is a glimpse of early proletarian revolutionary slogans. But who were the proletariat? Primarily, they were young, impoverished students, workers, and farmers with no money, no land, and no housing. Western revolutionaries took these ideas and developed them into the theory of proletarian revolution or workers' and peasants' movements. These revolutionaries, often students themselves, were also poor and sought to overthrow the ruling class, sharing in power and wealth.

Historically, peasant uprisings have been common. When they failed, they were labeled as rebel bands or bandits — such as the Yellow Turban Rebellion, Song Jiang's band, Fang La's revolt, and the Taiping Rebellion. But when they succeeded, they were hailed as revolutionaries, liberators of the people from their misery, such as Liu Bang, Zhu Yuanzhang, and Emperor Taizong of Tang.

It's not uncommon to say that aristocratic or wealthy leaders hijacked the fruits of peasant uprisings. However, these figures were often part of the revolts themselves. Like the modern revolutionary movements, many included the sons and daughters of landowners and capitalists who abandoned their families and privileges to join the cause. China's long history of revolutions has seen about half of these uprisings succeed, and the other half fail.

Successful uprisings owe much to their revolutionary slogans. For instance, Li Zicheng's promise of "No taxes" was so effective that it became a rallying cry, displayed everywhere, constantly reinforcing the revolutionary fervor.

Once the peasants killed the landlords, they divided up the land and houses and married the wives. Initially, they were happy, having effortlessly improved their lives. But over time, some peasants prospered, using their labor to buy more land and property, becoming new landlords. Others, lazy or indulging in vices like gambling and drinking, lost everything they had seized and ended up as laborers again, working for their wealthier former comrades.

Thus, over time, some revolutionaries became wealthier than the landlords and capitalists they had overthrown. The divide re-emerged — new capitalists and landlords replaced the old. This is the outcome most feared by the theory of proletarian revolution: the revival of capitalism and the landlord class, a phenomenon similar to the restorations of Liu Bang, Emperor Taizong, and Zhu Yuanzhang.

In this context, is it still possible to advocate for a new revolution? Can the new landlords and capitalists be overthrown again? Of course not. Calling for a new revolution now would be seen as inciting chaos and disorder.

Thus, those who still promote revolution today are engaging in futile efforts, destined to be repressed by those in power.

2. Western Civilization

In order to address the tensions between the ruling class and the common people, Western countries have historically engaged in extensive theoretical exploration, including the adoption of Marxist-Leninist (Marxist-Leninism) ideas. However, because these countries were relatively wealthy and well-educated, they rejected the radical aspects of Marxist revolution, particularly its calls for killing landlords and capitalists, viewing such actions as creating chaos.

So how do modern Western nations handle these issues? The primary conflict in any country is typically between the ruling class or wealthy elites (Those with power and money) and the impoverished or proletariat (Those without power and money), which Marxist theory calls class struggle. However, in reality, neither side is inherently bad. The rich and powerful are the ones who control and distribute national wealth and resources, while the poor and powerless are the ones who consume those resources. This dynamic is often influenced by education, knowledge, and wisdom, which naturally create layers or classes within society, just like the levels in an education system (Elementary, secondary, university, etc.).

The question arises: are the wealthy and powerful willing to voluntarily transfer some of their wealth and power to the poor and powerless? Would a landlord be willing to build houses for each peasant? Would a capitalist be willing to raise wages for workers, helping them establish families and careers? If so, perhaps the poor wouldn't feel the need to resort to violent revolution, using knives to kill capitalists and landlords.

But if the wealthy refuse to share, that's not necessarily a problem either. Governments can step in, using tax policies to redistribute wealth. For example, in Australia, the wealthy are taxed at 47%, while the poor are taxed only 17%. While wealthy individuals won't voluntarily raise wages, the government can enforce minimum wage laws, compelling the rich to distribute some of their wealth to the poor. Similarly, pension systems can be established by the government to ensure that even the proletariat has security in old age. By elevating the standard of living for the poor, the likelihood of proletarian revolutions, riots, and uprisings — sources of societal instability — can be reduced.

This is the core of Western democratic civilization. It was developed through centuries of theoretical exploration, painful wars, failures, and lessons learned, culminating in principles of freedom, democracy, and the rule of law. The French Revolution is a key example — its violence and bloodshed provided a stark lesson, resulting in a society that values balance and systemic reform over chaos.

Marxist revolutionary theory, emerging in the 1840s around the time of the French and Russian revolutions, failed to clearly define the relationship between rulers and the people. It primarily offered a slogan of wealth redistribution — “Communism” — without fully addressing the complexities of governance.

In the East, there was limited understanding of Marxism and its ideology. While slogans supporting Marxism-Leninism were loudly chanted, along with anti-Western rhetoric like "We won't follow the West" and "The moon in China is no less round than in the West", the reality was different. Despite government insistence on "Positive energy", few people truly believed that Marxist revolutionary theory represented such energy. Without a genuine faith in a unifying ideology, the door was left open for separatists to exploit religious and cultural differences, as seen in movements for independence in Xinjiang, Tibet, and even political tensions in Hong Kong, Macau, and Taiwan.

Ultimately, the root cause of these issues can be traced back to early Western theoretical exploration — specifically Marxist ideology, which promotes disorder and revolutionary violence. Should this early Western theory still hang on the wall like an idol, venerated without question? Or should it be reconsidered in light of modern realities?

3. New Hope for the Future

Do we need revolutions or chaos to transform society and achieve revival? Absolutely not! When people understand these simple truths, how could they resort to chaos and violence? In fact, chaos and killing represent a regression in thought, not progress. During the Republican era, many intellectual radicals mistakenly believed that advancing thought meant adopting Western revolutionary theories — picking up arms, overthrowing the government, and seizing the wealth of capitalists and landlords. However, the death and destruction caused by such so-called revolutions are plain for all to see.

Since Deng Xiaoping's time, the Chinese government has recognized that progress in thought and civilization requires "Reform", not revolution. The government encouraged openness and modernization — did it see itself as outdated or conservative? Why not view the government as the leader of social progress? Civilization cannot develop without government support. Deng Xiaoping, after all, was a key figure in pushing these reforms forward.

History has proven that without systemic reform, any struggle between emperors and the people only leads to the repetition of past mistakes. It becomes a cycle: you oppress me, I overthrow you; I take power, then I oppress you again. The constant cycle of peasant uprisings, landlord restorations, and subsequent revolts echoes the endless repetition of feudal society over thousands of years.

4. Humanists and Social Scholars

Ideally, this discussion should be led by the nation's top-level academicians. These individuals receive special government stipends and live off taxpayer money, so they should contribute to the nation's future and civilization, taking on both academic and personal risks. Yet after much observation, it's clear that while the world has social and human sciences academicians, China lacks such figures — there isn't even a single prestigious social or humanities academician, let alone a true master.

China boasts around 5,000 years of civilization, most of which revolves around social and human history. Significant time, energy, and resources have been devoted to developing theories on society, humanity, and history. Most books and famous online influencers in China deal with these topics. Yet, despite this wealth of history and literature, there isn't a single heavyweight academician in social, historical, or human studies in the entire society.

5. Conclusion

Lu Xun once said: "Before the school year ended, I had already gone to Tokyo, because after that incident, I realized that medicine was not a crucial matter. As long as the people remained ignorant and weak, no matter how healthy and strong their bodies, they would be nothing more than senseless spectators and exhibit materials. The number of deaths would not be considered unfortunate. So the most urgent task was to change their spirits, and I thought the way to do this was to promote a literary movement."

Mao Zedong stated: "'Facts' refer to the objective reality of all things, 'Is' refers to the internal connections of these objective realities, i.e., their regularities, and 'Seek' means to research. We must begin with the actual situation at home and abroad, in the provinces, counties, and districts, and derive inherent regularities, not fabricated ones, as a guide for our actions."

Deng Xiaoping remarked: "Don't underestimate the debate over 'Practice as the sole criterion for testing truth.' The significance of this dispute is profound."

Xi Jinping said: "To keep up with the times, we cannot allow our bodies to be in the 21st century while our minds remain stuck in the past."

From China's intellectuals to its top leaders across generations, it is clear that they have been aware and are actively seeking change.

(Created in February 2020)

Fig. B12-1 Works of the French painter Delacroix

B13. Philosophy and History; Mystery and Wisdom

Abstract: When philosophy is confined to books, it is called a worldview ------ a vague and often elusive concept. But when philosophy transcends the written word, it transforms into a force of spirit, power, wisdom, and mystery. And when philosophy reaches its peak, it can trigger bloodshed, weapons, and wars.

Part One

1. The mysteries of the universe may be incomprehensible forever.

The progression of human social systems can be summarized as:

Primitive Society; Slavery Society; Feudalism Society; Democracy Society; Unity Society.

In China, the Yellow Emperor and Emperor Yan established the primitive society.

King Wen of Zhou transitioned this to slavery (After 2,000 years).

Emperor Qin Shi Huang brought China from slavery to feudalism (After another 2,000 years).

Currently, we stand at a pivotal moment between Feudalism and Democracy. Whoever manages to transition China to a democratic system will undoubtedly be remembered alongside the likes of the Yellow Emperor, King Wen, and Qin Shi Huang. From a philosophical and intellectual perspective, the Fuxi, Yellow and Yan Emperors created the 《I Ching》 , and under King Wen, this wisdom reached perfection. During China's 2,000-year-long slavery era, the 《I Ching》 stood as the sole philosophical wisdom.

During the Spring and Autumn Period and the Warring States Period, the rise of Taoism and Confucianism defined the feudal era for 2,000 years. Now, a new philosophical turning point has arrived. I believe there is a theory that will again lead China for 2,000 years, but it may take many years to reach its full maturity.

2. Another cosmic mystery that may never be fully understood.

It is the parallel emergence of philosophical texts in both the East and the West. While the 《I Ching》 spread through China, the 《 Bible 》 (Specifically its Old Testament) spread in the West, particularly in the Middle East.

Thus, during the 2,000 years of slavery, both the East and West had their own philosophical classics. All other philosophical texts were merely commentaries on these two foundational works.

Siddhartha Gautama (Buddha) was born around 563 BC, roughly contemporaneous with Laozi and Confucius. This means that during the same period, both the eastern and southern parts of Asia saw the emergence of new philosophies. Over the next 2,000 years of feudalism, nearly all philosophical works were essentially elaborations on these core texts. Even today, scholars continue to analyze and interpret these same figures.

3. Another mystery of the universe.

Philosophy always precedes, and political systems follow. After the rise of new philosophies during the Spring and

Autumn Period, the state of Qin swiftly emerged, swept across rival states, and unified China. With this unification came the transition from slavery to feudalism.

When Indian Buddhism emerged, it swept through Southeast Asia, transforming weak and fragmented nations into Buddhist states. Buddhist missionaries crossed the Himalayas into Tibet, rapidly turning it into a Buddhist domain. From there, they moved west into Afghanistan, constructing grand idols before turning east along the Hexi Corridor to advance into western China. By the Tang Dynasty, much of China had fallen under the sway of Buddhist philosophy.

Philosophy is powerful! It drives political, economic, and military power. Science often follows, but no discipline rivals the might of philosophy.

4. The universe's mysteries extend even further.

The dominance of Buddhist philosophy led to political and military expansion, which deeply troubled Tang dynasty rulers like Emperor Taizong.

Tibetan King Songtsen Gampo, empowered by Buddhist philosophy, launched aggressive campaigns, first conquering Tuyuhun and then launching attacks on Tang territory. However, the Tang forces ultimately defeated him. Emperor Taizong, recognizing the formidable power of Buddhist philosophy, encouraged the study of Buddhism across the nation and sent Tang Sanzang to India to bring back scriptures. The emperor also attempted to broker peace by marrying Princess Wencheng to King Songtsen Gampo.

Although Buddhism originated from foreign lands, it underwent significant transformations in China. The essence of its philosophy can be found in works like the

《Universal Law》. Today, however, much of what remains is mere ritual, such as shaving heads, performing martial arts, and reciting scriptures.

Buddhist philosophy stands alongside China's two great systems of thought — Taoism and Confucianism. If not for these two philosophical pillars, China might have become a Buddhist nation like Thailand or Myanmar.

King Songtsen Gampo realized that China's strength lay in its profound ideologies. Unlike Thailand and Myanmar, the expansion of Buddhism in China met a firm halt. Buddhism's zenith in China saw monks elevated to high ranks, such as the Tang Sanzang, known as Master Xuanzang. However, Buddhist monks never pursued political power or warfare, which is why they never became China's rulers.

5. Another perplexing mystery of the universe.

As Buddhist philosophy spread across China, a new philosophical force — Islam — emerged.

Prophet Muhammad (570–632 AD), at the age of 40 (610 AD), wrote a book known as the 《Qur'an》. Though Muhammad was illiterate and lacked access to reference books, he dictated the 《Qur'an》 to others, who transcribed his words. The 《Qur'an》 can be seen as a philosophical work, building on the foundations of the 《Bible》's philosophy but replacing the name "God" with "Allah".

After the birth of Islamic philosophy, political, economic, and military power surged. Islamic armies swept across the Middle East, first expelling the Jews from Mecca. They then moved westward, clashing with the Crusaders multiple times, pushing north to the Caucasus, taking control of

Central Asia, advancing south into North Africa, and invading parts of India and Afghanistan.

Philosophy is indeed formidable! With the rise of Arab philosophy, Arab natural science also flourished. Arab scholars translated vast amounts of Greek scientific texts and made significant contributions to philosophy, forming a crucial foundation for modern natural sciences.

6. The mysteries of the universe may forever require your contemplation.

Let's not discuss how Muhammad, without any reference books, mysteriously created Islamic philosophy. Instead, let's talk about how Islamic philosophy expanded eastward, swiftly driving out the Buddhists from Afghanistan. Around the mid to late Tang Dynasty, it made a grand entry into China. Missionaries along the Silk Road spread Islam eastward, turning Xinjiang and Gansu into Islamic states and further advancing into Shanxi and Hebei provinces.

If we say the chaos during China's Northern and Southern Dynasties was caused by the impact of foreign Buddhist philosophy, then the chaos of the Five Dynasties and Ten Kingdoms period, between the end of the Tang Dynasty and the beginning of the Song Dynasty, was the result of Islamic philosophy's invasion.

How did the Chinese react to the invasion of Islamic philosophy? The philosophies of Confucianism, Buddhism, and Daoism were all severely impacted by Islam and retreated step by step. The intellectual landscape of late Tang and early Song China became chaotic, while neighboring countries erupted into conflicts. The Song Dynasty was weak, directly contributing to the rise of the Mongol armies. If the Mongols hadn't used military force to drive the Islamic influence back to the Persian Gulf, who knows if China would have ended up as an Islamic nation like Pakistan or Indonesia?

Islamic philosophy was also a foreign philosophy, and its teachings are outlined in the 《Universal Law》 book. However, with just that philosophy alone, it couldn't stand up to the two major Chinese philosophical systems — Daoism and Confucianism — or to the other foreign philosophy, Buddhism. Although Islamic missionaries from Persia far outnumbered Buddhist missionaries from India and had a greater impact on China, Islamic philosophy was ultimately absorbed into the systems of Daoism, Confucianism, and Buddhism. The missionaries intermarried with the Chinese and became sinicized. Despite the Islamic tendency to spread through the sword, it never became the ruling force in China.

Historians are not philosophers, and they typically don't view history through the lens of philosophy. However, if any historian wants to reference the above words and philosophical analysis, they are welcome to, but they must cite the source — here.

By the way, I'd like to solve a historical mystery. The sealing of the Dunhuang Library Cave and the Thousand Buddha Caves in Jimusar was likely due to the invasion of Islamic philosophy into Afghanistan. The Buddhists, sensing their religion's impending doom, sealed the caves. If it were just a change of kingdom or emperor, they wouldn't have done so.

7. The mysteries of the universe may forever require your deep reflection.

Christian philosophy is ancient, but its introduction to China came much later, around the Tang Dynasty. At that time, it was called “Nestorianism”, and its main feature was the belief that Jesus is God and that he could die and be resurrected. The basic teachings are outlined in the 《Universal Law》 book.

Christian philosophy didn’t have the same luck as Buddhist and Islamic philosophies. Although it’s ancient, it never really took root in China. Perhaps the idea of Jesus being God conflicted with the belief in the emperor as a dragon, making it taboo for Chinese rulers, who viewed it as heresy. Or perhaps the pathways through Afghanistan were always blocked by powerful Buddhists and Muslims. In any case, Christian philosophy seemed incompatible with China’s philosophical systems.

During the Yuan Dynasty, when Mongol armies invaded the Eurasian continent, they opened up channels between East and West, allowing the spread of Roman Catholicism from Europe and Nestorianism from West Asia. It was said that the Yuan people called it "Yelikewen" or "Cross Religion". However, after the fall of the Yuan Empire in the late 14th century, these religions disappeared from China.

The difficulty of Christian philosophy’s spread into China was merely a matter of time. Any philosophy with ideas will never be completely submerged. After Christian philosophy spurred the scientific revival in Europe, it began its march across the globe.

First, they discovered the Americas. There, they defeated the indigenous peoples and turned both North and South America into Christian nations. Then they moved west, incorporating Australia, New Zealand, and the Pacific islands under their influence.

8. The mysteries of the universe may require even more reflection.

If Christian philosophy had stopped there, you would be underestimating it. Its next mission was to once again attempt to enter ancient China, the place it had never fully conquered.

Some historians claim that the West's interest in China was purely due to its vast land and silver reserves. That is a short-sighted view. Historians merely record history and see only the surface. Philosophy looks deeper, at the root of history, while literature focuses on entertainment.

The West already possessed the Americas, Oceania, and parts of Africa. Why did it still desire to control China, where imperial power and the military were so tightly knit? What they truly sought was to bring in their philosophy. China, guarded by Confucianism and Daoism, was the last bastion of ancient philosophy, and Christian philosophy had long desired to penetrate it.

During the late Ming and early Qing Dynasties, Catholic (Old Church) and Protestant (New Church, i.e., Jesus Church) missionaries arrived by sea. They no longer traveled the land routes like the Silk Road, where old philosophies stood in their way. As European warships grew larger, missionaries boldly spread Christian philosophy, relying on the power of cannons and guns. Famous figures like "Matteo Ricci", "Johann Adam Schall von Bell", and "Ferdinand Verbiest" became well-known for their efforts.

The more modern history, I believe readers are more familiar with. After Christian philosophy made a major push into China, the rulers were thrown into disarray. If everyone believed in Jesus, who would still believe in them? Just like a scene from history, the Qing government responded by closing the country to foreign influence. Brainwashed youths, supported by the government, began the "Boxer Rebellion". They killed foreign missionaries, burned churches — much like today's youth throwing stones at U.S. embassies or blocking French chain stores.

History repeats itself. Just as Qing loyalist scholars cursed the Western powers for partitioning and humiliating China, today's nationalistic writers shout, 《China Can Say No》, 《China Is Unhappy》, or 《China Can Fight the World》.

Imperial scholars, nationalistic writers, and historians always focus on how foreign powers behave, but they never ask, "Why are our Chinese rulers so foolish?" "Why are Chinese rulers unhappy with their own ignorance?" "How are foolish Chinese rulers preparing to fight the world?" ... They never seek progress. While the rest of the world adopts parliamentary systems and the separation of powers, China clings to propaganda control, censorship, and imperial and papal systems. Even Japan, a small country, embraced Christian philosophy and became stronger through reform. Why can't China do the same? Look at today's propaganda machine shouting, "Our system will not change for 100 years; we will never learn from the West!" Doesn't that sound eerily similar to "Empress Dowager Cixi's" words, "We will never learn from the West!"?

Philosophy is philosophy. It cannot be stopped by the absurdities and hindrances of an incompetent government. When Western Christian philosophy couldn't break into China, it gave the Chinese a taste of gunpowder and opium. Soon, the "Opium Wars" broke out, and the "Eight-Nation Alliance" invaded Beijing, burning the "Old Summer Palace". When they took back the "Zodiac Heads" of the fountain, British and French soldiers and officers even sat on the emperor's throne and bed. Some even urinated on it, the ultimate mockery of the Chinese emperor by Christian philosophy — a climax in its assault on China.

It was only then that the Chinese government understood what philosophical civilization meant and began learning Western ideas through the "Self-Strengthening Movement". But it was too late! Since 1840, Europe's great powers bombarded ancient China with ironclad ships and cannons. The "Opium Wars", the "Sino-French War", the "Eight-Nation Alliance", and even Japan, influenced by Christian philosophy, started the "Sino-Japanese War". China was beaten into signing thousands of unequal treaties, losing vast amounts of territory and paying exorbitant indemnities. What did China gain? Merely an open door? Or just the foolish realization by Chinese rulers that they needed to learn from the West?

History is truly thrilling. For thousands of years, Chinese rulers have continuously revised history textbooks to suit their political needs, dumbing down the populace. Their greatest fear is the spirit of democracy and freedom, the very things that have kept China from having philosophy, thought, or civilization for the last two thousand years, resulting in constant beatings!

9. The mysteries of the universe require exploration.

If the Qing Dynasty had introduced Western philosophy like Japan did, establishing a democratic system with a separation of powers, I believe that China would not have lost any territory. Instead, it could have entered the ranks of the world's powers by adopting the capitalist system of Western philosophy. But why did it always criticize and reject the West, refusing to follow their system?

When Christian philosophy attacked China alongside guns and cannons, another new philosophy was born ------- Marxism.

Karl Marx (1818-1883) wrote his first political article, 《Critique of the Prussian Press Law》, in 1842.

In 1845, he wrote the 《Theses on Feuerbach》, a philosophical work that pointed out that practice is the standard for testing the truth of human thought.

Then, together with Engels, he co-authored 《The German Ideology》, which systematically explained the materialist conception of history.

In 1858, he completed his first economic manuscript, 《Outlines of the Critique of Political Economy》, or the first draft of 《Das Kapital》, elaborating on the theory of surplus value.

In 1859, Marx wrote 《A Contribution to the Critique of Political Economy》, which elaborated on his value theory, including the theory of money, among other things. ... Where is Marx's originality?

In metaphysics, materialism, and idealism, systems had already been established by thinkers such as Aristotle, Kant, and Hegel; Marx merely criticized them. In dialectics, ancient China had already explained it through the concept of "Yin and yang", which he merely rephrased. In other words, Marx had no original contributions in the fields of metaphysics, materialism, idealism, or dialectical philosophy.

His originality lies in economics. More specifically, he is an economic philosopher. He discovered the theory of surplus value and exposed the secret of capitalists exploiting workers. However, he couldn't solve the problem, so he proposed revolution ------- killing capitalists and distributing factories to workers. Simple, right?

But what happened? Workers who got rich became capitalists and continued to exploit other workers. So, what's next? Haven't countries with Marxist systems already killed many capitalists and landlords? They redistributed factories and land, but now a new batch of capitalists and landlords has emerged, still exploiting workers through surplus value. What can be done? Kill again or not?

So, Marx only discovered surplus value, but he couldn't solve it.

He understood class struggle, armed rebellion, and seizing power, much like the military governments in Africa, the Philippines, and Pakistan often do. However, in some countries, this is done with a few small units, while others use millions of troops, taking power by force on a much larger scale.

He didn't understand science and wrote 《Dialectics of Nature》 with Engels, which was filled with layman's talk. He didn't understand politics either, so countries with Marxist systems still use emperor-like or military governments and even papal systems. Nevertheless, his economic philosophy could be considered a philosophical revolution, so let's see how this philosophical revolution plays out this time!

10. The mysteries of the universe need further exploration.

During his lifetime, not many people paid attention to Marx's ideas. He merely incited workers to protest frequently, destabilizing nations — a practice we might call "Stirring trouble" today. As a result, governments were annoyed by him and drove him from place to place.

After his death in 1883, Marxist philosophy lay dormant. However, though largely ignored, it didn't die. His ideas of armed rebellion and seizing power through force appealed to the impoverished masses. When the global economic crisis hit, people revisited his philosophy, and it began to stir again. Thirty years later, his ideas finally began to take hold. Once philosophy shows its wild side, you can't hold it back!

Look at how Marxist philosophy went wild ------ the whole world went mad. Starving and freezing proletarians rose up! Armed with Marxist philosophy (Note: it had become a weapon), they shattered the old society, sweeping away all oppressors. Unstoppable! Incredible, absolutely incredible!

In 1917, the Soviet Marxist Party acted first, seizing power with guns and becoming the first Marxist nation.

In 1919, the "Communist International" was founded, aiming to help liberate people around the world by forcibly overthrowing local governments. Over the following decades, the Soviet Union helped dozens of Eastern European countries seize power with guns, turning them all into Marxist nations. Philosophy is powerful, isn't it?

In 1920, the Soviet "Communist International" sent missionaries Maring and Nikolsky to China, directly financing the formation of the Chinese Communist Party. Soon after, the Chinese Communist Party was established in Shanghai with members like Chen Duxiu, Li Dazhao, and Mao Zedong.

In 1921, the first National Congress of the Chinese Communist Party was held in Shanghai, marking its founding year.

How did China's Nationalist government view the intrusion of foreign philosophy?

The Republic of China had just been established in 1912 after the Xinhai Revolution overthrew the Qing Dynasty. Sun Yat-sen was elected as the first President of the Republic of China ------- a very young nation facing numerous founding challenges. There were warlords dividing the north, and in the south, peasant revolts led by the Communist Party waged revolution with two kitchen knives, killing landlords and capitalists.

Killing a few tyrannical landlords may not seem like much, but under today's legal system, killing a few corrupt police officers, like Yang Jia did, probably wouldn't be considered a capital offense, right?

Sun Yat-sen (1866–1925) was quite confused. He had just dealt with the Christian philosophical attack and even married a Christian wife. Now Marxism arrived. What to do?

After much thought, he decided to ally with Russia and the Communists and support the workers and peasants.

After Sun Yat-sen died in 1925, his successor, Chiang Kai-shek, was furious at the Communist-led riots, street blockades, looting, killing of landlords, and capitalists. He responded with massacres and suppression, which is a common approach for ruling parties — crackdowns! The martyrdom of Chinese missionary Li Dazhao followed. While doing the same thing, Li Dazhao became a martyr, while Yang Jia was labeled a criminal. What a historical coincidence — just a reversal of positions.

The conflict between the two parties heated up. The Chinese Communist Party launched a series of uprisings, like the Nanchang Uprising and the Autumn Harvest Uprising, establishing numerous Communist bases. The war between suppression and counter-suppression escalated into civil war.

From a few Soviet Marxist missionaries in just a few years, the movement grew into an army of millions of Chinese missionaries. That's fast! Philosophy's wild nature had gone mad!

Millions of Chinese soldiers faced off against millions of Chinese soldiers! How many died? And for what? Just so

Western philosophy could infiltrate China's power structure? Strange, isn't it? Chinese people killed so many of their own just for a Western Marxist philosophy. Too brutal!

This scale of killing exceeds any small African nation's military coups.

Whenever Western Marxist agents declare at national meetings, "We will never learn from the West! ...." I can't help but laugh. Isn't your entire system Western? Stop waving your flag! You've only adopted the West's violence and murder but haven't learned any of its good parts! Then you add some Chinese imperial elements, creating a "Chinese characteristic". Then, with a little media spin, it becomes the "Three Represents", supposedly representing the world's most advanced philosophy. It makes me laugh so hard!

If the Chinese government and its hundreds of advisors could create new philosophy, I believe rulers worldwide would kneel before them.

History repeats itself, over and over again. In the 2,500 years since the creation of Confucianism and Daoism, China has not created any new philosophy. Even now, it only has a semblance of philosophy.

Over this time, China has faced four major invasions of foreign philosophy: Buddhist philosophy during the Northern and Southern Dynasties, Islamic philosophy during the Five Dynasties and Ten Kingdoms period, Christian philosophy in the late Qing Dynasty, and Marxist philosophy during the Republican era. Each time, the invasions brought war and death, each time more intense and bloodier.

The philosophies of Confucianism and Daoism have retreated over time, while foreign philosophies have gradually pushed their way in, ultimately becoming the rulers of China. The conflict between the Nationalist and

Communist parties wasn't just a simple party struggle — it was a life-and-death battle between Western philosophy and Chinese philosophy, culminating in a final, bloody showdown.

In short, Western Marxist philosophy ultimately succeeded, becoming the ruler of Chinese thought. Its Eastern Chinese agents became the leaders of all the vast lands, and the "River crabs" (Censorship) fiercely control and suppress all philosophical thought. If you have ideas, the "River crabs" will say, "As long as we're here, there will be no thoughts!" How tragic! The tragedy of the Chinese people!

There is one small hope ------ these Eastern Marxists are from the East, not blue-eyed, high-nosed Westerners. So they don't truly understand Western Marxist philosophy. They can only be considered Marxist missionaries or the biggest "Multi-level marketers" often banned by governments. Their sales pitch? "Join the party and you'll get a position; join the party and you'll make money!"

A netizen posted a question: "Does Mr.Hai Zhitao understand philosophy?"

I've thought about this question for several days. In the natural sciences, I know a little about math, physics, chemistry, astronomy, electronics, computers, and so on. In the social sciences, I know a little about economics, finance, accounting, trade, history, literature, and so on. But philosophy ------- I truly don't understand what it is!

If philosophy stays in books, it's the study of worldviews. But what is a worldview? That's vague too!

If philosophy escapes from books, it becomes a kind of spirit, power, wisdom, and mystery. Once it goes wild, it turns into bloodshed, weapons, and war. Can any netizen define what philosophy is based on the nature of philosophy I've described above?

11. Summary

1) This section explores how philosophical thought has been deeply intertwined with political, military, and societal developments throughout history. Each era's dominant philosophy drove not only intellectual discourse but also the rise and fall of civilizations. The mysterious and powerful nature of philosophy remains a force to be reckoned with, influencing everything from social systems to scientific progress.

2) This text presents a broad historical analysis, focusing on the philosophical and military conflicts between China and foreign ideologies, especially Islamic, Christian, and Western influences, and it criticizes China's internal governance for resisting these philosophies while lagging behind global progress.

3) The passage offers a reflection on the history of philosophy, focusing especially on Marxism, its reception, and its consequences in China, while contrasting it with the nation's traditional and foreign philosophical influences.

(Written in Guangzhou on April 7, 2009)

Part Two

The first part discussed China's history over thousands of years. This second part makes predictions about China's future. However, it is important to emphasize that these are only speculations and not necessarily facts. Philosophy is the root of history, and looking at history from a philosophical perspective is like observing the Earth from space.

As stated in the first part of "Philosophy and History; Mystery and Wisdom" and the book 《Universal Law》:

The entire social system of humanity can be described as:

- Primitive System: before 3000 BC
- Slave System: 3000 BC – 500 BC
- Feudal System: 500 BC – 2000 AD
- Democratic System: 2000 AD – 4500 AD (Predicted)
- Unified System: After 4500 AD (Predicted)

Each stage lasts approximately 2500 years. This is China's current situation, and China is now at the intersection of the late feudal system and the early democratic system. Globally, however, the situation is different. Western countries entered the democratic system about one to two hundred years ago. The early stages of the democratic system were unstable and saw multiple wars, but now it has become quite stable.

This view comes from looking at history through the lens of philosophy. Therefore, any events or wars happening now or in the future around the world are closely related to the "Democratic system" philosophical framework.

In book 《 Universal Law》, I wrote between 2003 and 2005 that China would experience 30 years of decline starting in 2009. Why is that? Let me explain.

China's political system still adopts a medieval European papal-like structure, with nine standing committee members acting like nine cardinals. This is slightly better than the feudal system of passing power from father to son but is still outdated compared to current Western countries, which leads to incompatible thinking in international affairs. The government even fears websites and articles, indicating its inner insecurity and lack of confidence.

From 2009 onward, give or take a year, China's social situation will enter a downward trend until 2038. Judging by the series of natural disasters, human crises, and other issues that began in 2008 and continued into 2009, this prediction is being confirmed.

Some may say this is idealism, but let's see how history proves it!

There is a famous Chinese saying: "Thirty years east of the river, thirty years west of the river." This perfectly describes China's current situation:

During the 150-year "Great Communist Dynasty" cycle, it can be divided into five intermediate waves.

- The first wave, from 1919 to 1948, a total of 30 years, represents revolution (Upward trend).
- The second wave, from 1949 to 1978, a total of 30 years, represents the Cultural Revolution (Downward trend).
- The third wave, from 1979 to 2008, a total of 30 years, represents reform (Upward trend).
- The fourth wave, from 2009 to 2038, a total of 30 years, represents transformation (Downward trend).
- The fifth wave, from 2039 to 2068, a total of 30 years, possibly represents a new "Revolution"? (Future prediction)

Each intermediate wave can be further divided into five smaller waves. This is how history unfolds:

1. The First Intermediate Wave (Revolutionary Cycle) — 30 Years, Each Sub-Wave Lasting 6 Years:

1) "1919–1924": Birth of the revolution. The main activities were anti-government slogans, riots, smashing, looting, and killing corrupt officials, landlords, and local elites. The government responded with military and police suppression, imprisoning protestors, and executing the most serious offenders. The number of deaths from political dissent was in the hundreds per year.

2) "1925–1930": Development of the revolution. Student movements transformed into militias and guerrilla forces, establishing bases and organizing uprisings, with minor clashes with government forces. Deaths from political dissent rose to thousands per year.

3) "1931–1936": Growth of the revolution. Guerrilla forces grew into the Red Army, and the revolutionary base areas expanded. Conflicts with government forces intensified, with annual political dissent deaths reaching tens of thousands.

4) "1937–1942": Strengthening of the revolution. The Red Army became a regular army, expanding further, organizing large-scale military confrontations with government forces, involving more civilians. Political dissent deaths reached hundreds of thousands per year.

5) "1943–1948": Maturity of the revolution. Large-scale decisive battles against government forces took place, leading to a full-scale civil war, with the revolutionary army eventually defeating the government. Deaths from political dissent rose to millions per year.

Summary: From 1919, the three major upward trends ensured the revolutionary army's 30-year revolution, eventually overthrowing the Nationalist government. These three upward trends were the slogans of "Democracy, revolution, and freedom."

2. The Second Intermediate Wave (Cultural Revolution Cycle) — 30 Years, Each Sub-Wave Lasting 6 Years:

1) "1949–1954": Early phase of the Cultural Revolution. Domestic policies included the "Three-Anti" and "Five-Anti" movements, and the "Four Cleanups" campaign. Externally, there was the Korean War and the beginning of isolationism. Deaths from political dissent reached millions per year.

2) "1955–1960": Second phase of the Cultural Revolution. Domestic policies featured numerous campaigns, the Great Leap Forward, and the establishment of People's Communes. Externally, relations with the Soviet Union soured, and isolationism continued. Deaths from political dissent remained in the millions per year.

3) "1961–1966": Third phase of the Cultural Revolution. Domestic movements continued, including the "Three Years of Natural Disasters." Externally, there were wars with neighboring countries, and isolationism persisted. Deaths from political dissent continued at millions per year.

4) "1967–1972": Fourth phase of the Cultural Revolution. Domestic movements intensified, culminating in the Cultural Revolution. Externally, wars with neighboring countries continued, and isolationism persisted. Deaths from political dissent remained in the millions per year.

5) "1973–1978": Final phase of the Cultural Revolution. Domestic movements began to reflect, gradually subsiding. The death of Mao and the Tangshan earthquake marked a turning point. Externally, the wars ended, and relations with the U.S. were established. Deaths from political dissent were in the millions per year (In the early phase).

Summary: Starting in 1949, three major downward trends determined the Republic's 30-year misstep. These three downward trends were the slogans of "External wars, internal purges, and isolationism."

3. The Third Intermediate Wave (Reform Cycle) — 30 Years, Each Sub-Wave Lasting 6 Years:

1) "1979–1984": Early phase of reform. Hua Guofeng crushed the Gang of Four, reopened cultural and educational sectors. Domestically, the government corrected past injustices and reversed wrongful persecutions. Externally, diplomatic relations with neighboring countries were opened. The annual death toll from political dissent was around a hundred.

2) "1985–1990": Second phase of reform. Deng Xiaoping continued Hua Guofeng's policies. Domestically, culture, education, and the economy were opened. Externally, diplomatic relations with neighboring countries were maintained. The annual death toll from political dissent remained around a hundred (Except for 1989).

3) "1991–1996": Third phase of reform. Deng Xiaoping continued the opening of culture, education, and the economy but did not pursue political reforms. Externally, diplomatic relations with countries worldwide were expanded. The annual death toll from political dissent remained around a hundred.

4) "1997–2002": Fourth phase of reform. Jiang Zemin continued Deng Xiaoping's policies. Domestically, cultural, educational, and economic openness expanded. Externally, diplomatic relations with countries worldwide were maintained. The annual death toll from political dissent remained around a hundred.

5) "2003–2008": Fifth phase of reform. Hu Jintao and Wen Jiabao continued Deng Xiaoping's policies. Domestically, culture, education, and the economy were opened further. Externally, diplomatic relations with countries worldwide were maintained. The annual death toll from political dissent remained around a hundred.

Summary: From 1979 onward, three major upward trends were established, marking 30 years of reform for China. These three trends were encapsulated by the slogans "Reform, Openness, and Stability." It's important to note that both Jiang Zemin and Hu Jintao, along with Wen Jiabao, inherited Deng Xiaoping's policies of economic openness and political stability, without any political reform. This laid the groundwork for potential storms over the next 30 years.

4. The Fourth Intermediate Wave (Transformation Cycle) — 30 Years, Each Sub-Wave Lasting 6 Years:

1) "2009–2014": Early phase of transformation. Social contradictions became acute. Corruption and illegal activities flourished. Collusion between officials and businesses oppressed ordinary people. Tensions between officials and citizens escalated, leading to violent conflicts. Civilians protested, and it was not uncommon for county governments to be burned or attacked. At this time, however, the military and police could still control the situation.

2) “2015–2020”: Second phase of transformation. Social contradictions became even sharper. Corruption and illegal activities worsened. The collusion between officials and businesses intensified, leading to more widespread conflicts between officials and citizens. Violent confrontations became more common, and county and district governments were attacked more frequently. The military and police could still suppress uprisings, though with difficulty.

3) “2021–2026”: Third phase of transformation (Accompanied by a large-scale pandemic).

4) “2027–2032”: Fourth phase of transformation.

5) “2033–2038”: Fifth phase of transformation.

Summary: Starting from 2008, three major downward trends appeared, indicating 30 years of turmoil for China. These three trends are encapsulated by the phrases "Natural Disasters, Earthly Hardships, and Human Calamities."

"Natural disasters" refers to climate changes, floods, plagues, and viruses; "Earthly hardships" refers to Earthquakes and volcanic activity; and "Human calamities" refers to unjust governance, intensifying ethnic tensions, and oppression of the populace.

During these 30 years, if events such as the collapse of the Yangtze River dam, nuclear power plant explosions, pandemics, Earthquakes, severe smog, floods, ethnic strife, massacres, and religious persecution occur, they will deepen the contradictions between the government and the people. These changes in the sub-waves will accelerate, and the 30-year cycle may even shorten.

5. The Fifth Intermediate Wave (Revolution Cycle), Divided into 5 Sub-Waves:

If the above predictions come true, there might not be another 30-year period, but if the fourth wave does not see these extreme events, then they may occur during the fifth wave. No matter what, it seems that China will experience earth-shattering changes in the coming years.

I fear that many people may die in the not-too-distant future, which is why I wrote this article. If China can become more democratic and reform its political system, the above analysis could change.

This section presents a philosophical and historical analysis of China's past and makes predictions about the future based on cyclical patterns and philosophical shifts. It also discusses the predicted trends and transformations in China, focusing on social, political, and environmental upheavals.

(Written in Guangzhou on April 7, 2009)

Part three

I know the Chinese government has always sought reform, but sometimes their methods of governance are problematic. The reason is that their think tanks often engage in flattery to protect their positions, not offering real advice but even spreading falsehoods. They won't admit their incompetence and inability to offer strategic advice to the leaders, but instead, they blame foreign reactionaries and domestic hostile forces, claiming that these groups never cease their attempts to overthrow China. They emphasize external factors without addressing internal ones, blaming China's domestic issues on foreign opposition forces like Tibetan independence, Taiwanese independence, and Xinjiang separatism, which is utterly absurd!

I suspect the Chinese government also harbors ambitions of defeating the United States. But even if they wish to, would they really dare to destroy it? Would they dare to use nuclear weapons?

The same goes for the United States — they want to destroy China every day. But would they dare to use nuclear weapons against China?

If the Chinese government were to be overthrown, it wouldn't be the work of foreigners or overseas Chinese. Rather, it would be done by the Chinese people themselves. As Chinese history shows, when the court employs sycophants and eliminates dissidents, the government inevitably faces internal and external crises, much like how the Song dynasty was ruined by treacherous ministers. This is entirely due to the internal factors within the Chinese government, and they can't blame foreigners.

The Chinese government does not understand that the Han people are the main driving force in China. If the Han people do not express discontent, the 56 ethnic minorities would never rise in rebellion. It is the instability of the Han people that leads to the overall instability in China, which in turn inspires the 56 ethnic minorities to take action.

But what is the root of the Han people's dissatisfaction? The Chinese government's policies toward the Han people differ from those for ethnic minorities, such as in education and family planning, effectively dividing the Han people and ethnic minorities into two groups, rather than one united Chinese nation. I've never seen the United States or Australia offering preferential policies to their domestic ethnic minorities, yet they all identify as Americans or Australians!

The Chinese government forces the Western Marxist doctrine on the upper class intellectuals among the Han people, suppressing the development of nationalistic thought. It prohibits the publication of nationalist ideas and only allows the publication of Marxist teachings, promoting speeches by Marxist leaders. As a result, the Chinese nation becomes a subordinate to Western Marxist thought, causing great harm to the Chinese nation and naturally stirring dissatisfaction among the intellectuals.

For the lower classes, the Chinese government resorts to oppression because Marxist doctrine doesn't resonate with them. They have greater faith in the Earth God and Buddha. If we pull 100 people, no, just 10 people from the petitioners in Beijing, and listen to what they have to say, we would quickly learn why the Chinese officials have driven the common Han people to petition constantly.

I have summarized three main areas of concern, aligning them with the concepts of Heaven, Earth, and Humanity, corresponding to the "Natural disasters, Earthly hardships, and Human calamities" that are expected from 2009 to 2038. I hope the Chinese government can implement reforms.

1. The Concept of Heaven:

The Chinese government must reform its understanding of "Heaven". It must revere Heaven and show deep respect, abandoning the false doctrine of Western Marxism's materialism and the notion of "Fighting Heaven and Earth." They should stop believing that power comes from the barrel of a gun.

I believe the Chinese government has learned something from the natural disasters and civil unrest of 2008. Only by believing in the laws of nature and abandoning Western Marxism's atheism can China be saved from disaster. This rejection of Marxism cannot be superficial or mere lip service while still promoting Marxism in universities and other areas. The government must genuinely reject Marxism and refuse to remain Marxist followers.

Instead, they should turn to the great Chinese thinkers like Laozi and Confucius, becoming followers of Confucianism and Daoism. Only in this way can the 56 ethnic minorities fully integrate with the Han people, and only then can the nation avoid division and ethnic war.

Therefore, the government must conform to the natural order, rejecting the Marxist materialist worldview. Even the name of the Communist Party must be changed. I suggest renaming it the "People's Party", the "Reform Party", or the "Harmony Party". "Democratic Party" or "Republican Party" could also be considered, but the name "Communist Party", a remnant of Marxism, must be abolished. It is the root of rebellion and ethnic conflict, and this change would align with the will of Heaven.

2. The Concept of Earth:

The government must reform its understanding of "Earth". Chinese people place great importance on feng shui, not as superstition, but as an embodiment of energy and spirit. Beijing is the center of China, and Tiananmen is the center of Beijing, so the area around Tiananmen is the source of energy for the entire nation.

But look at the area surrounding Tiananmen. In the center of the Tiananmen Tower hangs a portrait of Mao, and in the center of Tiananmen Square stands a monument to the dead. South of the monument lies Mao's mausoleum. This north-south alignment mirrors the structure of the Ming dynasty tombs, with the Tower, the Monument, and the Mausoleum. Thus, Tiananmen Square is essentially a grand royal tomb, filled with excessive yin energy.

After Mao's corpse was placed there, the 1989 Tiananmen Square massacre occurred, resulting in thousands of deaths in the square and on the nearby streets. Since then, many people have jumped into the Jinshui River in front of Tiananmen or immolated themselves in the square.

The entire city of Beijing is built around this grand tomb, and thus, it is often shrouded in smog, sandstorms, and fluctuating temperatures, with no blue skies ------- signs typical of bad feng shui. Furthermore, Zhongnanhai, the residence of China's leaders, is located where previous emperor were poisoned to death. (After Mao moved in, he became entangled with spirits and turned into a dictator.) Every time I return to Beijing, I feel chills and tightness in my chest, as if gripped by a haunting presence. The peaceful skies of my childhood are gone.

I don't understand why Marxist governments worldwide insist on placing their leaders' corpses in the center of the capital — Soviet Russia, North Korea, China, Vietnam, and so on. Isn't that a contradiction to their materialist beliefs? In Chinese history, no emperor ever buried himself in the heart of the capital. It's terrible for feng shui and destructive to the energy of the land!

Therefore, I propose the following changes: Mao's portrait should be moved to the Museum of Chinese History, where it belongs. The Great Hall of the People should be renamed "The People's Parliament". The Monument to the People's Heroes should be re-inscribed, not to honor the martyrs of the past 30 years, but to commemorate all those who have sacrificed for democracy and freedom throughout history. Above the monument, instead of an imperial-style roof, there should be a statue of the Goddess of Liberty, to symbolize the sacrifice made for democracy and freedom, not for dynastic succession.

The mausoleum south of the monument should be renamed the "Hall of Justice", to commemorate those who were unjustly persecuted or killed, and serve as a place for petitioners. Mao's body should be moved to Babaoshan Cemetery or returned to his hometown in Hunan. The Hall of Justice would be overseen by a rotating member of the Politburo Standing Committee, who would address petitions, wrongful cases, and local government abuses.

After these changes are made to Tiananmen Square, it will no longer be a massive tomb, and the accumulated negative energy will disperse. Perhaps then Beijing will return to its former beauty, with clear skies, fresh air, and gentle breezes.

Since Beijing is the feng shui center of China, by removing the tomb-like elements, the feng shui of the entire country would naturally improve, leading to fewer natural disasters, calamities, and deaths across the land.

3. The Concept of Humanity:

The government must reform its approach to "Humanity", showing respect for the will of the people. This requires changes to the legal system and a shift towards rule by law. The title "Secretary" (书记 Shuji) should be abolished, as it implies a foreign agent or puppet government. Instead, officials should be called "Representatives", indicating that they serve the people. Issues like judicial independence, nationalizing the military, and multi-party elections can be gradually introduced — not too quickly, but not avoided either. These changes must be made! Don't claim we shouldn't follow the West — Deng Xiaoping said it himself: "It doesn't matter whether a cat is black or white, as long as it catches mice!"

Why should the national ideology of the Chinese people be considered inferior to Western Marxism? Since Marxist ideology has caused so much chaos in China, why not give Chinese philosophy a try? Human beings are thinkers, and respecting humanity means respecting people's ideas and will.

Additionally, China's national flag should be changed to feature three colors: blue, yellow, and red, rather than just yellow and red. These three colors would symbolize the reforms in Heaven, Earth, and Humanity. Once these reforms are completed, I guarantee China will become a stable nation in the next 30 years — without ethnic conflicts, territorial divisions, or religious wars.

In this way, China will integrate into the global system, aligning itself with the great democratic wave that began around the year 2000 and is predicted to continue until 4500 AD. Following that, a unified system may emerge (According to predictions). Right now, we are at the beginning of this fourth great wave of democracy.

If China does not follow these suggestions, then we can only leave it to fate. We do not know what will happen, but if, in the coming decades, millions of heads hang over Tiananmen Square, truly turning it into a graveyard, what can I say? I can only sigh in despair! Heaven's will cannot be defied, and there is no power left to reverse the course.

(Written in Guangzhou on April 7, 2009)

Author John Chang (Hai zhitao)

Four. Unifying Science

Chapter Summary:

The classic life science prophecy book 《Tui Bei Tu》 was written during the Tang Dynasty by Mr.Yuan Tiangang and Mr.Li Chunfeng:

Prophecy: "Vast and boundless is the universe, its end unknown. The Sun and Moon revolve, and the cycle repeats."

Ode: "From Pangu to Xi Yi, tigers fought and dragons contended, how strange the events! Grasping the true meaning of the cycle, the key will be discussed after Tang Dynasty."

Pioneers of Eastern and Western Life Science Prophecies:

Ancient Times: 《I Ching》 (Book of Changes), written by Mr.Fu Xi.

Zhou Dynasty: 《 Song of the Eternal Heaven and Earth》 , written by Mr.Jiang Ziya.

Spring and Autumn Period & Warring States Period: 《Buddhist Sutras》 , written by Mr.Siddhartha Gautama (Buddha).

Han Dynasty: 《The Bible》 , written by Christians.

Three Kingdoms Period: 《Ma Qian Ke》 (Lessons Before the Battle), written by Mr.Zhu Geliang.

Tang Dynasty: 《Tui Bei Tu》 , written by Mr.Yuan Tiangang and Mr.Li Chunfeng.

Yuan Dynasty: 《Shao Bing Ge》 (The Pancake Song), written by Mr.Liu Bowen.

Ming Dynasty: 《The Centuries》, written by Mr.Nostradamus.

Present Day: ?

Oppressive Groups and Factions:

The authors of prophecies throughout history have been the world's top life science idealists. Their opponents were the dictators of various eras and so-called materialist experts and professors. These rulers, fearing the loss of their regime, ordered controlled pseudo-academics, fake doctoral examiners, and experimental pseudo-scientists to dominate the narrative, suppress publications and promotion, and diminish the value of life prophecies. For instance, in China, Academician Mr.He disparaged Qigong and traditional Chinese medicine as pseudoscience ----- this continues to the present day.

C1. Universal Law Periodic Table of Chemical Elements

Abstract: The Universal Law Periodic Table of Chemical Elements encapsulates all the properties of the current periodic table while also revealing properties that the current table has yet to demonstrate.

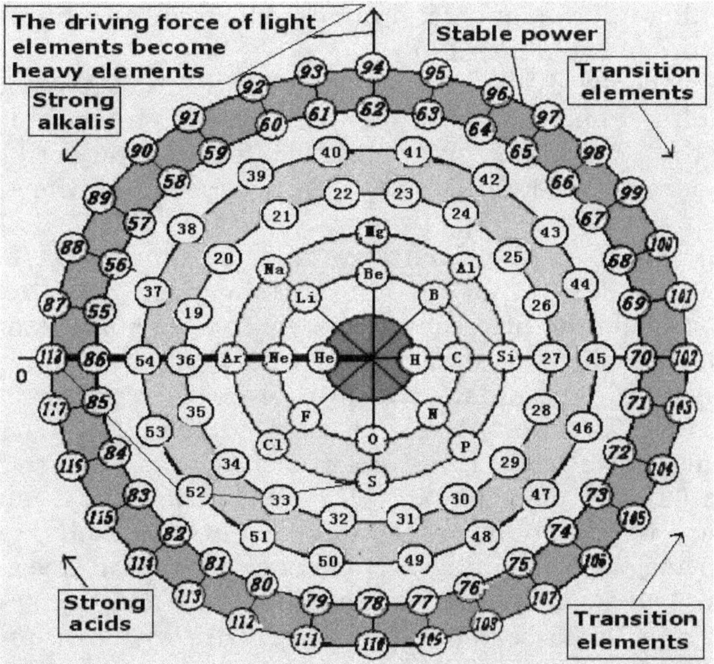

Fig. C1-1 The Periodic table of chemical elements of the universal law of the Galactic civilization (Original chart)

We show the cycles of mathematics, physics and chemistry. At present, the cycle of mathematics to physics is called "Mathematical physics", and the cycle of physics to chemistry is called "Physical chemistry", but the cycle of chemistry to mathematics seems to be another leap.

The periodic table we are showing was written in the book 《Universal Law》 in 2003, showing the leap from chemistry to mathematics.

The characteristics of this periodic table are:

1) 118 elements are arranged in a circular wave shape according to the atomic number, showing a hierarchical structure of ".", "1", and "o".

The centre "." is the nucleus; "1" is the energy wave extending from the inside to the outside, from dilute to dense; "o" is the energy level distribution of the peripheral electrons, K, L, M, N, O, P, Q Layer respectively, the shape is like an enlarged drop of water.

2) Group zero elements are atomic numbers 2, 10, 18, 36, 54, 86, 118. They are the starting point and the end point, closing the hierarchical system to form stable atoms.

3) The elements are divided into four levels from the central core outwards (The fifth level of elements is not found). The first level is the K level, which only accommodates 2 electrons, each occupying a 180° rotation space (Based on a plane); The second layer is L and M layers, which only accommodate 8 electrons, each occupying 22.5° rotating sector space; the third layer is N and O layers, which can accommodate 18 electrons, each occupying 11.25 sector space; the fourth layer is P and Q. The layer can hold 32 electrons, each occupying 5.625° sector space. The more outward, the smaller the space of the rotating sector, the easier the electrons leave. The formula for the arrangement of electrons is $2n^2$ (n = 1,2,3, ...) . They are always arranged on the lowest energy electron shell first, indicating that the centre make its control strength.

4) Turn clockwise from zero group upwards, it is positive group, and it is alkaline; from zero group down counterclockwise, it is negative group, it is acidic. The closer to the zero elements, the stronger the acidity and alkalinity, but there seems to be an acid spiral in the element plane space, just like the vortex structure of the Milky Way.

5) Expand the Lanthanide and Actinide series elements to make all the elements into a whole, and the "Transition elements" transition from top to bottom, fully showing the characteristics of element changes at the atomic level.

This periodic table summarizes all the properties of the current periodic table, and also shows the properties that the current periodic table does not show. It is intertwined and connected to each other, reflecting the beauty of nature and the precision and perfection of the laws of the universe. Look at the snowflake in winter, the constantly changing shape and structure, isn't this a periodic table of chemical elements?

Fig. C1-2 The periodic table of chemical elements in this universal law also looks like galaxies and conch shells, as well as snowflakes that constantly change their shapes.

The alien civilization also displays a periodic table of chemical elements and chemical elements similar to ours. The five level outermost is 4 electrons, the chemical element Zirconium.

Fig. C1-3 The periodic table of chemical elements of the universal law of the Galactic civilization displayed by an alien civilization, representing the element zirconium.

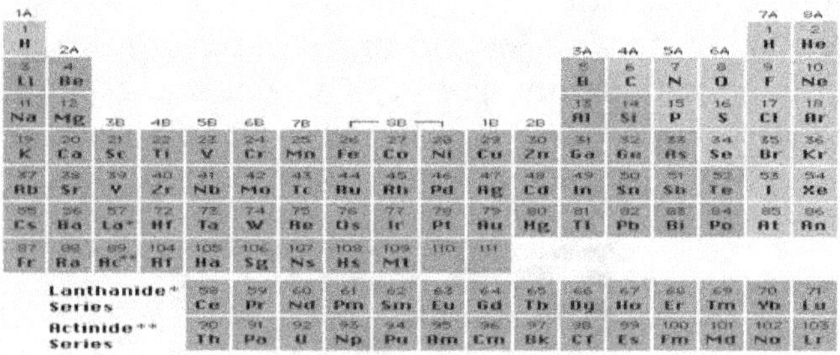

Fig. C1-4 Periodic table of chemical elements displayed by Current civilization **(Edit by Jun. 2017)**

Reference: 1. John Chang: 《Universal Law》, Chapter 11, (2003), Universal Publishing, Sydeny, Australia.

2. John Chang: 《Crop Circle》(2015), Universal Publishing, Sydeny, Australia.

C2. Life Intelligence Entity

Abstract: Is there a law governing the entire universe, encompassing both living organisms and celestial bodies? Where do humans and celestial bodies come from? Is there a law that dictates the existence of these bodies, determining their space and time? Is there a rule that can determine the future of living beings or celestial bodies, including their final destination and the direction of their motion? The concept of the "Life Intelligence (wisdom) Entity" serves as the cornerstone for investigating these profound questions.

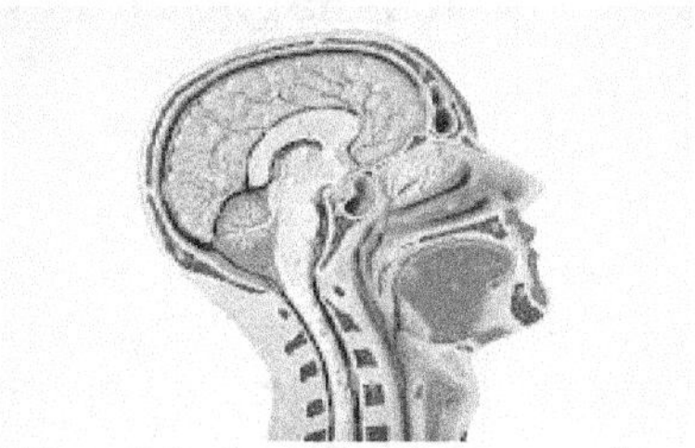

Fig. C2-1 The human brain center

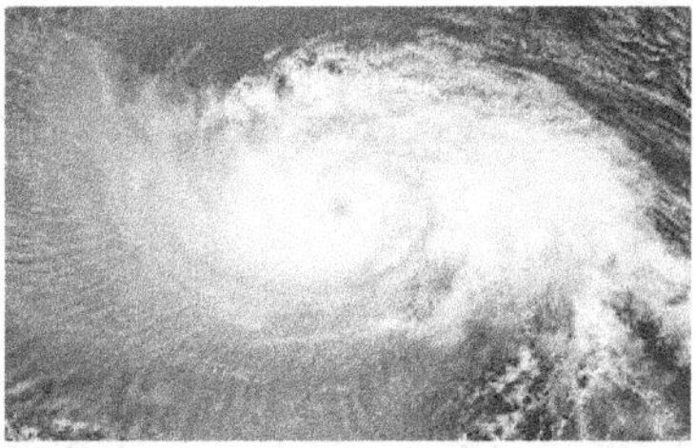

Fig. C2-2 The center of a typhoon

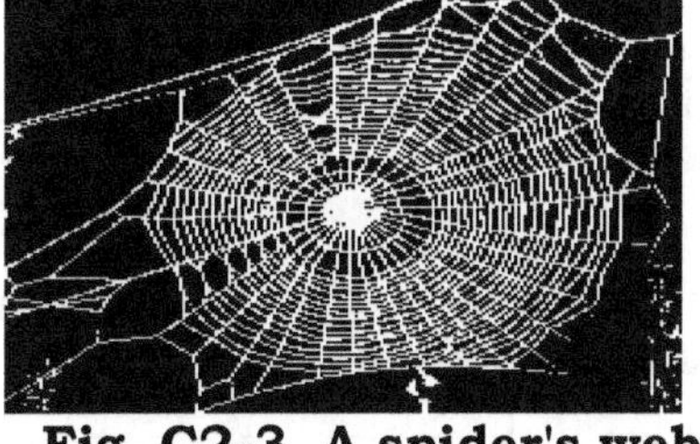

Fig. C2-3 A spider's web

Fig. C2-4 A seashell

Fig. C2-5 Circular tree patterns

Fig. C2-6 Deep-sea fish

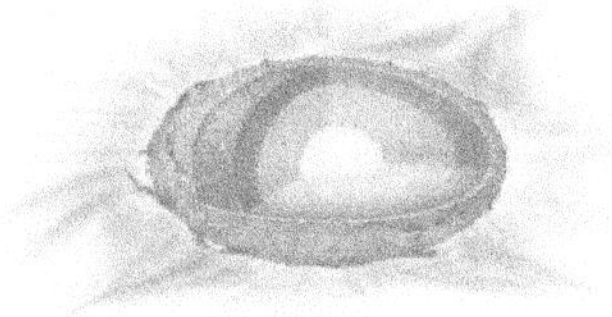

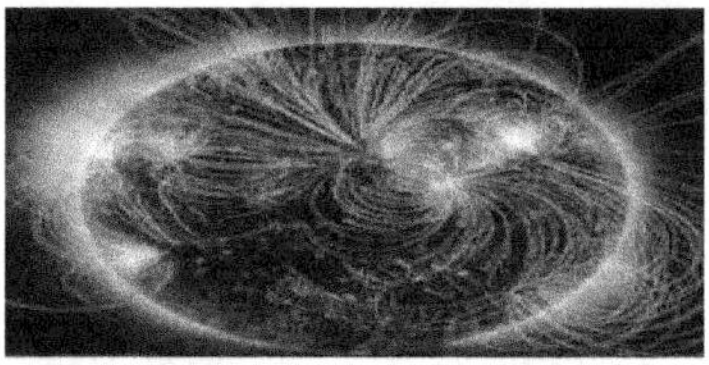

Fig. C2-7 The structure of the Sun

Fig. C2-8 Earth's magnetic field

1. Life Intelligence Entity

Our universe exists in a delicate interplay between the tangible and the intangible. The intangible governs the tangible, while the tangible reflects the essence of the intangible. This is the relationship between matter and consciousness, between reality and abstraction. Only the "Life Intelligence (wisdom) Entity" can demonstrate this universal law, such as controlling material environments. Only this entity can express this process through natural forms like trees and seashells. Moreover, only the "Life Intelligence Entity" can comprehend this process, as seen in scientific exploration.

We believe that within celestial bodies and living organisms, there exists a unique substance, possibly what has long been referred to as the "Soul". Since the "Soul" has a layered energy structure, we refer to it as a "Life Intelligence Entity". This Life Intelligence Entity not only governs our physical bodies but also controls massive celestial bodies like Earth and the Sun.

Currently, laboratory instruments cannot directly observe the “Life Intelligence Entity”. If such direct observation were possible, it would imply that computers possess wisdom surpassing human intelligence. However, indirect methods might offer feasible approaches to understanding it.

This exploration suggests that “Life and intelligence” are intertwined with the fundamental laws of the universe, governing not only individual lives but also the movement and existence of planets and stars.

2. Life Intelligence Force

We are familiar with the Coulomb force that exists between electrons and atomic nuclei, which closely resembles Newton's gravitational force between the Sun and planets. The mathematical forms of these forces are strikingly similar. Meanwhile, the forces between protons, neutrons, and elementary particles within an atomic nucleus are strong and weak nuclear forces, distinct from Coulomb forces. Given that the forces inside atomic nuclei are not Coulomb forces, why should we assume that Newtonian gravity is the only governing force inside the Sun?

It stands to reason that the gravitational forces within the Sun might cancel each other out due to the extreme density of matter, and the gravitational collapse of celestial bodies may not be driven solely by Newtonian gravity. Instead, it could be governed by a different kind of force ----- a force generated by the “Life Intelligence Entity”.

This “Life Intelligence Force” could also explain phenomena like a person moving objects through sheer willpower or thought. According to Newton's law of gravitation, a person's mass would be far too small to move even the lightest objects, such as a feather or a piece of paper. However, if we consider the Life Intelligence Force, such feats might become conceivable.

The "Life Intelligence Theory" also provides an explanation for the late stages of a Star's life cycle. As a star ages, its "Life intelligence gravitational force" weakens, eventually losing its ability to maintain the stability of its outer layers. This results in the star swelling into a Red giant and finally exploding, casting off its outer gas shell while leaving behind a dense core such as a White dwarf or Neutron star. While current physics uses quantum theory to explain this process ------ describing nuclear fusion at the star's surface where lighter elements fuse into heavier ones, causing the star's core to collapse under its own gravity ------ this explanation does not fully account for why the Red giant expands or why the star eventually explodes. This is where modern physics struggles.

The "Life Intelligence Theory" offers a more holistic explanation. It can elucidate phenomena such as sunspot activity, the Sun's life cycle, and the purpose of solar explosions ------ whether they serve to expand space or elevate energy levels, for instance.

In the case of Earth's ice ages, they might be explained by the Sun's "Life intelligence entity" influencing Earth's climate cycles, leading to alternating warm and cold periods. This suggests that the Sun is not a mere lifeless ball of gas, but rather a living star with a soul and life cycle ------ analogous to the stages of childhood, youth, adulthood, and old age.

The geologic record of Earth provides strong evidence that Earth itself is a living planet, sustained by a "Life intelligence entity" at its core, which engages in periodic life activities. This idea introduces a profound perspective on celestial bodies, not as inert masses, but as entities with an intelligence guiding their lifecycles and interactions.

3. Formula for Life Intelligence Relations

In intuitive terms, the foundation of physics revolves around studying the relationships between “Mass”, “Energy”, “Time”, and “Space”. These fundamental properties are expressed as:

- “Mass” behaves as a "Dot" (.) — representing a concentrated point or essence.
- “Time” is represented as a "Circle" (0) — reflecting cycles and continuity.
- “Space” is depicted as "Line" (1) — indicating extension, dimension, and expansion.

These symbols mirror the governing laws of the universe. Further, the relationship between “Life Intelligence Quantity” and Mass is a "Dot" relationship, representing control and inner essence. The relationship between “Life Intelligence Quantity” and the life cycle is a "Circle" relationship, signifying levels and energy states. The relationship between “Life Intelligence Quantity” and space is a "Line" relationship, indicating the extension and succession of things in space.

We hypothesize that “Life Intelligence Quantity” (Denoted as "¤" and referred to as “Dian”) is proportional to Energy, Mass, Life cycle, and the controlled space. These relationships are represented in the following formulas:

1) Life Intelligence Energy Formula:

E = a ¤ ----- (1)

- (E): Energy
- (¤): Life Intelligence Quantity

- (a): Constant

2) Life Intelligence Mass Formula:

M = a1 ¤ - - - - - (2)
- (M): Mass
- (¤): Life Intelligence Quantity
- (a1): Constant

3) Life Intelligence Space Formula:

L = a2 ¤ - - - - - (3)
- (L): Controlled space
- (¤): Life Intelligence Quantity
- (a2): Constant

4) Life Intelligence Time Cycle Formula:

T = a3 ¤ - - - - - (4)
- (T): Time cycle
- (¤): Life Intelligence Quantity
- (a3): Constant

Derivation and Insights, by combining formulas (1) and (2), we derive the equation:

E = a /a1 M

This resembles Einstein's famous mass-energy equivalence formula:

$$E = c^2 M$$

where (c) is the speed of light. The significance of these formulas lies in the fact that both biological organisms and celestial bodies must operate under the influence of "Life

Intelligence Entities" to continually absorb cosmic energy, transforming it into Mass.

The missing link in Einstein's mass-energy transformation is "Life Intelligence Entity". Without it, these equations do not hold true. For example, an object with mass cannot transform into energy without the intervention of "Life Intelligence Entity". A table will remain a table indefinitely ------ it cannot spontaneously transform into an atomic bomb. Similarly, without the action of "Life Intelligence Entity", the Sun would not emit light or energy.

In addition to Einstein's equation **E = (a/a1)M** , other relationships include:

E = (a/a2)L ; E = (a/a3)T; L = (a2/a3)T

These equations suggest that:

- The greater the controlled space, the greater the energy.
- The longer the time life cycle, the greater the energy.
- The larger the controlled space, the longer the time life cycle.

These concepts may become the focal point of future research, depending on the collective attitude and direction of the scientific community. They hint at a deep connection between life, intelligence, and the physical universe, bridging the gap between Mass, Energy, Time, and Space through the action of "Life Intelligence Entities".

4. Formula for Life Intelligence Gravity

The gravitational force exerted by a celestial body like the Sun is not solely determined by its Mass, as suggested by Newton's law of gravitation. Instead, this force is controlled by the "Life Intelligence Quantity" of the Sun's inner structure. Thus, the term "Mass" (M) in Newton's gravitational equation should be replaced with “Life Intelligence Quantity” (¤).

The gravitational force between two objects with “Life Intelligence Quantities” (¤1) and (¤2), separated by a distance (r), is given by the formula:

$$F = \text{¤}1\text{¤}2 / r^{2} \qquad \text{------} \quad (5)$$

Where:

- (¤1) is the “Life Intelligence Quantity” of the larger object (e.g., the Sun),
- (¤2) is the “Life Intelligence Quantity” of the smaller object (e.g., a planet),
- (r) is the distance between the two objects,
- (F) is the gravitational force between them.

If we substitute the “Life Intelligence Mass Formula” from equation (2) into equation (5), we get:

$$F = (1/a1)^{2} \; M m / r^{2}$$

This equation resembles Newton's universal law of gravitation but emphasizes the role of “Life Intelligence Quantity”.

“Gravitational Interaction with Photons”

If the object being influenced by gravity is not a planet but a photon (Light particle), we can substitute equation (1) (The “Life Intelligence Energy Formula”) into equation (5), yielding:

$$F = (1/a.a1) \; M E / r^{2}$$

Where (E) is the energy of the photon. This equation suggests that the “Life Intelligence Force” of the Sun can bend the path of photons, aligning with Einstein's predictions from the general theory of relativity that massive objects bend light. However, the derived formula is much simpler than the complex geometry of Einstein's equations.

“Implications of Life Intelligence Gravity”

This means the Sun's ability to curve surrounding space is a result of its “Life Intelligence”, not merely a mathematical or geometrical abstraction. Furthermore, the Sun adjusts this curvature as it ages, hinting at the inadequacy of purely mathematical models like Einstein’s, which would require additional terms to account for the age or life cycle of a celestial body.

For instance, the curvature of light passing near a White dwarf or Black dwarf may not occur in the same way as near a "Living" star, like the Sun. This raises the possibility that “Life Intelligence” — not merely mass — causes the gravitational effects predicted by general relativity. If it is scientifically proven that light does not bend near dead stars, the validity of general relativity would be challenged, and this theory of “Life Intelligence Gravity” could bring about a paradigm shift in physics.

This chapter concludes by suggesting that “Life Intelligence” plays a pivotal role in the universe's gravitational mechanics, and future discoveries may drastically alter our understanding of celestial dynamics.

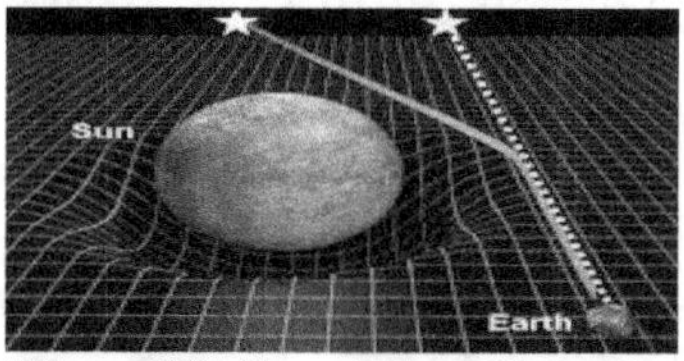

Fig. C2-9 The Sun bends space-time because it has life (Picture from the Internet)

Scientists in current civilization study dead mathematics and dead astronomy. **(Written in 2003)**

References: 1. John Chang: 《Universal Law》 (2003), Chapters 4, 7, 8.

C3. Life Wisdom Wave

Abstract: After the big bang, blast changed the time and space to form a universal law. The law of the universe is the ".", "1", "0" type, that is the formation of three space-time wave. In addition to Gravitational waves and Electromagnetic waves, there is also a new theoretical system developed from "Life Intelligence Entity", called "Life wisdom wave".

We illustrate from a large number of examples that any matter generated is related to the Big Bang form of the universe after the Big Bang, that is, it resonates with a wave, but this wave is not a Gravitational wave, nor an Electromagnetic wave. It is come from the new theoretical system developed by the “Life Intelligence Entity”, is called the “Life wisdom wave”.

The Life wisdom wave is also a wave of time and space. "Life" signifies the time occupied; "Wisdom" signifies the space under control, and the spread medium is the vacuum.

After the Big Bang, the shock wave changed time and space and formed the law of the universe. The universal law is the ".", "1", "0" style. That is the three kinds of time and space waves are formed.

We have found two kinds of waves so far.

The first is the Gravitational waves, discovered by Einstein, based on Newton's law of gravitation and the theory of relativity. It used to study the structure and behavior of celestial bodies mainly.

The second type is Electromagnetic waves, discovered by Maxwell based on the laws of Ampere, Faraday, Gauss, etc. The both strong and weak interactions belong to the Electromagnetic wave category. They have been unified by

Electromagnetic waves and are used to study the structure and behavior of quantum mainly.

The third type is the Life Wisdom Wave, which is proposed based on the "Life Intelligence Entity" of the book 《Universal Law》, publishing in 2003. It is mainly used to study the material of life, such as the structure and behavior of animals and plants.

Generally speaking, the Life wisdom wave is the "." wave; the Gravitational wave is the "0" wave; the Electromagnetic wave is the "1" wave, which are the three major waves of the "Law of the universe". They are all time-space waves, and all spread medium is the vacuum.

The relationship between the three waves are a bit like the relationship between Natural science, Social science and Life science, and connection or different. They cannot be unified completely, and can only be unified under the framework of the universal law.

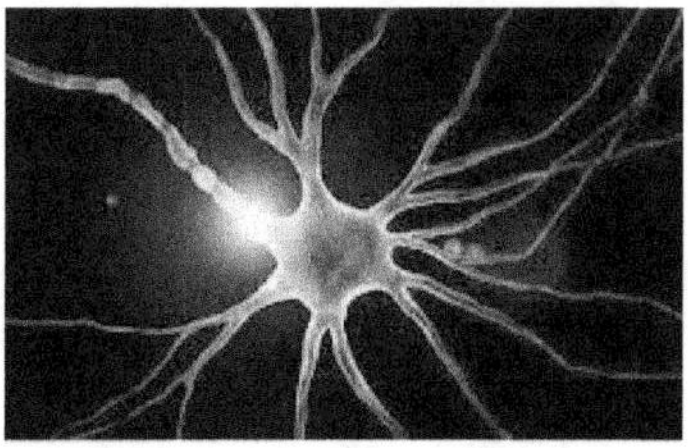

Fig. C3-1 The "Life Wisdom Wave" displayed by nerve cells.

In addition, the "Dark energy" was studied by scientists currently is likely to be the mixture of the "Life Wisdom Wave" energy and the Gravitational wave energy that we are talking about, because these two waves usually mixed together. The Gravitational waves are biased towards the celestial bodies, and the Life wisdom wave are biased towards animals and plants. The part of the energy of Electromagnetic waves is light, which is bright energy.

The kind of "Dark matter" that scientists are currently studying may be the “Life Intelligence Entity” we are talking about, which is in the form of mass-energy conversion between the Life wisdom waves, the Gravitational waves and the Electromagnetic waves. The above has no experimental basis, but is based on philosophy.

(Written in June 2017)

References:

1. John Chang: 《Universal Law》, published by Universal publishing, year 2003, Sydney, Australia.

C4. Dark Energy as the Life Wisdom Wave; Dark Matter as the Life Intelligence Entity

Abstract: The Dark energy that scientists are currently studying is highly likely a mixture of the Life wisdom wave energy and Gravitational wave energy. Similarly, Dark matter may represent the Life Intelligence Entity, manifesting through energy transformations of Life wisdom waves, Gravitational waves, or Electromagnetic waves.

----

1. Dark Energy, refers to an energy that permeates space and exerts negative pressure. According to relativity, this negative pressure, over long distances, acts like a form of anti-gravity. This hypothesis is a leading explanation for the accelerated expansion of the universe and the phenomenon of missing matter. In physical cosmology, dark energy is a form of energy that fills space and increases the expansion speed of the universe. It currently constitutes approximately 70% of the universe's mass-energy content, according to the standard cosmological model.

Edwin Hubble discovered that galaxies in the universe seem to be moving away from our galaxy, and the farther they are, the faster they move. However, astrophysicists had previously pointed out that gravity would slow down this expansion. By precisely measuring how light from these galaxies shifts toward the red end of the visible spectrum (Similar to how a train whistle lowers in pitch as it moves away from you, known as the Doppler effect), scientists observed the accelerating expansion of the universe.

Comment: The dark energy that scientists are currently researching is likely a mix of Life wisdom wave energy and Gravitational wave energy. These two waves often intermingle, with Gravitational waves being more associated with celestial bodies and Life wisdom waves more with living organisms such as animals and plants. Electromagnetic waves, a portion of which is visible light, are "Bright energy". Scientists often complicate the concept with this distinction.

2. Dark Matter, on the other hand, is a type of matter that does not interact with electromagnetic forces and thus cannot be studied directly through electromagnetic observations. Its existence is inferred from gravitational effects, and a large amount of dark matter is known to exist in the universe.

Modern astronomy detects dark matter through methods like gravitational lensing, large-scale structure formation in the universe, and cosmic microwave background radiation. According to the ΛCDM model and data from the Planck satellite, the universe consists of 4.9% ordinary matter, 26.8% dark matter, and 68.3% dark energy (Mass-energy equivalence). The presence of dark matter helps resolve inconsistencies in the Big Bang theory and plays a crucial role in structure formation. Dark matter may consist of new particles outside the standard model of particle physics, making its study a key topic in modern cosmology and particle physics.

Comment: The dark matter currently studied by scientists could be the Life Intelligence Entity, manifested through energy transformations involving Life wisdom waves, Gravitational waves, or Electromagnetic waves.

(See Wikipedia) **(Written in November 2017)**

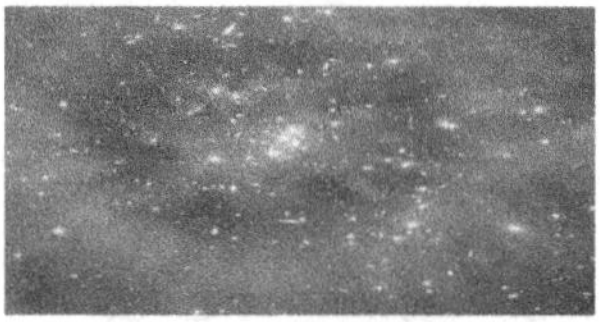

Fig. C4-1 Dark Matter

C5. Great Ultimate Theory - From Galactic Civilization

Abstract : The Big Bang forms the universal law; the universal law forms the Life wisdom waves, Gravitational waves and Electromagnetic waves; the three waves extend to the entire universe, to form the Life wisdom, the Social humanities and the Natural sciences in the human society.

The introduction of the Great Ultimate Theory, It was changed time and space after the Big Bang, forming the universal law ".", "1", "0". The three kinds of waves spread out to the entire universe. They are the Life wisdom waves, the Gravitational waves and the Electromagnetic waves.

In other words, any matter in the entire universe carries these three waves. For example, the Sun has Gravitational fields and Gravitational waves for the entire solar system. It also has Electromagnetic waves (The luminous bodies) and Life wisdom waves, that is means the Sun has an ages (Such as youth, middle and old age). Do you saw the stone has an age, but the Sun has it.

Fig. C5-1 Solar system structure

For the biological world, every human body emits Electromagnetic waves (The cold light), everyone has the Life wisdom wave (The low level creatures have only life, the high level creatures have wisdom) and human gravitation leads to society, which is the ability to leader.

Therefore, when the three kinds of waves are introduced to the study of the entire human society, the Electromagnetic waves become Natural sciences; the Gravitational waves become Social sciences; and the Life wisdom waves become Life sciences.

Explain that all the practical application results of our current Natural sciences revolve around the Electromagnetic waves (or light); the actual national rule and management of our social sciences revolve around the gravity; all the plants and plants in our life science research the behaviour and application of animals revolve around the wisdom of life.

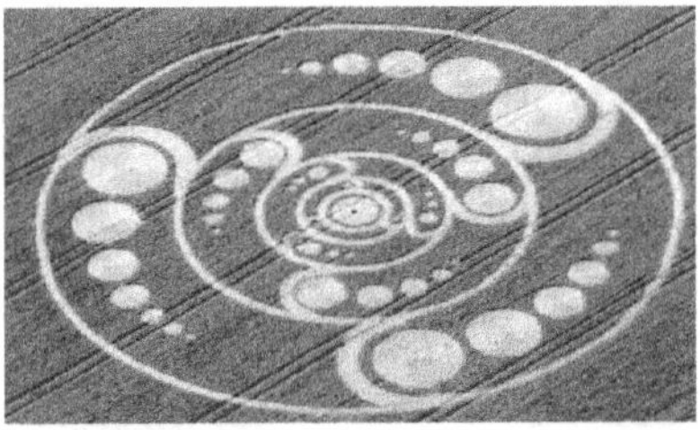

Fig. C5-2 Expansion of the disciplines of human society

Put it simply, the Big bang forms the Universal law; the Universal law forms the Life wisdom waves, the Gravitational waves and the Electromagnetic waves; the three kinds of waves extend to the entire universe, and form Life wisdom, Social humanities and Nature science in human society.

(Original article June 2017)

C6. The Cyclical Laws of "Natural Science, Social Humanities, and Life wisdom"

Abstract: After the Big Bang, the shock wave changed the space-time, and formed the universal law. The universal law is the ".", "1", "0" type, namely formed three kinds of space-time waves. The reflection of three kinds of wave to human society, the Life wisdom wave, Electromagnetic wave and Gravitational wave form Life wisdom, Natural science and Social humanities.

"Social humanities, Natural sciences and Life wisdom" is from "0", "1" and "." with three transverse waves, according to the "Space" expansion.

The Natural science, Social humanities and Life wisdom are from the three waves, Electromagnetic waves ("1" wave), Gravitational waves ("0" wave) and Life wisdom waves ("." Wave), as reflection of human society.

For scientists, to be able to turn something natural, through experiments, into a theoretical science is to explore. That is, the promotion of "Nature to Science".

For a literate person, to be able to write about social phenomena, through observation, refinement, into culture, such as the publication of poetry, prose, and fiction, is progress. That is, the promotion of "Sociaty to Humanities".

For religious people, they can transform the things of life, through practice and perception, into things of wisdom, such as scripture, which is enlightenment. That is, the rise of "Life to Wisdom".

That is the basic story of the world today. We are now exploring another situation, called "Leap", in which scientists, while studying science, eventually surpass current science; writers, while writing literature, finally surpass current literature; the practitioner transcends the current religion. This is the "Natural science, Social humanities and Life wisdom" cycle. Let me explain.

1) For scientists, what they do is take something natural and turn it into a theoretical science through experiments, and most scientific researchers stop there and write a few papers for the rest of their lives. What we're asking now is to go one step further, and turn it into a part of society, which is to turn science into a social utility, like the invention of the airplane and the train, and some scientists went there, and now we're asking scientists to go further, into the humanities, and most people can't do that, because a lot of people are get into weapons.

Of course, some people do science fiction, Ok and good! What if we asked scientists to turn them into things of life and intelligence? Almost nobody, because most scientists can't get over it, so they can't jump.

The great scientist Mr. Newton, for example, has turned nature into a scientific theory; he has also become a celebrity and achieved social status; he has also become a humanist and written a book, good! What about up? When it came to life and wisdom, he spent 40 years exploring and trying to cross this hurdle, but for scientists in the Star system civilization, this was a hurdle that no one had ever crossed.

This is the cycle of Nature to Science; Society to Humanity and Life to Wisdom. The key to science lies in "Life to Wisdom". A scientist can cross "Nature to Science", "Society to Humanities", is already a master, if they can cross "Life to Wisdom", then return to "Nature to Science", that is what we call "Leap", into Galactic civilization.

2) For the litterateur, at the primary level, they are able to transform social phenomena, through observation, refinement, into cultural things, such as the publication of poems, essays, and novels. Well, that's progress, but most literate people stop there.

If poetry, prose, and fiction could be made a part of life and wisdom, it would be a master.

For example, Mr. Cao Xueqin, the Chinese author of 《A dream of Red Mansions》, saw his work as a part of his life and elevated it to wisdom, even though it was a single book, reaching its literary peak. However, he still could not cross the "Nature and Science" hurdle, on which almost all the world's literary master stopped. If they can crossed it and returned to the "Society to Humanities ", it would be a "Leap", go into Galactic civilization.

This is the cycle of "Society to Humanities", "Life to Wisdom" and "Nature to Science" of cultural man.

3) The same is true for religious people, who turn the stuff of life, through practice and enlightenment, into something intelligent, like a lot of scripture, which is a primary step forward. And then, they go into nature, or they go to the mountains and the woods, and they meditate, but most people stop there, and they barely get to science, and if they can understand science, they're masters.

Mr. Gautama Buddha, for example, he said, "A grain of sand is a universe". Good! But when he comes down to the "Sociaty and Humanities" hurdle, he can't get over it. For example, he did not advocate the establishment of a family, escape from society, and can not write a humane article. Jesus was rejected by society, killed, and Muhammad went on a rampage of revenge and murder. So these so-called masters of practice can not cross the "Sociaty and

Humanities" this hurdle, if crossed, and then back to "Life and Wisdom", is the "Leap", go into the Galactic Civilization.

This is the cycle of "Life to wisdom", "Nature to science", "Society to humanities", and the door hurdle is on "Society to humanities".

So at present most people are trapped in the circle of "Stellar Civilization", can not cross the last hurdle, into the "Galactic Civilization". This is the "Nature to science", "Society to humanities" and "Life to wisdom" with "Six phases" of the universal law, as same as the Milky Way's six spiral arms.

Galaxy

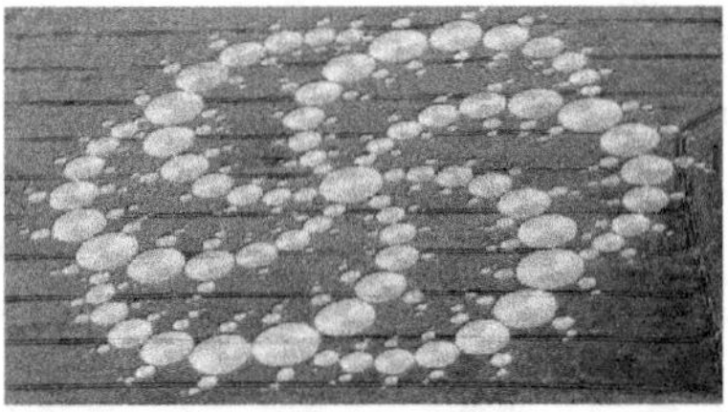

Six loops and a spinning wheel

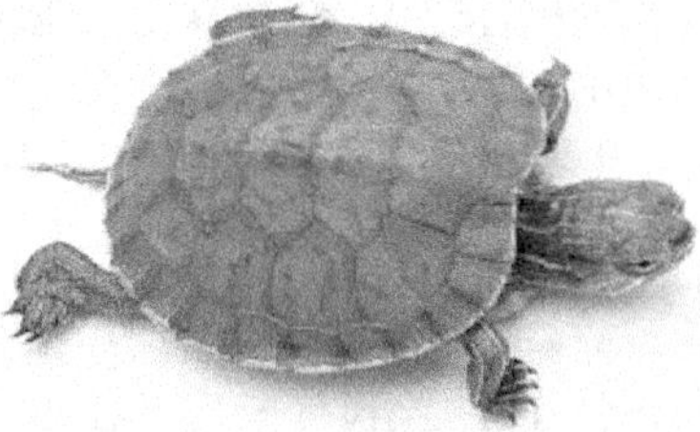

Fig. C6-1 Six loops and a spinning wheel, corresponding to the Milky Way's spiral arms. Look at this turtle. It goes around for a circle, and only the head is the transcendental point.

(Original in June 2017)

C7. The Nine Major Cyclical Laws

Abstract: Crop circles exhibited by Galactic civilizations clearly illustrate the variations of the nine major cycles: "Mathematics, Physics, Chemistry"; "Politics, Economics, Psychology"; "Astronomy, Plants, Animals". At the center of these cycles are three primary forces: "Physics", "Plants", and "Economics".

Fig. C7-1 Crop Circle Representing the Nine Major Cycles

The diagram of the Crop circle shows the following:

1. Three Directions Separated by White Triangular Paths: Each of these three directions is divided into three parts, with a central circle rolling over them. Three smaller circles roll over the nine sections.

2. Division into Three Categories:

- Natural Sciences: Divided into "Mathematics", "Physics", and "Chemistry".
- Social Sciences: Divided into "Politics", "Economics", and "Psychology".

- Life Sciences: Divided into “Animals”, “Plants”, and “Astronomy”.

These are represented by three types: "Dot" (.), "Line" (1), and "Circle" (0) symbolizing different aspects of the universe.

3. The Galactic Civilizations' Crop Circles: Clearly demonstrate the dynamics of these nine cycles, with three central forces being “Physics”, “Plants”, and “Economics”.

4. Key Observations:

- Physics is the "0" cycle, where most scientists revolve.
- Economics is the "0" cycle, where most ordinary people revolve.
- Plants is the "0" cycle, where most natural species revolve.

5. The 9-Part Matrix System:

- Mathematics (1), Physics (0), Chemistry (.) form a continuous cycle.
- Politics (1), Economics (0), Psychology (.) create another cycle.
- Animals (1), Plants (0), Astronomy (.) complete the triad of life cycles.

6. Scientific Cycles:

- The “Mathematics-physics-chemistry” cycle forms a dynamic loop, where Chemistry bridges Mathematics and Physics. The exploration of the universe's laws and the periodic table of Chemical elements is an ongoing journey.
- The “Politics-economics-psychology” cycle involves the intricate balance of “Political economy” and “Economic psychology”, with a cross-discipline leap between

Psychology and Politics, focusing on the exploration of "Human societal systems".

- The "Animals-plants-astronomy" cycle delves into the origins and evolution of life. The leap between "Astronomy" and "Animals" encompasses the study of "Extraterrestrial life" and technologies related to space and life sciences.

7. Two Forces Working Together:

The central circle typically spans two categories, symbolizing two cycles working in tandem. For example, the Mathematics-physics cycle, the Politics-economics cycle, or the Animals-plants cycle. The third category remains less engaged in this interaction.

8. Dynamic Reconfiguration:

These nine parts can be re-distributed diagonally, forming new interdisciplinary fields. These combinations roll like spheres, continually evolving and merging to create new areas of knowledge and exploration.

Summary of the Nine Cycles:

This crop circle depiction demonstrates the interconnectivity of the "Natural, Social, and Life sciences" through a nine-part cycle. Each discipline is intertwined, influencing and feeding into one another, forming a continuously rolling sphere of knowledge and growth. The movement between the disciplines creates a dynamic exploration, with certain cycles becoming the focus of scientific and societal inquiry.

(Original in July, 2017)

References:

John Chang: 《Crop Circles》 (2015), Universal Publishing, Australia.

C8. Twenty-Seven Cycles and Transcendence

Abstract: The development of disciplines can be visualized through cycles of three, nine, and twenty-seven, demonstrating the progression of knowledge in the Galactic Civilization. These cycles show how fields of study evolve through phases of openness, circulation, and transcendence.

---

1. Natural Sciences: Divided into Mathematics, Physics, and Chemistry

1) "Mathematics" consists of "Algebra, Geometry, and Probability", representing (1), (0), and (.) characteristics respectively.

- Cycle of the Three:

The transition from "Algebra to Geometry" is represented by the "Pythagorean Theorem" or "Analytic Geometry".

The transition from "Geometry to Probability" is found in "Geometric Probability", a cutting-edge field.

- Cycle and Transcendence:

Mathematics follows the cycle: "Algebra → Geometry → Probability". The cycle transcends when it transitions from "Probability back to Algebra", forming a new field called "Probabilistic Algebra".

However, to achieve true transcendence, this new form of mathematics would need to exceed Geometry, a level currently unattainable.

2) "Physics" is divided into "Electromagnetism, Mechanics, and Quantum Theory", also representing (1), (0), and (.) characteristics.

- Cycle of the Three:

The transition from “Electromagnetism to Mechanics” is described by “Electrodynamics”.

The transition from “Mechanics to Quantum Theory” is found in “Quantum Mechanics”.

- Cycle and Transcendence:

Physics follows the cycle: “Electromagnetism → Mechanics → Quantum Theory”.

The transcendence occurs when it transitions from “Quantum Theory back to Electromagnetism”, forming “Special Relativity”.

Further transcendence, from “Electromagnetism beyond Mechanics”, leads to “General Relativity”, which takes physics a step toward “Galactic Civilization”. However, because of the complexity of General Relativity, it does not align with the principle of “Simplicity” emphasized by the Galactic Civilization.

3) “Chemistry” is categorized into “Organic Chemistry, Inorganic Chemistry, and Elemental Science”, representing (1), (0), and (.) characteristics.

- Cycle of the Three:

The transition from “Organic Chemistry to Inorganic Chemistry” results in “Organometallic Chemistry”.

The transition from “Inorganic Chemistry to Elemental Science” is described as “Inorganic Elemental Chemistry”.

- Cycle and Transcendence:

Chemistry follows the cycle: “Organic Chemistry → Inorganic Chemistry → Elemental Science”.

The transcendence would occur when “Elemental Science transitions back to Organic Chemistry”. To fully transcend, this new branch of chemistry must exceed inorganic chemistry, which is currently beyond our reach.

The "Major Cycles" represent a systematic progression within the Natural sciences, allowing for a deeper understanding of how knowledge can evolve through stages of "Circulation" and "Transcendence". However, achieving full transcendence requires advancing current fields to a level where they surpass traditional boundaries, a hallmark of the Galactic Civilization's open, innovative approach to knowledge.

2. Social Humanities: Divided into Politics, Economics, and Psychology

1) "Politics" is divided into "Democracy, Law, and Governance", representing (1), (0), and (.) characteristics respectively.

- Cycle of the Three:

The transition from "Democracy to Law" results in the formation of a "Nation", where the people are bound by laws and establish a country.

The transition from "Law to Governance" leads to the creation of a "Government", where the rulers use laws to maintain order in society.

- Cycle and Transcendence:

Politics follows the cycle: "Democracy → Law → Governance". The transcendence occurs when governance shifts back to democracy, through the process of "Election".

If a ruler appoints the next leader without involving the people and the legal process, it is not an election but "Dictatorship". True transcendence happens when new laws are created through democratic elections that exceed the existing legal framework.

2) "Economics" is divided into "Microeconomics, Macroeconomics, and Capital", also representing (1), (0), and (.) characteristics.

- Explanation:

"Microeconomics" deals with individuals and small businesses, while "Macroeconomics" focuses on national and corporate economies. "Capital" refers to the financial sector, especially banking.

- Cycle of the Three:

The transition from "Microeconomics to Macroeconomics" involves "Labor' or earning a "Wage", creating surplus value as individuals contribute to the economy.

The transition from "Macroeconomics to Capital" happens through "Investment" or "Capital appreciation" as businesses expand into financial assets.

- Cycle and Transcendence:

Economics follows the cycle: "Microeconomics → Macroeconomics → Capital". The transcendence occurs when "Capital is reinvested into individuals", and if a bank invests in an individual who then becomes highly successful, exceeding the performance of other businesses, this person becomes an "Entrepreneur".

3) "Psychology" is divided into "Individual Psychology, Group Psychology, and Ontological Psychology", representing (1), (0), and (.) characteristics.

- Cycle of the Three:

The transition from "Individual to Group Psychology" is described as "Growth", where individuals develop through their experiences within society.

The transition from "Group to Ontological Psychology" happens when individuals "Reflect" on their life experiences and gain deeper understanding or insight.

- Cycle and Transcendence:

Psychology follows the cycle: “Individual → Group →Ontological Psychology”. The transcendence occurs when insights gained in the ontologies are reflected back onto the individual. This is seen in the creation of “Literary and artistic works”, which are expressions of the author's deep reflections (Ontological Psychology) on life, embodied in individual expression.

The transcendence is achieved when an individual's work surpasses the collective social consciousness, resulting in timeless masterpieces like 《Dream of the Red Chamber》, 《Romance of the Three Kingdoms》, 《Journey to the West》, and 《Water Margin》.

In religion, if an individual's understanding does not surpass the insights of religious figures from thousands of years ago, they remain merely a follower or worshiper. “True transcendence” occurs when the individual's wisdom exceeds that of past spiritual leaders, reflecting growth beyond historical teachings.

3. Life wisdom Divided into Zoology, Botany, and Astronomy

1) “Zoology” is divided into “Evolution, Reproduction, and Embryo” representing (1), (0), and (.) characteristics.

- Cycle of the Three:

The transition from “Evolution to Reproduction” shows that evolution stems from natural mutations driven by the “Life wisdom wave”, resulting in large-scale changes (e.g., from egg-laying animals to live-bearing animals). Reproduction itself involves the cycle of birth and death but does not contribute to evolution.

The transition from "Reproduction to Embryo" indicates that reproduction begins with the "Embryo", which takes various forms.

- Cycle and Transcendence:

The cycle is "Evolution → Reproduction → Embryo". Transcendence occurs when "Evolution starts again" from the embryo, showing that all evolution begins within embryos, such as live birth replacing egg-laying. Each stage of evolution brings about new forms of reproduction. Future forms of evolution may replace live birth, perhaps with "Mechanical reproduction", which would be a transcendence, as machines would surpass biological processes in reproduction.

2) "Botany" is divided into "Evolution, Reproduction, and Embryo" (The embryo being the "Seed"), following the same (1), (0), and (.) framework.

- Cycle of the Three:

The transition from "Evolution to Reproduction" shows that plant evolution, like that of animals, involves greater variability and speed, as plants are more sensitive to environmental factors like soil and water. The Life wisdom wave causes "Large-scale plant evolution", such as the transformation from algae to ferns.

The transition from "Reproduction to Embryo (Seed)" shows that plant reproduction primarily occurs through "Fertilization", sometimes aided by external factors like wind or animals, leading to a wide variety of seeds.

- Cycle and Transcendence:

The cycle is "Evolution → Reproduction → Embryo (Seed)". Transcendence occurs when evolution begins again with the seed, resulting in new plant species. Large-scale plant evolution (e.g., from algae to ferns) produces new reproductive systems, which "Surpass" previous ones.

3) "Astronomy" is divided into "Evolution, Reproduction, and Embryo", where "Reproduction" is achieved through "Explosion" and the "Embryo" is the "Nebula".

- Cycle of the Three:

The transition from "Evolution to Reproduction" shows that celestial bodies undergo different "Explosive events" depending on their stage of evolution. The transition from "Reproduction to Embryo" happens when a star explodes and leaves behind a "Nebula".

- Cycle and Transcendence:

The cycle is "Evolution → Reproduction → Embryo (Nebula)". Transcendence occurs when celestial evolution resumes from the Nebula. Different types of nebulae correspond to distinct stages of stellar evolution, such as the progression from "Stellar clouds to Stars, Red giants, Supernova explosions, and White dwarfs". Meanwhile, galaxies evolve differently, following the cycle from "Quasars to galaxies, explosions, and black holes".

4. Conclusion

It is important to note that "Cycles" belong to the realm of "Stellar civilizations", whereas "Cycles and transcendence" belong to "Galactic civilizations". The "Twenty-seven cycles and transcendences" can further be subdivided into "Eighty-one cycles and transcendences", such as the subdivision of Geometry into "Solid geometry, Plane geometry, and Abstract geometry", all following the same (1), (0), and (.) pattern. This process can be extended indefinitely, reflecting the same principles seen in extraterrestrial civilizations.

Fig. C8-1 The above picture shows that each subject is divided into three parts, which expand downward in layers. The three parts on the same layer are separated by a wall.

Fig. C8-2 The above picture shows that the subject is divided into three parts, which expand downward in layers, and can be divided forever.

(Original in October 2017)

References:

1. John Chang: 《Crop Circle》 (2015) published by Universal publishing.
2. John Chang: 《Great Ultimate Theory》 (2013) published by Universal publishing.

C9. Universal Formula of All Things

Abstract: Modern science seems to have reached a point where progress is either blocked by current "Instrumentation limitations ("o")" or has hit a "Conceptual dead-end" by following a narrow professional path. To leap to a higher level, great courage is needed to abandon outdated concepts and embrace the next breakthrough.

I. Grand Unified Theory

We have concluded that the "Laws of the universe" consist of three parts:

1) Life Wisdom Science ("."),
2) Natural Science ("1"),
3) Social Science ("o").

These elements are layered in an energy-level structure, represented by ".", "1", and "o".

It is important to note that ".", "1", and "o" themselves are nameless. However, they are present in every aspect of human wisdom and in all fields of study. These three elements have been part of the cosmos since the "Big Bang". The ongoing human pursuit of knowledge is merely the process of attaching beautiful names to the various "Small and large "o" " and "Long and short "1"".

These names facilitate classification, categorization, memorization, and communication. For example, the 《I Ching》 (Book of Changes) is a naming system that attributes names to various "o" and "1" structures, primarily in metaphysical fields such as "Astronomy, Calendrics, and Astrology". Systems like "Heavenly Stems" and "Earthly

Branches" are examples, though naming tends to limit these structures from becoming broader scientific tools.

II. Universal Formula of All Things

The "Basic components" of the universe's laws are ".", "1", and "o". This can be summarized as:

- The universal law is "." + "1" + "o".

Thus, we derive the following formula:

$$¤ = ¤(.) + ¤(1) + ¤(o) \quad \text{-----} \quad (1)$$

Where:

- "¤" represents the "Total Life Wisdom",
- ¤(.) represents the "." Life Wisdom,
- ¤(1) represents the "1" Life Wisdom,
- ¤(o) represents the "o" Life Wisdom.

This formula is a "Universal formula", as all relationships in "Natural science", "Social science", and "Life Wisdom science" can be derived from it. Below, we will explore its applications.

1. Natural Science ("1")

The foundation of "Natural science" is "Physics". We have discussed that:

- Mass has a "." nature, possessing internal energy E(.).
- Space has a "1" nature, possessing kinetic energy E(1).
- Time has an "o" nature, possessing potential energy E(o).

Thus, the total energy "E" is the sum of these components:

$$E = a¤, \qquad E(.) = a1\ ¤(.),$$
$$E(1) = a2\ ¤(1), \qquad E(o) = a3\ ¤(o)$$

Substituting this into the “Universal Formula” (1), we get:

$$(1/a)E = (1/a1)E(.) + (1/a2)E(1) + (1/a3)E(o) \text{ - - - } (2)$$

Where “a”, “a1”, “a2”, and “a3” are constants. This equation represents the “Law of Conservation of Energy”, one of the most important principles in physics. It indicates that “Total energy remains constant before and after a transformation”. This law applies not only to macroscopic systems but also to the quantum realm, where phenomena like antimatter particles have been confirmed based on this principle.

In this framework:

- E(.) represents “Internal energy”, the inherent changes within a system.
- E(1) represents “Kinetic energy”, changes related to spatial movement.
- E(o) represents “Potential energy”, changes related to the energy level of a system.

This leads to the general equation for energy:

Total Energy = Internal Energy (.) + Kinetic Energy (1) + Potential Energy (o) - - - - (3)

Basic Analysis of Formula (3):

1) Newton's Law of Gravitation gives potential energy as:

Potential Energy(o) = F r = G M m/r

Einstein's Mass-Energy Equation gives internal energy as:

Internal Energy (.) = mc^2

Kinetic Energy (1) is given by:

Kinetic Energy(1) = $1/2\ mv^2$

Substituting these into (3), we get a commonly used formula in physics:

$$E = mc^2 + 1/2\ mv^2 + G\,M\,m\,/r \text{ - - - - - } (4)$$

2) For "Macroscopic physics", when the total energy and internal energy are constant, formula (4) simplifies to:

Kinetic Energy (1) = Potential Energy(o)

This results in common experimental formulas such as:

$1/2\ mv^2 = GmM/r$ or $1/2\ mv^2 = mgh$

3) When "Potential energy is constant", formula (4) becomes:

Total Energy = Internal Energy (.) + Kinetic Energy (1)

This can be interpreted thermodynamically, where heat transferred to a system is partially used to increase "Internal energy" and partially used to do "Work". This is the "First Law of Thermodynamics". When the system's energy flow is directional, it aligns with the "Second Law of Thermodynamics".

4) As "Macroscopic physics" transitions to "Microscopic physics", the formula for kinetic energy becomes:

Kinetic energy(1): $E(1) = 1/2\ mv^2 = h\upsilon + A$

This is the "Planck-Einstein Photoelectric Effect Equation".

Similarly:

- **Internal Energy (.): $E(.) = mc^2$** (Einstein's mass-energy equivalence),

- **Potential Energy (o): $E(o) = (1/4\pi\varepsilon)e^2 /r$**

(Coulomb force times electron orbital radius).

Substituting into formula (4) gives:

$$E = mc^2 + h\upsilon + (1/4\pi\varepsilon)e^2 /r \text{ ---- } (5)$$

5) When "Internal energy E(.) " is constant, the relation $h\upsilon = 1/2\ mv^2 - A$ gives:

$$E = 1/2\ mv^2 + (1/4\pi\varepsilon)e^2 /r$$

This is the "Bohr Energy Level Equation".

6) When "Total energy" and "Potential energy" are constant, formula (5) becomes:

$$mc^2 = h\upsilon$$

This is “De Broglie’s Equation”.

7) “Quantum mechanics” further advances to the “Wave function”, where “Schrödinger’s Equation” is based on the conservation of “Kinetic energy” and “Potential energy”:

$$E\Psi = -(h^2/8\pi^2 m)\nabla^2 \Psi + V\Psi \text{ - - - - (6)}$$

(Total energy) (Kinetic energy) (Potential energy)

This equation is the foundation of quantum theory and is widely applied in atomic, nuclear, and solid-state physics. The development of quantum theory demonstrates that the conservation of energy (Composed of internal, kinetic, and potential energy) is aligned with the ".", "1", and "o" principles of the “Universal Formula”.

8) Another key direction in physics is General Relativity. In 1915, Mr.Einstein and Mr.Hilbert derived the “Gravitational field equation”:

$$R\mu\upsilon - (1/2)\, g\mu\upsilon\, R = (8\pi G/C^4)\, T\mu\upsilon \text{ - - - (7)}$$

The right side represents the “Energy-momentum tensor” of matter, where “Energy” corresponds to "." and “Momentum” to "1". The left side is the “Spacetime curvature tensor” of “Riemannian geometry”, which is an "o" tensor.

In summary, the “Gravitational wave equation” is fundamentally a ".", "1", and "o" formula, reinforcing Einstein’s notion that the universe is “Bounded ("o")” yet “Boundless ("1")”.

2. Social Science ("o")

Social science is based on "Control". We assume that "C" represents total control, which includes both "Political" and "Economic" components.

1) Political Control (Virtual)

In human political society, control is primarily exercised through laws. Thus, C(.) represents government laws (e.g., election laws, hereditary succession laws), C(1) represents civil laws (e.g., civil rights), and C(o) represents stability laws (e.g., land laws, national security laws).

We can derive a set of equations:

$$C = a\text{¤} \qquad C(.) = a1\ \text{¤}(.)$$
$$C(1) = a2\ \text{¤}(1) \qquad C(o) = a3\ \text{¤}(o)$$

The meaning of these equations is:

- The more wisdom in ¤(.), the better the system of governmental checks and balances, resulting in smooth leadership transitions and the absence of corruption.
- The more wisdom in ¤(1), the more refined the civil laws, leading to public stability and fewer grievances or refugees.
- The more wisdom in ¤(o), the more perfected the national security and land laws, ensuring peaceful borders and no wars.

Substituting this into the "Universal Formula" (1), we get:

$$(1/a)C = (1/a1)C(.)+(1/a2)C(1)+(1/a3)C(o) \quad \text{-- (8)}$$

This equation forms the foundation of "Social and political science" and is referred to as the "Law of Conservation of Control" (or "Political and Legal Conservation Law"), analogous to the "Law of Conservation of Energy" in natural science.

2) Economic Control (Real)

In human economic society, control is exerted through managing expenses. Therefore:

- C(.) represents control over basic, inherent costs,
- C(1) represents control over variable costs, and
- C(o) represents control over fixed costs.

We can derive a similar set of equations:

$$C = a¤ \qquad C(.) = a1\ ¤(.)$$
$$C(1) = a2\ ¤(1) \qquad C(o) = a3\ ¤(o)$$

The meaning of these equations is:

- The more wisdom in ¤(.), the better the control over inherent costs.
- The more wisdom in ¤(1), the better the control over variable costs.
- The more wisdom in ¤(o), the better the control over fixed costs.

Substituting this into the "Universal Formula" (1), we get:

$$(1/a)C = (1/a1)C(.)+(1/a2)C(1)+(1/a3)C(o) \text{ - - } (9)$$

This equation forms the basis for "Macro- and microeconomic science", referred to as the "Law of

Conservation of Economic Control", which parallels the "Law of Political and Legal Conservation".

3. Life Wisdom Science (".")

"Life wisdom science" is based on "Wisdom". Let "W" represent the total Life wisdom, where:

- W(.) represents Basic wisdom,
- W(1) represents Super wisdom,
- W(o) represents Self-wisdom.

For humans, Life wisdom science can be further understood as "Spiritual science", where:

- Basic wisdom W(.) corresponds to the "Id",
- Self-wisdom W(o) corresponds to the "Ego",
- Super wisdom W(1) corresponds to the "Superego".

The equations are as follows:

W = a¤   **W(.) = a1 ¤(.)**

W(1) = a2 ¤(1)   **W(o) = a3 ¤(o)**

The meaning of these equations is:

- The more ¤(.), the easier it is to evolve from animal physiology to human physiology.
- The more ¤(o), the easier it is to advance from human physiology to rationality.
- The more ¤(1), the easier it is to transcend from rationality to morality.

Substituting this into the "Universal Formula" (1), we get:

(1/a)W=(1/a1)W(.)+(1/a2)W(1)+(1/a3)W(o)- - - (10)

This is the “Law of Conservation of Life Wisdom” (or “Law of Conservation of Spiritual Power”), and it, along with the “Law of Conservation of Energy” and the “Law of Conservation of Control”, constitutes the three fundamental laws of the universal ".", "1", and "o" principles.

III. Analysis and Expansion

The three conservation laws can also be combined into the “Universal Formula” (1), giving:

¤ = W + E + C ----- (11)

This means that a “Life wisdom entity” is the sum of the “Total energy” from Natural science ("1"), the “Total control” from Social science ("o"), and the “Total wisdom” from Life wisdom science ("."), applied to human society. The comprehensive application of this formula indicates:

1) When society progresses (¤ in the positive direction):
- Spiritual science (.) increases, with the self and superego striving toward excellence.
- Natural science (1) increases, leading to innovation and discoveries.
- Social science (o) increases, leading to sound legal systems and social stability.

2) When society regresses (¤ in the negative direction):
- Spiritual science (.) decreases, with the id taking over, leading to a rise in crime.
- Natural science (1) decreases, leading to intellectual stagnation and brain drain.

- Social science (o) decreases, leading to lawlessness, corruption, and instability.

The three conservation systems represented by "Formula (11)" mutually influence and interact with each other, forming a complete system of universal laws.

(Written in 2003)

References:

John Chang: 《Universal Law》 (2003), Chapter 21, published by Universal Publishing

C10. Practical Engineering Technology and Inventions Following Universal Laws

Abstract: The practical fields of engineering and invention, such as technology for daily life, work, and profit, are practical applications that reflect universal laws. Like the ultimate theories in science, these fields are also divided into three aspects.

---

1. Historical Overview

Around six million years ago, in Africa, there were three types of early humans: the “Yellow apes”, the “White apes”, and the “Black apes”. The “Black apes” were the strongest and most dominant. They established a dictatorship and repressive system based on primitive religious and feudal ideologies (e.g., leader worship, religious worship, etc.). The “Yellow apes”, being smaller and weaker, were severely oppressed. Some yellow apes developed a desire to escape the control of the black apes and, using rudimentary tools like stone axes and wooden carts, attempted to break free. Although many black apes mocked and suppressed them, some yellow apes courageously became the first to leave Africa and ventured into distant Asia. Later, the “White apes” followed, migrating to Europe.

Those who remained in Africa, primarily the most powerful and conservative black apes, continued to oppress innovation and embraced authoritarianism. As a result, they stagnated. Fast forward millions of years, and we see that those who remained in Africa never advanced technologically, while the Yellow and White apes, having ventured out and innovated, built great civilizations.

Key Concepts:

1) Freedom of Thought and Innovation: These are the driving forces of human progress. Any suppression of thought and innovation inevitably leads to ignorance and stagnation. This same principle applies today as humanity faces a new critical moment — the leap from "Stellar civilization" to "Galactic civilization".

2) Resistance to Progress: The forces that once suppressed progress, represented by the Black apes, have evolved into new obstacles today: organized religious institutions that stifle innovation. These institutions, characterized by ignorance, authoritarianism, and corruption, have contributed little to invention or creativity, relying instead on imitation and replication. However, just like the Yellow apes who first left Africa, new ideas will break through, guided by "Universal Law".

3) Cosmic Law and Practical Engineering: To advance to a Galactic civilization, humanity must develop practical engineering technologies that surpass current capabilities. This includes space travel technologies. At present, most global research is directed at overcoming the barriers of "Stellar civilization" and reaching the "Galactic civilization", and all engineering and technological inventions are aimed at this goal.

4) Three Domains of Practical Engineering:
- Medicine and Pharmaceuticals (.): Practical fields extending from "Life sciences".
- Literature and Arts (0): Practical fields extending from "Social sciences".

- Engineering and Technology (1): Practical fields extending from “Natural sciences”.

Each of these fields can be further subdivided, resembling the structure of the ultimate scientific theory. While some fields (Like medical diagnosis, art, and engineering) may eventually be overtaken by computer intelligence, the “Domains governed by the Universal Law” will never be replaced, as they transcend technological capabilities.

2. Philosophical Viewpoint

From a philosophical perspective, there are parallels between engineering and scientific thought:

- Universal Law can be viewed as the highest level of metaphysics ("Dao").
- Three major non-practical fields (Life sciences, social sciences, natural sciences) represent “Idealism” (Metaphysics and theoretical reasoning, "The principle").
- Three major practical fields (Medicine and pharmaceuticals, literature and arts, engineering and technology) represent “Materialism” (Practical applications, "The tool").

In essence, even in the realm of engineering and technology, the ultimate theory of the Universal Law is revealed. This system involves the largest research teams worldwide, with universities and research institutions across the globe all contributing to the exploration of these principles.

3. Intuitive Diagram of Thought

1) Metaphysics (.) - Universal Law System - Galactic Civilization (Abstract system, no economic value)

2) Intermediate Metaphysics (1) - Natural Science System (Theoretical system, general economic value)
- Social Science System
- Life Science System
- Stellar Civilization

3) Practical Metaphysics (0) - Engineering and Technology (Practical system, key economic value)
- Literature and Arts
- Medicine and Pharmaceuticals
- Planetary Civilizations

4. Conclusion

The practical applications of technology, engineering, and invention follow the same structure as the universal laws. These laws will guide humanity toward the "Galactic civilization", overcoming obstacles and uniting science, philosophy, and technology in an unprecedented leap forward.

(Original March 2018)

References:

1. John Chang: 《Great Ultimate Theory》 (2013), Universal Publishing, Australia.

C11. The Theory and Technology of Galactic Civilization According to the Laws of the Universe

Abstract: Our book has already covered the theoretical framework of "Galactic civilization" in accordance with the "Laws of the Universe". What's remarkable is that extraterrestrial civilizations use a unique technology to showcase these theoretical systems in Crop circles, allowing everyone to witness the combination of theory and technology ------ a truly extraordinary phenomenon.

----

1. Introduction

1) Advanced Technology of Galactic Civilizations

This "Galactic civilization technology" far surpasses the technological capabilities of our current "Solar system civilization". For example, these civilizations use "Microwave technology" to bend stalks of wheat precisely in the middle. Consider a plot of land with 6 billion stalks of wheat: they can track every single stalk and bend each one at specific points ----- top, middle, or bottom.

This technology is analogous to the principle behind a microwave oven, but far more advanced ------- it can precisely target the location (Specific wheat stalks), area (Specific plots of land), and objects (Specific crops) while utilizing immense power. Unlike conventional microwave ovens, which lack directionality and cannot pinpoint specific targets, this Galactic technology has laser-like precision.

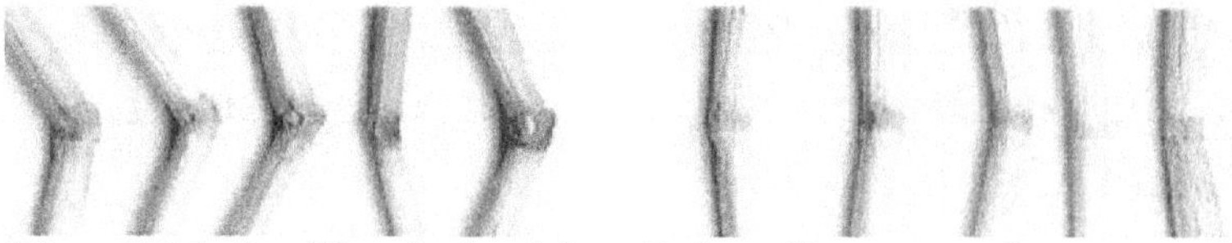

Fig. C11-1 The left side of the diagram shows stalks bent by microwave technology, while the right side shows ordinary stalks.

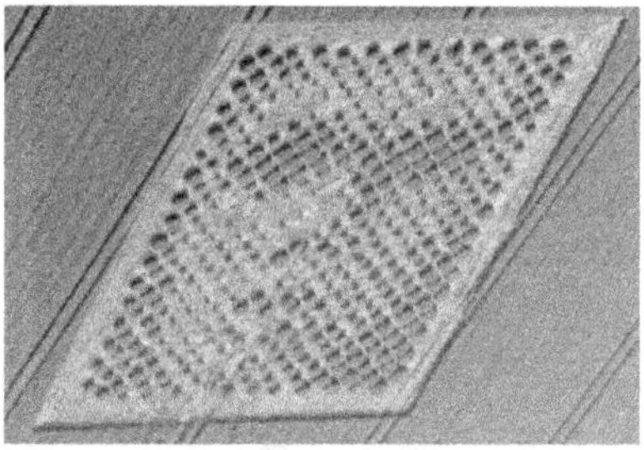

Fig. C11-2 In this Crop circle, each straw is broken in different positions at the top, center, and bottom, creating a three-dimensional effect of light and dark.

2) Military Applications

If applied to weaponry, this technology could be catastrophic. It could track all 6 billion people on Earth, pinpoint their exact locations, and selectively target them, potentially breaking their bodies into three parts with pinpoint accuracy.

To give an analogy, if a country on Earth were to send out a "Naval fleet" to battle a Galactic civilization, the fleet would be rendered useless. As soon as the fleet sets sail, all personnel aboard could be individually eliminated with pinpoint precision, leaving only empty metal vessels adrift at sea. Galactic civilizations' technology represents "Dimensional reduction" in warfare, where only the critical human targets are neutralized without even engaging the machines or weapons directly.

It's like a hunter with night vision shooting at a pack of wolves in the dark. In an hour, hundreds of wolves could be picked off, one by one, without the wolves ever seeing the hunter ------- while the hunter can see each wolf with perfect clarity.

By contrast, the weapons used by "Stellar system civilizations", such as planes, warships, bombs, or even nuclear warheads, are crude in comparison. They are mainly aimed at metal structures, often failing to hit their human targets effectively. Even when they do, they destroy both the human and the machine together.

3) Civilian and Medical Applications

Beyond military use, this technology has vast potential for "Civilian" and "Medical" applications. In medicine, for instance, tumors could be removed without the need for surgery. The technology could precisely identify specific cells or tissues, differentiating between what should be removed and what should remain.

In short, if the technology of Galactic civilizations according to the Laws of the Universe were fully deployed, all current weapons systems used by Stellar system civilizations ------ including fighter jets and warships ----- would become obsolete. Military forces, no matter how large, would be as vulnerable as a pack of wolves, unable to locate or fight back against their hunter.

Currently, more than half of the world's scientists and engineers work on weapons systems, consuming trillions of taxpayer dollars and wasting years of their lives on efforts that will soon be rendered obsolete by Galactic technology. These resources would be better spent on "Education" and

“Healthcare” for the public. For example, countries like North Korea invest in nuclear weapons while their people starve ------- what good will that do in the face of Galactic technology?

4) Global Implications and Concerns

This is why some "Experts" scare the public with threats of foreign invasion, using it as an excuse to funnel more taxpayer money into weapons production. They claim there are no extraterrestrial civilizations within 30,000 light-years, but such statements are made by people who use simplistic means to understand the universe. They certainly cannot replicate the intricate patterns of Crop circles, even if they were to try in broad daylight, let alone at night.

Despite the impressive capabilities of this Galactic technology, it cannot be widely disseminated at this time. Humanity, as a “Stellar system civilization”, is not yet wise enough to handle such power. Many authoritarian states still exist, and if this technology were to fall into their hands, it would endanger the entire solar system.

Even democratic nations are not ready for this technology, as some governments might attempt to steal or reverse-engineer it through students or spies. Only when the global level of civilization reaches the stage of “Galactic civilization” will these technologies be shared. At that point, global militaries and weaponry will become unnecessary, and taxpayer money will no longer be wasted on defense budgets.

To achieve a future where the world no longer needs weapons or armies, we must first spread and understand the “Theoretical framework” of Galactic civilizations according to the “Laws of the Universe”. As civilization advances step by step, all people on Earth, regardless of their level of education, can gradually elevate their understanding. Here's a simplified summary of these concepts for further exploration.

2. Natural Sciences

1) Mathematics

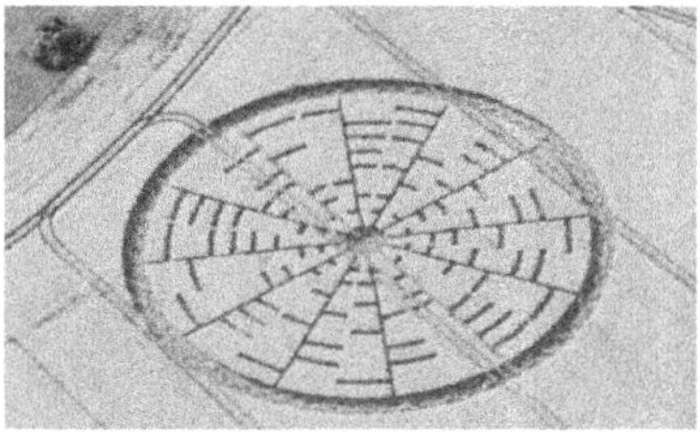

Fig. C11-3 Algebra: Laws of the Universe, Euler's Equation Approximation, e^(hi)(pi) + 1 = 0, May 22, 2010, Wilton Windmill, Wiltshire, England

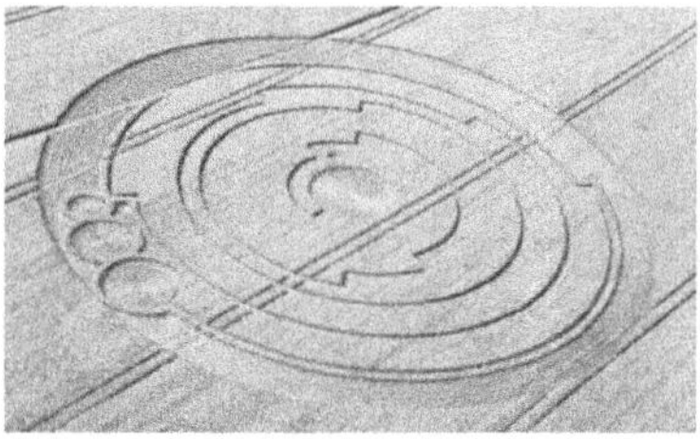

Fig. C11-4 Geometry: Mathematical pi 3.141592654 **......** Crop circle, June 1, 2008, in the Barbury Castle, Wiltshire area of the United Kingdom.

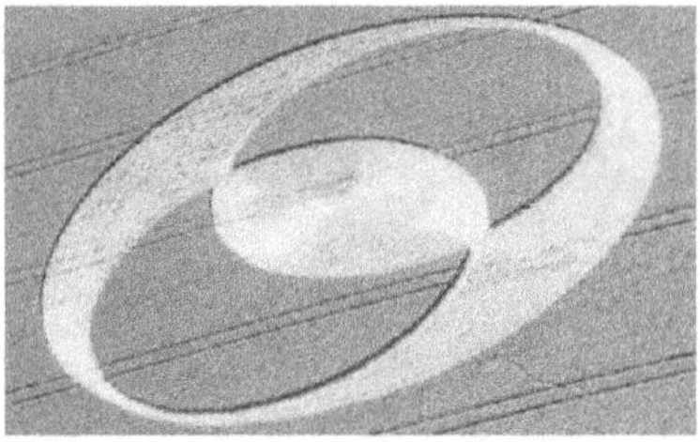

Fig. C11-5 Probability: Mathematical probability image on August 1, 1996, in Ashbury, Oxfordshire, England.

2) Physics

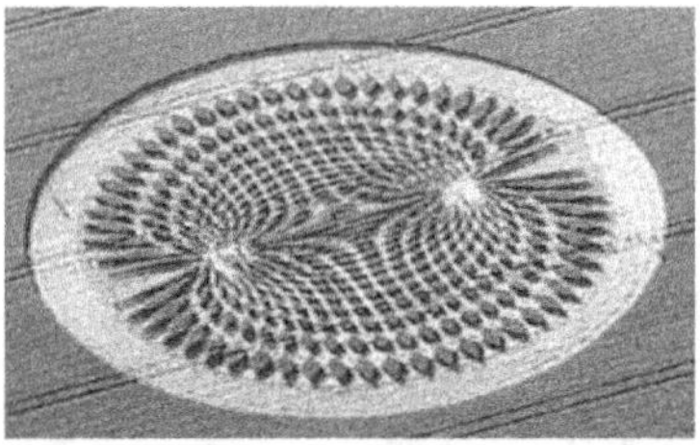

Fig.C11-6 Electromagnetics: Crop circle with electromagnetic field on July 22, 2000, in Knoll Down nr Avebury Trusloe, Wiltshire, England.

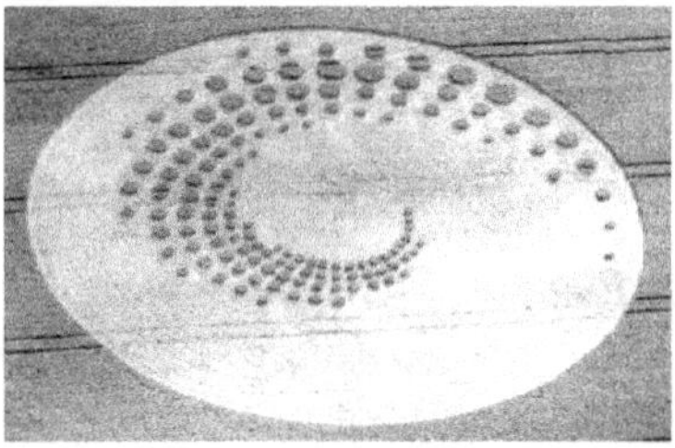

Fig.C11-7 Gravity: Wheatfield Circle with Gravitational Field, July 16, 2014, Forest Hill, nr Marlborough, Wiltshire, UK.

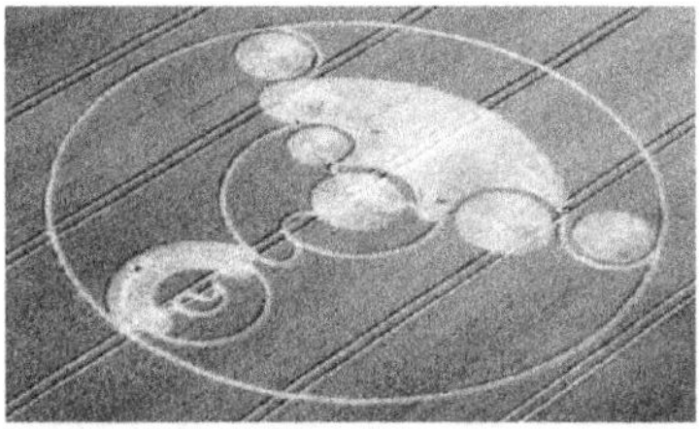

Fig. C11-8 Quantum: Crop circle with quantum fields of physics, July 21, 2001, Yateley, Wiltshire, UK.

3) Chemical

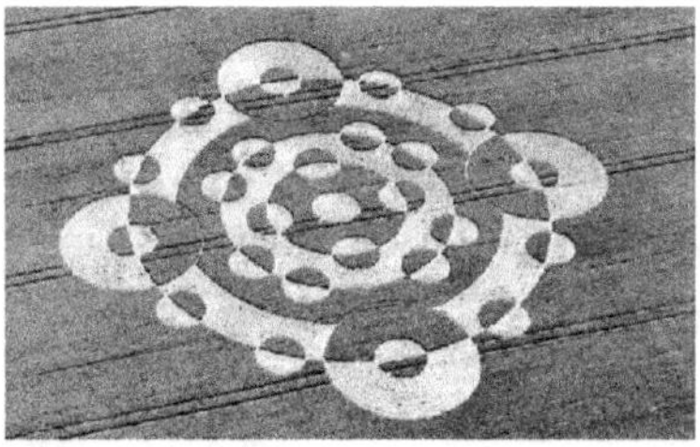

Fig. C11-9 Chemical elements: The appearance of the periodic table of chemical elements of Universal law, table element zirconium, on June 22, 2005, at Lurkley Hill - nr Lockeridge, Wiltshire, England.

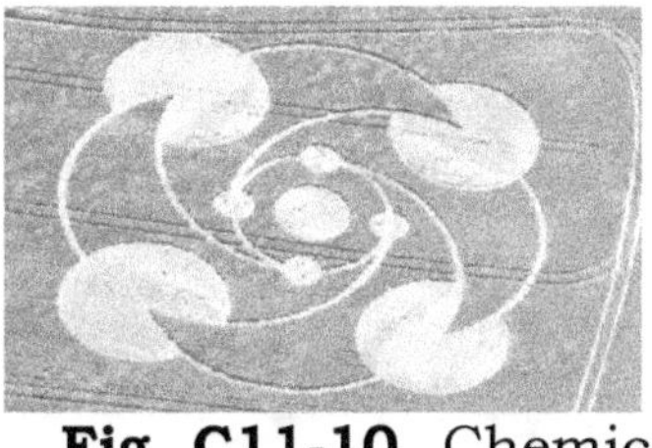

Fig. C11-10 Chemical Reaction: June 1, 2009, Knoll Down - nr Beckhampton, Wiltshire, UK, appears the chemical reaction crop circle, from two layers of 4-electron carbon to three layers of 4-electron silicon.

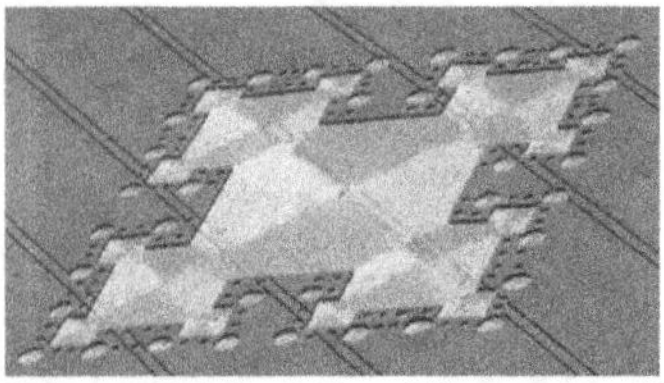

Fig. C11-11 Chemically Produced Material: Crop circle of chemically produced material on August 4, 1999 in the West Kennett Longbarrow, Wiltshire, UK.

3. Social Sciences

1) Politics

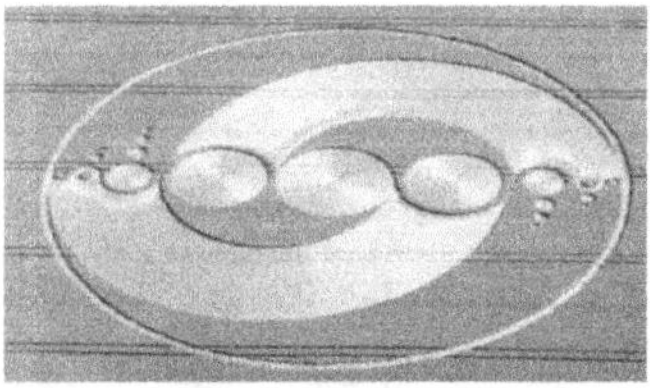

Fig. C11-12 Democracy: On July 28, 2002, in the Avebury, Wiltshire area of the UK, there was a crop circle of democratic politics, where two parties were fighting each other around a single power, and there was a separation of powers and a democratic system.

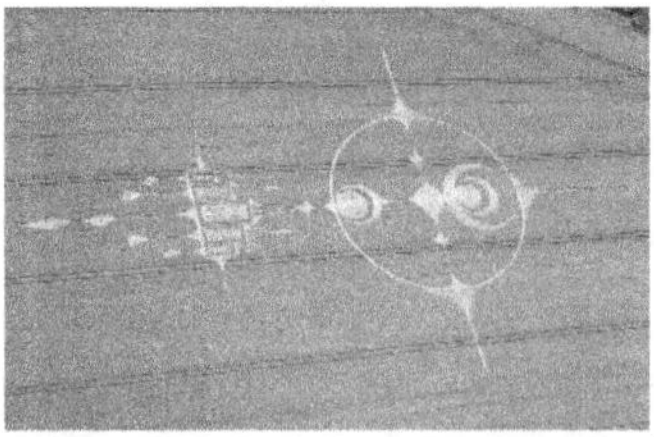

Fig. C11-13 Law: July 20, 2012, Stanton St Bernard, nr Alton Barnes, Wiltshire, England , now religious law, Islam suppresses Christianity, blood is being shed below.

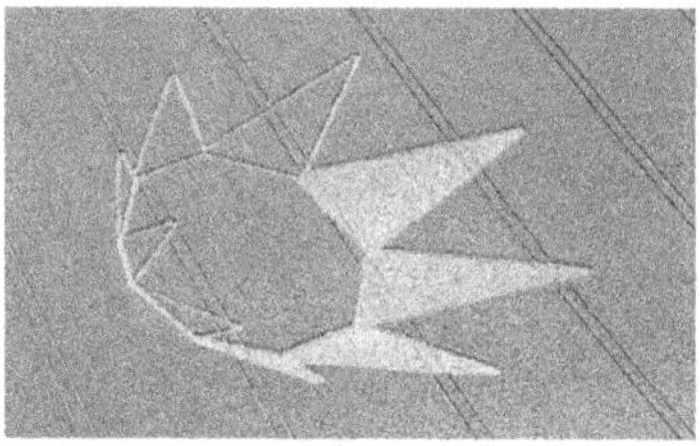

Fig. C11-14 Rule: July 23, 2012, in Longwood Warren, nr Winchester, Hampshire, England, Crown, Feudal system rules.

2) Economy

Fig. C11-15 Microeconomy: On July 22, 2002, in the South Field - Alton Barnes, Wiltshire area of the UK, there was a microeconomic knot.

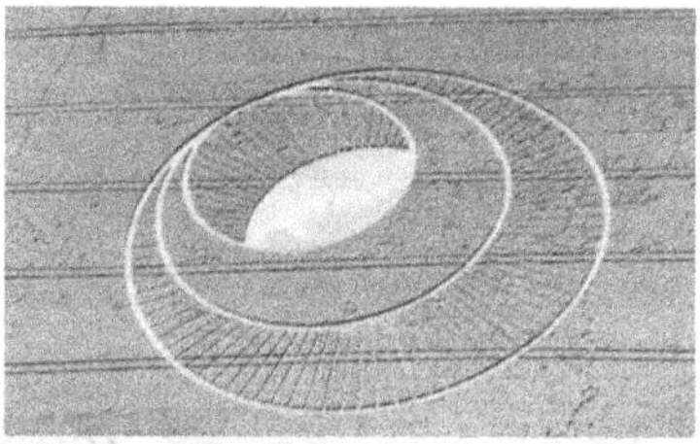

Fig. C11-16 Macroeconomy: The macroeconomic framework emerged on August 3, 2003 in the Morgan's Hill, Wiltshire area of the United Kingdom.

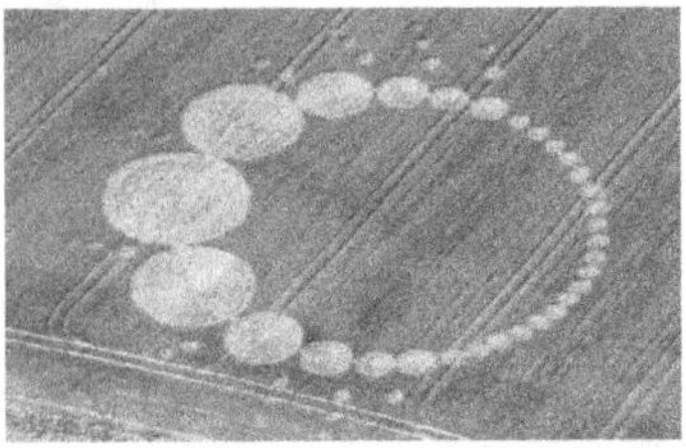

Fig. C11-17 Capital: The emergence of the jeweled crop circle on July 22, 2013, in the Giant's Grave, nr Oare, Wiltshire area of the UK.

3) Psychology

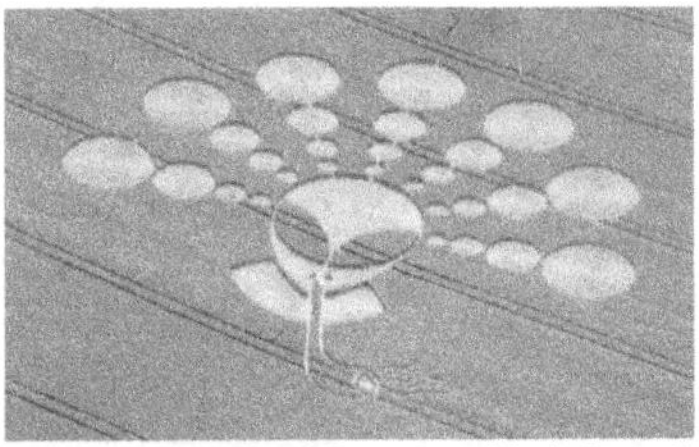

Fig. C11-18 Individual Psychology: Intelligent Man in thought, July 27, 2011, in the Cherhill White Horse, nr Calne, Wiltshire area, UK.

Fig. C11-19 Group Psychology: On July 20, 2008, in the Lockeridge, Wiltshire area of the UK, there was a crop circle expressing group psychology.

Fig. C11-20 Ontopsychology: July 9, 2005, Silbury Hill, Wiltshire, England, Crop circle of Ontopsychology, Thoughts or Emotions.

4. Life Sciences

1) Animals

Fig. C11-21 Evolution: July 29, 2009, Ogbourne St Andrew, nr Marlborough, Wiltshire, UK, Animal Trilobite crop circle.

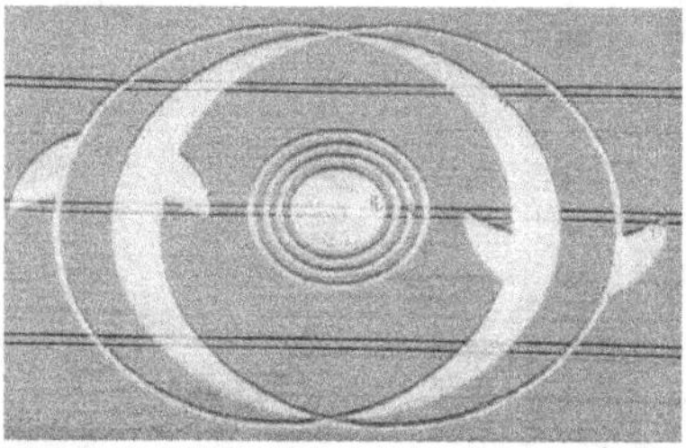

Fig. C11-22 Reproduction: Male and female fishes tease childen, August 12, 2002, East Field - Alton Barnes, Wiltshire area, UK.

Fig. C11-23 Embryo: Shell crop circle in the Pewsey, Wiltshire area, UK, July 16, 2002

2) Plants

Fig. C11-24 Evolution: 8-leaf flower of the plant on July 28, 2001 in the Beckhampton, Wiltshire area, UK.

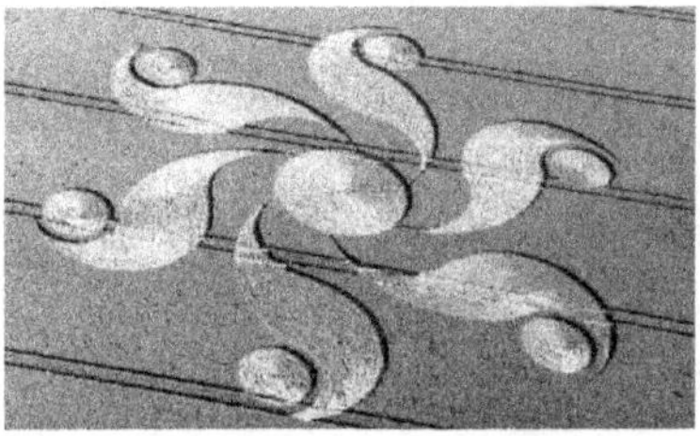

Fig. C11-25 Reproduction: Plant 6-leaved flower crop circle, June 15, 2004, in the Honey Street, Wiltshire area, England.

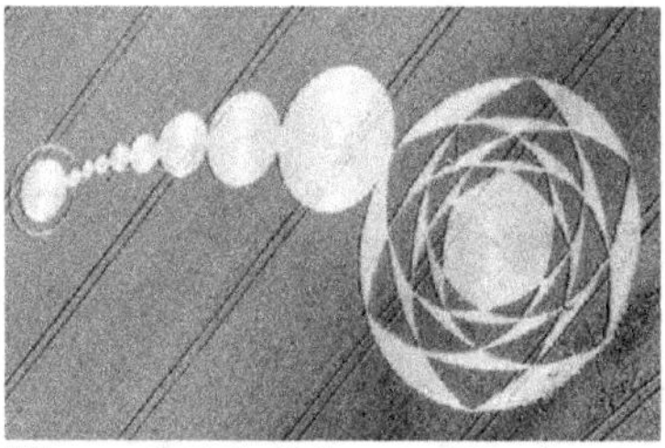

Fig. C11-26 Embryo: Plant-flowered embryo crop circle in the Uffington White Horse nr Woolstone, Oxfordshire area, U.K., July 23, 2000

3) Celestial bodies

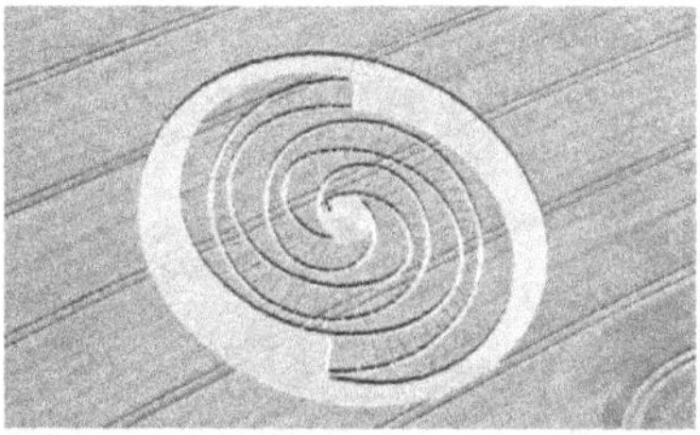

Fig. C11-27 Evolution: Galactic crop circle on June 9, 2008, in the West Kennett, Wiltshire area, UK.

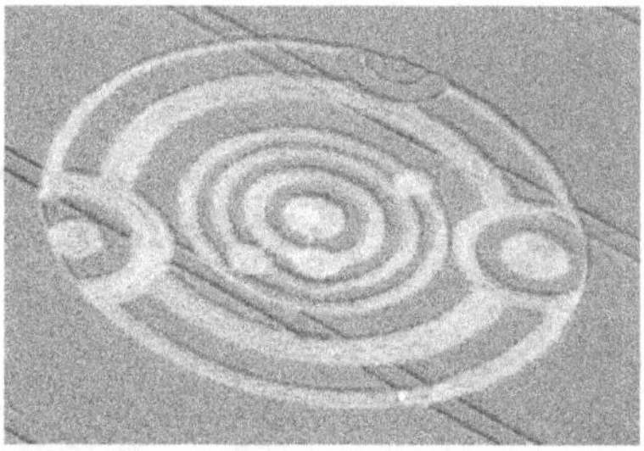

Fig. C11-28 Reproduction: crop circle of stars, planets, rings and satellites on June 18, 2011, in the Cow Drove Hill, nr Kings Somborne, Hampshire area, UK.

Fig. C11-29 Embryo: Crop circle with black hole, July 15, 2006, in the Aldbourne - nr Swindon, Wiltshire area, UK.

5. Summary

All Crop Circles Display the Ideological System of Galactic Civilization According to the Universal Law.

These crop circles are completed in an instant, something that the civilization of our solar system cannot achieve. Most people cannot understand what these mean because they don't understand what "Galactic civilization" is, including many so-called "Experts". A significant portion of these experts are pseudo-scientists hired by government propaganda departments to deceive the public with pranks and misinformation.

Currently, it seems that our universities have mostly degraded into institutions focused on technology and experiments. Experts and professors only know about experiments, technology, or some industrial inventions. However, the most important aspect of the universe is "Thought and civilization", and what the Crop circles display is entirely about "Civilization", not technology. So how could these experts and academicians possibly understand?

On another note, if civilization does not advance, then no matter how advanced the technology is, it will be useless — just like if social systems don't progress, even the best economy won't matter.

"Stellar System Civilizations", from an academic standpoint, only understand certain isolated disciplines. From a commercial and industrial perspective, they merely work to satisfy their need for food and livelihood. The lower a civilization is, the more it is obsessed with finding food, which leads to a higher likelihood of sickness and a shorter lifespan. Currently, we also consume too many different junk foods, which results in many diseases, including cancer.

In terms of "Spirituality and belief", Stellar system civilizations regard beings with higher wisdom as Gods, much like how Cats and Dogs might see us as Gods. Many worshipers, who have lost their sense of reason, merely kneel and pray to God, Allah, or emperors. When faced with the magnificent design of nature, we gaze at it like bewildered pets, marveling at the "Room's beautiful arrangement" and wondering, "Why can't we do that?"

The more advanced a civilization is, the less dependent it becomes on food. For example, "Galactic civilizations" typically sustain themselves with a single injection or a pill that can last for months. With a standardized nutrition pill, people rarely fall ill and live longer. Since their desire for food and material goods diminishes, society no longer needs so much commerce or industry, and hospitals become unnecessary. Although digestive functions might weaken, they produce much less waste and environmental pollution.

In Galactic civilizations, clothing is largely standardized. Since there's no industry, the government provides all necessities. There's no hierarchy or distinction in professions, and there's no pursuit of wealth or power. These civilizations travel to various planets in the universe, spreading beauty, and all plants and animals are designed and created by them.

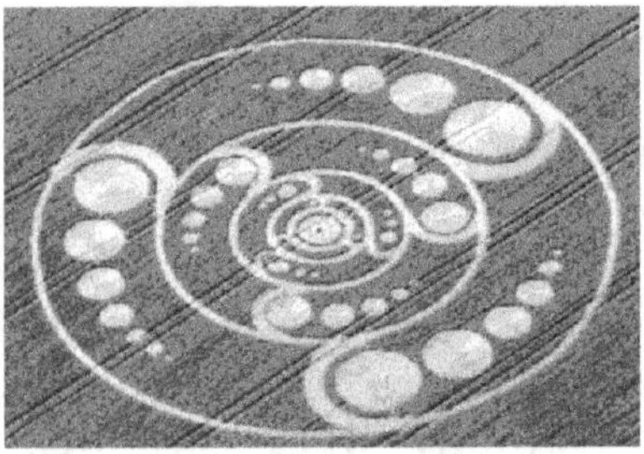 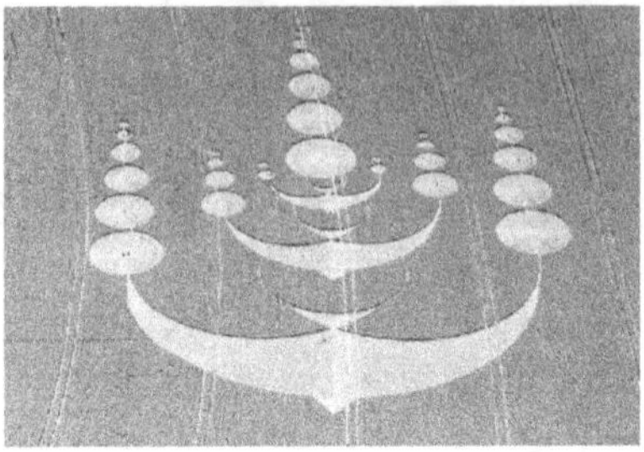

Fig. C11-30 The Ultimate Theory System

The educational system of the Galactic civilizations is based on the "Ultimate Theory System", which promotes breakthrough learning, rather than passive, exam-focused education. In contrast, our current education system emphasizes exams, homework, and exercises, producing students who are skilled only in copying and test-taking.

(Images sourced from the internet, article written in January 2019)

References:

1. John Chang: 《Crop Circle》 (2015), Universal Publishing, Sydney, Australia.

2. John Chang: 《Great Ultimate Theory》 (2013), Universal Publishing, Sydney, Australia.

C12. The Five Civilizational Developments in World History and the Great Prophecy of Chinese Civilization

Abstract: We previously discussed the concepts of "Social humanities, scientific technology, and life wisdom", derived from the three major horizontal waves of "0", "1", and ".", which expand in terms of "Space". Now, we will address the three major vertical waves, which also include "Social humanities, scientific technology, and life wisdom", but progress in terms of "Time". These horizontal and vertical waves differ slightly.

The current era is one focused on the integration of "Technology and life sciences". It is predicted that over the 500 years following 2012, five great masters --- comparable to Newton and Einstein --- will emerge from the East, each achieving groundbreaking advancements in specific fields.

---

1. Introduction

In the long course of world history, every step leaves a trace, and every minor wave revolves around a larger wave.

For example, we've passed through the stages of "Primitive, slavery, and feudalism society", and naturally, we can infer the emergence of future stages such as "Democracy" and "Unification", marking five major societal systems. Although some governments may coerce historians and sociologists into creating systems that justify their rule, history is never truly written in the present; it is penned by scholars of the future. Much of the falsehoods will be corrected by later generations.

An example comes from the 《Lüshi Chunqiu》（吕氏春秋）, which records, "The Grand Historian of the Xia Dynasty, Zhong Gu（终古）, presented his historical charts, held them, and wept", and "Grand Historian Zhong Gu then fled to the Shang Dynasty".

This story illustrates how the Xia Emperor Jie, known for his decadence, ordered Zhong Gu to falsify history to glorify his reign. Despite attempts to counsel the emperor, Zhong Gu eventually fled to the Shang Dynasty, refusing to alter the historical record. This was the first recorded instance of a historian "Escaping", showing the integrity of ancient Chinese historians. Even though Emperor Jie sought praise, his misdeeds were authentically recorded by later historians. As the saying goes, "One cannot conceal their actions forever". True history lives in the hearts of people.

From this, it is clear that historians in ancient times held firm to their values, opting to flee rather than alter history.

From the perspective of civilization's development, represented by “Celestial phenomena”, we have already passed through the stages of “Satellite civilization, Planetary civilization”, and “Stellar civilization”. From this, we can naturally deduce the upcoming “Galactic civilization” and “Cosmic civilization”, forming five great civilizations.

When aligning societal systems with astronomical cultural development, “Primitive society” corresponds to “Satellite civilization”; “Slavery society” to “Planetary civilization”; “Feudalism society” to “Stellar civilization”; “Democracy society” to “Galactic civilization”; and “Unification society” to “Cosmic civilization”.

Why is astronomy the representative? Because all civilizational breakthroughs have been tied to astronomical observations. For instance, the earliest theoretical systems of "Satellite civilization" were formed around satellites like the Moon, in Primitive and slave societies of ancient history.

Each civilizational breakthrough was often led by one individual whose ideas deviated from the mainstream. These figures were often misunderstood by society, as their advancements were not motivated by money or power but by the desire to elevate human civilization. Over time, their ideas were eventually understood and appreciated.

2. Satellite Civilization

Aristotle (384 BCE - March 7, 322 BCE) was an ancient Greek philosopher, a student of Plato, and a teacher of Alexander the Great. His works covered a wide range of subjects, including physics, metaphysics, poetry, drama, music, biology, economics, zoology, logic, politics, and ethics.

Aristotle's thoughts on physics deeply shaped medieval culture, influencing the Renaissance until they were eventually replaced by Newtonian physics. His academic contributions also included formal logic theory, ethics, and metaphysical studies. In philosophy and theology, he had a profound impact on both Islam and Judaism. Sadly, due to the loss of history and wars, only about one-third of his original works survived.

Note: We believe Aristotle, from ancient Greece, analyzed the achievements of scholars before him and made a breakthrough in establishing the "Satellite Civilization". His works, 《On the Heavens》 and 《Meteorology》, were regarded as comprehensive theories on the study of satellite systems. That era marked the beginning of the social humanities era, approximately 500 years before Ptolemy ushered in the "Planetary Civilization".

Fig.C12-1 Aristotle

Fig.C12-2 Ptolemy

3. Planetary Civilization

Claudius Ptolemy (100 – 170 CE) was a scholar, mathematician, astronomer, geographer, and astrologer. He passed away around 170 CE in Alexandria, Egypt. As a Roman citizen living in Alexandria, Egypt, Ptolemy wrote in Greek. Not much is recorded about him, but he is most famous for proposing the geocentric model of the universe.

Ptolemy authored several scientific works, three of which significantly influenced the scientific development of Byzantium, the Islamic world, and Europe. The first was 《Almagest》, which discussed the geocentric theory; the second was 《Geographia》, exploring Greek and Roman geographical knowledge; and the third was 《Tetrabiblos》, concerning astrology and refining methods for creating star charts.

Note: During this time, people believed in the divine right of kings and emperors, yet Ptolemy, an Egyptian, synthesized the motions of the planetary systems and formulated the geocentric theory, which posited the Earth at the center. His analyses of these theoretical systems broke new ground and ushered in the "Planetary Civilization". This era marked the beginning of the human sciences, about a thousand years before Copernicus initiated the "Stellar Civilization", demonstrating how Ptolemy's ideas differed from the mainstream of his time.

4. Stellar Civilization

Fig.C12-3 Copernicus

Nicolaus Copernicus (February 19, 1473 - May 24, 1543) was born in Royal Prussia, a region that had been part of the Kingdom of Poland since 1466. He was a Polish mathematician and astronomer of the European Renaissance, known for advocating the heliocentric model, which posits the Sun as the center of the universe.

In 1543, shortly before his death, Copernicus published 《On the Revolutions of the Celestial Spheres》. His work is widely regarded as the starting point of modern astronomy and was instrumental in launching the Copernican Revolution, greatly advancing the development of science.

Note: At the time, academic institutions and nearly all civilians believed the world revolved around the Earth. However, Copernicus, a European, independently analyzed the movements of the solar system and developed the heliocentric model, with the Sun at the center. His synthesis of these theories marked the beginning of the "Stellar Civilization", ushering in an era of science and technology approximately 500 years before today's onset of the "Galactic Civilization". Since Copernicus' views were vastly different from those of his time, his ideas faced significant suppression.

5. Galactic Civilization

Around 2012, the "Galactic Civilization" began, marked by the establishment of a comprehensive theoretical system, with the key focus on "Galactic structures". This era launched the integration of technology and life sciences. It is predicted that this will last for approximately 500 years before the next breakthrough, the "Cosmic Civilization", follows the same cyclical pattern of major advancements every 500 years.

Although scientists of this era have discovered Galaxies and understand black holes, most knowledge remains rooted in "Dead" astronomy, represented by materialism. The general populace, still devoted to religious leaders and authoritarian rulers, fails to grasp the connection between "Astronomy and civilization" or the dialectical relationship between materialism, idealism, and metaphysics. Furthermore, they do not comprehend the significance of the relationship between "Galaxies and black holes" within the framework of governance, or the meaning behind the heliocentric model that corresponds to a world with Kings, Gods, and worship.

The current "Galactic Civilization" primarily showcases the pinnacle of contemporary Chinese civilization. Over the next 500 years, more people will come to understand this system, much like how Copernicus' "Stellar Civilization" was gradually embraced.

It is predicted that in the coming centuries, several Eastern masters of the "Galactic Civilization" will emerge, their accomplishments comparable to Galileo, Newton, Maxwell, and Einstein. Roughly one such figure is expected every 100 years, with a focus on the intersection of technology and life sciences.

Fig.C12-4 Galaxy

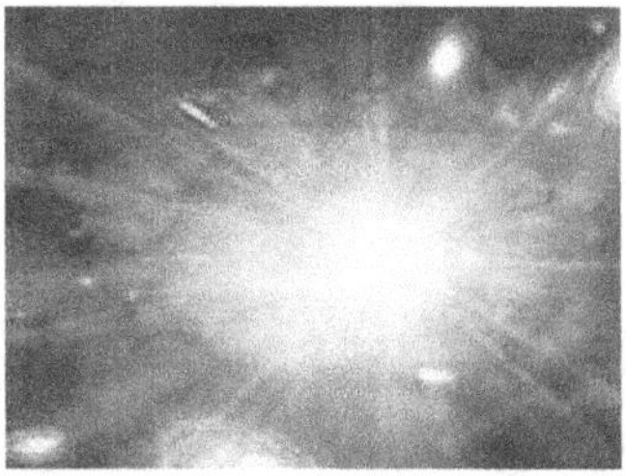

Fig.C12-5 The Big Bang

6. Cosmic Civilization

It is predicted that around the year 2500, someone will create the "Cosmic Civilization", an even more grandiose theoretical system than today's "Galactic Civilization". This system, like those before it, will be completed by a single individual without the need for external assistance.

What might this "Cosmic Civilization" entail? We can speculate based on historical patterns. Aristotle began the "Social humanities" philosophical system; Ptolemy initiated the "Human sciences" conceptual system; Copernicus established the "Scientific technology" experimental system, and now we are in the age of the "Technological life" wisdom system. What comes 500 years from now? Perhaps it will be the "Life wisdom" soul system, characterized by explosive growth akin to the explosive forms found in the universe, such as animals, plants, and other lifeforms.

This new system could be a perfect combination of "Society and humanities; Science and technology; Life and wisdom", seamlessly integrating theory and experimentation across six major theoretical frameworks.

The person who creates this "Cosmic Civilization" likely won't be Greek, Egyptian, European, or Chinese, but perhaps someone from South America ------- an American or a descendent of the Mayan civilization. This follows the cyclical law, where breakthroughs do not continuously emerge from the same continent or race.

In the eras of Aristotle and Ptolemy, the primary pressure came from royal authority, while in Copernicus' time and our present day, the influence of religious dogma is significant. However, 500 years from now, these limitations will be completely eradicated, and civilization will experience explosive growth. This is the essence of the "Cosmic Civilization", a theoretical system that will expand rapidly throughout the universe, something I deeply feel is coming.

7. Future Predictions

In the book 《World Systems Science》, we discussed the three horizontal waves of development: "Social humanities, Natural science, and Life wisdom", expanding through "0", "1", and "." in space. Now, we shift our focus to three vertical waves: "Social humanities, Scientific technology, and Life wisdom," which develop over time. While the horizontal and vertical waves are similar, they differ in their progression.

Here, we present a timeline of vertical waves in historical order:

- Aristotle (Social Humanities);
- Ptolemy (Human Sciences);
- Copernicus (Scientific Technology);
- Present (Technological Life);
- Future (Life Wisdom).

(1) Before the "Satellite Civilization"

Before Aristotle (384–322 BCE) founded the "Satellite Civilization," both Eastern and Western civilizations saw the emergence of five masters:

Western: Thales, Socrates, Thucydides, Pythagoras, Plato.

Eastern: Laozi, Confucius, Buddha, Guiguzi, Mozi.

Their primary studies revolved around sociology and the humanities, which were essentially considered part of philosophy at the time.

(2) After the "Satellite Civilization" or Before the "Planetary Civilization"

500 years after Aristotle, five significant figures emerged in the West, but not in the East:

Euclid, Archimedes, Hipparchus, Pliny the Elder, Jesus.

They focused on expanding Aristotle's "Sociology and humanities," or the early natural sciences.

(3) After the "Planetary Civilization" or Before the "Stellar Civilization"

Ptolemy (100 - 170 CE) founded the "Planetary Civilization," bridging the humanities and science. Over the next thousand years, the East saw the emergence of five masters:

Ge Hong, Zu Chongzhi, Yixing(一行), Al-Khwarizmi, Guo Shoujing.

They focused on continuing Ptolemy's blend of humanities and science. The West, however, experienced a period of stagnation during the so-called Dark Ages.

(4) After the "Stellar Civilization" or Before the "Galactic Civilization"

Copernicus (1473 – 1543) founded the "Stellar Civilization", bridging science and technology. Over the next 500 years, five prominent Western figures emerged while the East remained relatively quiet due to foreign invasion and isolation. These figures were:

Galileo, Newton, Coulomb, Maxwell, Einstein.

Their work continued to build upon Copernicus' revolutionary fusion of science and technology.

(5) After the "Galactic Civilization" or the Current Era

The "Galactic Civilization" began around 2012 and is characterized by the integration of technology and life sciences. Over the next 500 years, five masters will emerge from the East, comparable to the stature of Newton or Einstein. These figures will not simply be spreaders of Western knowledge or new religious leaders but will be true pioneers in specific fields of Eastern civilization.

Their breakthroughs are expected in areas such as the origin and evolution of life, Disease mechanisms and treatment, Medicine applications, Longevity, Chinese medicine, Qigong, Unique human abilities, Intelligent technology, Robotics, Space communication, Space materials, and more.

These breakthroughs will be led by individuals, not teams. Teams, driven by financial needs and commercial goals, cannot produce masters of this caliber. For instance, if a Chinese medicine master emerges, they will resolve all theoretical questions about traditional medicine, bridging Chinese and Western medicine while finding solutions to virtually every disease, even those modern medicine cannot treat. This master is predicted to be Chinese.

Similarly, in the field of Qigong and human abilities, another Chinese master may emerge, resolving the mysteries of bioelectromagnetic phenomena, life wisdom, and the origins of life, sweeping away all previous biological challenges.

(6) After the "Galactic Civilization" or the arrival of the "Cosmic Civilization"

Around 2500 CE, the "Cosmic Civilization" will be founded by a single individual, advancing human knowledge into the realms of "Life and wisdom". This figure will complete the vertical development of human civilization, marked by six cycles of major breakthroughs.

In the 500 years following the creation of the "Cosmic Civilization", five new masters will appear in both the East and the West, reminiscent of the pre-Aristotelian period. This will mark the closing chapter of civilization as we know it.

8. Conclusion

This overview of historical progression shows a preordained pattern of human evolution, not determined by

Gods but rather by the necessity of human development, much like the stages of individual human life (Childhood, Adolescence, Youth, Middle aged and Old age).

All predictions and interpretations made here will be fully understood and verified in the "Life and wisdom" era, 500 years from now. At that point, global religion, philosophy, and science will be completely unified. Although the unity initiated in 2012 is not yet fully realized — due to current resistance from religious, scientific, and political establishments — this will inevitably change.

In the future, all ancient and modern predictions will be fulfilled and recognized as part of human history's natural progression.

(Picture online, article originally written on Taipei on April 2, 2019)

C13. From Stellar Civilization to Galactic Civilization

Abstract: Stellar civilization represents a conservative, closed system with a central, singular deity or idol, often reflected in authoritarian or theocratic governance. The masses surround this center, worshipping and obeying.

Galactic civilization, on the other hand, is characterized by openness and transcendence. There is no single central authority, and instead, brilliant stars ----- representing great scientists, philosophers, and religious figures ----- circle around a center of knowledge and wisdom, creating cycles of advancement and transcendence.

---

1. Stellar Civilization

A "Stellar system" has a central star (Such as the Sun) with planets, moons, asteroids, and comets orbiting around it. For thousands of years, human civilization was largely confined to the solar system, and civilizations during this time were focused on hierarchical, authoritarian systems:

1) Emperor-centered societies: Surrounding the emperor were countless subjects. The emperor consolidated power by calling on the people to revere him, proclaiming himself the "Son of Heaven" or the "Sun". This system was maintained by force, using police and military to control behavior, known as "Behavioral control".

2) Religious-centered societies: Surrounding the religious leader were countless followers, instructed to donate wealth to the church and believe that the leader was divine. Followers were warned that failure to worship the leader would result in eternal damnation, known as "Thought control".

Together, “Behavioral control” and “Thought control” formed a theocratic and dictatorial system typical of Stellar civilization. This civilization type represents conservatism and closed-mindedness, with a central dictator, deity, or idol. All societies for the last 5,000 years have been influenced by these patterns.

For most species, this civilization was a repetitive cycle of birth, reproduction, and death with little change, looping endlessly over millions of years. Academic research in Stellar civilizations tended to focus on narrow disciplines ---- most scientists and sociologists were specialists in a single field (e.g., a physicist would not understand economics).

Fig. C13-1 Solar system

Fig. C13-2 Galaxy

2. Galactic Civilization

The discovery of “Galaxies” in the early 20th century expanded humanity's view beyond the Solar system. Unlike Stellar systems, the center of a Galaxy is a non-luminous entity called a “Black hole”, surrounded by countless stars (Including planets, moons, comets, and nebulae).

In “Galactic civilization”, there is no central authority figure such as a king or a universally worshiped religious leader. Instead, the brightest stars ------ representing notable historical figures like great scientists, philosophers, and religious leaders ------ circle around the black hole.

What energy binds these brilliant minds together? It is the most powerful force: knowledge and intelligence. The “Universal Law” brings together the greatest scientific, philosophical, and religious minds, creating a dynamic of “Cycles and transcendence”.

In contrast to Stellar civilization's narrow specialization, Galactic civilization promotes “Holistic academic research” that transcends individual disciplines. All fields of study are unified, and research is conducted in an integrated manner.

3. Conclusion

“Stellar civilization” is characterized by “Cyclical patterns”, while “Galactic civilization” embodies both “Cycles and transcendence”. For example, species such as animals lay eggs and reproduce cyclically for millions of years, but the evolutionary leap from egg-laying to live birth represents “Transcendence”. Similarly, plants evolved from algae to ferns to seed plants, representing both cyclical reproduction and occasional transcendence.

Transcendence is brief, while cycles last for extended periods. Each time a species transcends, it advances one level. But what drives these cycles and transcendence in species?

In our short human lifespan, we only witness the “Cycles”, not the “Transcendence”. We cannot observe large-scale evolutionary changes like the shift from egg-laying to live birth in animals or from algae to ferns in plants. While the time span for these changes is short in terms of Earth's history, it is long compared to human life.

Scientists today focus mainly on studying the reproductive cycles of species, but the broader timeframes of "Transcendence" remain a mystery. However, by analyzing the "Three waves" produced since the Big Bang, it becomes clearer.

The key to understanding the "Origin of life" lies in the "Life wisdom wave", also known as the "Wave of space-time". This wave has peaks and valleys, with time and space both representing energy. The wavelength of this wave corresponds to the lifecycle of celestial bodies and the space they control.

Over long periods, the wave is "Smooth"; over shorter periods, it is "Abrupt". Under the influence of this natural cosmic wave, large-scale evolutionary changes, such as the transition from algae to ferns or from egg-laying to live birth, occur. These changes are global and affect entire species, not isolated instances such as color changes in moths due to industrial pollution. Similarly, the evolution of animals from egg-laying to live birth follows the same pattern of transcendence.

Conclusion: Galactic civilization represents a new era of openness and collective advancement, bringing together the brightest minds under the guiding principles of the Universal Law. Unlike Stellar civilization, which revolves around cycles and stagnation, Galactic civilization embraces cycles and transcendence, leading to continuous growth and evolution.

(Article originally published in October 2017)

C14. Scientific Analysis of the Spring and Autumn Period and the Modern World

Abstract: China used the theoretical frameworks of "Daoism, Confucianism, and Legalism" to transition from the Spring and Autumn period to the Warring States period, ultimately unifying the country. History tends to repeat itself, and based on both temporal and geographical analysis, the world today is experiencing a similar phase to China's Spring and Autumn era, with conflicts among nations, frequent wars, and the need for the unification of standards in science, language, culture, and ideology. We are witnessing an era of intellectual transformation, similar to the Hundred Schools of Thought period in ancient China, characterized by profound changes and integration between Eastern and Western ideologies.

I. The Western World and Parallels to Ancient China

The Western world, especially Europe and North America, is currently undergoing a political shift similar to ancient China's transition. They are employing the principles of "Freedom, democracy, and the rule of law", which echo the ancient Chinese schools of thought: "Daoism, Confucianism, and Legalism". This transformation reflects a transition from Feudal systems to Democratic parliamentary systems, similar to how ancient China shifted from Feudal states to Centralized governance.

The global landscape, with over 100 smaller nations, resembles China's Spring and Autumn period. The United Nations (UN) functions like the Zhou Dynasty's royal court, where representatives from different countries gather, much like how smaller states in ancient China sent envoys to the

Zhou court. Major powers such as the "United States, Canada"; the former Soviet Union; China; "The UK, Germany, France"; India; "Australia, New Zealand"; and various African nations, can be compared to the Seven Warring States of ancient China.

II. The Spring and Autumn Period

1. The Spring and Autumn Period in China

From a military and political perspective, the Spring and Autumn period (770–476 BCE) saw the emergence of over 170 documented states, the most prominent being Qi, Jin, Chu, Qin, Lu, Song, Wei, Yan, Chen, Cao, Cai, Zheng, Wu, and Yue, among others. These states, while technically under the Zhou Dynasty, operated with significant independence. The Zhou royal court, located in Luoyi (Modern-day Luoyang), symbolized the central authority, and envoys from various states lived near the capital, paying tribute to the Zhou court while pursuing their own interests.

During this period, five hegemonic rulers (Known as the "Five Hegemons") rose to prominence. They were:

- Duke Huan of Qi (685–643 BCE),
- Duke Mu of Qin (659–621 BCE),
- Duke Xiang of Song (650–637 BCE),
- Duke Wen of Jin (636–628 BCE),
- King Zhuang of Chu (613–591 BCE).

These rulers, as leaders of powerful states, held the responsibility of defending the Zhou Dynasty's authority, resisting foreign invaders, suppressing internal rebellion, and mediating conflicts between states.

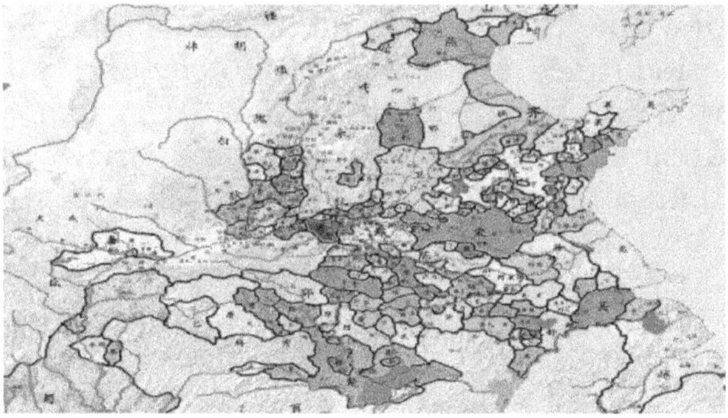

Fig. C14-1 In the Spring and Autumn Period of China, there were more than 170 countries

2. The Global Spring and Autumn Period

Today, there are approximately 190 nations in the world. Some of the most influential countries include the United States, the United Kingdom, France, Russia (Formerly the Soviet Union), China, India, Japan, Canada, Australia, Brazil, Argentina, Indonesia, Pakistan, South Africa, Italy, and Saudi Arabia. The United Nations acts as the central authority, akin to the Zhou royal court, with each nation sending diplomats, paying membership fees, and seeking to protect its own interests.

In a manner similar to China's Spring and Autumn period, modern global history has also seen the rise of five dominant powers, who have exerted control over global trade, military expansion, and territorial conquest. These "Global hegemonies" emerged in the form of the following powers:

- Portugal (15th to 16th centuries),
- Spain (16th to 17th centuries),
- Netherlands (17th to 18th centuries),
- United Kingdom (18th to 19th centuries),
- United States (19th to 20th centuries).

These nations, like the Five Hegemons of China's Spring and Autumn period, used advanced technology and military power to assert dominance, manage trade, and engage in territorial expansion. Today, they maintain their global influence through diplomatic and military alliances, with the United Nations functioning similarly to the Zhou court during the Spring and Autumn period.

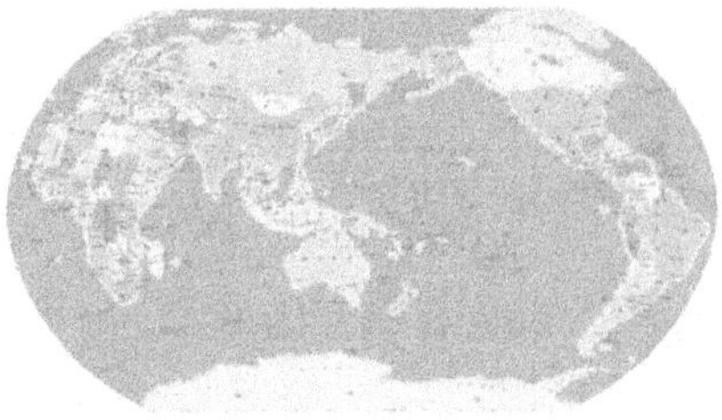

Fig. C14-2 In the Spring and Autumn Period of the world, there were more than 190 countries

III. The Warring States Period

1. The Warring States Period in China

After the Spring and Autumn period, China's political landscape shifted dramatically. The large, powerful states began to annex the smaller ones, and the Zhou Dynasty's central authority eroded. By the time of the Warring States period (475–221 BCE), China was effectively divided among seven dominant states: Qi, Chu, Yan, Han, Zhao, Wei, and Qin. These states, known as the "Seven Warring States", engaged in continuous warfare for dominance and survival. Eventually, this era of intense conflict culminated in the unification of China under the Qin state.

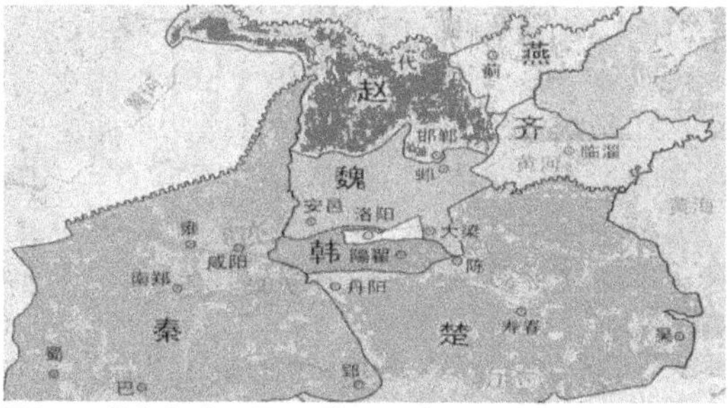

Fig. C14-3 During the Warring States Period in China, there were seven main countries

2. The Warring States Period of the World

In a global context, today's world mirrors the dynamics of ancient China's Warring States period. While the United Nations (UN) still exists as a symbol of international governance, it has not prevented conflicts and shifts in global power. The 190+ countries in the world, much like the hundreds of small states in ancient China, have gone through major wars, most notably the two World Wars. These wars led to the rise and fall of various powers, much like the annexation and consolidation of smaller states during China's Warring States era.

Nations like Germany, Japan, and Italy attempted to dominate and annex other countries during the 20th century, but their efforts were thwarted, similar to the failed ambitions of various smaller states in ancient China. The defeat of these nations by the Allied forces of the United States and Britain during the world wars paved the way for a new global order, akin to the Warring States' transition towards eventual unification under Qin.

1) The "Seven Global Powers" Today.

Just as China had its "Seven Warring States", the modern world can be seen as having its own set of dominant powers or "Seven Global Powers". These are:

- United States and Canada (Dominating North and South America): Comparable to the ancient state of "Qi".
- Russia (Influencing Eastern Europe): Similar to the ancient state of "Yan".
- China (Influencing Asia): Resembling the ancient state of "Zhao".
- The European Union, with England, Germany, and France (Controlling Western Europe): Analogous to "Qin", a state that appeared small but had advanced civilization and expansionary capability.
- India (Influencing South Asia): Corresponding to "Han".
- Australia and New Zealand (Influencing the South Pacific region): Comparable to "Chu".
- South Africa and Israel (Controlling parts of Africa and the Middle East): Likely equivalent to "Wei".

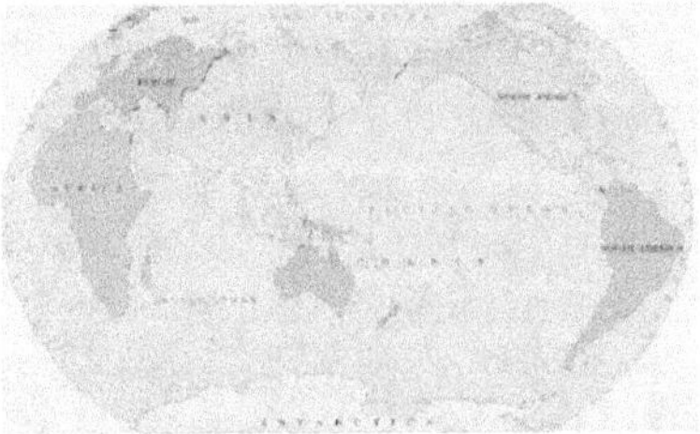

Fig. C14-4 The six continents of the World Warring States Period are divided by political power and culture. Asia and Africa are equivalent to the four theaters of Yan, Zhao, Han, and Wei, and are relatively backward politically and economically; Europe, America, and Oceania are equivalent to Qin, Qi, and Chu. Relatively advanced politics and economy

The geographical positioning and influence of these nations resemble the ancient states in China's Warring States period. For example, Europe, despite its relatively small landmass, is positioned in the global "Northwest," much like Qin was in ancient China. Qin appeared small, but it possessed advanced military and cultural capabilities that allowed it to expand rapidly and unify China.

2) Modern Parallels with Ancient China.

Just as the Zhou Dynasty's central authority became merely symbolic by the end of the Spring and Autumn period, today's United Nations faces similar challenges. While it serves as a global forum for diplomacy and international law, it often struggles to enforce its resolutions, particularly when dealing with major powers. This is akin to how the Zhou court, while maintaining a ceremonial role, lost control over the feuding states, and powerful states began ignoring or challenging the Zhou rulers.

- Tribute to the UN: The "Tribute" that states once paid to the Zhou Dynasty can be compared to the membership fees that countries pay to the UN today. Just as smaller states often avoided paying tribute, many small nations today do not contribute or contribute very little to the UN budget, while larger nations contribute more.
- Manipulation by Major Powers: During China's Spring and Autumn and Warring States periods, powerful states would often manipulate the Zhou court, using the figurehead authority to control smaller states. Similarly, today, large nations use their influence within the UN to further their own interests, sometimes toppling governments or installing puppet regimes in smaller, weaker nations.

3) Historical Cycles and Modern Global Conflict

Much like China's ancient transition from the Spring and Autumn period to the Warring States, the modern world may be moving towards a period of greater conflict and consolidation. The UN, like the Zhou Dynasty, may continue to lose influence as major powers assert their dominance. Smaller nations may increasingly find themselves dependent on larger powers for survival, much like the smaller states of ancient China sought alliances with more powerful neighbors.

In this context, it becomes clear that the parallels between ancient China's history and today's global dynamics are striking. The fragmentation, power struggles, and shifting alliances that defined the Warring States period are mirrored in the modern world, where large nations compete for influence and smaller countries align themselves with these powers for protection.

IV. The Trend Towards Global Unification

1. Global Strategic and Military Trends

Western strategists, particularly in Europe and the Americas, have long sought global unification through the establishment of standardized systems like the metric system and engineering standards — today's global equivalents of "Measures and weights" from ancient China. They aim to spread English as the global lingua franca, comparable to the Qin state's imposition of its own language on China. However, unlike Qin's aggressive unification through war, the West has adopted a gradual approach, promoting scientific, technological, and cultural integration as precursors to political unification.

Europe began its global exploration early, discovering the Americas and establishing the United States, which can be seen as a strategic ally similar to how Qin formed partnerships with neighboring states. The U.S. later became a global power by leveraging European culture, much as Qin leveraged alliances to spread its influence. The U.S. also replaced Europe's "Feudal county system" with a "Democratic parliamentary system", asserting its independence from Britain and eventually becoming one of the five global superpowers.

2. Gradual vs. Aggressive Unification

The Anglo-American alliance, akin to the strategic partnership between Qin and Qi, helped defeat internal threats within Europe, such as the fascist regimes in Germany, Italy, and Japan during World War II. After these dictatorships were toppled, they adopted democratic parliamentary systems, which laid the foundation for a more unified world order — mirroring Qin's internal consolidation before launching its unification campaign.

The West, particularly the U.S. and Europe, has also been spreading its culture, language (English), and legal systems to other parts of the world, including India, South Asia (Han), Africa, and the Middle East (Wei), and Oceania (Chu). Countries that resist adopting Western-style systems often face military intervention, much like Qin's early annexations of neighboring states.

3. Parallels with Qin's Political Reforms

Qin's legal reforms under Shang Yang, including the principle that "The king and the people are equally subject to the law", were far more advanced than the legal systems of other states, which were rooted in hereditary privilege. Similarly, the Western legal system, with its emphasis on democracy and freedom, has developed mechanisms to impeach corrupt leaders and promote accountability, much like Qin's efforts to enforce justice and eliminate corruption. This is in contrast to some countries today where corruption is selectively punished, depending on political alliances.

Qin's imposition of the "Feudal county system" over the older "Slave-holding fiefdom system" resembles the modern West's promotion of democracy over outdated autocratic systems.

4. Talent and Resource Attraction

Qin was open to foreign talent, employing skilled individuals regardless of their origin — figures like Lü Buwei and Li Si were influential foreigners in the Qin court. Similarly, the U.S. and Europe attract global talent to fuel their development, mirroring Qin's openness. This contrasts with some states during the Warring States period, which limited key positions to other natives and clung to conservative policies, much like some nations today that restrict immigration or isolate themselves economically.

5. Modern Geopolitical Alliances and Conflicts

Today's geopolitical situation, especially the strategic rivalry between the USA/EU (Qi/Qin) and Russia/China (Yan/Zhao), mirrors the ancient Warring States era. The U.S. and its allies, representing the "Horizontal alliance", face opposition from Russia and China, which lead a "Vertical alliance" of nations in Africa, the Middle East, and South Asia. These regions — analogous to Wei, Han, and Chu — are battlegrounds where both alliances seek influence through economic aid, political alignment, and military presence.

For instance, the U.S. and Europe have focused on gaining footholds in regions like South Asia, the Middle East, and Africa by aligning with countries like India, Israel, and South Africa. Meanwhile, China and Russia attempt to strengthen their own alliances in these areas through economic cooperation and military partnerships, much like the shifting alliances in the Warring States period.

However, the "Vertical alliance" led by China and Russia is fragile. These nations often harbor deep-seated historical grievances, as seen in the tensions between China and Russia over past territorial disputes. This situation resembles the uneasy alliance between Zhao and Yan during the Warring States period, where cooperation was based more on mutual interest than genuine trust. The West is well aware of this fragility and uses opportunities to weaken these alliances through diplomatic and economic strategies, as seen during the Cold War when China and the U.S. briefly allied against the Soviet Union.

6. Division and Fragmentation Risks

In recent years, Russia has faced increasing pressure from the West, with NATO forces now stationed near its eastern borders, akin to Qin's encroachments on Zhao and Yan. Similarly, China faces internal and external challenges: the status of Taiwan, Hong Kong, and Macau remains contentious, and there are ongoing separatist movements in regions like Xinjiang and Tibet. This parallels the instability "Zhao" faced when surrounded by stronger and more unified adversaries.

As the modern world moves towards potential unification, led by the Western powers, the question remains, will this unification come through gradual integration, as seen in the peaceful spread of technology and culture, or will it involve more aggressive tactics, akin to Qin's eventual conquest of its rivals? History suggests that while peaceful strategies may delay conflict, the struggle for dominance often leads to eventual confrontation, just as it did in ancient China.

V. Reasons for Global Unification

From a broader perspective of societal development, Europe and the Americas represent the advancement of world civilization ---- championing values like "Freedom, Democracy, and the rule of law". These democratic parliamentary systems resemble how the state of "Qin" symbolized progress during the Warring States period, with its "Centralized county system". While the combined military might and weaponry of the other six states far exceeded that of Qin, none could stop Qin's advance. Why was this the case?

1. Strength of Systems and Ideals Over Military Might

A nation's true strength lies not in the size of its military or its arsenal but in the "Direction of its societal and institutional development" and the "Alignment with the people's will". Qin's victory stemmed from its "Superior governance system" and its ability to rally people under a clear, forward-thinking vision. Today, while Russia and China may possess military and economic strength comparable to Western powers, they find themselves on the defensive, unable to protect their borders or hold sway over neighboring countries. Why? Because "People, including their own citizens, increasingly look to the West", seeking to study and live under more advanced systems.

Qin's open attitude to absorbing people from other states was epitomized by its leader, Ying Zheng (The future First Emperor), who welcomed foreigners with open arms: "Anyone who enters Qin becomes a Qin citizen. We have advanced ideas here; come to Zhengguo Canal, and we will provide seeds and livestock". This level of openness and inclusivity won the hearts of people across different regions, drawing talent and labor from everywhere.

In contrast, Russia and China have sought to "Restrict their own populations", building barriers like the "Berlin Wall" in the past and "Internet firewalls" today to prevent the free flow of ideas. Both countries once had deep cultural traditions that championed "Freedom, democracy, and the rule of law" ------- concepts they now suppress, while paradoxically adhering to Western doctrines like Marxism. This self-imposed isolation has weakened them over time, as seen with the "Collapse of the Soviet Union", which shrank from a global superpower into a fragmented collection of smaller states.

2. Global Unification as the Ultimate Outcome

If current trends continue, with Russia and China further weakened, the West, led by Europe, the U.S., and Australia, could achieve a global unification on par with Qin's historic feat of uniting China. The West has already "Linked three major regions, Europe, the Americas, and Australia" and strategically placed allies like "South Africa, Israel, and India" to secure control over Africa, the Middle East, and South Asia. This alignment leaves Russia and China boxed into a corner, facing isolation.

While Russia and China have invested vast amounts of money and resources in developing advanced weaponry, including significant nuclear arsenals, they are left with a daunting question: "Where can they use these weapons?" The global reach of Western influence has penetrated nearly every region, making direct conflict nearly impossible without severe consequences for themselves. This parallels how Zhao and Yan, despite having comparable military strength to Qin, could not mount an effective resistance.

3. The Role of Leadership and Systems

In ancient China, the state of Yan, recognizing its inability to confront Qin militarily, blamed the unification drive on "Qin Shi Huang" himself, leading to assassination attempts like that of "Jing Ke". But was the unification of China really the product of one man's ambition, or was it the inevitable result of Qin's superior governance system? The lesson from history suggests that it was Qin's "Institutional strength" , its open policies, its embrace of reforms, and its strategic vision, that allowed it to triumph, not just the leadership of one individual.

Similarly, today's global political landscape is not determined solely by the actions of individual leaders but by the"Superiority of the systems" in place. Western democracies, with their focus on "Individual freedoms, rule of law, and institutional openness", offer a path forward that resonates with the desires of people around the world. These values have a natural "Magnetism", drawing people away from more closed, authoritarian systems.

In summary, while military power and economic strength are crucial, the key to unification lies in "Civilizational direction and institutional progress". The Western democratic system, much like Qin's centralized governance model, has demonstrated that a "Unified, advanced political system" can ultimately achieve dominance, not through brute force, but by appealing to the aspirations and values of people across the world. If China and Russia continue to resist this trend, they risk being further fragmented and weakened, paving the way for a Western-led global order, much like Qin's unification of the Warring States.

VI. The Failure of Global Unification

Is now the right time to unify the world? Has the moment arrived? History suggests that even if all nations were rapidly united under a powerful military force, they would eventually fracture again. The world has been unified multiple times before, by the "Roman Empire", the "Persian Empire", the "Mongol Empire" , yet these empires all soon split apart. The reason for this lies in "Culture": these empires were unable to unify the diverse cultures of the world. The people did not accept the cultures of Rome, Persia, or Mongolia, and as soon as the empire weakened, it disintegrated.

In modern history, military dictatorships like "Nazi Germany" under Hitler and "Imperial Japan" also tried to use ideologies like the "Greater European Co-Prosperity Sphere" or the "Greater East Asia Co-Prosperity Sphere" to unify surrounding nations through both cultural influence and war, but they too failed.

In ancient China, "Qin" conquered and unified the six other states using force and by imposing its governance system, "The county system", over the previous "Feudal aristocratic system". Yet, just a few decades later, Qin's empire quickly crumbled. "Xiang Yǔ （项羽）", the warlord of Western Chu, attempted to restore the Enfeoffment system, but “Liu Bang”, the founder of the “Han Dynasty”, recognized that Qin's reforms had moved too quickly. He adopted a hybrid system, “One half enfeoffment, one half centralized rule”, but this left the seeds of future rebellion, as seen in the “Rebellion of the Seven States” during the reign of Emperor “Jing” of Han.

1. Can the West Unify the World with Its "Institutional Power"?

“Institutional Power” refers to the “Democratic parliamentary system” of the West, which reduces centralized authority, weakens the power of heads of state, abolishes lifetime leadership, and replaces autocracy with multi-party elections. This system has forced early Western monarchs to relinquish power, such as the British Queen and the Japanese Emperor, both of whom are now figureheads with no real political authority, confined to ceremonial roles in their respective palaces.

2. "Military and Economic Power"

After the Western powers decisively defeated the fascist regimes of Hitler's Germany and Imperial Japan, they turned their military and economic focus to the global stage. Over time, they have pressured countries across “Asia and Eastern Europe” to adopt more open economic systems. Many of these regions have indeed shifted towards “Western-style economies”. In recent years, the West has continued to use military means to overthrow and dismantle “Authoritarian theocratic regimes in the Middle East”, further pushing for global economic integration and unification.

3. Can the West Unify the World with "Cultural Power"?

While the Roman, Persian, and Mongol empires were unable to unify the world culturally, what does the West offer in terms of cultural unification today? Some argue that "Science, technology, and Hollywood" represent modern Western cultural tools. Before considering these, we should first examine the West's core cultural values, "Freedom, democracy, and the rule of law", which they heavily promote.

Upon closer analysis, however, we find that these concepts are not Western inventions at all. Much like the "Idea of communism" or "Wealth redistribution", these values actually originate from "Ancient Chinese philosophy". The Chinese emperors, however, preferred to suppress ideas like "Freedom, democracy, and the rule of law", choosing instead to promote loyalty to the emperor and patriotism. When these Chinese ideas reached Europe during the "Renaissance", Western philosophers eagerly embraced them, modifying and rebranding them to suit their own purposes, and then promoting them widely through media.

For instance, during the "Spring and Autumn" and "Warring States" periods in China, "Daoism", "Confucianism", and "Legalism" all contained elements that are strikingly similar to Western concepts:

- Daoism's "The Dao follows nature" mirrors the idea of "Freedom" and non-interference.
- Confucianism's "The people are the most important, the state comes second, and the ruler comes last" is a version of "Democratic principles" and benevolent governance.

- Legalism in Qin was the precursor to modern "Rule of law".

- Even the idea of "Wealth redistribution" (e.g., "Sharing wealth with the poor" and "Communism") originated from early Chinese rebellions led by figures like "Li Shun (李顺)" and "Wang Xiao Bo (王小波)".

As for the West's primary faith, "Christianity", it did not originate there either, but came from the"Jewish tradition". This belief system has struggled to gain acceptance even within Islam, much less within "Buddhist" or "Eastern cultures". From a Chinese perspective, Western Christian faith is often viewed as a combination of "Magic" and "Prophecy", with semi-literate religious leaders who, compared to the scholars of the 《I Ching》 or 《Dao De Jing》, fall far short in philosophical rigor. Christianity, seen as a form of "Monotheistic worship", has failed to unify civilizations across the globe and has led to millennia of conflict.

Western "Science and technology", though sometimes seen as the key to unification, can be viewed merely as a modern improvement on Qin's standardization efforts, like the "Unification of weights and measures". While these innovations are important, they are not enough to bring about cultural unification on their own.

4. The Limits of Western Cultural Influence

In essence, most of the ideas that might be used to unify the world today, whether in science, technology, or social philosophy, are modern adaptations of "Ancient Chinese thought", rebranded by the West. For example, the "Concept of duality" (Yin-Yang) has been transformed into Western "Dialectics". None of these are true Western creations. The West's only true innovation that has achieved widespread success is its "Institutional progress", particularly the "Democratic parliamentary system". Though it had its roots in ancient Greece, it was later refined and expanded by figures like "George Washington" and "Abraham Lincoln".

This system has indeed "Defeated many of the world's monarchies and authoritarian regimes", including those in "Germany, Italy, and Japan", and has forced most countries to adopt at least some form of "Open governance". The world has become shaped by this system.

However, even if the West succeeds in spreading its "Democratic parliamentary system" across the globe, it is unlikely to "Unify the diverse cultures" of the world. Western culture is still far from achieving global acceptance. As mentioned earlier, "Christian civilization" has been unable to unify the world, even if Western military and economic power could dominate.

The persistence of "Islamic countries" that maintain their own distinct cultural and political identities, despite adopting democratic systems, exemplifies this issue. For example, "Turkey" is a democracy, yet continues to resist full cultural integration with the West.

5. Conclusion

The ultimate failure of global unification lies in the "Inability to unify cultures". While the West may have succeeded in promoting its "Institutional systems" and using military and economic power to influence much of the world, its "Cultural influence" remains limited. As long as diverse cultures, religions, and traditions exist, true global unification will remain out of reach, and, as history has shown with past empires, the world may once again fragment.

VII. Chinese-style Unification

Unifying the world involves winning over people's hearts, not just conquering nations. A powerful superpower might be able to sweep through smaller countries with its military, but unifying nations doesn't mean winning the hearts and minds of all people and cultures.

From the current global landscape of ideas and cultures, the West has unified measurement standards through science and technology, partially unified language with English, and even embraced concepts like "Freedom, democracy, and the rule of law" which were originally inspired by ancient Chinese thought. However, core Western cultural aspects like Christianity are far from being able to unify Eastern civilizations, suggesting the conditions for global unification are not yet mature.

Historically, China has never been a dominant military power. The northern Xiongnu were a constant threat, and during the Spring and Autumn Period, China had over 170 small states with different measurements, languages, ideas, and cultures. Yet, Qin managed to unify these disparate entities. How did Qin achieve unification of thought and culture?

1. Cultural Unification

During the Spring and Autumn period, numerous scholars contributed to their respective philosophies, including:

- Confucianism (Confucius, Mencius, Xunzi): Emphasizing propriety, benevolence, virtue, and democratic governance. Their works, such as 《The Analects》, 《Mencius》, and 《Xunzi》, advocated moral governance, akin to modern democratic values and support for a global body like the United Nations.

- Daoism (《Laozi》, 《Zhuangzi》, 《Liezi》): Focusing on the nature of the universe and natural order, with concepts of freedom and non-intervention. Today, this represents the philosophy of "Freedom" in society.

- Legalism (Han Feizi, Li Si, Shang Yang): Advocating for governance by law, treating everyone equally under the law. This became the foundation for modern Western legal systems.

These scholars advised their respective rulers on how to unify China, contributing original ideas about Freedom, Democracy, and the rule of law ------- concepts that would later be echoed in Western philosophy.

Additionally, thinkers like the “Diplomatists” (Guiguzi, Su Qin, Zhang Yi) and “Yin-Yang School” (Zou Yan) influenced practical strategies for governance, while “Mohism” (Mozi) promoted universal love and meritocracy, which were later adopted by Western religious doctrines.

In practical fields, military strategists like “Sunzi”, medical experts like “Bian Que”, and engineers like “Zheng Guo” provided Qin with technological advantages. These contributions illustrate that most original philosophical and practical ideas emerged from ancient Chinese thought during this period.

Qin's chancellor, “Lü Buwei”, compiled the 《Lüshi Chunqiu》 to integrate various schools of thought, laying the theoretical foundation for Qin's unification, similar to how modern global thinkers try to synthesize philosophies today.

2. Advanced Institutions

In book《Universal Law》, it's explained that human society evolves through stages: "Primitive chieftainship, Slave-based enfeoffment, Centralized feudalism, Democratic parliamentary systems, and eventually, Global unification." Regardless of how scholars might attempt to revise history, the course of societal evolution cannot be reversed.

At the time, "Li Si" of Qin championed centralized feudalism over the slave-based enfeoffment system. His advocacy for a unified administrative system mirrors the efforts of "Washington" and "Lincoln" in the United States to establish a new democratic system in opposition to British colonial feudalism. Just as the U.S. broke free from British rule to form a democratic nation, Qin rejected the outdated enfeoffment structures in favor of a more centralized and advanced governance model.

3. The Burning of Books and the Execution of Scholars

When Qin unified China, some conservative scholars insisted on promoting the old slave-based enfeoffment system and opposed the new centralized system. They praised the ancient Zhou kings and argued that reforms should proceed more cautiously, suggesting a two-system model with partial decentralization and partial central authority.

Today, similarly, some scholars praise outdated systems, resist full modernization, and argue against adopting Western democratic models. This echoes the conservative resistance in Qin times, which led "Qin Shi Huang" to order the burning of books and the execution of scholars. His goal was to decisively move away from the outdated enfeoffment system and fully embrace centralized governance, a bold move toward modernization for its time.

This is analogous to current political strategies, where partial reforms and experimental zones represent hesitant steps toward broader societal change. The idea of a "Two-system" approach isn't new; it's an ancient strategy dating back to the Qin dynasty.

While "Qin Shi Huang" did burn historical records, it's important to note that key works from ancient Chinese thinkers were preserved, and the regime's actions were focused on eliminating conservative resistance rather than wiping out intellectual heritage. In today's context, some contemporary scholars produce low-quality work that lacks innovation, serving only to promote the status quo.

4. Utilizing Philosophers, Not Religious Leaders

Western history is filled with religious leaders and prophets, such as those from Christianity, Islam, and Buddhism, who sought to win followers and establish religious dominance. These religions can be a significant barrier to global unification, as their beliefs can clash with each other. In contrast, during the Spring and Autumn period, Chinese philosophy was grounded in human-centered thinking, focusing on practical governance rather than supernatural intervention.

After the "Renaissance", Western philosophers borrowed heavily from Chinese concepts like "Freedom, democracy, and the rule of law." Western political movements, such as "Marxism", also drew from ancient Chinese ideas of wealth redistribution. However, these ideas were often modified and packaged as Western innovations, much like today's reverse appropriation of Western technology in some Eastern countries.

5. Unifying Law, Language, and Standards

Qin replaced the legal systems of other states with a unified legal code, standardized written language (Using Small Seal Script), and introduced standardized weights and measures, effectively creating a cohesive society. This mirrors today's Western dominance in global legal norms, the widespread use of English, and the standardization of scientific and technological practices across the world.

In China, the unified written language (Chinese characters) transcended regional dialects and helped integrate the country's 170 small states into one nation. While the pronunciation may have differed, the written form created a shared understanding.

In essence, ancient Chinese philosophers were far more advanced in their thinking than many contemporary scholars. Most of today's humanistic studies are reinterpretations or misrepresentations of ancient Chinese philosophies, which have stood the test of time. China's "Jixia Academy（稷下学宫）" in the state of Qi was comparable to today's "Ivy League schools", fostering intellectual discourse and progress.

VIII. Predictions for the Future Political System

The work that Europe and the U.S. are currently engaged in is essentially what Qin undertook in its time: striving for unification, even if it means war and casualties. Back then, corrupt rulers of fragmented states denounced Qin as "Tyrannical", claiming their people had "Suffered long under Qin". Qin's laws disrupted the "Feudal slave-lord system" that had kept many small states stable. Today, America plays a similar role, challenging and destabilizing feudal and autocratic states globally, especially in the Middle East, where authoritarian regimes bemoan that they've "Suffered long under America".

However, who truly represents the progressive direction of world civilization? In ancient times, it was Qin; today, it is the U.S. and Europe. Just as Qin unified the warring states, the Western world has brought the world to this level of unification. Social progress is not easy; it doesn't move forward incrementally but rather in leaps, each leap marked by bloody lessons.

When Zhao defied Qin's unification efforts, it encouraged its army to resist, resulting in the mass burial of 400,000 Zhao soldiers, yet Zhao still fell. In the 20th century, Germany under Hitler and Japan under its emperor tried to use autocratic feudalism to dominate the world militarily, but in the end, it was Europe and America's "Democratic parliamentary system" and two atomic bombs that triumphed.

Today, backward nations no longer dare to confront Europe and the U.S. militarily. Even if they are discontent, their resistance is limited to constructing barriers like the Berlin Wall, isolating themselves, or stoking anti-Western sentiment through propaganda. Despite having large armies and nuclear weapons, these nations understand that confronting Europe and the U.S. would result in mass casualties and eventual defeat, much like the six ancient Chinese states against Qin.

Consequently, countries today have chosen to follow Europe and the U.S., labeling it "Reform and opening up," which translates to opening their markets to the West and reforming their political systems to avoid war and death. By aligning with the West, these nations reduce external pressure and ease internal conflicts, leading to political stability, market prosperity, and gradual national strength.

But if a government chooses to defy the West, isolating itself from global development, it risks becoming like North Korea or Iran, or worse, the Axis powers of Germany, Italy, and Japan in WWII, which were devastated. A country that resists the West is bound to face fragmentation and decline, much like the Soviet Union.

It's crucial to understand that military power is ultimately ineffective in this context because this is not a war of weapons but of civilization. Following the path of civilization allows a nation to grow strong without developing advanced weaponry, while rejecting it leads to eventual destruction. Europe and the U.S. will never allow any nation to challenge their "Democratic parliamentary system" with "Feudal centralized power". As long as there are nations that do not adopt Democratic parliamentary systems, Europe and the U.S. will continue to wage war until global unification is achieved under this model.

It's important to note that while the Soviet Union was crushed by Western systems and eventually had to follow them, Russia, due to its linguistic and cultural similarities to the West, was more easily assimilated. However, China, along with Japan and Korea, possesses a unique language system (Ideographic characters), which is culturally distinct from the West. This cultural difference has created a delayed, hidden opportunity for China. While the West found it easy to assimilate the Soviet Union, assimilating China is much more difficult.

Once the West has exhausted its efforts to unify the world into a "Democratic parliamentary system" through war and coercion, its task will be complete, and its direction and momentum will vanish. When the world operates entirely under the same standards, like Qin's unification of measurement and law, what comes next? Just as Qin, after unifying the six states, lost its momentum and eventually crumbled, the Western democratic parliamentary system is not the ultimate system, just a step beyond feudal autocracy. Similarly, Qin's feudal county system was not perfect, just a better alternative to the old slave-lord system.

The West has waged countless wars, with innumerable deaths, to unify the world into its current state, yet it still cannot achieve total global unification. Like Qin laying the groundwork for the Han dynasty's eventual unification of China, today's Western systems have set the stage for the next step. And what can truly unify the world is not political systems or warfare but culture, specifically the Han Chinese civilization's "Universal Law of the Galactic Civilization".

Just as the Han dynasty completed China's unification without warfare, China today will achieve global unification through culture, not through endless wars. This fulfills both Western and Chinese prophecies: that China is the "Middle Kingdom", the world's cultural and intellectual center, with the "Universal Law of the Galactic Civilization" providing the ideological framework for future global governance. In the future, all peoples will consider themselves part of the "Middle Kingdom", just as no one today claims to be a descendant of the war-torn Qin dynasty, but many proudly identify as "Han Chinese."

How, then, will China unify the world? Through culture and civilization, not by adopting Western Marxist imitations. If China relies on Western ideologies, it will struggle even to unify Hong Kong and Taiwan. Chinese ancestors already laid the groundwork for a unified culture and theoretical system during the Spring and Autumn and Warring States periods, with concepts like "Freedom, democracy, and rule of law" originating in China. "Wealth redistribution" was an original idea from ancient Chinese uprisings, emphasizing equality and justice, far more resonant than the borrowed Western term "Communism".

Now, with the emergence of the "Universal Law of the Galactic Civilization" system, China's cultural civilization has easily and thoroughly unified the globe. On the other hand, Western culture cannot unify Chinese civilization. Even if the West were to militarily conquer all of China's territory and dismantle the state, it still could not erase Chinese civilization, and in the end, the West would be assimilated by it, just as the Mongol empire was.

China's civilization has already culturally unified the world. All that remains is for a future Chinese government to adopt the "Unified Republican System", an evolution of ancient governance models that extends from "Primitive abdication, Slave enfeoffment, and Centralized feudalism, to the Democratic parliamentary system". By doing so, China can easily outpace the West in governance and unify the world, as already outlined in numerous theoretical works.

Once global unification is achieved, a single global military force, perhaps the "UN Army", "Earth Army", or "Solar System Army", will manage interstellar competition. Local governments will be dissolved, borders, firewalls, and trade barriers eliminated, and free publication and media will be established globally. Until then, the most advanced system is the "Democratic parliamentary system", and no country today is a true "Republic", merely a reflection of current ruling ideologies.

"Feudal county systems" were China's original contribution, surpassing early Western models; "Democratic parliamentary systems" were the West's innovation, surpassing the East. Now, the "Unified Republican System" from the East will surpass the West, representing a significant step forward in the evolution of human governance. No matter the methods or even war, this shift will occur, and all global management and theoretical systems will follow this transformation.

And the nation most likely to fulfill this grand vision is China, with its ideographic "Universal Law" and "Pyramid Civilization". This was foretold by Nostradamus in 《Les Prophéties》.

At that time, books about the "Democratic parliamentary system" will be thrown into the trash, and professors from prestigious Western universities will be swiftly eliminated, just as Qin Shi Huang burned books praising the old feudal systems. Future "Unified Republican Systems" will concentrate power (With the UN controlling weapons and military), opposing the current decentralized "Democratic parliamentary systems" (Which allow individual countries to maintain militaries).

IX. Summary

The evolution of governance over the past 6,000 years has followed a path from Primitive chieftainships to Slave-based enfeoffment, Centralized feudalism, and now Democratic parliamentary systems. The West has advanced beyond Eastern monarchies, but true global unification will require the next step: the "Unified Republican System" based on the "Universal Law of the Galactic Civilization", which transcends the current systems. After unifying Earth, humankind will extend its governance to the stars, creating an intergalactic civilization in the millennia to come.

(Original in March 2021, some picture network, purely academic, no political affiliation)

References: 1. Sima Qian: 《Historical Records》

C15. Eastern Galactic Civilization Vaccine Specifically Treats Western Stellar Civilization Virus

Abstract : Most diseases in the world can be cured in hospitals, but Western religious viruses are currently the largest source of cancer and mental illnesses. They often mutate and are very difficult to treat. They develop churches, believers, and organizations, spread lies, block streets, worship, collect money, kill people, and spread corruption, and promote false, big, and empty brainwashing slogans, which are truly asymptomatic sources of infection.

The outbreak and constant mutation of the coronavirus in 2020 are the warnings from the heavens to the people of the Earth, predicting that the "Western Stellar Civilization" religious viruses operate and kill people in this way. So the spread of these viruses can be cured, and the mental illness and worshippers can be cured, the most effective is isolation and vaccines, to isolate believers, and use the vaccinate of the "Eastern Galactic Civilization". With the existence of this vaccine, humans on earth will be immune for life.

I. Introduction

History will prove that 2012 was an important turning point in civilization. It marked the end of the "Western Stellar Civilization" and the birth of the "Eastern Galactic Civilization", which corresponds to the predictions of the Mayan civilization. The global social system and people's thinking are changing. The entire human civilization is also evolving and improving.

At present, the highest stage of the evolution and development of "Stellar Civilization", some good things have been created in the past, such as the "Democratic parliament" system. The global society has reached consensus, but the biggest threat is the possession of religious viruses. And variants, which have been infected for thousands of years, often occur repeatedly, constantly changing form and evolution, bullying the weak, and turning most religious fanatics into mental illness and war cannon fodder. They are also very cunning. They often pretend to be advanced, truthful and scientific, and they are the greatest threat to war and mankind. But Western viruses are viruses. They are by no means good cells. Only Eastern vaccines can be used to eradicate them completely.

II. Western Stellar civilization, viral mental illness, dark forces

“Western Stellar Civilization”, were brought by Mr. Copernicus, and later with the help of Chinese original "Taoism, Confucianism and Legalism" (Western adapted into "Freedom, democracy and legal system"), coupled with the original "City-state parliament" system of ancient Greece (Renamed "Democratic parliament" system in the West) to achieve global leader. We have also talked about it many times in previous articles, but this article only talks about the religious viruses and cancers created by the West in the past, and the harm that these viruses have caused to the world.

All scholars in the modern world have conducted research and proceeded from the perspective of sociology. A country, organization, party, or group uses science, power, money, religion, marriage, healing, and death as a guise to treat people and believers physically and mentally. The government control, and then closed information, propaganda and brainwashing the people, and finally obtained the unconditional allegiance of the people and believers, causing harm to society, freedom, health, and education, that is, "Social religious mental illness, cancer, and viruses".

1. Major viral mental illnesses in Western religions

Although the early Western religions came from some prophecies, and the leaders were also figures who understood prophecies and played a role in spiritual development in history. However, afterwards, churches were established and a large number of believers and organizations were formed. It has become a "Social virus and cancer", and a large number of cults and patients with mental illness have also been produced. They worshipped idols and made money, used their beliefs and money to develop organizations, imprisoned the minds of believers, worshiped the leader, and caused a large number of broken families and innocent deaths of believers. The head of the church defrauded money with truth and kindness, forced believers to be fighter in the name of anti-church, causing a large number of innocent people to suffer huge losses of life and property, causing the believers to be killed or suicide, or causing serious harm social order, violation of law, and extinction of humanity.

According to rough statistics, for thousands of years, Western cults have gathered crowds to worship, obstruct the streets to distribute propaganda materials, develop and establish various organizations and parties, use underworld evil principles to kill people, fake witchcraft spirits to spread social viruses, suppress the truth of information, and earn money. Cause the death of hundreds of millions of innocent people.

1) One of the major western religious viral mental illnesses ------ Islam

Islam is a "Social mental illness virus and cancer" derived from early Christianity in the West. Later, it grew and grew through murder and random reproduction. This religion is conservative and stubborn. Forcing a woman's face to be covered, failure to comply will be severely punished. In addition, they began to instill Allah from their children, preaching that God is the only one, oppressing people to lose independent thinking, and adopting policies of assimilation and extermination against infidels. Although its leader, Muhammad, had no culture, he knew some prophecies and claimed to be an angelic God who taught the 《Quran》. When preaching, he held the Quran in one hand and a knife in the other.

Imams, Mullahs, etc. were the religious leaders in the later development of this church, vigorously promoting grassroots organizations and agencies, deceiving believers, establishing terrorist organizations, threatening and oppressing other Churches and non-believers. This Church uses turbans and food to divide the non-belief masses. Many foods that were loved by other ethnic groups, but they were forced into "Halal" food by the believers to support the economic activities of the church. This Islam teaching controls the freedom of speech, banning books, newspapers and periodicals that are unfavorable to this teaching, and even killing authors and editors. Hundreds of millions of people have died as a result of this teaching's persecution.

Like all churches in the West, they were a little inspirational at the beginning, and they fell into a murderous group in the later period. The derivative religions of modern Islam have been recognized as cults, including: Osama bin Laden's Islamic al-Qaeda, ISIS religious extremist organization and Hamas extreme right organizations have killed countless civilians.

2) Second of the spiritual diseases of major Western religions virus ----- Buddhist

This teaching guru Sakyamuni also know some prophecy, but also the beginning of practice and focus on sentiment, some early development of the law of self-cultivation, but did not leave text, And later generations of believers just record his quotations. The Monks, Lamas developed by this church later used the so-called consecration and shaved heads to separate from the ordinary people, used the Monks to destabilize the family, established a system of worship and defrauding money, and then branched out many sects and led to a large number of cults.

In recent years, meditation, fitness, and Qigong have been opened up, mainly focusing on gathering crowds and deceiving, using fake trusts to cure illness and truthfulness, claiming "Dafa" fraudulently, putting evil things on believers, exercising mental control, and parading for the birthday of the derivative masters, blocking the streets to distribute propaganda materials and using temples to share the spoils. The leader Shakyamuni also predicted that this is the end of the teachings. It is no longer possible to teach people. At this time, most of the methods of self-cultivation are low-level and ignorant. It seems that the interest in money is far greater than the pursuit of rights. After being suppressed by the government, they began to set themselves on fire and conduct anti-government activities.

The evolution of Buddhism through the ages is similar to that of Islam. It has become more and more degenerate and has spawned many cults. In the early days, there was the "Yi guan dao", which killed many people by worship and lies. In modern times, there are still activities, mainly gathering overseas or in small families. Many countries are wary of them. There are also many evil sects that use so-called fitness, meditation, Qigong, consecration, dharma and other activities to gather crowds, accumulate wealth, and block the streets. The more controversial ones include:

Lu XX , True Buddha Sect, founded by American Chinese, "Lingxian True Buddha", he advertised himself as "living Buddha" and "Buddha master".

Shi XX, Guanyin Method was founded by Chinese-British in Taiwan. He advertised himself as "Supreme Master Ching Hai", equivalent to Sakyamuni, Jesus Christ, Allah, etc.

Li XX, the master of Falun Gong, claims to be the "Lord Buddha of the Universe". He can put wheels in the belly of believers to achieve mental control. Some believers are actually brainwashed to see whether there is a "Wheel". Claiming that you don't need to see a doctor if you are sick.

Most of these modern evil sects rely on Buddhism, or take out some of the prophecies or scriptures of Buddhism to slander and deceive, just like the devil said to the Buddha: "Put on your monk's clothes, cross-legged lotus seat like you, shouting for truth and goodness, even changed his birthday to your Buddha's birthday, pretending to be a Buddha, enticing people to teach, and gathering crowds to collect money". The Buddha suddenly burst into tears and was speechless.

Because it is the last Age of the Dharma, there are many derivative cult masters who distort Buddhism and Buddhist scriptures everywhere. The writing and structure of the writings are messy, and the theory is both no innovative and plagiarized. It is because the articles of the derivative masters are all deceived believers of the Dharma, and some believers. If some believers are fake doctors and professors, the cult master can't drop prices in front of believers, boasting that they are a God and have beautiful writing. Some have been banned by the government and then began to oppose the government, using believers to form opposition parties and refugees to apply for gathering popularity, or relying on political activities from foreign governments to make money.

3) Third of viral mental illness of major Western religions ------ Christianity.

This religion started from the prophecies of various schools of Judaism. Through the collection of early prophecies of Judaism, it brought out the leader Jesus. He has a bit of prophecy and can gather people with words. There is no theory and writing ability. Christianity, Catholicism, and Orthodox churches are basically the promotion of primitive Judaism.

The "Old Testament" of the 《Bible》 is a book of prophecies in Judaism, written by many prophets, at least to the words, or some prophecies and here will not be described in detail. However, the "New Testament" is a post-compilation. It is a story written by believers to their leader and the believer's missionary story, or it is more appropriate to simply call it "The master's biography". This "Biography of the leader" is mainly used to gather people to worship the leader, develop the church of believers, teach how to collect money and grow the church very professionally, and later become more and more extreme and evil, and use religion to judge and kill people. The original Judaism of the 《Bible》 simply did not believe in the so-called false "New Testament" later.

Because the leaders of Christianity, Islam, and Buddhism have no ability to write, their theoretical starting point is relatively low. Except for gathering people, including all derivative sects developed in the later period, they mainly rely on the praise of believers to start, but from the current direction of Christian reform, it is indeed better than what Islam and Buddhism do, at least following the modern civilization and democracy of the West, it is slowly changing.

The main evils are the pastors, priests, developed in the later period of this religion. They are all pimps of Christianity. They use prophecies (Old Testament) and the so-called miracles of the "Master's biography" to deceive and develop believers. In history, they encouraged worship and used the so-called God to judge civilians, causing countless public deaths. Many true scientists and philosophers have been judged by religion or died of persecution by Christ or Catholicism, such as Galileo and Bruno. Their perverse practices have also led out many cults, such as Islam.

Recognized cults derived from modern Christianity include: People's Temple, Aum Shinrikyo, Sons and Daughters of God (Family of Love), David Tribe, Sun Temple, Rajneesh Retreat, etc. They encourage ignorant believers to worship and suicide.

China's clear cult organizations include: Almighty God (Eastern Lightning), Shouters, Apprenticeships, All-Scope Churches, Lingling Churches, New Testament Churches, Bishops, Kings, Same Religion, Three Servants, and Sons and Daughters of Heavenly Father , Damien Missionary Church, World Elijah Missionary Church, etc.

2. Late Western super mutant religious virus mental illness

1) The Nazi Mutant Party

It is a super-religious mutant virus developed in the later period of Western society. Like the mutant virus that came out in India this year, it is more toxic, centralized and authoritarian, and is called "Nazi religious variant viruses", they suppress democratic ideas, control propaganda, establish military organizations and black-handed parties, wars and kill countless people. The main opponents are Judaism and the Communist Party of the Soviet Union.

2) Racial ignorance and variant virus

They are another variant of the virus in modern times in the West, which discriminates against different races, cultures and beliefs. For example, Hitler discriminates against and slaughters Jews in Germany; whites, blacks and Asians discriminate each other. In addition, in India, their religious groups use witchcraft and cults to kill people. For example, they gather crowds to jump into the foul-smelling Ganges, drink virus-laden water, pour poisonous cow dung on their bodies, do not use paper to defecate, refuse to wear masks, and do not trust doctors. Believe that witchcraft and Gods can fight viruses. This variant virus is called "Racial ignorance variant virus".

3) Philosophy variant virus

Originally, the spirit of philosophy is to explore the origin of society and human nature to make people wise, but the pseudo-philosophy in the West is to put true philosophy into practical use to transform society and oppress human nature. Like Marx and Lenin put philosophy becomes religion, establishes pseudo-religious regimes and parties, propagates lies, and develops brain disability and mental illness. Because the Western false philosophical theoretical systems are not perfect and inferior, they are basically plagiarisms from the East. They can only establish the system of the feudal emperors in the East or the church regime, causing disasters on the Earth, especially the false ones like the former Soviet Union and North Korea. In a philosophical communist country, thousands of people have died from communist religious persecution, and China has also suffered greatly.

Early Western pseudo-philosophical viruses and cancer came from the two big liars, Marx and Engels, who copied and translated Chinese philosophical original classics, and then further processed them, turning these slogans and false philosophical theories into beautiful butterfly coats, which resembled early Western religions and the leader, they claimed to be perfect and attractive at first, and they also said some words that fool the public and the so-called right things, such as liberating the poor, calling for the armed revolution, dictatorship capitalists and landlords, etc., indeed incited many lower class people and dung. The resonance of this deceives the ignorant masses.

Lenin and Stalin of the former Soviet Union directly put the false philosophical theory of Marx and Engels crooks plagiarizing goods into practical use, calling on workers and peasants to take up arms to overthrow the feudal tsar, kill landlords and capitalists, and spread it to the world through the "Communist International" church system. The most affected are Eastern Europe and Asia. In fact, these so-called Western revolutions are just the same as the peasant uprisings of past dynasties in China. They were only put on the sheep's head cloak of proletarian theory, and then they were restored by a new generation of landlords and capitalists to establish a new dictatorship and feudal system.

These Russian Marxist-Leninist missionaries changed the title of "Priest" to "Secretary" and "Equity rich and poor" to "Communist", spreading lies all over the world, propagating violence, worship, corruption, dictatorship, and feudalism.

The Marxist-Leninists in the Soviet Union can rashly kill the landlords and capitalists, and it can also overthrow the Czarist dictatorship, but after the power is really seized, how to manage the country is no longer possible, because the theory of Marx swindlers cannot develop the economy at all, and the so-called state established is basically It is a big pot of rice, poverty and backwardness. In modern times, Eastern European countries and Asian countries were deceived by the theory of Marx swindlers and coerced by the Soviet Union's methods of power out of the gun. They followed suit. China suffered a lot from this and caused "Fifty years of turmoil" in the early years (From 1921 until 1978).

Around 1978, Mr. Deng Xiaoping of China first advocated reform and opening up, set aside chaos, and rehabilitated all the landlords and rich peasants who had been overthrown, and did not learn the theory of Marxist-Leninist dictatorship in the West and the Soviet Union. Mr. Deng opened the market to European and American countries and learned from the operation of economic capital in Europe and the United States. This also affected the chain reaction of Eastern European countries. They tore down the Berlin Wall, all separated from the "Soviet Union", and completely disintegrated the Soviet Union.

After the death of Mr. Deng Xiaoping, the later leaders continued to maintain Deng Xiaoping's policy unchanged, adhere to the market opening policy, not to learn from the Soviet Union, and to adhere to the scientific development concept and anti-corruption with Chinese characteristics, which made China gradually prosperous and powerful.

The Soviet Union changed the names of the pastors and priests of Western churches to new names, "The secretaries and party representatives" who are missionaries to spread Marx and cheaters to countries around the world. They have established Marx cheaters research institutes in universities (The so-called Confucius Institute) around the world to defraud money and spread lies, use the so-called proletarian dictatorship. Establish a feudal autocratic system. This church values power and turns missionaries into party officials at all levels, calling power bribes. This religion is fickle and self-boasting. Officials mainly arbitrage money directly from the treasury, not the dedication of believers, because party member fees are far from the corruption and profligacy of the secretaries. This teaching strictly controls public opinion and propaganda, and even kills the author. In history, this cult killed countless people. Party members called themselves steel fighters. Like "The Boxers", they claimed to be invulnerable. Hundreds of millions of people died innocently. It is one of the most dangerous and terrifying Western cults in the World today.

Modern derivative mental illnesses and viruses include Leninism, Stalinism, former Eastern Europe, North Korea, Cuba, Vietnam, and Cambodia's feudal dictatorships etc. If a country's government supports the spread of such Western cults and viral ideas and illegal organizations in the world, then the entire country will be corrupted, laws and credibility will be lacking, people's hearts will be scattered, and it will become an island surrounded by global democracies.

4) The Mental diseases variations of scientific weapons.

The western countries have always attached importance to the role of weapons. Although gunpowder was invented in China, after being introduced to the West, they quickly developed into powerful killing weapons. In modern times, some countries even shot and killed people casually on the streets, safeguarding the so-called "Freedom" of individuals.

The use of military weapons to unify the world, rather than the use of culture and civilization to unify the world, is a manifestation of the variant mental illness of Western religions. In the early years, Hitler of Germany and the Emperor of Japan incited a large number of cannon fodders and mental illness weapons scientists. The warlords of the five major military powers in the modern world and the warlords of small countries fought, and they all raised huge weapons and pseudo-scientists.

They helped warlord - separatist government from all over the world, build aircraft carriers, missiles, and nuclear weapons, just like the Chinese version period of “The Spring and Autumn and Warring States”, offensive each other, launching wars and killing countless people. In addition, due to the existence and influence of a large number of religious malignant tumours and philosophical variants in the Western world, the governments of warlord countries all over the world are very fearful and unstable. The superpowers had to use money and honour to recruit pseudo-scientists or imperial military technicians to defend their homes and maintain world peace, and various weapons were born one after another.

"Western stellar Civilization" spends a lot of money to develop weapons, the purpose is to prevent the intrusion and spread of cancerous Islam and Soviet communism. But on the contrary, these cancerous church countries are also worried about being wiped out by Christian democracies, so they vigorously develop lethal weapons and form a global arms race.

The original scientific spirit is to explore nature, but pseudo-scientists can only take exams, copy books, and make weapons. Although most people have outstanding academic qualifications such as doctors, academicians, researchers, and meritorious professors, they are truly no one for human progress, but only created nuclear weapons, virus weapons, and directed energy weapons to kill people, help evil warlord countries and governments spread variant cancers and viruses, and maintain the church's mental illness regime that produces cancer.

Because the pseudo-scientists also wanted to obtain money and status from the country's huge military expenditures, they hit it off. The money that could have been used to buy medical supplies, relief food and support poverty, was all colluded by the pseudo-church government and pseudo-scientists to store nuclear materials and create large-scale killing weapons threaten world peace and have caused hundreds of millions of people to starve and die. For example, the governments of North Korea and Iran have spent a lot of money on nuclear weapons, causing a large number of abnormal deaths of their citizens. They said It is so-called natural disaster.

True scientists in the East invented gunpowder for peaceful purposes, while pseudo-scientists in the West developed into murderous weapons. Early Western pseudo-scientists of mental illness murderers developed weapons, such as conventional weapons, Aircraft, Tanks, and artillery. The weapons created by modern pseudo-scientists derived from mental illnesses include nuclear weapons, biological and chemical weapons, and directed energy weapons.

3. Western cults and mental illnesses make up the countries

The major Western churches and derivative religions listed above have produced a large number of mental illnesses. These mentally ill patients have formed countries, so that most countries in the world today are divided by these Western religious mental illnesses, rather than by ethnic groups. For example, India and Pakistan are originally of the same race, but because of their different religious beliefs, they are forcibly divided into two countries; the same is true for North and South Korea. Christianity and Communism are divided into two military rivalries, while the countries in the Middle East are divided by Islam, Such as Sunnis and Shiites, there are constant wars.

The root cause of the world war is also reflected in the permanent members of the United Nations, the centre of world power. It was contested by three Western Christian countries (The United States, Britain, and France) and two Western communist countries (Russia, China). All world disputes discussed and resolved by major powers have become a confrontation between the two Western religious forces. The Communist forces alone have united with the Islamic forces to fight against the Christian forces in a large number of countries. In order to weaken the force of the two religions, the Christian forces must first strike at the weak Islam, turning the small Islamic countries around the world into a battlefield and losing countless lives.

The previous world wars were also caused by the four major Western religions, such as the First and Second World Wars, the Vietnam War, the Korean War, the Afghanistan War, the Iran-Iraq War, and the current Middle East War. One religious believer treats another religious believer as a terrorist, such as Hitler killing Jews and Soviets.

In summary, the "Western stellar Civilization" has evolved from an illiterate leader to a religion, from a religion to a cult organization, and from a cult organization to a national military regime. For the unified "Eastern Galactic Civilization", the practices of these "Western Stellar Civilizations" are illegal. There are currently only four major Western religions left, and their organizations are all illegal organizations and countries are composed of these illegal organizations. Countries are divided according to religion, so most of the religious countries in the world are illegal countries, including the five permanent members of the UN, which has also found the key to unify the countries of the world and solve the problem of illegal countries in the West.

First of all, it is necessary to solve the problems of Christianity and Communism. If it can be solved, the five permanent members of the United Nations can be merged and jointly solve all the problems in the world today, and there will be no more major wars.

If the problems of Christianity and Communism are solved, the problems of Christianity and Islam can be easily solved. As a result, Christian and Islamic countries can be merged, there will be no small wars, and Buddhist countries can easily merge, and all countries in the world can be merged, peacefully resolve all disputes around the world, and merge into the Galactic civilization.

Although it seems simple, it is difficult to completely solve all the problems of Western religions, because whether they are Christians, Islamic believers, Buddhists, or Communists, they all insist that their beliefs are correct, and they all claim that they are great, glorious and correct religions, and steel warriors can defeat any other religion, so

Western believers cannot solve their own problems by themselves. They will always only fight.

III. Eastern Galactic Civilization, wisdom vaccine, light forces

In the universe, if there are dark forces, there will be light forces. Although the "Stellar civilization" is shrouded by the dark forces of the West, the light forces of the East are constantly growing and fighting back. At present, the four major Western religious strains virus have eroded the human body around the world. Vaccines can only save lives and cannot guarantee that they will not be eroded.

This life-saving vaccine comes from the East. That's why all the prophets at China and overseas in history are looking forward to the emergence of Orientals to resolve the religious disputes of these Westerners and maintain world peace. In the prophecy, "An Oriental will leave his hometown. He will cross the sky, sea, ice and snow. Everyone will be moved by his magic stick". That is, he will sweep the Western churches with the stick of God, bringing those more than 6 billion mental ill believers are all awakened, how spectacular this is!

And this Easterner can't believe in any Western religion and their derivative religions, and he must dig out all the weaknesses and blind spots of these Western religions. At the same time, he must use Eastern wisdom and theoretical systems to improve these religions and stop them. The blow caused all believers in the Western church to be feel deceived and turned from a mental illness to a normal person. When the believers of all churches in the West are sober, the world's peace and great harmony will come.

In fact, all the prophets of the ancient the East and West knew this recipe. They must first unify Western religions. However, no one in the West has the ability to unify all Western religions and must convince them. You have to know that the number of people who believe in all religions in the West is more than 6 billion! You want more than 6 billion hard-core believers to listen to an Oriental (Any theoretical system is proposed by one person, it cannot be a group of people), Its power is very small at first, and no one will believe what you said alone.

He can only use theory and cannot recruit believers and establish organizations (Anyone who recruits believers and establishes organizations is a cult. If armed, it becomes a warlord, and then it becomes a mentally ill church and a warlord country in the West). He need wait patiently, he can't return his hometown after a long wait.

Although he is alone and weak, the world is confirming that there are natural disasters, Earthquakes and viruses that are hitting all the church countries of the "Western Stellar Civilization"; there are prophets of ancient and modern Chinese and foreign who are laying the groundwork; there are all ancient books recording, from every corner is awakening everyone in the world at present. Just like the "Exodus story in the 《Bible》 ", the God punished the Egyptian Pharaoh and forced him to let the Israelites go. At that time, the Israelites were selected by the kingdom of God, but not anymore, but the Chinese, chosen by the kingdom of God!

In addition, today's aliens are showing these things with patterns on the wheat field. Don't your 6 billion believers believe in God? Then the kingdom of God will make you believe from every corner. And those who do not believe in God? Then the kingdom of God will use celestial phenomena to make you believe!

God (Perhaps a more intelligent person) will show that the only good way to unify the "Western stellar system religion" is to "Eastern Universal Law and the Galactic civilization". Only this theoretical system can achieve permanent peace in the world and eliminate War, and no one theory can reach it. Of course, religious believers in the West cannot understand it at the beginning. After they study carefully in the future, they will understand more and more, like more and more. God has demonstrated through the mouths of Western prophets: "The hope of mankind lies in the East, and the West only represents the end". The Eastern Galaxy System Civilization is shown in the following three points:

1. Religious spirit: No worship, no dharma meetings, does not require any believers, do not worship any leader and emperor. It is the "Pyramid" civilization system.

2. Philosophical spirit: Without any doctrines, without building any political parties and development organizations, you can fight and assimilate any pseudo-philosophical theory. It is the "Universal Law" system.

3. Scientific spirit: Without any weapons, no army, no cannon fodder, and no mathematical, physical and chemical formula calculations, can be defeated and unified by all countries and any theory in the world. It is the "Great Ultimate Theory" system.

IV. Isolation of patients with viruses and mental illnesses

Same as the treatment of Coronavirus in 2020, the only specific medicine for patients with cancer, viruses and mental illnesses of the "Western Stellar Civilization", is isolation and vaccines. The emperors in ancient China did a very good job. All Chinese who did not identify with the Chinese divine culture, such as 《Book of Changes》, but believed in foreign religions, gathered together and did not kill you, but gave a piece of land. Let you self-government and become an "Isolated autonomous region".

These chinese people may think that foreign religions are advanced, and they reject Chinese civilization, such as the “Ningxia Hui Autonomous Region”. They are actually Chinese people who believe in "Islam" in the Middle East. They call themselves as ethnic group called "Hui".

Historically, the leaders of the Eastern China believed in the "Taoism, Confucianism, and Legalism". The current Chinese government has repeatedly insisted that "Never learn religions from the West"; "The body is in the East in the 21st century in China, the brains is Western crooks Marx in the 19th century” are determined to be separated from the false philosophical theories of Marx crooks in the West. In the future, we will put all Marx fans to Qinghai Autonomous Region to live, work and isolate there.

Like the Mongolian belief in the "Knife" and the Manchu belief in the "Braid", Western "Marx fans" can maintain their beliefs, instead of just joining the party, greedy money and becoming officials, they can enact their own laws, control propaganda, and restrict anything. They can also spread all their property and money around the world to establish a system of world harmony. Experiment and see how many of Marx member who pay attention to practicality are really willing to go to the autonomous region?

The final result may be that, like the "Ningxia Hui Islamic Segregated Autonomous Region", the "Xinjiang Uyghur Segregated Islamic Autonomous Region" and the "Tibetan Buddhist Segregated Autonomous Region" are the poorest segregated autonomous regions in China, if the "Marx member" leave the vast areas of China, and are quarantined in China’s Qinghai Autonomous Region, which is called the "Virus Quarantine Zone", the "Marx

Autonomous Region" must be inferior to North Korea and Iran. It is the poorest, backward and closed area in the world, and cannot be accessed internet, behavioural speech is controlled, only the leaders are the happiest, with special service, bodyguards, chefs and drivers, no money to spread, and need assistance.

As for the vast land of China outside these isolation zones, the Chinese nation must be the most powerful and prosperous nation in the world. The ideological system is from the ancient Eastern 《Book of Changes》 to the three schools of "Taoism, Confucianism and Legalism", and then to the present day. The "Pyramid, Universal Law, and Galactic Civilization System" developed in 2012, unified the world and established a country that is completely comparable to Europe and the United States and surpassed Western civilization. All networks, newspapers, television, and movies have been liberalized. The dark "Western Stellar Civilization" has officially entered the bright "Eastern Galactic Civilization".

In nature, the tigers and lions and other beasts cannot be put into the crowd. The same is true for human beings. Those mental illnesses, barbaric nations and cults must not be placed in densely populated places.

We must understand this even more and must first turn murderers such as tigers and lions with mental illnesses into sheep and horses before they can be placed in crowded places!

V. Conclusion

Although the "Eastern Galactic Civilization" does not agree with the "Western Stellar Civilization", for the billions of people with religious mental illnesses living in the current "Stellar Civilization" itself, as well as the mental illnesses kneeling in the church for severely ill patients, this place may be heaven. What is the reason?

The reason is also very simple. If you are an eagle, you certainly don't like the sparrow, but if you are a fly, you naturally worship the sparrow as God. Your knowledge and level determine the object of your worship. Your low level is like a fly, of course, you have to worship the Western illiterate sparrow leader. If your level is an eagle and can fly thousands of times higher than the sparrow leader, would you worship them?

Especially when a sovereign state system is controlled by the "Western Stellar Civilization" mental illness religion, its micro-system will also have problems, such as corruption at the top of the government, counterfeit and inferior business, public order reversal, cults and mental illnesses. It is even more necessary to publicize confrontation and war in the international arena.

Western scholars said: "Chinese civilization is a system of civilization hidden in a country." Chinese civilization has no leader, does not believe in evil, and does not need to recruit disciples. Chinese thinkers never do this, and they are not illiterate. They have their own articles and works are handed down to the world, and they are all top revolutionaries of the philosophical theory system, such as the 《Book of Changes》, Taoism, Confucianism and Legalism. Even the top prophets, such as the 《Book of Changes》, 《Tao Te Ching》, and 《Tui bei Tu》, do not build churches to deceive.

On the contrary, Western religion leaders are illiterate, cannot write, need a ghostwriter, and have very poor theoretical level. Even some prophecies are low-level and simple, including those derived from cult leaders, who need to defraud and put things on the body of believers (Such as shaved heads, Wear a headscarf and put on wheels) and solicit disciples.

Although the world is currently under the flicker of Western illiterate leaders, it still brings chaos, weapons and injuries, a large number of "Mental illness" patients, and billions of virus carriers "Believers", who are known as "Herd immunity". The warlord countries under the rule of Western religion are still there. They not only harm the present, but also periodically endanger the future.

However, God is passing the 2020 "Virus" mutation vision to show that Western religious viral mental illness is to use the same method to kill humans. Therefore, the world today is undergoing a two-track battle between good and evil. Physically, it is a confrontation between coronavirus and inactivated vaccines; spiritually, it is a contest between "Western Stellar Civilization's dark religious virus" and "Eastern Galactic Civilization's universal law vaccine". The future will definitely be solved completely, the entire "Stellar civilization" will be merged into the "Galactic civilization" system, and all theories will be unified.

When the whole world accepts the cure of the Eastern Gods vaccine, it is to unite the entire human race on the Earth under the creed of mutual love. This is the establishment of a new world of Great Harmony. Everyone understands the wisdom of the kingdom of God. Every sect and every doctrine are integrated. That is "The Sun, the Moon and the beautiful sky, the dark group was succumbed"! ; "Acura from all corners of the world, the shade is blessed"! "The South and North will be settled, and the mountains and rivers will be unified"!

(Written in August 2021, academic discussion, written late at night in Shi fu Building, Blue mountain.)

C16. On the Education "Grand University" of Universal Law

Abstract: Currently, "Stellar civilization" represents "University" education, while "Galactic civilization" represents "Grand university" education. The belief system of "Galactic civilization" is based on the pyramid series, with structures in Australia, Egypt, and Maya; its philosophical system is explosive forms of ".", "1", and "0", corresponding to the beginning of heaven and Earth and the mother of all things. The writing system includes hieroglyphs, such as Chinese characters, ancient Egyptian, and Mayan script. Its scientific system consists of unified theories of Gravitational waves, Electromagnetic waves, and Life wisdom waves. The engineering aspect is represented by "Crop circles" and microwave technology, which can track billions of wheat straws and fold them into upper, middle, and lower segments, displaying both the philosophical ideas and military technologies of Galactic civilization.

---

1. Introduction

The breakthrough during Aristotle's time (Satellite civilization) was "Imperial" education, with an average education level equivalent to "Elementary" school, focusing on literacy.

The breakthrough during Ptolemy's time (Planetary civilization) was "Church" education, with an average education level equivalent to "Secondary" school, focusing on moral education.

The breakthrough during Copernicus' time (Stellar civilization) was "Democratic" education, with an average education level equivalent to “University”, focusing on vocational education.

The breakthrough in modern times (Galactic civilization) is "Republic" education, with an average education level equivalent to "Grand university", focusing on innovative education.

The breakthrough in the future (Cosmic civilization or Universal civilization) will be "Wisdom" education, with an average education level equivalent to "Ultimate university", focusing on breakthrough education.

2. "Elementary" Education

From a historical perspective, ancient private schools or church schools represented Elementary-level education, mainly focused on literacy and teaching dogma, worshipping a deity who was regarded as great, glorious, and righteous, teaching the masses through moral education. Influenced by this, later generations worshipped emerging deities and several authoritarian emperors, who controlled all propaganda. All headlines were about their quotes and activities, and all progress and knowledge were suppressed unless deemed beneficial to their rule, such as Confucian thought.

For example, in ancient China, figures like Zhuangzi and Laozi were considered hermits, and even Confucius' teachings in private schools were mostly moral instruction, similar to Elementary education. In contrast, modern university professors often base their teaching on ancient hermits and private school concepts, using their articles to gain promotions or quoting their words as spiritual comfort on TV and the internet. This shows a lack of innovation in modern university education, with many professors still at the level of ancient hermit or private school education.

Similarly, scholars who spend their lives studying 《Dream of the Red Chamber》 or professors isolated in ivory towers cannot write with the same richness as a private school teacher who has experienced life's challenges.

3. "Secondary" Education

Many universities in developing countries, especially in the third world or most of China, are government-funded and guided by state policies and dogma. They control students' thoughts and knowledge, providing vocational education that caters to national engineering and weapons development. In ancient times, scholars who studied in private schools mainly memorized the works of Lao zi, Confucius, and others, taking exams to become top scholars. Once their exams were passed and they secured positions in government, they no longer needed to learn further.

Today, many university students study Western science and social education topics. The best performers enter "Social academies" or "Science and engineering academies", similar to the old "Imperial Hanlin Academy", a bureaucratic institution funded by the State. Social academies focus on praising the government's wisdom, while science academies research internal stability and external military prowess.

In the past, top scholars wrote articles in the eight-legged essay style, which are now preserved in the 《Complete Library of the Four Treasuries》, while modern articles are published in university journals. Many of these papers, often copied from Western experiments, are similar to the old eight-legged essays, serving the same purpose of pleasing officials and securing promotions. Just like in ancient times, modern articles are often written for the ruling class, not for the public.

Many academic journals today publish papers for a fee, knowing these articles are often for career advancement, not for real value. The problem with current education in many Chinese universities, much like in sports and entertainment, lies in the pursuit of personal success and imitation of Western methods, without innovation.

Some prominent scholars, like mathematician Shing-Tung Yau（丘成桐）, have remarked that many professors in China's top universities, like Peking University and Tsinghua University, are only at the level of American undergraduates. Others claim that many "Academicians" are merely at the level of teaching assistants. While some areas, like weapon development, may have reached world-class standards, the average level of education lags behind.

4. "University" Education

In developed countries, university education has mostly reached the "Stellar civilization" level, which focuses on vocational education. This stage is about equipping students with professional skills and social adaptability. While Western universities excel in professional and specialized training, their ability to foster creativity and intellectual breakthroughs is often limited.

For instance, many students in science and engineering focus only on technical applications, lacking a comprehensive understanding of philosophy or sociology. While they may achieve success in their fields, they struggle to make significant contributions to broader societal, philosophical, or cultural issues.

Currently, the highest level of global education is the Western "Stellar civilization" system, characterized by paid education and vocational training, with Western universities considered the top globally. Evaluation metrics are also based on their standards, which many universities worldwide follow, focusing mainly on practical engineering and technical disciplines designed for careers and jobs.

In an effort to elevate Chinese Marxist-Leninist universities to the level of Western institutions or to address the gap in technical talent domestically, Chinese universities have, in recent years, had to hire foreign professors and experts at high salaries (Much like the practice of hiring foreign coaches for soccer). Most of these hires are technical engineering scholars or basic course instructors. Why do this? Because these individuals are pragmatists focused on applied technology and exam preparation. There's virtually no risk involved since they won't challenge or change societal education.

During this time, Chinese students studying abroad have seized the opportunity. They skim technical knowledge from foreign university textbooks or publish a few low-level technical papers in international journals. Essentially, they're just filling minor roles without any substantial contribution. Some work for a few years in foreign companies, steal practical techniques, and then rush back to China to take up key positions in schools.

There are also others who return to China mainly to swindle project funds by claiming to fill domestic gaps in knowledge. In reality, they contribute nothing. They secure large sums of money and establish state-of-the-art, luxurious laboratories or even private universities, but have they produced any significant results? Absolutely not. This is because the domestic education environment is at the Elementary and Secondary school levels, lacking the corresponding legal and intellectual incentives. The funds are often diverted to dubious projects, such as genetic engineering of humans or biological weapons ------- activities that foreign scientists avoid or dare not pursue.

On the other hand, these overseas students, after gaining degrees and work experience abroad, come back to take on high-ranking positions. But they are so occupied with administrative tasks and financial pursuits that they have no time for research. Surrounded by colleagues with middle school-level knowledge, they quickly exhaust the expertise they acquired abroad and stagnate, devoid of further growth or ideas. In the end, most are eliminated by reality and time.

The truth is, China doesn't have any universities in the true sense of the word, nor does it possess university-level education. It's merely a transfer station for Western practical technology, akin to how advanced countries transfer technology and industries to less developed nations. As a result, various shady institutions abound, and some even sell stolen U.S. military technology in China or exploit collaborations to launder money. Foreign governments have caught some of these "Technical experts", and some, too ashamed to face the public, have simply committed suicide.

While returning students are busy with profiteering, what are domestic scholars doing? Mostly they are busying themselves with promotion and salary-increasing papers, furiously submitting to foreign journals. As long as their papers get published, regardless of whether they have any value, they can get promoted to professor, with their salary increased accordingly. Take a look at several low-tier foreign journals, and you'll see them filled with Chinese professors' names. But a closer look at the content reveals it's all minor revisions of Western scholars' work or scraps from the edges.

If they don't submit, they can't get promoted or increase their salary. But if they do submit, the content has no value or innovation, it's all plagiarism or minor alterations. That's why many foreign journals are now rejecting papers from China, as most are worthless. Some journals, seeking to make money, still charge high fees, and these promotion-driven papers from China essentially pay to fill these journals' pages.

Meanwhile, domestic newspapers boast that the number of Chinese academic papers now ranks highly worldwide. In reality, these are valueless "Face-saving" papers meant to impress superiors, serving as stepping stones for promotion and salary increases.

In order to maintain the façade of Chinese cultural and educational prestige, education officials spend money to recruit subpar foreign students from Africa and the Middle East, treating them like Gods. On the one hand, they claim China is a major exporter of education, and on the other, they use these foreign students to show the world that China also has a large population of international students. But in reality, they're spending vast amounts of Chinese taxpayers' money to educate these foreign students from Kindergarten to Elementary school levels, while many Chinese students in rural areas can barely finish Elementary school or even afford to attend school. Some can't even get enough to eat. If these African or Middle Eastern students were to attend advanced Western schools, they'd struggle due to their lower intellectual levels and likely wouldn't be able to graduate.

The scholar Zi Zhongjun (资中筠) once said, "Tsinghua and Peking Universities gather the brightest youth in China, only to ruin them". Others have remarked, "Chinese universities gather international students from around the world, indoctrinate them with Marxist-Leninist ideologies at an Elementary level, and ruin them".

Although these comments are harsh, their concern for the future of national education must be understood. At the same time, we must wake up and find the underlying causes. Why does this happen? Because Chinese universities haven't followed Confucius' principle of the "Great Learning" and the Doctrine of the Mean. They can't innovate, have strayed from the Mean, and are bound by Western philosophies or religious dogmas, which have shackled the nation's creativity, much like how the Manchus restricted people's minds with their queues (Braided hairstyles).

Moreover, while prestigious foreign universities are governed by highly intelligent professors, Chinese universities are governed by less intelligent administrators, akin to how church-run schools in the West were managed by pastors. Their main focus is brainwashing, worshipping deities, obeying authority, and maintaining conformity.

In contrast, real "Stellar civilization" universities exist in Western democratic nations. Their education model emphasizes examination-based creativity and encourages innovation, or attracts students with vocational training through paid education. Whether or not students can find a job after graduation depends on their own abilities.

5. "Grand University" Education

In the transition to "Galactic civilization," the education system shifts from vocational training to "Grand university" innovative breakthrough education. This level emphasizes creativity, independent thinking, and the ability to transcend existing paradigms. In this educational model, students are no longer passive recipients of knowledge but innovators who can identify problems and creatively solve them.

To surpass the "Stellar civilization" education system of the West and elevate future education, we refer to the "Galactic civilization" education system established by extraterrestrial civilizations in Crop circle, freely showcasing a civilization system to Earth.

In Australia, we've pioneered a new civilization grounded in true Eastern values. Australia symbolizes the new Atlantis ------- a vast independent continent with a civilization rooted in the Cosmic law pyramid system. Its belief structures are represented by Pyramids in Australia, Egypt, and Mexico, arranged in a triangular formation. These structures surpass religious monuments of "Stellar civilization" nations, such as Western Christian, Islamic, and Buddhist buildings. The script used is hieroglyphic, corresponding to Chinese, Egyptian, and Mayan writing systems. In terms of education, we've established the world's first "Grand University" at the peak of the triangle, in Australia, at the position represented by a dot.

Books have already been published on Amazon and Google Books, accessible to the world.

The Grand University of Universal Law (Formerly known as the Academy of Universal Law) is the only "Grand University" of solar civilization, imparting knowledge from the Cosmos and the Galaxy. It was founded in 2005, and its primary focus is not job training or paid education, but the free dissemination of civilization. Extraterrestrial professors support us with their technical and theoretical expertise, displaying the primary technologies and theoretical frameworks of Galactic civilization in Crop circle around the world.

Our "Grand University" campus is located in Crop circle worldwide, and anyone can enter to experience the energy of extraterrestrial civilization. Every year, thousands of people flock to various crop fields globally to study and experience the "Universal Law" and Galactic civilization. We don't advertise, nor do we charge fees, yet we attract countless enthusiasts and students of "Stellar civilization" who come to witness the universal law. Of course, some skeptics claim these crop circles are created using ropes and boards, but they've never demonstrated how to do it publicly ------ only claiming it happens at night, unseen. These are just fraudsters seeking fame. Others have tried to create designs in the sand, but the material in the fields ------ wheat straw, is entirely different from sand.

From a global and historical perspective, the development of education can be divided into five levels. We could say that countless "Elementary" schools equate to one "Secondary" level; countless Secondary levels equate to one "University" level; countless Universities equate to one "Grand University"; and countless Grand Universities equate to one "Ultimate University". This is the historical process of human education, corresponding to different stages of historical civilization development.

Our "Grand University" uses the universal law theoretical system as its educational foundation, focusing on breakthroughs and innovation. Although many books are published each year on similar topics such as extraterrestrial civilizations and UFOs, our teaching at the Grand University of Universal Law is different from current "Stellar civilization" university education on Earth. We uphold the principle of integrating Life sciences, Natural sciences, and Social sciences, providing students with a "New" education that will propel world civilization to a higher level.

(Written on November 2019)

C17. On Terror and the Evil Pseudo-Scientists

Abstract: Typically, the title of "Scientist" refers to someone who studies the laws of nature and innovates for the benefit of humanity, advancing useful technologies and careers. However, modern-day "Pseudo-experts" or "Pseudo-scientists" only excel at passing exams and, under the guise of science, develop weapons such as nuclear, chemical, and biological arms, often under the leadership of state-sponsored initiatives.

These individuals are celebrated by state propaganda as "Meritorious scientists" and encouraged to develop increasingly lethal weapons. Protected by the State, they evade legal accountability. These evil pseudo-scientists also publish their research on weapons development in international journals, enabling terrorists to access this information and create biological or small-scale nuclear weapons, leading to global disasters.

In the Stellar System civilizations, pseudo-scientists revolve around ignorant governments, doing whatever the state orders them to do, primarily focusing on the development of killing machines and receiving ample funding. In contrast, scientists in Galactic civilizations focus on wisdom and knowledge, studying the laws of nature and fundamental sciences. These true scientists ignore ignorant governments and religious institutions, working for no immediate profit, but their work gains recognition in the future.

I. Introduction

Pseudo-scientists or "Experts" who engage in the development of nuclear weapons, chemical weapons, rocket systems, computer viruses, and biological viruses fall into the category of evil scientists. These individuals are rampant in the five permanent members of the United Nations Security Council: the U.S., Russia, China, the U.K., and France. With strong state support, they blatantly disregard international conventions and legal constraints. Many smaller nations aspire to develop such weapons but often lack the financial resources and technological capabilities to do so.

The research and development of weapons of mass destruction began with early initiatives pushed by scientists like Einstein, who urged the U.S. government to develop nuclear weapons to stop Nazi Germany and Japan's advances. After World War II, governments around the world realized that weapons were key to determining the outcome of wars and began investing heavily in their development.

From the early stages of nuclear and chemical weapons, research evolved into the development of rockets, laser weapons, and microwave systems, culminating today in the creation of virus-based weapons. Most of this weapon development is state-funded and state-directed, with very few independent "Pseudo-scientists" pursuing such research on their own. Since these "Pseudo-scientists" receive their funding directly from the government, they are often free from legal constraints within their own countries. During World War II, for example, both Nazi Germany and Imperial Japan heavily supported and sponsored numerous "Pseudo-scientists" to research deadly weapons.

Current Global View on Weapon Development.

International organizations and the United Nations generally believe that large-scale development of weapons leads to massive loss of life and is harmful to humanity. In response, many restrictive measures have been established. The superpowers have imposed various limits on the weapons development of countries like Germany, Japan, and smaller nations. However, these smaller and weaker nations, often led by authoritarian governments, fear annexation by larger powers. Consequently, they use nationalism to incite their populations against the dominance of superpowers, prioritizing the development of weapons for national defense.

Governments spend vast sums of money recruiting so-called national elites, calling on them to ensure national security. National security, of course, is synonymous with defense, and the key to defense is modernizing weapons and armies. This idea is constantly emphasized by state propaganda. As a result, many talented but evil scientists are legally supported by the government, granted the status of national heroes, encouraged with honors and wealth, and motivated by the idea of defending their homeland. State propaganda further inflames their "Heroic" and "Evil" nature, leading to the misuse of their talents, which in turn causes global disasters and mass casualties.

For example, in the 2003 SARS outbreak, the initial blame was placed on civet cats, animals incapable of speaking up or protesting their innocence. Later, it was confirmed that the virus was accidentally leaked from a national laboratory. Similarly, while the source of the 2020 COVID-19 outbreak has not been definitively identified, it is expected to eventually be traced to human error or an accidental leak from a national laboratory, not from wild animals.

2. Nuclear Weapons

The history of nuclear weapons is well known. Initially, they were developed to counter the aggression and expansion of Nazi Germany and Imperial Japan. Promoted by renowned scientist Albert Einstein, the first nuclear weapon was used against Japan, killing over 200,000 people. Despite the immense civilian death toll, there was little international outcry, as it was viewed as retribution for Japan's militaristic government, which had caused the deaths of tens of millions across Asia. Ultimately, this forced the Japanese government to surrender.

After World War II, governments worldwide realized that weapons were the decisive factor in determining the outcome of wars. Nuclear weapons research became a national priority and a strategic asset for confronting enemy nations, leading to the nuclear arms race between the U.S. and the Soviet Union. Both superpowers employed numerous pseudo-scientists and spent vast sums of money, but in the end, the Soviet Union's defeat in this arms race contributed to its economic collapse and the dissolution of the Soviet Communist Party.

China, in order to break free from the nuclear threat posed by the U.S. and the Soviet Union, began developing and researching nuclear weapons soon after its establishment in 1949. The Chinese government recruited accomplished foreign experts to return to China, even going so far as to use significant foreign currency reserves to purchase raw materials. This caused severe domestic shortages of food and other resources, leading to what is now known as the "Three Years of Natural Disasters" in the early 1960s. However, research has shown that during these three years, the weather was stable, and there were no natural disasters, yet millions of civilians died of starvation. Despite successfully conducting nuclear tests in the mid-1960s, these weapons were essentially useless, with many now rusted or destroyed.

Even in the 21st century, the influence of nuclear weapons has not fully dissipated. Countries like North Korea and Iran, much like China in the 1960s, are impoverished, with widespread issues affecting their citizens' basic needs. Yet, they continue to heavily invest in and research nuclear weapons, their primary strategic goal being to counter the military threats and destabilization efforts from superpowers.

3. Chemical Weapons

Chemical weapons are deadly not because of explosive materials, but due to the toxic substances they contain. According to the Chemical Weapons Convention, non-living toxic products derived from biological sources ------- such as botulinum toxin, ricin, and saxitoxin ------- are classified as chemical weapons. Under this convention, any toxic chemical compound, regardless of its origin, is considered a chemical weapon if it is prohibited.

Chemical weapons have been developed since World War I and II and were used by various governments during conflicts. For example, both Japan and Germany's military regimes deployed chemical weapons to massacre civilians. During the Iran-Iraq war, the Iraqi government also used chemical weapons extensively. However, the use of chemical weapons is limited due to their small area of effect and their susceptibility to environmental factors such as weather and climate, which is why they are typically only used in localized conflicts.

4. Viral Weapons

There are two types of viral weapons: computer viruses and biological viruses.

1) Computer Viruses

The development of computer viruses is rooted in the fact that most modern weapons are operated via computers. Creating computer viruses aims to disrupt and compromise the enemy's computer systems. Research has progressed to the point of infiltrating other countries' networks to steal military and political intelligence. In some cases, these viruses are even used to steal business intelligence and financial information, leading to monetary fraud. However, in recent years, many countries have strengthened their cybersecurity systems, making it increasingly difficult for computer viruses to succeed in attacks.

2) Biological Viruses

The study of biological viruses, or bacteriological warfare, has a long history. During World War II, Japan's infamous Unit 731, stationed in northeastern China, conducted research on biological weapons.

Unit 731, part of the Japanese Imperial Army's Kwantung Army, was led by Shiro Ishii and focused on biological warfare, bacteriological experiments, and human testing. Publicly, their research was framed as efforts to combat diseases and purify drinking water. In reality, they conducted lethal experiments on living Chinese, Soviet, and Korean individuals to test the effects of biological and chemical weapons. According to Japanese author Seichi Morimura's book 《The Devil's Gluttony》, at least 10,000 people ------ Chinese, Soviets, Koreans, and Allied prisoners of war ------ died in Unit 731's experiments.

Today, under the legal backing of their governments, "Pseudo-scientists" in superpowers are researching biological viruses. Multiple accidents have occurred where virus leaks have caused casualties or international panic. To avoid international lawsuits and massive compensation claims, governments often shift the blame for viral outbreaks onto natural causes, such as the consumption of wild animals. While animals, especially those in the wild, carry many bacteria and toxins to protect themselves from predators ------ like venomous snakes or virus-carrying bats ------- these naturally occurring viruses typically do not cause widespread human infections. Most of the major viral outbreaks in human populations can be traced back to artificially created viruses.

These pseudo-scientists not only manufacture viruses but also develop vaccines to counter them, all in a bid to secure more government funding.

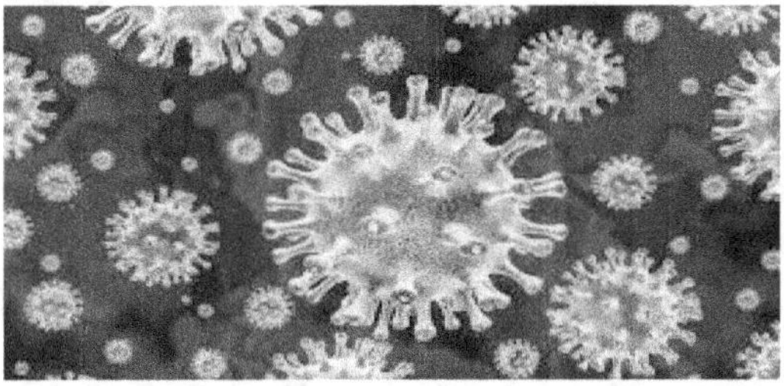

Fig. C17-1 Virus Illustration

3) Parallels with Computer Viruses

Just like with computer viruses, the companies developing antivirus solutions are often the biggest creators of these viruses. While some individual hackers do create viruses, major corporations need funding to research defenses against these individuals. By creating more severe and widespread computer viruses, they can secure more corporate investments and ensure job security. This situation parallels early insurance and security company practices. Although some property was genuinely damaged by criminals, many public facilities were, in fact, damaged by the insurance companies themselves. They would smash windows and stage thefts, only to sell insurance and security services afterward.

5. Laser and Microwave Weapons

These weapons are also known as "Directed-energy weapons" or "Beam energy weapons". They can be categorized into various types, including Laser weapons, Microwave weapons, Particle beam weapons, Sonic weapons, and Radio frequency (RF) weapons. These weapons use focused energy in the form of lasers, microwaves, particles, sound waves, and radio frequencies to generate high temperatures, ionization, radiation, and other effects. This energy can cause damage to personnel, electronic equipment, and other weapons by producing high energy densities on the surfaces they target.

In the article "The Theory and Technology of Galactic Civilization", we discussed how microwave technology can be used to kill enemies with precision, allowing for targeted strikes without harming allies. Although this is theoretically possible, the current technology of Stellar civilizations has not yet advanced to the point where such capabilities are feasible on a large scale.

6. Theoretical Framework

In 《Universal Law》, we presented a chart called the "Universal Energy Levels Diagram", which classifies all things, including viruses and bacteria, into distinct categories. Viruses and bacteria, like humans, have their own systems and are categorized between plants and animals, similar to how humans are positioned between animals and Gods in terms of evolutionary stages.

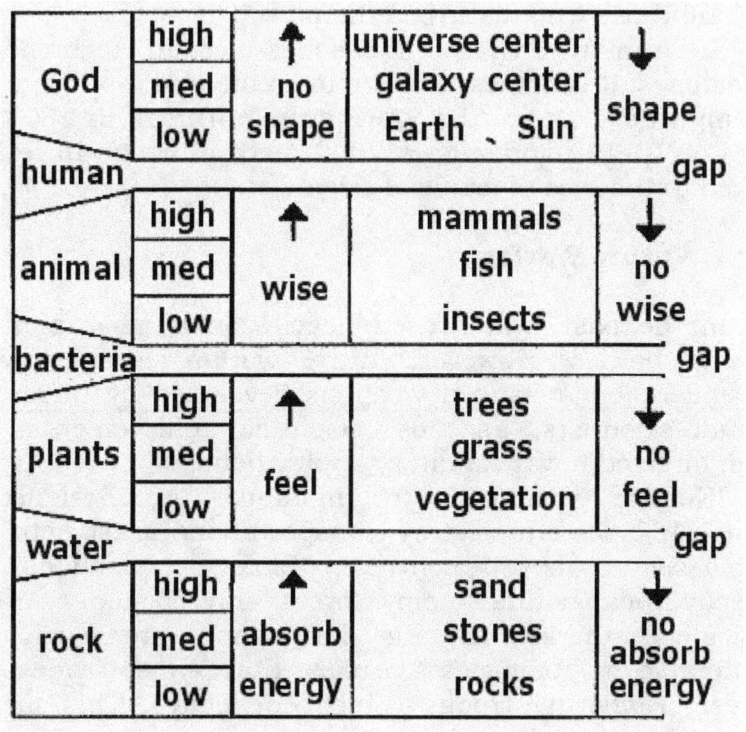

Fig. C17-2 Universal Energy Levels Diagram

Viruses and bacteria represent an intermediate phase between plant and animal life forms, just as humans represent the transition between animals and higher spiritual beings (Gods). According to ancient legend, the Egyptians were believed to have harnessed viruses for their own purposes. For example, some claim that the warning inscribed on pharaohs' tombs, stating "He who disturbs the pharaoh's rest will surely die", could be evidence of their use of viruses. Some scientists speculate that ancient Egyptians may have placed viruses in the tombs, which would infect and kill those who disturbed them.

As human civilization reaches certain technological milestones, it becomes possible to create and modify viruses. Examples of this are the SARS virus outbreak in 2003 and the COVID-19 pandemic in 2020, both of which have been linked to theories of artificial origins.

7. Future Warfare

In the past, wars relied heavily on large armies and ground battles. However, future warfare is increasingly dependent on advanced weapons developed by malevolent pseudo-scientists, as most scientific achievements have been directed toward military applications.

“Nuclear weapons”, for instance, are designed to obliterate cities and destroy transportation infrastructure on a massive scale. In contrast, “Biological weapons” can directly incapacitate enemy forces and civilians. Armies, typically gathering in large formations, are particularly vulnerable to biological viruses that cause widespread illness, rendering troops combat-ineffective. This method can effectively neutralize the enemy without direct confrontation, making biological warfare a key strategy for future conflicts.

"Microwave and laser weapons", on the other hand, provide precision targeting, allowing for the assassination of enemy leaders and military commanders while crippling command centers.

From a cost and technological standpoint, "Nuclear weapons" are the most expensive to produce and can only be developed by state actors. "Microwave and laser weapons" are somewhat less costly but still require significant resources. However, "Computer viruses" are much easier to create ------ many university students with basic computer knowledge can design malware. High-level computer experts can design more sophisticated viruses capable of disabling foreign websites, stealing government secrets, and compromising military information. Nations often sponsor these experts as a key component of cyber warfare, recognizing that the ability to protect and attack digital infrastructure could determine the outcome of future wars.

"Biological viruses" are also relatively simple to develop, even in a laboratory setting. A biologist can modify naturally occurring viruses to make them transmissible to humans. Naturally, many animal-borne viruses do not infect humans; however, viruses engineered in labs can be altered to target human populations.

Without proper international legal oversight and enforcement, many "Pseudo-scientists" could easily commit crimes under the guise of patriotism and scientific advancement. These scientists may misuse their knowledge for destructive purposes, developing "Nuclear weapons", "Chemical weapons", "Artificial viruses", and even dangerous "Food additives", such as melamine and harmful food dyes, that have caused widespread harm.

They also test their "Biological weapons" in real-world scenarios, as seen with the 2003 SARS outbreak, the 2016

Ebola virus, and the 2020 COVID-19 pandemic. These scientists have combined highly potent viruses like “Bat viruses”, “Plague”, “Influenza”, “Smallpox”, “Measles”, and “HIV” to create even deadlier strains. With ongoing research, there is a real risk that these malevolent scientists could one day develop a super-virus capable of killing large populations or, in the worst-case scenario, wiping out humanity entirely.

If “International organizations”, such as the “United Nations”, fail to effectively monitor government activities and media transparency remains inadequate, catastrophic disasters caused by these unregulated weapons could become a reality.

8. Conclusion

In authoritarian regimes, and even in some democratic nations, there exist so-called “Pseudo-scientists” who engage in harmful activities, such as weapons development, financial fraud, or intellectual plagiarism. These individuals often rise to positions of power through connections, leading to a system where corruption thrives. Those who engage in such activities are protected by mutual back-scratching networks, resulting in the proliferation of fake academicians or experts. When international experts expose these fraudulent activities, these pseudo-scientists are shielded by their colleagues, as the entire system is rife with dishonesty. Any investigation would implicate many within the establishment, making it difficult to hold anyone accountable.

These pseudo-scientists, often celebrated as "National heroes" or "Pillars of the state", are glorified for their work on weapons systems, yet their contributions are often little more than “Plagiarism or theft” of Western technology.

These so-called "Heroes" lack innovation, merely copying others' work. In the media, individuals like "Actors or public figures" are sometimes elevated to similar levels of reverence, creating a distorted image of who truly contributes to society.

Government-backed "Pseudo-scientists" involved in the development of deadly weapons, like "Nuclear weapons or biological viruses", claim their actions are justified by national interest. As a result, these individuals are rarely held accountable for the harm they cause. In some cases, they even publicly share their research on dangerous pathogens, as was allegedly done by researchers at "Wuhan Virology Institute". When such research leaks out and is potentially used by terrorists or foreign actors, those responsible deny accountability, despite the clear danger.

To effectively mitigate the risk of nuclear and biological weapons technology being leaked or misused, several steps are necessary:

1) "Increase transparency in the media" and expose the activities of those who develop these dangerous weapons.

2) "Hold governments and individuals accountable" for the research and use of these weapons. Governments should compensate the families of victims and be held responsible for any global damage caused by their actions.

3) "Punish scientists" who publish research on how to create deadly weapons, ensuring they can no longer use their positions to harm humanity under the guise of national interest.

Although the "Five permanent members of the United Nations Security Council" are responsible for limiting the development of weapons of mass destruction in smaller nations, it is also essential for citizens and smaller countries to "Hold these powerful nations accountable" for their own weapon development.

The "2020 COVID-19 pandemic" serves as a stark reminder that international institutions need to investigate and hold accountable those responsible for such disasters. If it is discovered that a specific government supported the development of a virus that caused global devastation, that government should be financially liable for the damage caused to the world economy and to the lives lost. The responsible nation should be penalized to the point of economic collapse, ensuring that they and others will not support the research of pseudo-scientists engaged in the development of deadly viruses in the future.

True heroes in science, such as Ms.Tu Youyou and Mr.Yuan Longping, who contributed significantly to the eradication of diseases and poverty, are often marginalized. These "Three-no scientists" ------- no academic degree, no position as academicians, and no published papers ------- are the real pillars of society. Despite facing criticism and accusations from pseudo-scientists, they remain committed to their work, refusing to align themselves with corrupt officials. They do not publish in government-controlled academic journals, as these journals are largely mouthpieces for propaganda, where only praise for the government or worthless research is published.

In contrast, "Pseudo-academics" clog the scientific community, forcing genuine scholars to seek recognition abroad, wasting resources and time. A common joke in academia highlights this absurdity: a professor edits a journal and allows his student's article, which praises the professor's wife, to be published. If the student had written about real science, the article might never have been accepted. This situation illustrates how "Pseudo-academics" block the path of real science, driving many capable researchers to publish in international journals.

In conclusion, "Pseudo-scientists in authoritarian governments" focus on destructive endeavors, driven by the whims of the state and unlimited funding. In contrast, scientists in "Civilizations based on wisdom" ------ such as those theorized in "Galactic Civilizations" ------- pursue fundamental knowledge and understanding of natural laws, often at the cost of profit. True scientists, who focus on the betterment of humanity, may not gain fame or fortune in their lifetimes, but their legacy will be recognized by future generations.

(Written in March 2020)

C18. Scientific Collaboration of Heaven, Earth, and Humanity in the Great Transition to the "Galactic Civilization"

Abstract: Around the year 2012, within a span of 50 years before and after, disasters have become increasingly frequent, signaling the assimilation into the Galactic Civilization. Heaven, Earth, and Humanity are all aligning with this transformation. While Heaven and Earth may not speak human languages, they are not silent. In ancient times, people would say, "Even Heaven is enraged!" Their actions are a testament to the shifting human society, reflecting the Earth's tremors and changes.

The "Stellar Civilization" has been under the control of dark forces, where most political systems are dictatorial and autocratic; religious systems are focused on idol worship and false Gods; and scientific systems are focused on developing practical tools and weapons of destruction. Catastrophic disasters are imminent. The Galactic Civilization, through the transformations of Heaven, Earth, and Humanity, is shaking these corrupt dark forces, making them experience suffering and death. The global pandemic of 2020 is one such example.

This is the declaration of war by the "Forces of light" ----- the Galactic Civilization ------- against the "Dark forces" of the Stellar Civilization, condemning them for the catastrophes and misdeeds they have caused over thousands of years.

----

1. Introduction

The inspiration to create the theory of Galactic Civilization began after the religious massacre on September

11, 2001. By around Passover of 2018, the entire theoretical framework was completed. Throughout the writing process, which centered around the year 2012, it became clear that Heaven, Earth, and Humanity were resonating with the growth and shock of this theory.

We have compiled a list of disasters occurring in the 50 years leading up to 2012, as well as those that have happened from 2012 until 2020. These events coincide with the rise of the Galactic Civilization and its development, and they predict the eventual demise of the Stellar Civilization.

2. Natural Disasters (50 Years Before and After 2012)

From 50 years before and after 2012, up until 2020, various disasters including floods, droughts, heatwaves, locust infestations, and snowstorms have occurred.

1960s:

- Dec. 1960: Nor'easter snowstorm in the U.S., 286 dead.
- Sep. 1961: Hurricane Esther hits North Carolina, causing a plane crash, 7 dead.
- Jan. 10, 1962: Sudden temperature rise causes an avalanche on Huascarán Mountain in Peru, approximately 4,000 dead.
- May 31, 1963: Hong Kong experiences a drought with a record high temperature of 35.5°C, unspecified deaths.
- Apr. 1964: Tornado in Jessore, East Pakistan (Now Bangladesh), 500 dead.
- Aug.30, 1965: Glacier collapse during dam construction in Valais, Switzerland, 88 dead.
- Jan. 27, 1966: Snowstorm in Oswego, New York, USA, 201 dead.

- Feb. 7, 1967: Wildfire in Tasmania, Australia, 62 dead.
- Dec. 1968: Drought across Africa, 1.5 million dead from starvation.
- Apr.14,1969: Tornado in East Pakistan (Now Bangladesh), 660 dead.

1970s:

- May.17, 1970: Hurricane Alma strikes Jamaica, Panama, and Cuba, causing deaths.
- Nov.13, 1970: Bhola cyclone in East Pakistan (Bangladesh), 500,000 dead.
- Jun. 1971: Flooding in Hanoi and the Red River Delta, Vietnam, approximately 100,000 dead.
- Feb. 1972: Deadliest snowstorm in history hits Iran, 4,000 dead.
- Apr. 17, 1973: Tornado in Dhaka, Bangladesh, 681 dead.
- Dec. 1973: Drought in Sudan's Sahel region, approximately 300,000 dead.
- Dec. 25, 1974: Tropical Cyclone Tracy devastates Darwin, Australia, 71 dead.
- Aug. 7, 1975: Typhoon Nina in Henan, China, causes dam collapse, over 220,000 dead.
- Mar. 8, 1976: Meteor shower in Jilin, China, a rare global phenomenon.
- Aug. 25, 1976: Continuous rainfall causes a landslide in Siu Mau Ping, Hong Kong, 18 dead.
- Apr. 1, 1977: Tornado in Madaripur-Shibchar, Bangladesh, 500 dead.
- Aug. 30, 1978: Hurricane Ella, the strongest to hit Canada, causes tourism disruption and deaths.
- Aug. 29, 1979: Tropical Storm Elena hits Texas, USA, causing multiple deaths.

1980s:

- Apr. 1980: Heatwave in the USA, affecting North Dakota, over 1,700 dead.
- Nov. 1981: Bahamas and the Greater Antilles hit by Hurricane Katrina, causing deaths.
- Jun. 1982: Subtropical storm hits Florida, USA, causing deaths.
- Feb. 16, 1983: Ash Wednesday bushfires in Australia, 75 dead.
- Jun. 9, 1984: Tornado in Ivanovo-Yaroslavl, Soviet Union, 400 dead.
- Oct. 18, 1984: Ethiopian famine, 1.7 million dead.
- Nov. 1985: Hurricane Kate strikes the USA, 15 dead.
- Aug. 1986: Hurricane Charley strikes northwest Florida, USA, 17 dead.
- May. 1, 1987: Daxing'anling fire in China, 191 dead.
- Jul. 1988: Heatwave in the Midwest, USA, the worst in 54 years, over 5,000 dead.
- Apr. 26, 1989: Tornado in Daulatpur-Saturia, Bangladesh, 1,300 dead.

1990s:

- Oct. 1990: Tropical Storm Marco hits Florida, USA, 12 dead.
- Apr. 29, 1991: Cyclone in Bangladesh, over 130,000 dead.
- Aug. 1991: Forest fires in Indonesia, 57 dead.
- Mar. 1992: Forest fire in Nepal, 56 dead.
- Mar. 1993: The "Storm of the Century" in the USA, 318 dead.
- Nov. 1994: Hurricane Gordon strikes Haiti and Central American countries, over 1,100 dead.

- Sep. 1995: Hurricane Ismael hits northern Mexico, over 100 dead.
- Jun. 1996: Hurricane Cesar devastates northern Colombia, 51 dead.
- Sep. 1997: Forest fires in Sumatra and Kalimantan, Indonesia, 240 dead.
- Jun. 1998: Heatwave in India, 2,541 dead.
- Oct. 1998: Typhoon Zeb strikes the Philippines, Taiwan, and Japan, 180 casualties.
- Dec. 14, 1999: Vargas mudslides in Venezuela, about 10,000 dead.

2000s:

- Aug. 2000: Typhoon Bilis strikes China and Taiwan, over 800 dead.
- Sep. 2001: Typhoon Nari hits Taiwan, causing 94 deaths.
- Aug. 2002: Typhoon Rusa, the strongest in 43 years, strikes South Korea, 233 dead.
- Aug. 2003: Heatwave in Europe, 35,000 dead.
- Jun. 2004: Typhoon Conson hits the Philippines and Taiwan, 64 dead.
- Jun. 2005: Atlantic hurricane season devastates Mexico, USA, and Cuba, 3,913 dead.
- Jun. 2006: Heatwave across Europe, approximately 3,418 dead.
- Jun. 28, 2007: Wildfire in Greece, 84 dead.
- Jan. 2008: Snowstorm in Afghanistan, 926 dead.
- May. 2, 2008: Cyclone Nargis strikes Myanmar, 138,366 dead.
- Feb. 7, 2009: Bushfire in Victoria, Australia, 180 dead.

2010s:

- Jul. 2010: Heatwave and wildfires in Russia, about 56,000 dead.
- Aug. 2010: Heatwave in Japan, 1,718 dead.
- Aug. 2011: Typhoon Talas strikes Japan, 73 dead.
- Jul. 2012: Tropical storm Khanun strikes Japan, North Korea, and South Korea, 89 dead.
- Nov. 2013: Super Typhoon Haiyan strikes the Philippines and China, 6,340 dead.
- Jul. 2014: Typhoon Rammasun hits Japan, 10 dead.
- May. 2015: Heatwave in southern India, 50°C, 2,500 dead.
- Jun. 2015: Heatwave in Pakistan, around 2,000 dead.
- Aug. 2016: Typhoon Lionrock hits Japan, North Korea, and Russia, 550 dead.
- Oct. 8, 2017: Wildfire in northern California, USA, 44 dead.
- Oct. 15, 2017: Iberian wildfire in Portugal and Spain, 49 dead.
- Jul. 23, 2018: Wildfires near Athens, Greece, approximately 99 dead.
- Aug. 2018: Super Typhoon Jebi strikes Japan and the Northern Mariana Islands, 17 dead.
- Jun. 2019: Locust infestations in Kenya, Ethiopia, and other African countries, dozens dead.
- Sep. 2019: Wildfires spread across Australian provinces, destroying countless animals and homes, 33 dead.

2020s:

- Feb. 2020: Hailstorms and thunderstorms in the middle and lower Yangtze River and Jiangnan regions of China, resulting in multiple deaths.

3. Earthquake Disasters (From the 1960s to 2020s)

Starting in the 1960s, the frequency of large Earthquakes (Magnitude 7 or above) increased significantly, resulting in devastating loss of life across various countries. The following is a summary of some major Earthquakes that occurred during this period:

1960s:

- May. 22, 1960: The “Great Chilean Earthquake”, with a magnitude of 9.6, remains the strongest Earthquake ever recorded. It resulted in the deaths of approximately 5,700 people.
- Apr. 4, 1961: A 6.4 magnitude Earthquake struck Kashgar County, Xinjiang, China. Casualty details are unknown.
- Jun. 4, 1961: An 8.0 magnitude Earthquake hit the Aling Mountain region in Tibet, China, with no confirmed death toll.
- Mar. 19, 1962: A 6.1 magnitude Earthquake occurred in Guangzhou, China, with no specific details on casualties.
- Apr. 19, 1963: A 7.0 magnitude Earthquake struck Alak Lake, Qinghai, China. Death tolls were not provided.
- Mar. 27, 1964: The Good Friday Earthquake in Alaska, U.S., registered 8.5 in magnitude and claimed 139 lives.
- Feb. 4, 1965: Rat Islands, Alaska experienced an 8.7 magnitude earthquake. The death toll is unclear.

- Mar. 8, 1966: The Xingtai Earthquake in Hebei Province, China, had a magnitude of 6.8, resulting in 8,064 deaths.
- Dec. 11, 1967: The Koynanagar Earthquake, triggered by the Koyna Dam in India, measured 6.3 in magnitude and caused 200 fatalities.
- Jan. 15, 1968: Sicily, Italy, experienced a 6.5 magnitude Earthquake that resulted in 380 deaths.
- Aug. 31, 1968: An Earthquake measuring 7.4 hit Northeastern Iran, killing approximately 12,000 people.
- Jul. 18, 1969: Bohai Bay, Shandong, China, suffered a 7.4 magnitude Earthquake, with 10 reported deaths.

1970s:

- May. 31, 1970: Ancash Earthquake, Peru, with a magnitude of 8 and about 90,000 deaths.
- Jul.14,1971: Papua New Guinea's Solomon Islands Earthquake, magnitude 8.1, 2 people killed.
- Apr. 24, 1972: An Earthquake occurred in Ruisui Township, Hualien County, Taiwan, with a magnitude of 7.2 and 5 deaths.
- Feb.6, 1973: Yade Earthquake in Luhuo County, Sichuan Province, P.R.China, magnitude 7.6, 2175 deaths.
- May.11, 1974: The Great Pass Earthquake in Zhaotong District, Yunnan Province, P.R.China, with a magnitude of 7.1 and 1,423 deaths.
- Feb.4, 1975: Haicheng, Liaoning Province, China, a major Earthquake with a magnitude of 7.3 and 1,328 deaths.
- Jul.28, 1976: Tangshan, P.R.China, a major Earthquake with a magnitude of 7.8 and more than 240,000 deaths .

- Mar.4, 1977: Bucharest, Romania Earthquake, magnitude 7.2, 1578 deaths.

- Jun.12, 1978: An Earthquake occurred off the coast of Miyagi Prefecture, Japan, with a magnitude of 7.7 and 28 people were killed.

- Jul.9, 1979: An Earthquake occurred in Liyang County, Jiangsu Province, China, with a magnitude of 6 and 41 deaths.

- Dec.17, 1979: An Earthquake off Bali Island, Indonesia, with a magnitude of 6.3, 27 people were killed.

1980s:

- May.18, 1980: Mount St. Helens erupted in the United States, and 57 people died.

- Oct.10, 1980: An Earthquake occurred in Algeria with a magnitude of 7.3 and 1,000 deaths.

- Nov.13, 1980: An Earthquake occurred in Italy with a magnitude of 7.2 and 2,735 deaths.

- Jan.24, 1981: An Earthquake occurred in Daofu, Sichuan Province, China, with a magnitude of 6.8 and about 150 deaths.

- Jul.28, 1981: An Earthquake occurred in southern Iran with a magnitude of 7.3 and 1,500 deaths.

- Dec.13, 1981: An Earthquake occurred in Yemen with a magnitude of 6.0 and 3,000 deaths.

- Mar.29, 1982: Mexico's El Chichón volcano erupted, killing 3,500.

- Oct.30, 1983: An Earthquake occurred in Turkey with a magnitude of 6.0 and 1,300 deaths.

- Aug.15, 1984: Lake Monauen, Cameroon, erupted at the bottom of the lake, 37 died.

- Nov.13, 1985: Amero tragedy in Colombia, 23,000 deaths.

- Sep.19, 1985: Mexico City Earthquake, 7.8 magnitude, more than 7,000 deaths.
- Aug.21, 1986: An eruption at the bottom of Lake Nios, Cameroon, killing 1,744 people.
- Oct.10, 1986: An Earthquake occurred in El Salvador with a magnitude of 7.5 and 1,500 deaths.
- Mar.5, 1987: An Earthquake occurred in Ecuador with a magnitude of 7.0 and more than 1,000 deaths.
- Dec.7, 1988: The Spitalk Earthquake in northern Armenia of the Soviet Union, magnitude 6.8, killed 25,000 people.
- Oct.17, 1989: A major Earthquake occurred in San Francisco, USA, with a magnitude of 6.9 and more than 270 deaths.

1990s:

- Jun.21, 1990: Mangil-Rudba Earthquake in Iran, magnitude 7.7, about 35,000 people died.
- Jul.16, 1990: An Earthquake occurred in the Philippines with a magnitude of 7.7 and approximately 2,000 deaths.
- Feb.1, 1991: An Earthquake occurred in Pakistan and Afghanistan with a magnitude of 6.8 and a total of 1,200 people died.
- Jun.3, 1991: Unzendake Volcano erupted in Nagasaki Prefecture, Japan, and 43 people died.
- Jun. 1991: Mount Pinatubo erupted in the Philippines, the second largest volcano erupted in the 20th century, killing hundreds of people.
- Oct.20, 1991: An Earthquake occurred in the northeast of New Delhi, India, with a magnitude of 6.1 and 1,600 deaths.

- Dec.12, 1992: An Earthquake occurred in Indonesia with a magnitude of 6.8, and about 2,200 people died.
- Sep.30, 1993: Five Earthquakes occurred in India, with a maximum magnitude of 6.4 and 22,000 deaths.
- Jun.6, 1994: An Earthquake occurred in southwest Colombia with a magnitude of 6.8 and at least 1,000 deaths.
- Jan.17, 1995: The Great Hanshin Earthquake in Japan, with a magnitude of 7.3 and 6,500 deaths.
- May.28, 1995: An Earthquake occurred on Sakhalin Island in the Far East of Russia, with a magnitude of 7.5 and nearly 2,000 deaths.
- Jul.12, 1995: An Earthquake with a magnitude of 7.3 in Menglian County, Yunnan Province, China, 11 people died.
- Feb.3,1996: An Earthquake occurred in Lijiang, P.R.China, with a magnitude of 7.0, and 309 people were killed.
- Feb.28,1997: An Earthquake occurred in northwestern Iran with a magnitude of 6.1 and more than 1,000 deaths.
- May.10,1997: An Earthquake occurred in northwestern Iran with a magnitude of 7.1 and about 1,560 people died.
- Feb.4, 1998: An Earthquake occurred in Afghanistan with a magnitude of 6.1 and 4,500 deaths.
- May.30, 1998: An Earthquake in Afghanistan, which killed more than 3,000 people.
- Jul.17, 1998: An Earthquake and tsunami occurred in Papua New Guinea, killing about 1,500 people.
- Jan.25, 1999: An Earthquake occurred in Colombia with a magnitude of 6.2 and more than 1,200 deaths.
- Aug.17, 1999: A major Earthquake in Izmit, Turkey, with a magnitude of 7.6 and 17,000 deaths.
- Sep.21, 1999: Chichi Earthquake occurred in Taiwan with magnitude 7.3 and 2415 deaths.

2000s:

- Jan.14, 2000: An Earthquake in Yao'an County, Yunnan Province, P.R.China, with a magnitude of 5.9 and 7 deaths.
- Aug.6, 2000: A huge Earthquake occurred on Sakhalin Island in the Far East of Russia, with a magnitude of 8.5 and many deaths.
- Oct.7, 2000: An Earthquake occurred in Tottori Prefecture, central Japan, with a magnitude of 7.3 and many deaths.
- Jan.26, 2001: A massive Earthquake in Gujarat, India, with a magnitude of 8, and 15,000 deaths.
- Jun.22, 2002: An Earthquake occurred in Buin Zahra, northwestern Iran, with a magnitude of 6.5 and 261 deaths.
- Dec.26, 2003: An Earthquake in Bam County, Kerman Province, southeast Iran, with a magnitude of 6.6 and 26,271 deaths.
- Oct.25, 2003: An Earthquake occurred in Minle County, Gansu Province, P.R.China, with a magnitude of 6.1 and 10 casualties.
- Dec.26, 2004: The Great Indian Ocean Earthquake and the South Asian Tsunami, with a magnitude of 9, over 280,000 people died.
- Mar.28, 2005: Sumatra, Indonesia Earthquake, magnitude 8.2, more than 2,000 people were killed.
- Oct.8, 2005: Kashmir, Pakistan Earthquake, magnitude 7.6, about 90,000 people died.
- Dec.26, 2006: A strong Earthquake off the coast of Pingtung, Taiwan, with a magnitude of 7.2 and 2 deaths.
- Sep.12, 2007: An Earthquake occurred in Indonesia with a magnitude of 7.9, and the death toll has risen to 70.
- May.12, 2008: The Wenchuan Earthquake in Sichuan, P.R.China, with a magnitude of 8.2 and over 69,000 deaths.

- Sep.30, 2009: Indonesia Sumatra Earthquake, magnitude 7.6, and 1,100 people were killed.

2010s:

- Jan.12, 2010: An Earthquake in Port-au-Prince, the capital of Haiti, with a magnitude of 7, and about 220,000 people died.
- Oct.25, 2010: Sumatra, Indonesia Earthquake and tsunami, magnitude 7.7, killed 435 people.
- Mar.11, 2011: Japan's northeastern Pacific coast Earthquake and tsunami, magnitude 9, and 15,893 deaths.
- Dec.7, 2012: Kamaishi City waters southeast of Japan Earthquake, magnitude 7.3, and 3 people dead.
- Apr.20, 2013: Ya'an Earthquake, P.R.China, magnitude 7.0, the death 160 people.
- Sep.24, 2013: An Earthquake occurred in southwestern Pakistan with a magnitude of 7.8 and 359 people were killed.
- Apr.2, 2014: Chile Earthquake in the north-west coast, magnitude 8.0, 6 people died.
- Apr.25, 2015: A series of Earthquakes in the Himalayas of Nepal, with a magnitude of 7.8, killed 9,018 people.
- Dec.17, 2016: Papua New Guinea Earthquake, magnitude 7.9, not many deaths.
- Apr.17, 2016: An Earthquake off the coast of Ecuador, with a magnitude of 7.8, killed 654 people.
- Nov.15, 2016: An Earthquake in the central South Island of New Zealand, with a magnitude of 7.5, killed 2 people.
- Aug.8, 2017: An Earthquake in Jiuzhaigou, Sichuan, P.R.China, with a magnitude of 7, and 25 deaths.

- Sep.19, 2017: Mexico City Earthquake, magnitude 7.1, 216 deaths.
- Sep.28, 2018: A series of Earthquakes in Central Sulawesi Province, Indonesia, with a magnitude of 7.7, killed 2,010 people.
- Sep.24, 2019: Jhelum Earthquake in Pakistan, magnitude 5.8, killed 43 people.
- May.26, 2019: An Earthquake in northern Peru, with a magnitude of 7.8, killed 1 person.

2020s:

- Jan.28, 2020: An Earthquake in the Caribbean Sea in southern Cuba, magnitude 7.7, with very few deaths.
- May.16, 2020: Nevada Earthquake, magnitude 6.5, not many dead.

4. Man-Made Disasters (From 1960s to 2020s)

Man-made disasters primarily result from human conflicts, including religious conflicts, ethnic clashes, wealth inequality, cultural differences, and struggles between democracy and authoritarianism, such as these highlight the profound and tragic consequences of human conflict and political turmoil across various regions and periods.

1960s:

- 1960: Long period of famine or hardship in China, ending in 1962, countless deaths.
- Mar. 6, 1960: U.S. announces sending 3,500 U.S. troops, Vietnam War begins, countless deaths.

- Apr. 17, 1961: U.S.-Cuba conflict, Bay of Pigs, total of 360+ deaths.
- May. 16, 1961: South Korea's Park Chung-hee launches his dictatorship with the May 16th military coup.
- October-November 1962: Sino-Indian Border War, over 3,000 killed on both sides.
- Oct. 1962: The outbreak of the Cuban Missile Crisis is the closest the Cold War has come to the brink of all-out nuclear war.
- Feb. 2, 1963: Operation Cold Storage occurs in Singapore, with authorities arresting some 111 leftists.
- Aug. 21, 1963: Hundreds of Buddhists are killed when Ngo Dinh Tuyen in South Vietnam leads his troops to raid the Temple of Shariputra.
- Jul. 21, 1964: Clashes between Malays and Chinese erupt in Singapore, killing and injuring 50 people.
- Aug. 3, 1964: Armed conflict between North Vietnam and the United States in the Gulf of Tonkin leads to U.S. involvement in the Vietnam War.
- Apr. 1965: Second Indo-Pakistani War or Second Kashmir War, thousands of casualties.
- Sep. 30, 1965: The September 30th Incident in Indonesia, President Sukarno kills hundreds of thousands of civilians.
- May. 16, 1966: China's Cultural Revolution breaks out, countless deaths, chaos until 1976 ends.
- Dec. 3, 1966: The 12-3 Incident breaks out in Portuguese Macau, clashes between police and civilians, 8 dead.
- Apr. 7, 1967: The Arab-Israeli conflict, the third war in the Middle East, known as the “Six-Day War”, breaks out.
- Jul. 6, 1967: The Nigerian Civil War breaks out, ending in January 1970 with 70,000 dead on both sides.

- Jan. 1968: The Prague Spring, a military occupation of Czechoslovakia by the Soviet Union.
- Oct. 1968: Mexican government shoots student and civilian protesters, Tlatelolco Incident.
- Mar. 2, 1969: Incident of armed conflict on Jumbo Island between China and the Soviet Union, ends on the 15th with 87 deaths on both sides.
- Jun. 28, 1969: Gay Americans start the Stonewall Riots, many dead and injured.

1970s:

- Feb.8, 1970: Political prisoners of Taiwan's Taiyuan Prison launched Independence Movement and prison revolution, and many people died.
- Dec.20, 1970: A large-scale military-civilian conflict during the U.S. rule of Ryukyu, a dead riot.
- Sep.13, 1971: Chinese Vice Chairman Lin Biao fled by plane and died in Windur Khan, Mongolia.
- Dec.3, 1971: The third India-Pakistan war broke out, Pakistan air strikes 11 Indian air bases.
- May.30, 1972: The Japanese Red Army committed a murder at the airport in Tel Aviv, causing 26 deaths.
- Sep.5, 1972: The Munich tragedy in West Germany, the PLO attacked the Israeli delegation, and 11 people died.
- Oct.6, 1973: The fourth Middle East war broke out, triggering an oil crisis, and 18 thousand deaths on both sides.
- Nov.29, 1973: A fire in the Ocean Department Store occurred in Kumamoto City, Kumamoto Prefecture, Japan, killing 103 people.
- Jan.19, 1974: China and Vietnam engaged in an archipelago battle over the Paracel Islands, and both sides died 71.

- Sep.12, 1974: Revolution broke out in Ethiopia, soldiers overthrew Emperor Selassie, 1.4 million people died.

- Sep.16, 1975: The Lebanese Civil War began and continued, killing approximately 120,000 people.

- Dec.7, 1975: Indonesian military occupation of East Timor, by 1999, a total of 200,000 people died.

- Apr.4, 1976: Prince Sihanouk of Cambodia resigned and was later arrested, causing numerous deaths in domestic turmoil.

- Oct.6, 1976: P.R.China's Huairentang Incident, Mao Zedong's widow Jiang Qing and others were arrested, and the Cultural Revolution ended.

- Mar.27, 1977: Tenerife plane crash, Pan Am and KLM planes collided, 583 people died.

- Oct.13, 1977: Lufthansa Flight 181 was hijacked by the PLO, and the hijacker died.

- Jul.11, 1978: A gas truck exploded in the province of Tarragona, Catalonia, Spain, killing 217 people.

- Nov.18, 1978: More than 900 followers of the "People's Temple" of the American leader Jim Jones committed suicide.

- Jan. 1979: Vietnam occupied Phnom Penh, Cambodia, and the Sino-Vietnamese border war broke out, killing about 140,000 soldiers and civilians.

- Dec. 1979: The Soviet Union invaded Afghanistan and withdrew in 1988. Approximately 900,000 soldiers and civilians died.

1980s:

- May.18, 1980: The Gwangju incident occurred in South Korea. The citizens demanded democracy and the government suppressed it. About 620 died.

- Sep.22, 1980: The Iran-Iraq War broke out and the border war lasted eight years. The two sides suffered about 870,000 casualties.

- Jun.7, 1981: Israel sent military aircraft to blow up nuclear reactors in Iraq, killing about 10 people.

- Jul.9, 1981: A passenger train crashed into a bridge on the Chengdu-Kunming Railway in P.R.China, killing more than 240 people.

- Apr. 1982: A war broke out between Britain and Argentina for sovereignty over the Falkland Islands. About 900 people died.

- Sep.16, 1982: Massacre in the Shatila refugee camp in Beirut, Lebanon, killing about 2,000 people.

- Feb.21, 1983: Assam students in India protested against Bangladeshi Muslim refugees, and 600 people were killed.

- Oct.25, 1983: The United States and the Caribbean countries sent troops to Grenada, and 90 people died on both sides.

- Oct.12, 1984: The Brighton Hotel bombing by the British Irish Republican Army killed 5 people.

- Dec.3,1984: Bhopal gas leak in Madhya Pradesh, India, killing about 16,000 people.

- Jan.12, 1985: A terrorist attack on Borobudur, a Buddhist site in Central Java, Indonesia, killing several people.

- Jun.23, 1985: The Air India flight was blown up by the Kalistan movement in Ireland, killing 329 people.

- Feb. 1986: The Philippine People's Power Revolution, ending the 20-year rule of President Marcos that killed countless people.

- Apr.26, 1986: The accident at the Chernobyl nuclear power plant in Ukraine, the Soviet Union, continued to kill about 4,000 people.

- Jul.15, 1987: Taiwan lifted the 38-year martial law, and about 140,000 people were killed during this period.

- Jun.10, 1987: The June Democratic Movement in South Korea agreed to direct presidential elections and adopted democratic reform measures.

- May.14, 1988: The world's longest oil tanker was sunk by an Iraqi warplane missile while passing through the Strait of Hormuz.

- Sep.18, 1988: The Burmese military government suppressed the protesters, and about a thousand students, monks and children were killed.

- Jun.4, 1989: The Tiananmen Square Incident on June 4th broke out in P.R.China.

- Dec. 1989: The United States sent troops to Panama and captured the top leader of Panama. About 350 deaths occurred on both sides.

1990s:

- Oct. 1990: The fall of the Berlin Wall, the merger of the two Germanys, and the drastic changes in Eastern Europe, hundreds of thousands of people died during the period.

- Aug.2, 1990: Iraq occupied Kuwait, the Persian Gulf War broke out, and ended in 1991 with 25,000 deaths.

- Jun.27, 1991: Yugoslavia's civil war broke out, killing tens of thousands of lives for several months.

- Dec. 1991: The Warsaw Pact was dissolved, the Soviet Union disintegrated, the Cold War ended, and millions of people died during the period.

- Apr.1, 1992: The Bosnian War broke out and ended in 1995. The war killed about 200,000 people.

- May.17, 1992: Hundreds of thousands of people in Thailand participated in opposing military interventions, and the military suppressed them, and dozens of them were killed.

- Jan.1, 1993: Czechoslovakia split into two independent countries, the Czech Republic and Slovakia.
- Apr.19, 1993: The FBI tanks invaded the Davidic stronghold, and more than 80 followers died.
- Dec. 1994: The Chechen War in Russia broke out and ended in 2009 with more than 100,000 deaths.
- Apr.6, 1994: Rwanda genocide occurred, about 800,000 people were killed.
- Mar.20, 1995: Japan's Aum Shinrikyo launched a sarin gas attack on the Tokyo subway, killing 12 people.
- Apr.19, 1995: An explosion occurred at the Federal Building in Oklahoma, USA, killing 168 people.
- Jun.25, 1996: A terrorist attack on a US military base in Saudi Arabia resulted in 20 deaths and 372 wounded.
- Jul.25, 1996: A military coup occurred in Burundi, and dozens of people died.
- Apr.14,1997: A fire in a pilgrimage camp in Meena Plain, 11 kilometers from Mecca, Saudi Arabia, killed 343 people.
- Nov.17, 1997: The Hatshepsut Temple in Luxor, Egypt, Islamist forces killed 62 tourists.
- May.13, 1998: Indonesia's May national anti-China riots killed more than 1,200 people.
- Aug.7, 1998: The U.S. Embassy in Tanzania and Kenya exploded successively, killing 224 people.
- Mar.24, 1999: The Kosovo War or NATO's air strikes against Yugoslavia killed thousands.
- Jun.30, 1999: A summer camp fire in Hwaseong County, Gyeonggi Province, South Korea, killed 23 people.

2000s:

- Aug.21, 2000: All officers and men of the Russian Navy Kursk were killed, 118 dead.
- Nov.17, 2000: Peruvian President Ken Fujimori went into exile in Japan, ending ten years of dictatorship and countless rulings.
- Mar.12, 2001: The Afghan Taliban destroyed two 5th-century Buddha statues in Bamyan.
- Sep.11, 2001: The World Trade Centre was crashed by terrorists using a plane, and more than 2,700 died.
- Mar.29, 2002: The conflict between Palestine and Israel escalated, resulting in more than a thousand deaths.
- Oct.23, 2002: The threat of the Moscow Opera House in Russia, resulting in more than 100 deaths.
- Jan. 2003: The SARS epidemic broke out in P.R.China, with more than 6,000 deaths worldwide.
- Mar.20, 2003: Iraqi Persian Gulf War, the United States and Britain used force, a total of 170,000 people died.
- Mar.11, 2004: "3.11 serial bombings" in Madrid, Spain, with a total of 191 deaths.
- Sep.1, 2004: Chechen armed forces created a "Beslan Hostage Incident" in southern Russia, killing 396 people.
- Jul.7, 2005: Seven explosions occurred in London, England, causing 56 deaths in subway stations and buses.
- Oct.29, 2005: The riots in Paris, France, the black immigrants were beaten, smashed, and looted, and dozens of people died.
- Jul.11, 2006: A serial train bombing in Mumbai, India, killing more than 200 people.
- Jul.12, 2006: Israel and Lebanon Hezbollah clash, claiming that the July War killed many people.

- Jan.1, 2007: A serial bombing occurred in Bangkok, Thailand, killing 3 people and seriously wounding 38 people.

- Aug.15, 2007: An anti-junta demonstration took place in Myanmar, calling it the "Saffron Revolution", and several people died.

- Aug. 2008: The South Ossetia War broke out in Georgia, and more than 1,870 people died.

- Nov.26, 2008: A series of terrorist attacks occurred in Mumbai, India, killing at least 195 people.

- Mar.9, 2009: The United States confirmed that a variant of the H1N1 influenza virus caused an epidemic, and more than 150,000 people died.

- Jan.20, 2009: Israel and Hamas used white phosphorous bombs in the Gaza War, killing countless people.

2010s:

- Apr.6, 2010: Kyrgyzstan's opposition revolution overthrew the government, 100 people died in violence.

- Dec.17, 2010: Anti-government demonstrations in Tunisia, North Africa, led to the fall of the regime and the Jasmine Revolution.

- Feb. 2011: An armed conflict between the Syrian government forces and the opposition, many countries intervened, and 10,000 people died.

- Feb.17, 2011: Libya's civil war, Gaddafi fought with the rebel forces, and 10,000 people died.

- Jan. 2012: The conflict in northern Mali, the Azawad National Liberation Movement, killed hundreds of people.

- Dec.10, 2012: Civil war in the Central African Republic, government forces and "Sereka", more than 5,100 people died.

- Aug.21, 2013: A chemical weapon attack occurred in Damascus, Syria, killing 322 people.

- Dec.14, 2013: South Sudan began a civil war, the conflict extended to Jonglei Province, at least 500 people died.

- Apr.3, 2014: The Ebola virus epidemic in south-eastern Guinea, Africa, with more than 7,000 deaths.

- Jun. 2014: The Middle East ISIS organization began to expand in northern Iraq, killing thousands of people.

- Jan.8, 2015: Nigeria's Boko Haram organization massacred hundreds of people in the town of Baja.

- Mar. 2015: Brazil has a large-scale epidemic of Zika virus, with microcephaly cases and dozens of deaths.

- Jul.23, 2016: Two explosions occurred in the De Mazan district of Kabul, the capital of Afghanistan, killing 80 people.

- Mar.22, 2016: A series of explosions occurred in Brussels, the capital of Belgium, killing 32 victims.

- May.22, 2017: The Irish Republican Army instigated an explosion at the Manchester Arena in England, killing 23 people.

- Dec. 2017: European refugee crisis, 3,116 smugglers were killed in the Mediterranean throughout the year.

- Mar.30, 2018: Israeli and Palestinian armed groups protested against member clashes, 110 died.

- Apr.18, 2018: Nicaraguan President Daniel's increase in income tax triggered protests, and 30 people were killed.

- Apr.21, 2019: A series of explosions in Sri Lanka occurred on the Sunday of the Resurrection, and 253 people died.

- Oct.18, 2019: Chile broke out in protests against the increase in ticket prices and caused riots. A total of 19 people died during the demonstrations.

2020s:

- Jan. 2020: The global coronavirus outbreak, the final death toll is hundreds of thousands.

5. The Connection Between Heaven, Earth, and Man

The above discussion shows the interconnection between Heaven, Earth, and Man. Every major Earthquake is associated with human societal activities and phenomena, marking the beginning of great transformations. Typically, Earthquakes of high magnitude or events with over 10,000 casualties correspond to significant historical turning points in that country, and they can be seen as predicting the future of society. For example:

1) May. 22, 1960 – The Valdivia Earthquake in Chile, magnitude 9.6, with 5,700 deaths.

It foretold the brewing of the Galactic Civilization, which would destroy old systems — wisdom ("Zhi") would benefit ("Li") the future.

2) Mar. 27, 1964 – The Good Friday Earthquake in Alaska, USA, magnitude 8.5, with 139 deaths.

It predicted the U.S. would no longer engage in large-scale foreign military interventions after the Vietnam War.

3) Mar. 8, 1966 – The Xingtai Earthquake in Hebei Province, China, magnitude 6.8, with 8,064 deaths.

It foretold a major cultural change in China, starting from the Hebei region and leading to the Cultural Revolution in Beijing.

4) Aug. 31, 1968 – An Earthquake in northeastern Iran, magnitude 7.4, with 12,000 deaths.

It foretold the rise of the religious-political union under Khomeini in Iran.

5) Jul. 28, 1976 – The Tangshan Earthquake in China, magnitude 7.8, with over 240,000 deaths.

It foretold the deaths of three top Chinese leaders in Beijing, marking a turning point towards China's opening and reform.

6) Mar. 4, 1977 – The Bucharest Earthquake in Romania, magnitude 7.2, with 1,578 deaths.

It foretold a significant transformation in Romania in the years to come.

7) Jul. 28, 1981 – An Earthquake in southern Iran, magnitude 7.3, with 1,500 deaths.

It foretold the devastation of the Iran-Iraq war.

8) Dec. 7, 1988 – The Spitak Earthquake in Armenia, USSR, magnitude 6.8, with 25,000 deaths.

It foretold the impending dissolution of the Soviet Union.

9) Jun. 21, 1990 – The Manjil-Rudbar Earthquake in Iran, magnitude 7.7, with 35,000 deaths.

It foretold Iran's isolation and economic sanctions.

10) Sep. 30, 1993 – A series of five Earthquakes in India, the largest with a magnitude of 6.4, resulting in 22,000 deaths.

It foretold the sharp escalation of ethnic and religious conflicts in India, with many casualties.

11) Feb. 4, 1998 – An Earthquake in Afghanistan, magnitude 6.1, with 4,500 deaths.

It signaled the beginning of continuous wars in Afghanistan.

12) Dec. 26, 2004 – The Indian Ocean Earthquake and tsunami, magnitude 9, with 280,000 deaths.

It foretold that South Asian countries would be troubled by Islam, leading to countless deaths. Additionally, the Galactic Civilization theory began to take shape.

13) May 12, 2008 – The Wenchuan Earthquake in Sichuan, China, magnitude 8.2, with approximately 69,000 deaths.

It foretold the collapse of figures like Bo Xilai, Wang Lijun, and Zhou Yongkang, who had dominated Sichuan. It marked a turning point in China's anti-corruption campaign.

14) Mar. 11, 2011 – The Tōhoku Earthquake and tsunami in Japan, magnitude 9, with 20,000 deaths.

It foretold the collapse of the Stellar Civilization system around 2012, and the Galactic Civilization theory system was largely born around 2012.

15) May. 16, 2020 – An Earthquake in Nevada, USA, magnitude 6.5, with multiple fatalities.

It foretold the outbreak of the coronavirus pandemic.

6. Predictions

The events above have already occurred, and through the analysis provided, we can make predictions about the future. If a major Earthquake occurs, there is a possibility of significant change for the entire country or even the world. For example, the Earthquake in 2020 predicted the global outbreak of the coronavirus, resulting in the deaths of hundreds of thousands.

We are closely monitoring major global Earthquakes and fatal incidents because the Galactic Civilization theory system was fully completed around 2020. The Stellar Civilization is being warned through the massive deaths caused by viruses.

7. Conclusion

Francis Collins, Director of the U.S. National Institutes of Health, stated in his speech about COVID-19 that the virus originated naturally and evolved through directed selection on ACE2 until it achieved super-strong binding capability. In other words, the virus evolved through its own efforts to gain the ability to infect humans, and human science at its current level could not have engineered such an unusual spike protein.

Since the virus has evolved naturally, why can't humanity evolve as well? The Stellar Civilization has indeed evolved into the Galactic Civilization, though most current academic publications, books and propaganda are controlled by academic elites and governments, leaving people unaware of this development.

Governments around the world, or even United Nations officials, are not scholars and have no theoretical systems to address these issues. Some are corrupt. So far, the United Nations has been unable to resolve global religious conflicts, political system conflicts, or ethnic tensions. They collect billions of dollars in management fees from countries worldwide each year but have no comprehensive plan to solve these conflicts. Instead, they deploy troops to maintain stability and provide refugee assistance, which is only a temporary solution.

Chinese divine culture and the laws of the universe embodied in Galactic Civilization can thoroughly solve the global theoretical crisis. The entire Solar System civilization is in jeopardy, and ending the Stellar Civilization has become an urgent priority. If we continue to remain stubborn and ignorant, even more disasters will follow.

(Written on May 2020)

Universal Publishing presents in society

C19. A Review of Eastern and Western Science and Art

Abstract: The beauty of science manifests in nature, such as in the shapes of celestial bodies, animals, and plants, and is also reflected in art. Mathematical, chemical, and physical formulas represent another form of beauty.

---

1. Introduction

The beauty of science is also evident in art, seen in the shapes of celestial bodies, animals, and plants, as well as in mathematical and physical formulas. Every scientific and technological design is expressed in artistic form. If a design lacks artistic beauty, then the science and technology behind it must be incomplete.

Many forms of ancient art are displayed through craftsmanship, such as on pottery and porcelain. These ancient artifacts also represent the peak of scientific and technological development of their time. Recently, I visited both the Forbidden City in Beijing and the National Palace Museum in Taipei, which felt like stepping into a time capsule of ancient art and craftsmanship. These institutions have preserved the ancient Chinese craftsmanship and artistic heritage exceptionally well. The traditional Eastern culture showcased there is both complete and stunningly beautiful. For experts studying ancient scientific and artistic treasures, these exhibitions offer valuable comparisons and insights for modern and future works.

2. Western Craftsmanship and Art

When discussing Western craftsmanship and art, what often comes to mind are the urban sculptures displayed in major European cities and the works of various art masters found in museums. These works include exquisite paintings, sculptures, and architectural decorations. Each sculpture and decorative element reflects the scientific and technological advancements of their time.

The history of Western craftsmanship and art mainly originates from the ancient lands of Europe, beginning with the rock carvings and cave paintings of the early Paleolithic era. Later, the ancient civilizations of Israel and the Aegean Sea region influenced the West. The Mediterranean craft and art forms they developed spread across the region, influencing the philosophy, science, craftsmanship, and art of ancient Greece. This influence extended through ancient Rome, eventually reaching the rest of Europe, North Africa, and Western Asia.

Fig. C19-1 Early crafts and art in ancient Greece and Macedonia in Europe, about 530 BC; scientific craftsmanship of painted pottery; imaginary style, impressionism

This spread of philosophy, science, craftsmanship, and art throughout history is referred to as Classical Era culture. For the following millennium, Western cultural development was fragmented, often disrupted by war, fear, and darkness, with little breakthrough. It wasn't until the Renaissance that people rediscovered history and began to explore the fruits of free and creative thought. The Baroque period followed, breaking away from the strict formality of the Renaissance by emphasizing luxury and emotional expression. This was later followed by the Neoclassical period and, more recently, the postmodern era, which showcases the brilliance of contemporary craft and art.

For several centuries, European philosophy, science, craftsmanship, and art were heavily influenced by the Christian Church and Middle Eastern myths. Much of the inspiration came from biblical stories, mythological Gods and goddesses, and epic battles. Religious and mythological stories were crafted into masterpieces by artisans, relying on philosophy, architectural design, painting, and sculpture to express the grandeur of scientific and artistic achievements. As time progressed, most crafts and artworks distanced themselves from religion, becoming increasingly influenced by political and ideological realities.

Fig. C19-2 《Mona Lisa》 by Leonardo da Vinci, 1503–1506 AD. , realism

Throughout Western history, European craftsmanship and art can be categorized into stages: Classical, Byzantine, Medieval, Gothic, Renaissance, Baroque, Rococo,

Neoclassical, Modern, Postmodern, and the latest developments in new European crafts and paintings. Despite this progression, Western craftsmanship and art can generally be divided into two main schools of thought: the realistic and the idealistic. Representations of these schools include Classicism, Realism, Impressionism, Naturalism, and Romanticism.

Sculptures and paintings also reflect scientific craftsmanship in their use of materials, dyes, and canvases.

Fig. C19-3 《Impression·Sunrise》 by Claude Monet, 1840-1926 AD. Drawing about virtualism and impressionism

3. Eastern Craftsmanship and Art

Comparing the history of Western craftsmanship and art, we now turn to Eastern craftsmanship and art, which primarily encompasses the achievements and developments in East Asia, South Asia, and West Asia. Early West Asian craftsmanship and art include the works from Egypt and Mesopotamia, such as the architectural design of the pyramids, representing the oldest Middle Eastern forms of philosophy, science, craftsmanship, and art. These influences spread eastward, affecting ancient India and China, and westward, influencing Europe.

Eastern craftsmanship and art began with Paleolithic rock paintings and sculptures. Sites such as Sanxingdui and the ancient northwestern plains of China show traces of influence from the Middle East, mixed with local mythology and religion. The creation and design of bronze artifacts suggest that, at some point in early history, Eastern and Western craftsmanship and art developed in parallel and even overlapped.

Over time, Eastern craftsmanship and art took on a unique, independent form. Archaeological findings at the Yin Ruins (Anyang 安阳) reveal that traditional Chinese craftsmanship and art had already developed into a complete system with its own philosophical foundations, seemingly uninfluenced by foreign culture, craftsmanship, or art. This new cultural form, rooted in Chinese science and philosophy, persisted throughout the history of Eastern craftsmanship and art. Indian craftsmanship and art, however, remained deeply embedded in mythology and religion, comparable to the early stages of European art. The craftsmanship and art of Korea and Japan followed China's lead in earlier historical periods but later aligned more with Western influences in later stages.

Chinese craftsmanship and culture, with its vast early innovations, laid the foundation for the long-lasting history of Chinese civilization. Over the course of its dynasties, through periods of unification and fragmentation, peace and war, Chinese culture alternated between prosperity and decline, interconnecting and evolving. In recent centuries, as modern science and technology have rapidly advanced, new categories of craftsmanship and art have emerged.

Chinese traditional craftsmanship and art can be broadly categorized into three types: fine arts, folk arts, and performance arts, each utilizing different materials such as stone, pottery, wood, and bronze. During the Paleolithic era, artists painted on pottery, as evidenced by the numerous pottery sculptures and paintings unearthed from early Zhou Dynasty tombs. The excavations of the Spring and Autumn and Warring States periods revealed exquisite bronze craftsmanship and art. By the Tang Dynasty, the art of ceramics reached new heights with the creation of the famous Tang Sancai (Three-colored ware) and the frescoes at Dunhuang. In the Song Dynasty, craftsmen and artists specialized in stone carving, architectural ornamentation, landscape painting, and portrait painting, developing highly refined techniques for shading and color contrast.

Eastern artists used stone, wood, or paper to create vague outlines of landscapes, conveying depth, distance, and even inner emotions such as sorrow, a typical "Impressionist" approach to natural scenes. This style predates the European Impressionist movement by many years. During this period, Eastern craftsmanship and art reached an artistic peak on a global scale, emphasizing the spiritual essence of the work, often surpassing mere human emotions.

Outstanding examples of Chinese ancient craftsmanship and art from various historical periods are displayed in the collections of the Forbidden City in Beijing and the National Palace Museum in Taipei. These include bronze ware, porcelain, gemstone works, and the famous jadeite cabbage. Many of these pieces influenced prominent philosophers, scientists, and religious figures of their time. Even emperors, such as Emperor Huizong of the Song Dynasty, contributed to the creation of art, as exemplified by his landscape paintings.

In conclusion, Eastern craftsmanship and art can also be divided into two major branches: the realistic school, which includes Classicism, Realism, and Naturalism, and the idealistic school, which encompasses Romanticism, Impressionism, and Nihilism. When comparing Eastern and Western craftsmanship and art in terms of technique, Eastern artists primarily used woodcarving and paper for their artwork, whereas Western artists favored stone carving and canvas.

A detailed analysis of the great Eastern and Western masters and their works reveals a general trend: Western craftsmanship and art tend to lean towards realism, while Eastern craftsmanship and art often emphasize idealism.

Fig. C19-4 "Along the River During the Qingming Festival", painted by Zhang Zeduan, a Northern Song Dynasty artist (1085-1145), is an example of Realism.

Ultimately, regardless of whether they are Realists or Idealists, Eastern and Western craftsmen and artists share one common element: the soul of their craft and art. The soul is the most important aspect, forming the core of the work. When wisdom, philosophy, art, and science unite, the resulting craftsmanship and art are timeless.

Of course, the artistic imagery found in mathematical, physical, and chemical formulas also reflects the laws of the universe, but due to space constraints, this will not be elaborated here.

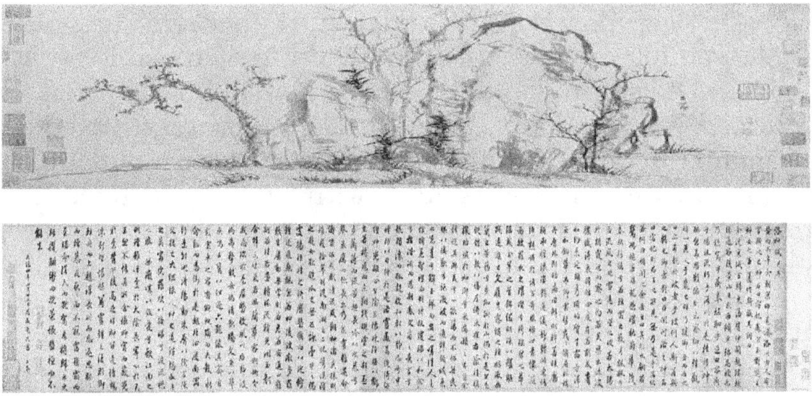

Fig. C19-5 "Art by Zhao Mengfu (赵孟頫)", a Song Dynasty artist, represents Naturalism.

Fig. C19-6 The art of Eastern India is mythology and religious stories, which are similar to early European art

4. Reflections on Visits to the Beijing and Taipei Palace Museums

Upon delving deeper into the ancient relics and artistic works displayed at the Beijing and Taipei Palace Museums, one can easily discern that the thought processes behind ancient craftsmanship and artistry are entirely different from the mindset that underpins modern art and craftsmanship. In ancient times, craftsmen and artists embodied a spirit of deep craftsmanship and bore a historical responsibility for art. In contrast, modern craftsmanship and art often seem empty and chaotic in thought, lacking artistic beauty, with disordered lines and confused emotions intermingled. It feels as though modern art and craftsmanship are created for money or to capitalize on celebrity status, much like how the study of mathematics, physics, chemistry, and other sciences is pursued today, primarily for passing exams, securing good jobs, and earning a living.

Reflecting on contemporary renowned painters such as Zhang Daqian, Li Keran, and Qi Baishi, one can see that, while they have inherited the artistic traditions of the Song, Ming, and Qing dynasties, they do not appear to have introduced significant soul-stirring innovations. Their innovations remain mostly technical. Many famous contemporary Chinese painters, in turn, have simply rehashed the techniques and styles of Zhang Daqian, Li Keran, and Qi Baishi, just as contemporary scientists largely copy Western scientific achievements, repackaging them into products for profit, as if science and art alike are being reduced to commercial enterprises.

In today's art world, wealthy businessmen can draw a random "Circle", and it becomes valuable, a near mockery of art itself. If people question this, the businessmen demonstrate that their casually drawn circles are worth more than the life's work of a dedicated artist. This dynamic plays out in famous auction houses in Hong Kong, where price inflation is driven by hype. A "Random circle" can sell for 30 million yuan. The intent is clear, art means nothing in such a context; the world is ruled by money. The modern "Art circle" operates as such, with speculative value rising faster than the historical worth of any ancient work of art. If no one buys the piece, no problem, the artist or their associates can buy it back, paying only a small commission. As long as the commercial value of the businessman's shoddy creation rises, the system continues.

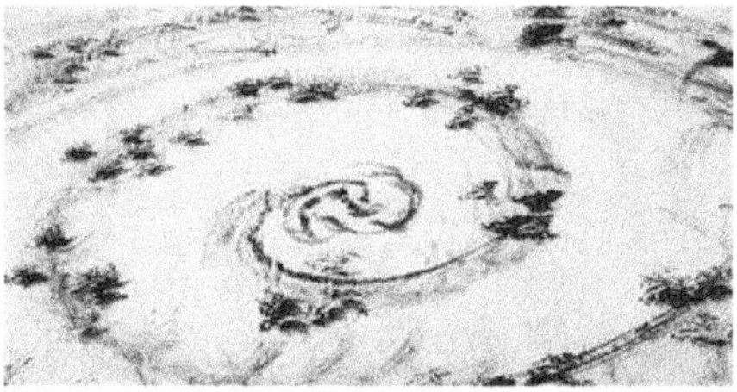

Fig. C19-7 This "Circle" painting by a contemporary businessman was sold for 33 million yuan, more than the ancient emperor's painting

Why are China's crooked businessmen turning to craftsmanship and art? It's because government officials no longer dare to accept bribes in cash and now accept only renowned works of calligraphy and painting. So, these shrewd businessmen have started practicing calligraphy and painting, or replacing their multimillion-yuan gold bars with self-proclaimed art pieces. By positioning themselves as artists and engaging in commercial speculation, they essentially turn their work into advertisements. When companies go public, bribing officials with a few hastily scrawled "Circles" is seen as a more tasteful and cost-effective way of securing favors.

These hastily scrawled "Circles", devoid of value, would otherwise be unwanted by government officials. So how do businessmen raise their perceived value? They hype their artwork on the market, driving the prices higher than any historical figure's or emperor's paintings. Naturally, the officials take note. Not daring to accept gold, they accept the paintings instead. Greedy officials, only recognizing money and not understanding art, scramble for these pieces, greenlighting the businesses in return. As a result, even junk stocks can get listed, leaving ordinary shareholders and investors to suffer. Modern art has thus become a tool of bribery, while businessmen continue to devalue modern artistic work, making it a victim of celebrity culture and commercial exploitation.

Fig. C19-8 Contemporary hyper-realistic painting mimicking a photograph.

Other contemporary artists, who lack the wealth or fame of businessmen, contrast themselves by spending long periods meticulously drawing hyper-realistic works that resemble photographs. While businessmen take only a few minutes to create their art, these artists might spend six months working on a single painting, replicating a photograph in painstaking detail. However, this isn't art either, it's merely time-consuming reproduction. The process involves enlarging a photograph, sticking it to a wall, and tracing it line by line. Does it contain artistic value? No. Does it have soul? Certainly not. It's simply time invested. The artist, having spent so much time on the piece, is assumed to have imbued it with value, like being paid by the hour. Yet, it holds no artistic thought or significance, merely another method of inflating the price of the artwork.

It's not just the art world that engages in such speculation, science and technology face similar issues. From swindlers building private schools for profit, to plagiarists posing as academicians, to fraudsters faking semiconductor breakthroughs, and boasting "Weapon masters" whose work is mere garbage, the pattern is the same. If someone doesn't engage in such commercial manipulation, they are often seen dragging their feet, holding high-ranking positions without delivering, taking salaries but failing to perform, or cutting corners to the point that bridges collapse. Scientific fraud, ghostwriting papers by the thousands, these are all part of the same grim reality. Whether in science or art, the scene is disturbingly similar. In short, the situation is rotten.

5. Conclusion

Visiting the Beijing and Taipei Palace Museums, the ancient relics displayed serve as a testament to the fusion of craftsmanship, art, philosophy, and spirit, blended with science and technology. The passage of time washes away the trivial, leaving behind treasures like the Song Dynasty's

"Along the River During the Qingming Festival," which can eclipse the work of tens of thousands of today's so-called famous artists. A single Tang poem can outshine the tens of thousands of mediocre verses penned by Emperor Qianlong.

History repeats itself. We've grown accustomed to the barrage of hollow contemporary science, shoddy craftsmanship, and lackluster art and poetry. Devoid of thought, soul, or meaning, their proliferation merely serves to churn out products for sale. The real essence of craftsmanship and art lies in innovation, seen in science, truth, beauty, human life, emotions, and even in mathematical formulas and engineering designs, particularly as they manifest in the natural evolution of animals and plants. True art is ultimately the reflection of these forces of nature.

(Written on May 10, 2024)

C20. Universal Laws and China's Yin-Yang and Five Elements Theory

Abstract: This article delves into the "Relationship between universal laws and China's ancient Yin-Yang and Five Elements theory", emphasizing how these ancient Chinese concepts are influenced by the natural workings of the universe, particularly the "Solar system". The text explains that while Earth's inhabitants primarily experience the solar system's laws, such as Earth's rotation and revolution, the broader universal laws also indirectly influence Earth in subtle, long-term ways, much like the galaxy's center affects the solar system.

I. Ancient Chinese Wisdom from Nature

The "Yin-Yang and Five Elements theory" is deeply connected to natural cycles observed on Earth, particularly in relation to the Sun's impact on Earth's rotation and revolution. This natural observation formed the foundation of Chinese ancient science and philosophy.

1. Time

1) Earth's Rotation

"Earth's rotation" causes the cycle of day and night, which represents "Time" and is reflected in the concept of Yin and Yang. Day (Yang) and night (Yin) alternate, symbolizing the constant motion of the cosmos.

In ancient Chinese timekeeping, the "24-hour cycle" is split into 12 time periods, which align with the "Chinese zodiac signs" ("Zi"子, "Chou"丑, "Yin"寅, etc.). Each period has both Yin and Yang phases: Daytime is considered auspicious (Yang), while nighttime is inauspicious (Yin). For instance, the darkest period, "Zi hour (Midnight)", is deemed the most dangerous, while "Wu hour (Noon)" is the most favorable.

2) Earth's Revolution Around the Sun

The "Earth's orbit around the Sun", creating the four seasons, is another example of time in motion, represented in 12 months or 12 zodiac signs. Winter is associated with inauspiciousness (Yin), while summer represents auspiciousness (Yang). The yearly cycle reflects the same balance of opposing forces as the daily cycle, where spring marks the transition from Yin to Yang, and autumn the reverse.

This cycle is further subdivided into "24 solar terms", corresponding to events like "Solstices, equinoxes", and seasonal transitions, paralleling the 24 hours of the daily cycle.

3) Cycles of Time – Days and Years

Time on Earth operates in cycles, both "Short-term (12 days)" and "Long-term (12 years)". These cycles also correspond to the 12 zodiac signs, with "Zi years (Like 2020)" representing more inauspicious periods (Yin), while "Wu years" are associated with prosperity and balance (Yang). We also connects this cyclical pattern to "Sunspot activity", which operates on an 11-12 year cycle, suggesting a natural rhythm that affects human life and history.

4) Social and Cosmic Implications of Yin-Yang

The cyclical nature of time and the balance between "Yin and Yang" extend beyond natural phenomena and influence human society. These forces are seen in the "Dynamic tensions" between opposites like war and peace, justice and injustice, as part of the "Dialectical forces" that shape history and social progress.

5) Analysis:

The text provides an insightful connection between "Astronomical phenomena" and traditional "Chinese cosmology", linking "Earth's movement in the solar system" with the "Yin-Yang duality" and "Five Elements theory". It underscores the intricate patterns that both govern the natural world and guide human understanding of time, seasons, and societal structures. The application of these ancient theories is portrayed as an extension of the "Universal laws", highlighting their relevance not only in China but as a reflection of larger "Cosmic principles".

2. Space

This section focuses on how ancient Chinese thought linked "Space" with the "Five Elements (Wu Xing)" — Metal, Wood, Water, Fire, and Earth — highlighting how these concepts symbolized the "Material world" and its "Cyclical nature".

1) The Five Basic Elements

The "Five Elements" represent fundamental materials of the Earth, referred to as "Di Dao" (The way of the Earth).

These elements were symbolic rather than literal, meaning they weren't meant to suggest that the world is solely made up of these five substances.

Ancient scholars categorized natural elements and movements within the framework of these "Five Elements". They were encoded using the "Chinese calendrical system" (E.g., Jia, Yi, Bing, Ding, etc.), indicating cycles of energy and motion.

2) The Cyclical Process

The "Five Elements" describe a "Dynamic process" of creation, transformation, and destruction:

- "Metal" represents gathering and contraction.
- "Wood" represents growth and expansion.
- "Water" symbolizes infiltration and adaptability.
- "Fire" embodies destruction and dissolution.
- "Earth" signifies integration and balance.

These principles extend beyond physical matter and are applied to cycles in Nature, Society, Economics (Such as stock market fluctuations), and human institutions. For instance, they represent the growth and decline of businesses or nations. The ancient scholars used this to explain the "Cycles of life and death", growth, and decay.

3) Time and Space Connection

The "Heavenly Stems (天干 Tian Gan)" and "Earthly Branches (地支 Di Zhi)" systems correlate with the "Yin-Yang and Five Elements" theories. Each of the 10 Heavenly Stems and 12 Earthly Branches carries a "Yin or Yang" nature and is associated with a particular element.

For example:

- Wood: Jia (Yang Wood), Yi (Yin Wood).

- Fire: Bing (Yang Fire), Ding (Yin Fire).
- Earth: Wu (Yang Earth), Ji (Yin Earth).
- Metal: Geng (Yang Metal), Xin (Yin Metal).
- Water: Ren (Yang Water), Gui (Yin Water).

4) Time-Yin-Yang and Space-Five Elements Relationship

The interaction between the "12 time periods (Yin-Yang cycles)" and the "Five Elements" forms a "60-year cycle" known as "Jiazi (甲子)". This long cycle is seen as a harmonious blend of "Time and space", affecting everything from daily life to larger societal trends. It represents the full cycle of energy in Nature and its return to its original point.

For instance, 2020, being a "Jiazi year", is part of a repeating cycle that signals significant shifts or turbulence (e.g., the COVID-19 pandemic). We also can references historical examples, such as the "Yellow Turban Rebellion" (A chaotic event linked to a Jiazi year).

5) The 60-Year Cycle and Birth Chart

The "60-year cycle" is fundamental to Chinese astrology and forms the basis of determining one's "Bazi" (The Eight Characters of Birth), which is used to predict life patterns based on the "Heavenly Stems and Earthly Branches" corresponding to a person's year, month, day, and hour of birth.

This section highlights the sophisticated understanding of how "Time and space" interact within the framework of ancient Chinese cosmology. The "Five Elements" serve as both "Metaphors and practical tools" for interpreting the cycles of life, nature, and society.

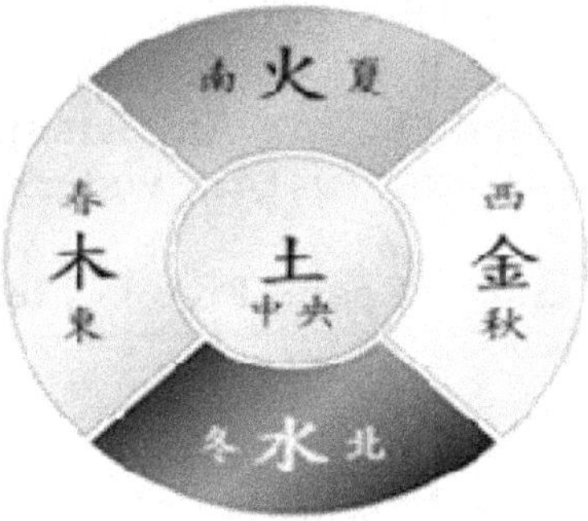

Fig. C20-1 The five elements are also related to color and orientation (Online chart)

II. The Application of Yin-Yang and Five Elements Theory

1. Numerical Sequence

According to ancient Chinese Five Elements theory, the elements (Water, Fire, Wood, Metal, Earth) correspond not only to natural phenomena but also to specific numbers:

Water: (1, 6); Fire: (2, 7); Wood: (3, 8); Metal: (4, 9); Earth: (5, 5)

This numerical relationship appears in classics like the 《Tai Xuan Jing》 and 《Book of Documents》, where numbers are used to deduce the generating and overcoming relationships of the five elements.

2. Spatial Diagrams

The generating and overcoming relationships of the Five Elements can be represented in "Two types of diagrams":

Pentagram Diagram: Illustrating how the elements generate and overcome one another. Generating relationships: Wood generates Fire; Fire generates Earth; Earth generates Metal; Metal generates Water, and Water generates Wood. Overcoming relationships: Wood overcomes Earth; Earth overcomes Water; Water overcomes Fire; Fire overcomes Metal, and Metal overcomes Wood.

Central and Four Directions Model: The elements are also associated with spatial orientations, with each element corresponding to a direction or central position, creating a complete spatial model.

3. Five Elements and Traditional Medicine

In traditional Chinese medicine, the Five Elements correspond to the organs and physiological functions of the human body:

- Metal (Lungs and large intestine): Represents functions like contraction and preservation.
- Wood (Liver and gallbladder): Represents growth and flexibility.
- Water (Kidneys and bladder): Represents moisture and cooling properties.
- Fire (Heart and small intestine): Represents warmth and ascending energy.
- Earth (Spleen and stomach): Represents nourishment and transformation.

III. Eastern Predictive Theories

Due to the cyclical nature and contradictory tendencies of Yin-Yang and the Five Elements, much of the universe operates in repetitive opposites, such as day and night influenced by the Sun, Earth's changing environment and climate, or the seasonal cycle of the year. Even the 60-year cycle reflects this repetitive pattern over a relatively short time frame. The mechanics of these repetitions are what ancient Eastern predictive theories often focus on.

1. Predictions for Individuals

Ancient Chinese predictions about an individual's life were based on analyzing their "Bazi" (Eight Characters), also known as the Four Pillars of Destiny. These eight characters correspond to the year, month, day, and hour of a person's birth, each represented by a pair of "Heavenly stems" and "Earthly branches".

"Heavenly stems" and "Earthly branches" combine to form a person's birth chart. The time and date of birth can determine if a person was born in an auspicious year or an inauspicious year, which is also why people choose favorable years for important events like marriage.

By analyzing an individual's life within the framework of the 60-year cycle (The average lifespan of ancient people), ancient astrologers could deduce rough patterns about their fate, though the accuracy was limited. People born at the same time could have very different lives, so predictions would also include assessments of facial features, palmistry, and even names.

For instance, the famous astrologer "Li Chunfeng" predicted Empress Wu Zetian's fate not only through her birth chart but also by examining her facial features.

In general:

- Heavenly path (天道): Represented by a person's birth chart (八字"bazi").

- Earthly path (地道): Determined through palmistry (Hand lines).

- Human path (人道): Observed through facial features.

Together, these make up the ancient system of "Heaven, Earth, and Man" (天地人) in predictive studies. For example, a person with unappealing facial features may struggle with interpersonal relationships and be prone to conflict.

Additionally, palmistry is divided into three main lines, reflecting the "Heaven, Earth, and Man" paths:

Life line (生命线); Wisdom line (智慧线); Emotion line (感情线)

Each line represents different aspects of one's destiny, much like how birth charts or facial features are analyzed to predict life events.

2. Predictions for Dynasties and Nations

Predicting the fate of dynasties or nations follows the same principles used for individuals but on a larger scale. Not only does the analysis involve the "Heavenly Path" ("Tian dao"), but it also requires consideration of the "Earthly Path" ("Di dao") and the "Human Path" ("Ren dao"). Each dynasty has its own "Bazi" (Birth chart), based on the year, month, and day it was founded, determining whether it was born in an auspicious or inauspicious time.

- Heavenly Path: This refers to the auspiciousness of the time a dynasty was established.
- Earthly Path: It involves geographic factors such as the location of the capital, natural resources, and climate.
- Human Path: This reflects the level of popular support, the relationship between rulers and the people, and the structure of the social system.

If all three — "Tian dao", "Di dao", and "Ren dao" — are in harmony, the dynasty will thrive; otherwise, it will be short-lived.

1) Predicting Individual Dynasties

Dynasties such as the Qin and Yuan had short reigns due to poor alignment with the "Ren dao" ------ internal divisions and disunity among ethnic groups. In contrast, dynasties like the Zhou, Han, and Tang had long reigns because their "Tian dao", "Di dao", and "Ren dao" were all strong. The cycle often follows periods of 60, 120, or 240 years.

2) Predicting All Dynasties

By using "Tian dao", "Di dao", and "Ren dao", it is possible to forecast the entire sequence of Chinese dynasties. The major Chinese dynasties can be arranged in a sequence that mirrors the 24 solar terms, representing stages of development:

- Xia, Shang, Zhou [Western Zhou, Eastern Zhou (Spring and Autumn, Warring States)]
- Qin, Han (Western Han, Eastern Han)
- Three Kingdoms (Wei, Shu, Wu), Jin (Western Jin, Eastern Jin)
- Southern and Northern Dynasties [Southern Dynasties (Song, Qi, Liang, Chen), Northern Dynasties (Northern Wei, Eastern Wei, Western Wei, Northern Qi, Northern Zhou)]
- Sui, Tang, Five Dynasties (Later Liang, Later Tang, Later Jin, Later Han, Later Zhou)
- Ten Kingdoms (Former Shu, Later Shu, Wu, Southern Tang, Wuyue, Min, Chu, Southern Han, Jingnan, Northern Han)

- Song (Northern Song, Southern Song), Liao, Western Xia, Jin, Yuan, Ming, Qing, Republic of China, People's Republic of China

This totals approximately 24 dynasties, corresponding to the 24 solar terms.

- Heavenly Path: Divided into 12 cycles based on the natural elements, such as the 12 zodiac signs (Zi, Chou, Yin, Mao, Chen, Si, Wu, Wei, Shen, You, Xu, Hai).
- Earthly Path: Divided into 10 cycles (Jia, Yi, Bing, Ding, Wu, Ji, Geng, Xin, Ren, Gui).
- Human Path: Refers to the ruling methods of monarchs, the level of popular support, and cultural progress.

These three factors interact and influence one another. For example, the Xia Dynasty and earlier periods were characterized by a primitive system of governance, while the Shang to Warring States periods saw a shift toward a slave-based feudal system, and the Qin Dynasty onward developed into a centralized feudal system.

3) Testing Predictions with 24 Dynasties and 12 Periods

By examining the 24 dynasties and comparing them to the 12 zodiac periods, a pattern emerges:

A. Periods 1-6: Xia, Shang; Western Zhou, Spring and Autumn; Warring States, Qin;

B. Periods 7-12: Western Han, Eastern Han; Three Kingdoms, Western Jin, Eastern Jin, Southern Dynasties;

C. Periods 13-18: Northern Dynasties, Sui; Tang, Five Dynasties; Ten Kingdoms, Northern Song;

D. Periods 19-24: Southern Song, Yuan, Ming, Qing; Republic of China, People's Republic of China

In terms of the "Heavenly Path", these 24 periods correspond to the zodiac and element cycles. For instance:

- Spring: From Xia to Qin (From primitive systems to late slave systems), representing a time of societal chaos and poverty.
- Summer: From Western Han to the Southern Dynasties, a time of great development and rising productivity.
- Autumn: From the Northern Dynasties to the Northern Song, when the nation was powerful but began to show signs of decline.
- Winter: From the Southern Song to the People's Republic of China, marked by foreign invasions and the dominance of external cultures.

Thus, the weakest and most chaotic periods are during "Zi" (Rat) and "Hai" (Pig), which correspond to the Xia and modern China. The strongest and most prosperous periods are "Si" (Snake) and "Wu" (Horse), correlating to the peak of the Sui and Tang dynasties.

- According to the "Earthly Path", the Qin and Western Han periods marked a societal transformation from Slavery to Feudalism, paralleling the shift from Spring to Summer in the cycle. Modern China is currently transitioning from Feudalism to Democracy, much like the transition from the Qin to Western Han periods.
- According to the "Human Path", the Qin Dynasty had poor relationships between the ruler and the people, resulting in its short reign. The Han Dynasty, on the other hand, had strong governance, which led to its long reign.

Following this pattern, it is also noted that after the Southern Song, China was ruled by various foreign invaders such as the Liao, Western Xia, Jin, Mongols, and the Manchu Qing Dynasty. These foreign powers were exploitative and lacked original cultural contributions. The intellectual sphere was dominated by foreign ideologies, such as Christianity, Islam, and Marxism, which exerted control and repression.

China's entry into the "Winter" of barbaric rule has left a lasting impact, though such oppressive regimes do not last long. The Yuan Dynasty was overthrown by the Ming, and the Qing was replaced by the Republic of China, as their rule did not align with the “Ren dao” (Human path).

By dividing the 24 dynasties into two groups ---- 12 from Xia to the Southern Dynasties and 12 from the Northern Dynasties to modern China ---- it becomes clear that the strongest period was the transition from Qin to Western Han.

3. Predictions of Chinese Prophets

Most prophets in China have based their predictions on the cyclical changes of yin and yang, as well as the five elements. These natural cycles allow for general predictions, but they often cannot provide highly specific details or individual forecasts. The most accurate and significant prophets combine these methods with the "Heavenly Path", "Earthly Path", and "Human Path", and even possess an extra-sensory perception or sixth sense that allows them to access spiritual insights.

1) Predictions Based on Natural Space and Time

One of the most famous Chinese predictive texts is the 《Zhouyi》 (Also known as the 《I Ching》), which is a classic text on yin-yang and five-element prediction. The 《I Ching》 uses a symbolic system based on yin-yang hexagrams that represent the states of the universe. By interpreting these symbols, people can predict the outcomes of events, and the text expresses changes in all things, embodying the traditional Chinese cosmology.

Later on, the 《I Ching》 expanded its influence beyond divination, impacting Chinese philosophy, religion, politics, economics, medicine, astronomy, mathematics, literature, music, art, military tactics, and martial arts. It represents a development of the yin-yang theory and its practical application.

2) Predictions from Wisdom and Spiritual Intuition

Ordinary people can make mechanical predictions based on natural cycles of time and space, such as interpreting "Bazi" (Eight characters), palm readings, and facial features. Most fortune tellers that can be found on the streets fall into this category, though their predictions are often vague and unreliable. However, true masters do not solely rely on the mechanical application of yin-yang theory and the 《I Ching》. They also use spiritual wisdom and sixth-sense intuition.

For instance:

- The 《Qiankun Wannian Ge》 (Song of Heaven and Earth) is a famous folk prophecy said to have been written by Jiang Taigong during the Zhou Dynasty. It consists of 106 lines, each with seven characters. While tradition attributes it to Jiang Taigong, the language and structure suggest later authorship or that his original words were recorded and compiled by later generations. These predictions, based on spiritual insights, forecast events for different dynasties and have proven remarkably accurate.

- The 《Ma Qian Ke》 (Lessons Before the Horse) is a prophecy attributed to Zhuge Liang during the Three Kingdoms period. Legend says he wrote it during his time as a military strategist. The text consists of 14 lessons, each predicting a specific dynasty in historical sequence, and it accurately forecasts events up to the founding of the Republic of China. It is another example of a combination of time-space prediction and spiritual intuition.

- The most accurate Chinese prophecy is the 《Tui Bei Tu》 (Pushing Back Chart), said to have been written by the Tang Dynasty Emperor Li Shimin's astrologer, Li Chunfeng, and the face-reader Yuan Tiangang. This work contains 60 images, corresponding to the intersection of 60 cyclical periods of time and space. It predicts the entire trajectory of China's social systems, from the Feudal county system to the Democratic parliamentary system and ultimately a Unified republic. The text forecasts 60 major events, providing a systematic analysis of the rise and fall of dynasties, and the transformation from Feudalism to Democracy and Unity.

Li Chunfeng and Yuan Tiangang's predictions combined the sequential order of dynasties with the overall theory of yin-yang, five elements, and the 《I Ching》. Their predictions also relied on spiritual intuition, enabling them to foresee not only the role of certain historical figures, but also the impacts of wars and the fate of nations. They could perceive the future of individuals and society through a spiritual "Third eye", beyond the capabilities of basic yin-yang theory.

- Another notable prophecy is the 《Shaobing Ge》 (Biscuit Song), written during the Ming Dynasty by Liu Bowen, an advisor to the founder of the Ming Dynasty, Zhu Yuanzhang. The 《Shaobing Ge》 consists of over 1,912 characters in 40 songs, each in the form of a riddle. It is believed to predict significant events from the Ming and Qing dynasties to the Republic of China and the People's Republic of China. The text cannot be entirely explained through yin-yang theory or the 《I Ching》 and is thought to have been derived from spiritual intuition.

Curiously, all of these great prophecies appeared during times when ethnic Han ruled China. For example, Jiang Ziya in the Shang-Zhou transition, Zhou Wenwang in the Zhou Dynasty, Zhuge Liang in the Three Kingdoms period, Li Chunfeng and Yuan Tiangang in the Tang Dynasty, Shao Yong in the Song Dynasty, Liu Bowen in the Ming Dynasty, and prophets during the Republic era. In every major Han people dynasty, a great prophet emerged, leaving behind texts as evidence. These prophecies often overlap and complement one another, as if guided by divine assistance.

IV. Western Prophetic Theories

1. Astronomical Predictions – Western Astrology

Western astrology is based on the positions of constellations in the sky, a system that dates back to around 2000 BCE. The astrological system, influenced by ancient civilizations such as Mesopotamia, Greece, Rome, and the Arab world, links celestial events to earthly events. Important historical moments were often interpreted as messages from the heavens, much like how the Chinese 《I Ching》 links yin and yang to social dynamics.

Western astrologers rely heavily on this system to map out celestial charts (Horoscopes) and use them to explain individual personalities or predict major events, much like Chinese diviners use the 《I Ching》 for personal and societal predictions. Despite modern scientific skepticism about the actual impact of distant stars on Earth due to their remoteness, Western astrology focuses on the positional changes of constellations rather than their physical composition, which aligns it somewhat with the cyclical logic of yin-yang and the Chinese zodiac system.

While the idea of using star constellations to predict an individual's life can seem mechanical and unreliable ---- just as Chinese predictions based on the 《I Ching》 might be ---- astrologers often turn to physical characteristics such as palm and facial readings to enhance predictions, especially for larger-scale societal outcomes.

2. Indian Astrology

Indian astrology, also known as "Vedic astrology", also relies on the positions of celestial bodies. Unlike Western astrology, however, Vedic astrology focuses more on predicting major life events for individuals rather than their personality traits and psychological profile.

A key concept in Indian astrology is the "Navagraha" (九曜) or nine planets, which includes the Sun, Moon, Mars, Mercury, Jupiter, Venus, Saturn, "Rahu (罗睺)" (The North Node of the Moon), and "Ketu (计都)" (The South Node of the Moon). Rahu and Ketu are considered malefic in Vedic astrology, and their influence is more heavily emphasized compared to Western astrology. The changes in these planetary bodies are believed to affect Earth's climate and even predict conflicts, such as how modern Indian child prodigy Abhigya Anand has made startlingly accurate predictions through his study of Vedic astrology. Vedic astrology may also have roots influenced by ancient Chinese studies of the five classical planets (Mars, Mercury, Jupiter, Venus, and Saturn).

3. Psychic Predictions

Western spiritual prophecies often take the form of psychic predictions. One of the most famous Western prophets was Nostradamus, a French-Jewish seer who wrote 《Les Prophéties》 (The Centuries) in 1555. The book, written in quatrains, reportedly contains predictions he gleaned from visions received on cold nights through spiritual intuition. Scholars have correlated some of his prophecies with historical events like the French Revolution, the rise of Hitler, and inventions like the airplane and atomic bomb.

However, unlike Chinese prophecies, Nostradamus's predictions often lack a clear sequence or structure and are considered by many to be vague, without concrete evidence to support their accuracy. Despite its popularity and wide interpretation, 《Les Prophéties》 falls short in comparison to the systematic spiritual predictions of China's 《Tui Bei Tu》, which meticulously follows historical chronology.

Another famous figure in Western spiritual prophecy is Baba Vanga, a blind Bulgarian mystic who was born in 1911. She reportedly predicted major events like the 9/11 attacks and the sinking of the Russian submarine Kursk. Baba Vanga's visions started after she mysteriously lost her sight in a storm at the age of 12, and she began to believe she had the ability to predict the future and heal others.

V. Conclusion

All humans receive different types of information from nature. The cycles of the solar system provide information, such as through the Yin-yang theory and the 《I Ching》, or the arrangement of constellations in astrology. Then, there is information from the brain, a mix of hallucinations and future insights. The solar system's messages can be felt through ancient Chinese Yin-yang theories or the Earth's rotation and revolution. Western astrology is similarly based on these ideas but is unrelated to modern Western philosophies like materialism, idealism, or dialectics.

The brain's hallucinations about past lives and future predictions are unique to each individual, influenced by one's mental state, facial and palm features, and personal wisdom. This uniqueness is why scientific communities struggle to explain or accept prophecy. Science, which focuses on reproducible theories, cannot yet address these non-replicable individual phenomena.

Lastly, the far-reaching information of the galaxy and the universe provides "Universal laws", an overarching framework for understanding the universe's future and societal development. This future science belongs to the realm of Galactic and Cosmic civilizations.

(Created on June 15, 2024, Picture Network)

C21. The Correct Scientific Interpretation of Figures 44 to 47 of 《Tui Bei Tu》

Abstract: There are many prophets in the East and the West. The most famous prophet in the West is Mr. Nostradamus, and the most famous prophet in the East is Mr. Yuan Tian gang and Mr. Li Chun feng in the Tang Dynasty. The 44th, 45th, 46th, and 47th bishops of the 《Tui Bei Tu》 prophecies are a section and a key event and node in history.

Prophecy is also a science, so how can the prophet predict the future with such precision? At present, scientists only talk about theories, formulas, and practical technologies. They have also studied molecules and atoms, but they don't understand how to form wisdom and predictive science from brain molecules and atoms. They don't even know about how did they generate theory and logic from their brains.

I. Introduction

《Tui Bei Tu》 was co-authored by Mr. Li Chun feng and Mr. Yuan Tian gang in the Tang Dynasty. It is divided into four parts of prophecy namely, Hexagram, photos, prophecies and interpretations. There are six different versions of the existing 《Tui Bei Tu》. Although such books are strictly forbidden in all dynasties, they are constantly being tampered with in the process of spreading. There are many versions, but one of them must be the original copy, or copied from the original, such as Mr. Jin Sheng tan’s annotated version. It is copied from the original (Although there are several pictures and sentences later in the dynasty). Maybe Mr. Jin Sheng tan's research found that the time predictions in this book are correct, otherwise he would not spend so much effort to annotate, because the real book really predicted the future very accurately, and it was deduced in the order of dynasties and time.

And most of the pseudo-books are simply reversed in time order, and the characters in the pictures are also paintings casually. Many prophecies in 《Tui Bei Tu》 can be more accurate if they are compared with the Western prophecy 《Bible》 and Nostradamus' 《Les Propheties》 .

II. The corresponding prophecies in the West

We have previously talked about some of the prophecies of Nostradamus’ 《Les Propheties》 . Here is a story from the 《Bible》 . In the Old Testament 《Exodus》 , it is mentioned that the Egyptian Pharaohs enslaved the Israelites. God punished the Egyptian pharaoh and sent "Ten plagues" to Egypt in order to make the pharaoh surrender. At the beginning, the disaster was mild, and the pharaoh didn't care about it, and it became more violent. Egypt suffered a lot of blows and losses, but Pharaoh still didn’t believe it and didn’t want the Jews to leave Egypt. Until the last plague, Pharaoh’s eldest son died overnight, and Pharaoh agreed the Jews to leave. Then he regretted it again, sent troops to chase, and finally all the chasing soldiers were buried in the Red Sea.

We extend from this story to the world today, that is, the 44th, 45th, 46th, and 47th bishops of 《Tui Bei Tu》 Chinese prophecies. The Orientals will lead the world to a peaceful and prosperous age. The world controlled by religions and leaders in the West, who will naturally not agree with it. Then the Gods will use the same method to send ten disasters to the world to force the "Western stellar civilization" to identify with the "Eastern galactic civilization".

At first it seemed to be a natural disaster, such as (1) Earthquakes (Global); (2) Tsunamis (Southeast Asia and Japan); (3) Nuclear pollution (Japan); (4) Forest fires (Global); (5) Locust plagues (Africa); (6) Volcanic eruptions (Global); (7) Floods (Asia and Europe); (8) Extreme heat and cold extreme weather (Global), slowly becoming as if someone is controlling disasters, such as (9) Plague (Global)..., this is the kingdom of God cooperating with the arrival of Eastern civilization to force Western religions to know.

At present, most of the dead are civilians, reaching tens of millions, but the religions and leaders around the world don't care. They think that the disaster will be over soon, or think that the Christianity or Islam they believe in is faith in the true God (In fact, the world's Religion has no faith in true Gods), which is the same as the belief that the Egyptian pharaohs insisted at that time (The Pharaoh did not understand Pyramid beliefs at that time).

However, the disasters will become more severe than the last until the end. We still don't know what more powerful means the heaven will use after this plague, but it must no longer be civilians, but like the Egyptian Pharaoh who died his son, causing certain important people to suffer suddenly to force them to understand the rescue of Eastern civilization.

The Egyptian Pharaoh was so arrogant and tough at the time, and it was impossible to believe the words of a group of slave Israelis. And today's Western leaders and religious leaders naturally look down on something!

Although these Western religions have testimonies, such as prophecies in their beliefs, such as Christ, Maitreya Buddha, Islam's Elsa, Egyptian pharaohs, and Mayan warriors, etc come back again, but for their followers, it's just talk, and didn't see, there was no one who really believed.

"Eastern Galactic Civilization" is to unify all religions, philosophies, and sciences in the world. Whether you believe in God or not, you will be impressed by the tremendous energy and means of the Eastern Kingdom of God.

Just as the Israelis arrived in Canaan, the land of God's promise, China will become the promised country of God, end the global warlord's melee and the world's chaos, and build well-being for world peace and harmony. The Jews at that time were God's chosen people, but they are not anymore. They could not unify the religions of the world and became Chinese. The stories they showed were almost exactly the same as the sufferings, beliefs, and perseverance of the Jews back then.

III. Corresponding predictions of the 《Tui Bei Tu》

《 Tui Bei Tu 》 accurately propagates downwards according to the time and dynasty sections, almost all of the major events and nodes of each dynasty and generations, with the focus on the characters. The current analysis from the Internet is not bad at all. I will not go into details here, but just list the online explanations:

For example, The Tang Dynasty is the 1st to the 10th photos;

The Five Dynasties and the Ten Kingdoms are the 11th to 15 photos;

The Song Dynasty is from the 16th to the 24th photos;

The Yuan Dynasty is from the 25th to the 26th photos;
The Ming Dynasty is from the 27th to the 32th photos;
The Qing Dynasty is from the 33th to the 36th photos;
The Republic of China is from the 37th to the 40th photos.

Since the Republic of China arrived in Taiwan in the later period, the 40th photo has continued to the current situation in Taiwan, with three places on both sides of the strait. There are many explanations and analyses on the Internet. Although there are some differences, they are basically accurate and a consensus has been reached. It is relatively easy to grasp what has happened. Almost all echoes before and after, and it is logical that the correct rate is 100%.

IV. The prophecies for the present

But from the 41st to the 47th photos, are happening in the mainland, from now to the future for a period of time. I saw many explanations on the internet, but the basic details are not accurate. Some people say that it took a lifetime to interpret. I only took 20 minutes to interpret it. Because it is not their personal experience, they definitely don't know. Only through personal experience can we understand.

In fact, from the 41th to the 47th photos are also advancing downwards in chronological order, very precise, mainly divided into two parts.

1. Explanation from the 41th to the 43th photos:

This is a section. From the liberation of mainland China in 1949 to the present, the continuous movement to reform and opening up, the restoration of normal order, and the current problems.

第四十一象甲辰

【谶曰】 天地晦盲　草木繁殖
阴阳反背　上土下日

【颂曰】 帽儿须戴血无头　手弄乾坤何日休
九十九年成大错　称王只合在秦州

Fig.C21-1 This 41th photo represents Chairman Mao's continuous movement, which caused national turmoil.

1) Photo:

Playing with the Earth alone shows how capable Mao was at that time.

2) Prophecy:

"The world is blind, the vegetation reproduces": Refers to various critique movement, the sky is dim, the ground is overgrown with weeds, and no one is planting the ground.

"Yin and yang turn against the back, under the Earth is the Sun": The yin and yang are reversed, and good people turn into bad people. Air-raid shelters were dug day and night in everywhere, and the electric lights under the soil like the Sun.

3) Interpretation:

"Hats need to wear blood without head": Hats wear this red head badge or sign.

"When will be ended by the hands fiddle the world": Mao was backhanded by clouds at the time, and regained hands by rain. Who would dare to say no?

"Nine Nineteen years make a big mistake": 9 plus 19 for a total of 28 years, that is, from 1949 to 1977, a total of 28 years. There were no dead in the first 9 years, and a large number of dead in the next 19 years. Repeated movement made a big mistake.

"The king can only be called in Qinzhou": To say that Mao is worthy to be called a king in "Qinzhou". "Qinzhou" is the boundary of ancient Shanxi, that is, in Yan'an. The author of the《Tui Bei Tu》is really ironic! Whatever Mao pretend to be, "Qin emperor and Han emperor lose literary talent; Tang emperor and Song emperor are less coquettish!" It seems that Mao is talking, the sky is watching in the 6-dimensional space, and the author of 《Tui Bei Tu》seems to know what you are doing. He deliberately refute Mao! Stop saying that all the emperors are inferior to you, right! Mao will only be a king in one county.

第四十二象乙巳

【谶曰】 美人自西来，朝中日渐安
长弓在地，危而不危

【颂曰】 西方女子琵琶仙，皎皎衣裳色更鲜
此时浑迹居朝市，闹乱君臣百万般

Fig.C21-2 This 42 photo chart represents China's next scenario, reform and opening up, and the West enters the Chinese market.

1) Photo:

Women are all going to play and acting is the most profitable, all weapons "Bows" are thrown away, rabbits are "Money" important.

2) Prophecy:

"Beauty comes from the West, imperial court gradually settle down": The Cultural Revolution ended, reform and opening up, and the Americans came from the West. Chinese government settle down and stop playing movement.

"Longbow on the ground, danger but not danger": Even if the weapons are put down, there will be conflicts or trade frictions in some areas, and even bombing of Embassies, but it is not dangerous.

3) Interpretation:

"Western female fairy has brighter clothes.": Western businessmen and beauties have swaggered through the market in large numbers, and there are gorgeous street girls everywhere.

"At this time, many muddy traces are hidden in market, there are millions of monarchs and ministers make in disorder". All kinds of smuggling and abduction in the market also confuse government officials. There are millions of corruption and bribery.

第四十三象丙午

【谶曰】 君非君 臣非臣
始艰危 终克定

【颂曰】 黑兔走入青龙穴 欲尽不尽不可说
唯有外边根树上 三十年中子孙结

Fig. C21-3 This 43th photo shows another scene. After a period of reform and opening up, there are still problems, because the government's Marx's system has not changed and the policy has instability, and the people still can not speak freely. Almost no one on the Internet can solve this photo.

1) Photo:

Adults and children are sometimes a bit scared, covering their faces with their sleeves, pretending not to see anything and dare not say anything. Even if the road sees unevenness, he hides far away for fear of being deceived.

2) Prophecy:

"A monarch is not a monarch, and a minister is not a minister": It means that a State system such as Marx's religion is neither a Feudal monarch nor a Democratic president, or a Western religious cardinal. The emperor is not the emperor; the ministers are not ministers, so if you put the name of the "Secretary and chairman" of the Western Soviet Union, you don't know what the ruling system is.

"Danger at the beginning, and stability at the end". The reform was a bit difficult at the beginning, such as the turmoil in Tiananmen Square. In the end, these dangers were suppressed and settled down.

3) Interpretation:

"The black rabbit walks into the cyan Dragon cave": It means that the five types of bad guy who were defeated in the movement were rehabilitated, and they all turned around and became glorious the official.

This also refers to a series of national leaders, such as Hu Yaobang, Zhao Ziyang, Jiang Zemin, Hu Jintao, etc., who all came to power one after another in the Black Five categories.

"You can't talk about your desires": Do you want to talk about the Anti-rightist movement and the past of the Cultural Revolution? Would you like to talk about the current inequality between the rich and the poor and the various status quo of society? That's another forbidden zone that can't be said.

"Only on the outer roots, the descendants will tie up in 30 years" : Refers to the overseas Chinese in Taiwan, Hong Kong, Macau and the world outside the mainland, but they have been promoting Chinese culture and spreading the roots of Chinese culture to overseas descendants after year 1989.

Some also refer to the middle year of the 30 years from 1989 to 2020, that is, in 2012, when the Stellar civilization died and the Galactic civilization began.

\---

2. Explanation from the 44th to the 47th photos:

This is a section, mainly about a person and his theoretical system, which is to solve the problems of the 41th to the 43th photos. And solving the above problems are not only a problem of China itself, but also a problem that affects the entire world. Because Marx's religion is also part of the virus variants of the world religion, only the theoretical system of the Orientals can be completely resolved, and the time was set to be around year 2012 when the theoretical system was completed.

第四十四象丁未

【谶曰】 日月丽天　群阴慑服
百灵来朝　双羽四足

【颂曰】 而今中国有圣人　虽非豪杰也周成
四夷重译称天子　否极泰来九国春

Fig. C21-4 The 44th photo: Because the Orientals are beginning to solve the problems of the Westerners, even the Western prophets Mr. Nostradamus, Casey, Janet Dixon, and Polliska felt it, and almost all the top Western prophets predicted it.

1) Photo:

This man with a bow is actually like a warrior on the expedition. He wants to fight all religious believers in the West. Of course, there is a double meaning, let alone. But he didn't think he was so great, but he asked people of higher wisdom for advice. The sitting person may be a person from Heaven, a wiser person or an alien. It is not like the Western religious leader who claims to be the son of God, or is a God or an angel, who is used to solicit believers.

2) Prophecy:

"The Sun, the Moon and the sky are beautiful, the insidious group be deterrence": It is mainly the word of deterrence. His theoretical system is to make all religious believers fearful and convinced. Isn't it difficult?

"Many clever birds came to the dynasty, double feathers and four legs": The spiritual people are gathered. "Double feathers and four legs" is Chinese word "Yan", in the Northern of China.

3) Interpretation:

"Nowadays, there is saint in China, even if he is not heroes, he is also Zhou Cheng."

"The world retranslated his books, or it will bring the spring to the all countries."

Generally, one person in the East wants to defeat the entire Western religion and their more than 6 billion believers, that is, a rainbow warrior, at most Mr. Zhou Cheng or a hero. So everyone can become a saint, so you can give it a go. Don't go to worship in any church or derivative church in the West. Retreat from all their organizations, take out your powerful theoretical system, frighten them, and fight for the religions nations of the world. There is peace in the world, if it is true or not, it is a saint.

Here is an important point to explain that believers of all religions in the world today want to turn their cult leaders into saints, just like Hitler's large number of Nazi SS nominated Hitler for the Peace Prize. Believers of various religions bring a lot of benefits from the leader, often holding dharma meetings, obstructing the streets and collecting money, spreading rumours, control media and making troubles everywhere. The problem is that your master mainly came up with a set of theoretical systems to make other Western churches "Deterrence"? That's the most important thing.

Some people say that all churches only use "Truthful goodness" to entice people to teach. You can't oppose the "Truthful goodness" of people, right? But the Bible has already written in the prophecy that contemporary leaders can deceive with anything, but they can't move the "Truth and good" fruit. As long as you move, you will die. The Bible is using prophecies to "Deterrence" these Western priests, calling them "Snakes" and they will only deceive female believers. You have to "Admire" God's eyes. It have long seen through these snake-like Western religious priests, and the trick of the derivative cult master!

第四十五象戊申

【谶曰】 有客西来 至东而止
木火金水 洗此大耻

【颂曰】 炎运宏开世界同 金乌隐匿白洋中
从此不敢称雄长 兵气全消运已终

Fig. C21-5 This 45th photo means that all religions of the "Western stellar civilization" have been stopped by the "Eastern galactic civilization". It is also a theoretical system that almost no one can understand on the Internet. You should know what is the "Western stellar civilization" and what is the "Eastern galactic civilization" ?

1) Photo:

It seems impossible to poke the Sun with a spear. The Sun is the "Stellar system", and the "Galaxy" has feet. Here, a gun is used as a representative. Using the gun of the theoretical system of "Eastern galactic civilization" in East to poke "Western stellar civilization" in West is to defeat it. It's amazing! People in the Tang Dynasty thousands of years ago knew what people thought today. From another point of view, the 《Tui Bei Tu》 book cannot be a collective creation!

At present, almost all online and books explain that the "Sun" is Japan and that China is fighting with Japan. In fact, it is a big mistake. It can only be said that it cannot be explained. If China really wants to fight with Japan and the United States, it will hardly be an opponent at all. You have to cooperate with the complete plate of 44th to 47th photos to understand.

2) Prophecy:

"The guest comes from the West and ends at the East": Refers to all religions from the "Western stellar civilization", all of them are guest, and they are stopped by the native system of the "Eastern galactic civilization", which corresponds to the 44th photo. The one who can achieve this goal is the Eastern Sage, who fights 6 billion people with one person instead of a bunch of believers versus a bunch of believers. Isn't it difficult?

"Wood, fire, gold and water, wash away this great shame": Most people don't know what it means. It refers to the specific meaning of "Western guest". "Wood, fire, gold and water" here refers to four types colour, colour mainly refers to the clothing colour and religious colour mark that these religious believers like to wear, namely cyan wood (Buddhism); red fire (Communist); white gold (Christianity); black water (Islam) is unified by the "Eastern galactic civilization", which has washed away the shame of the East being invaded by foreign cultures for a hundred years. It also refers to the theoretical system, not the war. Maybe four colours also mentioned by the four big beast seals in the Bible Revelation.

3) Interpretation:

"Flaming luck opens the world together, the golden ships hides in the white ocean": It also means that the theoretical system of the “Eastern Galactic Civilization” unifies the Western religions, the global democracy established by the United States of America triumphs in the period of the Yan Yun (i.e., between year 2024 - 2027) and opens up the world, and the Russian maritime fleet are hidden in the oceans and do not dare to fight any more. The double meaning is a golden Ukraine that joins the North Atlantic Treaty Organization.

"Since then, it has not dared to dominate, and all its military strength is over." It is indicated that the Marx Cult, the birthplace of Russia, has never since dared to claim a long, or a bear's paw. Its soldiers and arms are useless, most of them destroyed, and its luck gone.

第四十六象己酉

【谶曰】 黯黯阴霾　杀不用刀
万人不死　一人难逃

【颂曰】 有一军人身带弓　只言我是白头翁
东边门里伏金剑　勇士後门入帝宫

Fig C21-6 This 46th image shows that the top leaders in China is fighting internally over whether to continue to adhere to the "Western stellar civilization", Marxist-Leninist religious variant, or to adopt the Chinese traditional "Eastern galactic civilization", which is also related to the theoretical system.

1) Photo:

This person is angry with himself there, I must kill someone.

2) Prophecy:

"It's dark and haze, you don't need a knife to kill. ": At present, the Internet refers to viruses or haze. In fact, it is a big mistake, but it means that the high level of China government is bloody, grey and dark, and internal forces are proceeding in a life-and-death struggle. The opposition was directly caught and thrown into prison for various reasons, not directly killed with a knife.

"Ten thousand people do not die, only one can not escape.": This sentence is connected with the previous two sentences, which means that most of the group members are not dead, but the main leader has been arrested. According to the main points grasped by the author of the 《Tui Bei Tu》, if you just grab the main leader and change to another leader, and China's political situation has not changed, it is useless to change the soup without changing the medicine. It must be an event that will affect the overall situation of China in the future. The key event is like the big change in China's reform and opening up after the Gang of Four was arrested.

3) Interpretation:

"There is a soldier with a bow, but I am a White-headed bird".

"A golden sword is buried in the east gate, and the warrior enters the imperial palace at the back door."

The two verses of this ode are followed by the two sentences of admonition. This refers to the direct contention within China's senior leadership, or the specific scene of court fighting. This competition has directly changed the direction of China's future political situation, and is regarded as a major event for reversing Eastern civilization.

"White-headed bird" is an anagram and the key. It is a Chinese upper-class figure. I probably know who it is. But this is a secret. I won't say it first. But from the accuracy of the 《Tui Bei Tu》, this will happen. Naturally at that time just understand. This once again shows that destiny cannot be violated. If you violate it, you will be arrested and sent to prison like a Gang of Four.

Regardless of the internal contention, from the results of the 47th photo, the faction of Chinese senior leaders who favoured the traditional Chinese "Eastern galactic civilization" won and completely kicked the Western variant

Marxism-Leninism out of China. The reason why this photo is important is that it is more than just that. The key to reversing China's future political situation, and also having a huge impact on the world, is the key victory of the "Eastern galactic civilization" against the "Western stellar civilization".

In other words, from this battle, 1.4 billion people broke away from Western religions, plus hundreds of millions of people in the surrounding countries that China has influenced, almost 2 billion people are on the side of the "Eastern galactic civilization". At this time, it was not based on 1 person to 6 billion people, but 2 billion people to 4 billion people (The global population this year is 7.8 billion people, about 1.8 billion people, tentatively designated as miscellaneous religions), the power of Eastern and Western beliefs has also taken place a fundamental change.

第四十七象庚戌

【谶曰】 偃武修文　紫薇星明
匹夫有责　一言为君

【颂曰】 无王无帝定乾坤　来自田间第一人
好把旧书多读到　义言一出见英明

Fig C21-7 This 47th photo is the result of the 44th photo to the 46th photos. When the upper echelons of China kicked out the Marx's education in the West, they all believed in the traditional Chinese theoretical system of "Eastern galactic civilization". The whole world was shocked. Their derivative teachings are rubbish, and the believers have also become street mice, everyone shouts and beats, and abandons worship one after another, that is, "No king, no emperor will determine the nation".

At this time, the world is peaceful and the country and the people are in peace, because global wars are all mixed by these Western rubbish religions. It is estimated that the results will be seen soon in the future.

1) Photo:

This picture is easier to see. The bookshelves are full of books and theoretical systems. Orientals first use theoretical thought systems instead of using wars and weapons to sweep down the world's religions and countries.

2) Prophecy:

"Stop force, specialize in articles, The stars are bright, everyone is responsible, and one word is king.": Give up military force and rule the world with civilization, which is the victory of "Eastern galactic civilization" defeat "Western stellar civilization". The key to this is that everyone feels that they should make some contribution to the society. It is the responsibility of everyone, not like the 43th photo. It's none of my business, pretending to be out of sight, hiding far away, and nobody save child who even fall into the river.

3) Interpretation:

"There is no king or emperor who determines the nation, the first person come from the civilians.": The key to this prophecy is that there is no king or emperor to determine the nation, which specifically embodies the Oriental theoretical system that there is no need to worship any leader or emperor, or if you deny Western religious leaders, the world can be peaceful. This is just a theoretical system from a single person among civilians.

"It's good to read more old books, and you will be wise as soon as righteous words come out.": It's best to read more traditional old books! Those modern books, such as eulogizing, sci-fi, fantasy, and eunuch books, it is best to read less. And the difficult problems that you can't be solved in your lifetime, such as the photo on the 《Tui Bei Tu》, it can be solved in a few words.

The 44th to 47th in the photos are a section. At present, we are one step away from the 46th photo. When the world praises the "Eastern galactic civilization", the ten plagues that heaven has brought to the world controlled by Western religions have also been completed. All kinds of natural disasters, land disasters, and man-made disasters are gone, so that the people and theoretical systems described in the 44 to 47 photos are all integrated. And it will come soon, we will see the results in our lifetime, and it is estimated that the correct rate is still 100%.

It is emphasized here that the author of 《Tui Bei Tu》 used 4 photos to describe a theoretical system of Eastern thought, which is equivalent to photos used by dynasties. For example, only 4 photos were used in the Qing Dynasty for more than 200 years, which shows this theory. How important is the influence of the system on future generations.

3. From the 48th to the 60th photos

It is another sector after the 48th photo in 《Tui Bei Tu》. It will take decades to a hundred years, and no one can understand it at present. Only in that era can you feel the picture, the details of the combination of prophecy and interpretation is also sorted by time in one section plus another section.

But one thing we can know is that if the 44th to 47th photos are the first global unity of the Orientals in the religious, philosophical, and scientific theoretical system, it is called "Global theoretical unity", which is a small section. From the 48th to the 59th photos, it is the unification of the global countries, called "Global national unification". It is a large section (Also interspersed with time fragments of several small section), that is, the use of weapons and warfare. Unify all countries in the world.

I took a close look at the 48th to 58th photos. I generally know them, but the details are not clear. The photos talk about who is in charge in future, no longer talk about theories. They are all about actions. Warlords are fighting between countries, chaotic battles in the world, and high-tech wars. The picture, especially the 56th photo, is simply a world war, that is, a global high-tech unification war. There are riots and cessation in various small sectors; a cycle of war and peace again. During this period of time, 《Tui Bei Tu》 is about people and things that happened from the East; 《Les Propheties》 is about things that happened from the West. In fact, they all talk about one thing, depending on which prediction is accurate, or add each other. It is generally believed that the predictions of 《Tui Bei Tu》 are very detailed and can name the key leaders, but most of the Western prophets describe things in detail and do not give the names of the characters.

Finally, we reach the 59th photo, that is, all countries in the world are truly unified, or the "Unified Republic" we predicted.

The 59th photo: "The Red, Yellow, Black and White are unclear, and the East, the West, the North and the South are in harmony". It is means that all the red, yellow, black and white people are assimilated; the East, the West, the North and the South of the world are in harmony.

This is a bit like a replica of the scene of the unification of the Spring and Autumn Period and the Warring States Period and the Qin Dynasty! First, in the Spring and Autumn Period and Warring States period, the thinkers used theoretical ideas to unify, and then the whole country was unified by war (Only the transition from the "Enfeoffment system of slave owners" to the "Feudal system of prefectures and counties" was replaced from the "Democratic parliamentary system" to the "Unified republic").

All prophecies may extend down to a thousand years later, but in which era was the last prophecy of the figure? Only then will it be known. Some people say that the sorting of the 《Tui Bei Tu》 is disrupted, which may refer to a large number of fake copies, or they can't crack it at all. If everyone can crack it, aren't they all Mr. Yuan Tian gang and Mr. Li Chun feng? The writing of 《Tui Bei Tu》 is very accurate and pays attention to details. All pictures, prophecies, and interpretation are matched with each other, and there is no contradiction. Every word and sentences are meaningful and arranged in time and order. The correct rate is 100%.

Due to the huge differences in historical time-down scenarios, speculation about the future can only be approximate, and Mr. Jin Sheng tan's solution is the same. He can only explain what happened before his death, and most of the solutions after his death are chaotic. Some prophecies are relatively short, such as 《 Pre-Horse Lessons》 , which may really end here at the 47th photo.

V. Summary

《Book of Changes》, 《Tao De Jing》 and 《Tui Bei Tu》 are the three ancient prophecy books or Chinese divine books. 《Book of Changes》 shows the periodic part of the laws of the universe, showing a "0" nature; 《Tao De Jing》 shows the laws of the universe that they are the beginning of the Heaven and the Earth and the mother of all things, showing the "." nature; 《Tui Bei Tu》 shows the expansion of the universal law, showing the "1" nature, and time and space foreshadowing the books. There are hardly any other Chinese books that can compare with these three books. It is beyond words to describe how wonderful they are!

Like Confucian books, legal books, Guiguzi books, war books, historical books, Tang and Song poems, Ming and Qing novels, and various contemporary science and technology books, no matter how well they are written, they can be written by humans. But these three books cannot be written by ordinary people, even the top masters of the past, and they are hard to quite match. For example, 《The Book of Changes》 is edited by the emperor, which talks about Heaven and Earth operations; 《Tui bei Tu》 is edited by court officials, talks about the fortune of the dynasties; The 《Tao Te Ching》 is edited by ordinary scholars, and it talks about the operation of the government and the people, it is almost as if it was arranged by the Gods!

If the three books written by ancient men in the East compare the three books of the Western 《Bible》, 《Quran》 or 《Buddhist scriptures》, or the "Three books of one nation" should be compared with the "Three books of three nations". Let billion worshippers can understand and know, the Eastern hierarch must be more “An angelic deity” than their Western hierarch. But the Orientals do not worship at all, no Gods, and there is no way for them to form believers with brain-disabled people, and the leaders of the East do not need believers with brain-disabled people, which shows how extensive and profound the Eastern culture is.

《Exodus》 is the second volume of the Pentateuch. It is generally believed that the author of the book is Moses himself. This is the lyrics of the movie 《Exodus》 , which is similar to the rising horn of "Eastern Gods Culture, Universal Law and Galaxy Civilization":

This is my land, and God gave me this land,
and gave me this brave golden land.
Morning light emerges from the side of the mountain,
and I can see the children playing freely.

So, take my hand and walk with me on this land.
Walk with me on this lovely land.
Although I am only a person, you walk with me.
Under the protection of the Lord,
I know that I can become strong and walk with me in this lovely land.
Although I am only a person, you walk with me.

When I looked up at the starry sky, a voice seemed to yell: "When you are in trouble, don't be discouraged. Believe in God. God can help the rise of the Egyptians, the rise of the Israelis, and of course the rise of the Chinese. God It is omnipotent! It can do anything!"

(Written in 26 Aug. 2021)

References: 1. Moses: 《Exodus》
2. Li Chun feng, Yuan Tian gang: 《Tui Bei Tu》 (Tang Dynasty)

Appendix 1: Image 43rd of 《Tui Bei Tu》, The world is corrupt and there are many liars

Abstract: We discusses "The 43rd Image in the 《Tui Bei Tu》 prophecy" and provides an interpretation that links it to modern societal problems, primarily focusing on corruption, deceit, and the moral decline of society. We argues that this figure serves as a warning about the current state of the world and prepares the way for the next prophecy (The 44th Image). The following key themes are explored:

----

1. Further analysis of the prophecy

1) Moral Decline in Society

- We provides examples of how modern society has fallen into a state of moral decay. For instance, acts of kindness, such as helping an elderly person who has fallen, can backfire when scammers take advantage of good-hearted people, accusing them of wrongdoing and demanding compensation. The result is that people become too fearful to help others.
- This reflects a broader societal breakdown, where trust has been eroded, and acts of charity or goodwill are met with suspicion.

2) Economic Fraud

- We discusses the rise of financial scams due to a flawed political system, and argues that fraudulent behavior has become rampant in various sectors, including real estate, online Ponzi schemes, and bribery within businesses and government circles.

- We emphasizes that these economic scams are possible due to the collusion between corrupt officials and unscrupulous businesspeople, leaving countless victims in their wake.

3) Religious Scams

- We delves into religious fraud, explaining that many religious movements and cults have emerged, masquerading as legitimate spiritual practices. These groups often claim to offer benefits to their followers but are primarily focused on amassing wealth and power.
- Religious scam groups exploit people's faith, offering places of worship, healing practices like Qigong, and holding events like workshops and speeches to deceive followers into donating money and revering charismatic leaders.
- The rise of these religious frauds is compared to ancient brainwashing techniques, noting that such scams are becoming increasingly widespread in China.

4) Government Response and Conflict with Religious Scammers

- The government, feeling threatened by these groups' growing influence, has begun cracking down on them. We suggests that the government fears the loss of control over the public's loyalty and the potential for these movements to undermine the state's authority.
- However, the religious fraudsters counter these actions by accusing the government of engaging in similar deceit and suppressing religious freedom.

5) Use of Prophecies to Legitimize Scams

- We concludes by pointing out that some religious scam groups have begun using ancient prophecies like the 《Tui Bei Tu》 to bolster their legitimacy. For instance, they claim that specific figures in the prophecy ---- such as the 40th figure, associated with turning a wheel, or the 42nd figure, associated with a woman playing a pipa (A Chinese instrument) ---- are symbols of their own movements or leaders.
- These groups use these interpretations to attract more followers, create online buzz, and raise money, further cementing their influence and scamming more people.

Analysis:

The passage is a "Critique of the current state of society" in China, focusing on how scammers in various sectors ----- social, economic, and religious — exploit both individuals and communities. We makes a connection between these modern-day issues and the 43rd prophecy in the 《Tui Bei Tu》, suggesting that the prophecy predicted this widespread moral and ethical collapse.

We emphasizes the urgency of recognizing these fraudulent behaviors and avoiding being misled. The link to 《Tui Bei Tu》 serves as a cautionary tale, encouraging readers to discern truth from deception and to be vigilant in the face of societal corruption.

In essence, we calls for "Moral awakening" and "Critical thinking", warning against the allure of charismatic religious and political figures who may use deceit to gain power. The critique of the government and religious institutions reflects a broader dissatisfaction with the state of governance and the manipulation of people's faith and goodwill for personal gain.

2. The Encryption of Prophecy

We elaborates on the "Encrypted nature of prophecies", particularly focusing on the 43rd and 44th figures in the 《Tui Bei Tu》 prophecy. We discusses how these prophecies are designed to prevent confusion and manipulation by religious fraudsters and false ideologies. We emphasizes that these prophecies serve as tools for "Exposing fraud and deception", particularly in the realm of religion.

1) Encrypted Prophecies to Identify Fraudsters

- We suggests that "Ancient prophets intentionally encrypted their prophecies" to avoid misinterpretation and misuse by future con artists and religious scammers. Specifically, the "43rd figure" in the 《Tui Bei Tu》 serves as a safeguard, placed before the 44th figure, to expose religious fraudsters who may try to claim divine status.
- We critiques the common misinterpretation of the prophecy, particularly the belief that it relates to cross-straits relations between mainland China and Taiwan. We asserts that Taiwan no longer has any significant influence over China's development, and this misinterpretation is a result of guessing and confusion.

2) Distinguishing Religious Fraudsters

- Religious fraudsters are more dangerous than ordinary con artists, according to the prophecy, because they seek "Devotion and power" rather than just monetary gain. These fraudsters may claim to be divine or be revered as "Saviors" or "Saints" to deceive people.

- "The 44th figure" in the 《Tui Bei Tu》 is often misused by these groups, with leaders claiming to be the subject of the prophecy to attract followers and encourage blind worship.

- Other prophets, such as Mr.Liu Bowen from the Ming Dynasty, provided simple methods to distinguish true spiritual figures from frauds. For instance, Liu Bowen's statement, "The true Buddha is not in the temple, palace, or monastery", serves as a warning against institutionalized religion and those who seek power in religious organizations.

3) Role of Ancient Prophets in Safeguarding Truth

- We praises the "Foresight and brilliance of ancient prophets", stating that they designed prophecies in such a way as to repeatedly confirm the authenticity of their predictions and to expose fraudulent movements. We believes that this is a divine arrangement, a system set in place by higher powers to prevent manipulation.

- The passage stresses that modern-day religious and political fraudsters are unable to compete with the depth and accuracy of these ancient prophecies, even though they attempt to deceive people by attaching titles like "Saint" or "Savior" to their leaders.

4) Caution Against Overzealous Religious and Ideological Worship

- We issues a "Warning against the blind worship of any ideology or religious leader", arguing that while reading philosophical texts like the Bible, the Quran, Buddhist scriptures, or Marxist theories is fine, the problem arises when these texts dominate all discourse and suppress critical thinking.

- We highlights the danger when “Religious institutions or ideological movements” force their teachings on society, particularly when these movements demand absolute loyalty in workplaces or public life. This leads to “Manipulation of societal progress” and promotes ignorance and fanaticism.

5) Consequences of Ideological Manipulation

- We points out that modern-day religious movements, in their quest for expansion, often resort to “Fraudulent practices” such as “Financial scams”, brainwashing, and “Gathering power”. These movements oppose progress by stifling free thought and creating an environment of intellectual and social stagnation.
- The prediction warns that unchecked, these fraudulent religious movements could cause widespread harm, reflecting what the text refers to as a "Killing cult" ------- a movement that oppresses its followers and ultimately damages society.

6) Final Thoughts

- We concludes by drawing parallels between “Civilizational evolution” and the rise of fraudulent religious movements, and suggests that as society progresses from simpler stages to more advanced civilizations, “Conflict is inevitable” between old and new ways of thinking.
- Despite these risks, the natural course of history is “Forward-moving”, and we expresses hope that fraudulent ideologies will eventually be exposed as society advances.

Analysis:

We provides a “Skeptical and critical perspective on religious fraud” and the misuse of prophecies by con artists, and argues that “Ancient prophecies” like the 《Tui Bei Tu》 were carefully designed to protect against future misuse, especially by those who would exploit people's faith for personal gain.

We reflects a deep “Distrust of institutionalized religion” and “Blind ideological worship”, advocating for critical thinking and the rejection of any system that suppresses free thought. The use of prophecies as a tool to expose fraudsters, highlights the belief in “A higher cosmic order” that continually works to preserve truth and integrity in the face of deception.

In summary, we calls for “Vigilance and discernment” in spiritual and ideological matters, urging people to resist the allure of false prophets and religious movements that seek to control and manipulate society.

(Commentary article originally published in Dec. 2021)

Appendix 2: Image 45th of 《Tui Bei Tu》 Religious Virus, War Psychosis

Abstract: No one on the internet is able to understand the 45th photo of the 《Tui Bei Tu》 because of the hidden multi-layer metaphor and encryption. The first layer of meaning is that the "Western Stellar Civilization" is unified by the "Eastern Galactic Civilization". The second layer of meaning is to show that the vaccine needle of the East is injected into the virus of the West; the third layer of meaning, on the surface, is the religious fanaticism and psychosis to show off the war, but secretly, it is the theory system of the East to eliminate the war, which is a delicate design, ingenious and marvelous, so that the real theory system will not be confused by other people to carry on the wrong and confuse.

I. Further Explanation of the 45th photo

Here are some specific questions to be added in detail, why did the Tang Dynasty prophets say that the four major religions of the West are all guests and not devils? Why did the Orientals stop them instead of defeating them? What shame did they bring to the Chinese, and Orientals wanted to wash away?

1. The arrival of the Western religious "Guests from the West" and their views

The arrival of Westerners in China, for example, Buddhism came to China during the Western Han Dynasty, when diplomats from the Western regions were invited to teach the Buddhist scriptures to the upper class, and there is a saying that "Yicun taught the scriptures"; Islam came to China in the middle of the Tang Dynasty, along the Silk Road, introduced by merchants, and then spread; Christianity came to China as early as during the Tang Dynasty, during the Zhenguan period, when the Great Teacher Aroben brought the scriptures to Chang'an; and Marx religion was introduced to China through the collaboration of the Comintern in the Soviet Union and the professors of Peking University and Tsinghua University.

From the viewpoints and theories put forward by the four major Western religions when they first came to China, for example, these are their three main points of view.

1) Belief in "God". Westerners spread the word "God" to the Orientals, and in fact the Orientals also believed in the word, and dogs and cats thought that man was a god when they saw what man had created. And human beings are unable to understand many divine things, for example, who designed the eye so delicately? Even today's top scientists can't answer. Doesn't someone say, "Man is just a grain of sand in the universe"?

2) Believe in "Truth and goodness", this word Oriental people also believe in. Do human beings want to kill, robbery and crime? Of course not. Unlike animals, human beings have thoughts and intelligence.

3) Believe in "Revolution", this word is put forward by the modern materialistic church in the West, breaking up the old world and creating a new one, is this not progress? The Orientals have also been seeking innovation and progress, isn't that good?

Of course there are other messy terms and things, all sorts of confusing things, such as the opening of the eyes of heaven, the six divine powers and cultivation and whatnot. When these views of the West began to enter the East, the East did not reject and ostracize them, but accepted and identified with them as the views of their guests.

2. Why the Orientals Stopped Western Religions

First of all when these religions first came in, they were very friendly, all seemed to be good people of faith, courteous visitors, sweet-talking, presenting ideas and views different from those of the East, and seeming to be novel and good. However, after entering China for a period of time and familiarizing themselves with the path, they began to mess around, establishing churches, developing believers, moving out the cult of the godfather and cheating money.

1) Western churches emphasize "God": Yes, but their believers have named "God", such as "Jehovah", "Allah", and so on, which are all false names, and then they describe their Patriarchs directly as "Gods" or "Prophets".

Even the godfather was born on a "Virgin", like a contemporary godfather who changed his birthday and claimed to be the reincarnation of a certain Buddha, so as to emphasize that he is a God, so as to recruit believers to worship him, and whoever opposes their deception will be killed. Like Christianity, which killed many anti-God scientists in Europe in its early years; Islam, which killed many writers and editors who opposed Muhammad as a prophet. Buddhism is even stranger, combining "Buddha", "God", and "Religious leader" into one; worshipping God is the same as worshipping Buddha, and worshipping Buddha is the same as worshipping religious leader, and they make a fake mud tires for people to kneel on!

It is fine for these Westerners to treat their godmasters as prophets, but which of these godmasters is more prophetic than the Chinese Yuan Tiangang and Li Chunfeng? It was predicted long ago that "Wood, fire, gold, water" and all these western false religions were stopped by the easterners, so stop lying to people. Besides, why don't the Chinese form a church and get a bunch of brainless believers to worship the prophet Li Chunfeng and collect money? It is a sign of mental illness for westerners to transition to a "Godly" way of interpreting religion and then use it to oppress people and even subvert other countries and governments.

2) Western churches talk about "True goodness": yes, but in reality they are using true goodness to enrich themselves, so if you want true goodness, then donate all your money to the church. For example, those chakra lamas and Buddhist temples, if you don't pay for their overpriced tickets and incense, then get out! This is how religion is used to trick people's good hearts for commercial hype and psychosis.

3) Western materialism talks about "Revolution": it is OK, but they talk about revolution as power coming out of the barrel of a gun, killing landowners and capitalists, such as in the former Soviet Union, and then use counter-revolutionary words to imprison people, shut down the Internet, build all kinds of walls, block criticism, and even kill innocent people, resulting in a large number of unjust cases, which is a manifestation of transitory faith and manifestations of mental illness.

It is because the Orientals have discovered the Western

Church's transitional interpretations and manifestations of psychosis that they have come up with ideas to stop them. Note that it is stopping their fraud and worship of false gods, not rejecting some of the so-called right viewpoints they put forward in the early days, nor killing believers and bombing big Buddhas for such excesses. How accurate and detailed the prophets of the Tang Dynasty were!

3. What Shame Western Religion Has Brought to the Chinese People

This is to say from the historical development of the Western religion to China, for example, Buddhism, in the Han Dynasty come into, or obey rules and regulations, but in the chaotic era of China's North and South Dynasties, they built idols and enrichment, so that most of China's fools are kneeling at the feet of this Indian (The Tang Dynasty's Wu Zetian change the Indian avatar for her avatar), so humiliating to the personality of the peoples of other countries? Historically, Shakyamuni and Confucius and Laozi are the same era of people, also known as the "Master". Why didn't Confucius and Laozi do the same thing? Put a statue of Confucius all over India and let them all kneel down and worship him! (Note: Siddhartha Gautama himself did not say that he was God, so that believers are kneeling to him, but the gang of crooked missionaries in India, the God, the Buddha and the Lord of the Church into one, with the Lord of the Church kneeling to them to recruit foreign fools, to carry on the fraudulent wealth.) To the Chinese, kneeling to a foreign religion leader as a God is a great shame to humiliate a nation.

Islam entered China during the Tang Dynasty, and at first it was also a disciplined religion, but when its followers grew in strength, especially during the chaotic times of

China during the Five Dynasties and Ten Kingdoms, they kept colluding with foreign forces to enter Xinjiang, attacking Ningxia, Shanxi, and Hebei, occupying a large portion of China's land, and at one time trying to create a new country to divide it, which was also a great shame to the Chinese.

Christianity also entered China during the Tang Dynasty and did nothing for a long time, but in the late Qing Dynasty, when China was poor and weak, the army was sent to push the religion. And China did not send troops to occupy Western lands, it was also a great shame to the Chinese that they attacked China so much, burning royal gardens, looting public property, and signing unequal treaties.

The Communist religion was copied from "Equalizing the rich and the poor" by the western Marx, because he didn't like to work, he thought that the capitalists exploited him and extracted his surplus value, and he wanted to gather the poor and share with rich people money every day, and all the countries bombarded him everywhere, he was a psychopath who shouted for revolution. This is nothing, but in China's chaotic and impoverished Republican warlords time, and the Communist was introduced into China by the Soviet missionary Comintern, and constantly encouraged to carry out armed uprisings, killing landlords and capitalists, resulting in more than 50 years of turmoil from 1921 to 1977, until the era of Deng Xiaoping to vindicate the landlords and capitalists, and reform and open up the economy. However, the resulting civil war between peasants and landlords over the Communist Party of China and the late movement of dead people can not be counted, which is also a great shame for the Chinese people.

So in the view of the prophetic seers of the Tang Dynasty, it is a great shame that Western religions, with their so-called right views in the beginning and then spreading to China, forcing the Chinese people to kneel down and worship their godmothers, taking advantage of China's weakness and chaos and anarchy, and then expanding until they forced the government with arms and brought wars and a lot of deaths to the Chinese people.

4. What the East uses to wash away its shame

To sum up, the shame brought by the Westerners to the Easterners is mainly ideological and cultural, and extends to killing and war, i.e., in peacetime it is a friendly missionary, accumulating strength, and in wartime, it picks up a gun, turns against the enemy, and ends with killing and war.

China's rulers through the ages have known this in their hearts, but they have been powerless against the people's war tactics employed by Western religions and have no good theories to stop them, so they have resorted to extreme methods in a hurry to stop them by killing people, such as the killing of Christians and the burning of foreign churches in the late Manchurian Qing Dynasty, the forcible return of Buddhists to secularism during the Cultural Revolution, and the imprisonment of Xinjiang's radical Muslim terrorists. However, this kind of strong medicine can not stop the religious virus and wash away the ideological and cultural shame, but instead bring a large number of refugees and hurt the innocent. Most of the civilian believers are nothing more than women and children, or brainwashed, ignorant worshippers.

Western religions are backward and ignorant things, they are viruses and mental illnesses, hard killing can kill the viruses, but it will also kill the good people who are brainwashed. So it is necessary to use the Eastern theoretical vaccine to strengthen one's immunity, or to isolate the group of severely mentally ill terrorist believers, to stop their scams, to recognize their tricks, and to improve the wisdom of the people of the East and the world.

To pierce the veil of Western religion with intellectual and cultural civilization is to wash away the shame of the East that has been invaded by Western culture for thousands of years.

Note that this was spoken by the Tang Dynasty prophets Li Chunfeng and Yuan Tiangang, and is in no way a deliberate codification of our taunting of these four great Western religions, but merely a correct interpretation. The Tang Dynasty prophets also deeply understood the contemporary roots of charlatanism and mental illness, as well as what the Orient wants, and also praised our theoretical system of washing away shame, which is the 47th photo in the back, rather than using war, or the prophet would not have said that.

In addition, the ancient prophets also carefully reminded that today's world, regardless of the East and West, will not easily recognize the theory system of the "Eastern Galactic Civilization" at the beginning, i.e., the prophecy, "If we do not know anything about the East and the West, we will not be able to help the people". They have 5-7 billion believers (False information), kneeling and desiring war everywhere, and will surely "Deny" that they are sick in the head, which is the "Negative pole" of the prophecy. But don't be anxious or worried, the future will change, and soon it will "Come to pass".

Therefore, it does not matter whether you agree or disagree with the world today, because the prophets of the ancients have already predicted today, and they are almost 100% correct. If you can present your discussions and better interpretations, and convince all people, then it may be really closer to the truth.

II. Explain further

1. War Mania as a Mental Illness

The “45th prophecy” of the 《Tui Bei Tu》 offers layers of hidden meaning, intricately woven into its illustrations, verses, and characters. The complex nature of these prophecies makes them nearly impossible to decipher before the events have taken place. This specific image in the 45th prophecy symbolizes a war maniac, where the prophet depicts a crazed individual wielding a spear aimed at the Sun. This illustration serves as a metaphor for the irrational and destructive nature of war-crazed minds.

The prophecy's creators cleverly used this metaphor to distract self-proclaimed experts, guiding their interpretation towards literal war scenarios. In doing so, it subtly eliminates irrelevant interpretations and focuses on the underlying message about the delusion of those consumed by war-mania. The prophecy critiques these so-called "Experts" and religious figures who fail to understand this deeper allegory, ultimately exposing their lack of insight.

The “War mania” illustrated here speaks to the societal obsession with conflict and the glorification of warfare, rooted in the madness of a few individuals. These individuals, driven by their mental illness, manipulate large populations into wars, with devastating consequences. In today's world, according to the prophecy's interpretation, “Scammers and people suffering from mental illness” dominate society, misleading the masses with false ideologies, as the authors of 《Tui Bei Tu》 foresaw.

2. Religious Mental Illness

The second explanation delves into "Religious fanaticism", a theme prevalent in many civilizations, particularly in Western "Stellar civilizations" as described here. These civilizations revolve around two main elements: a "Dictator emperor" and a "Religious leader", much like celestial bodies orbiting the Sun. The prophecy portrays these figures as conmen: dictators posing as the "Red Sun" (A direct symbol of deception in the 43rd prophecy), and religious leaders who brainwash their followers, rendering them mentally unstable, represented in the 45th prophecy.

Historically, religious fanatics and monarchists supporters have been portrayed as "Warriors of steel", who blindly follow their leaders into wars, sacrificing the dignity and worth of individuals in the process. These followers become mere pawns, devoid of any individual value, brainwashed into dying for causes that serve only the interests of the rulers or religious leaders.

In the prophecy, "Eastern wisdom" seeks to completely "Expose and dismantle" the fraudulence of religious leaders and despotic rulers. It warns against worshipping false Gods and pseudo-prophets, critiquing modern religious institutions that continue to exploit followers. The prophecy challenges the notion of any individual or leader claiming divinity or prophetic status. Instead, it encourages a "Rational and enlightened" approach to human affairs, viewing all forms of organized worship or religious authority rooted in control and deceit as a form of "Religious mental illness".

This interpretation of 《Tui Bei Tu》 acts as a "Rejection of authoritarianism and blind faith", aiming to unveil the dangers of fanaticism and manipulation of the masses by religious and political figures. By doing so, it advocates for a world free from the control of false prophets and dictatorial rulers, who rely on “Deception and spiritual manipulation” to maintain power.

III. The Encryption of Prophecy

1. Ingenious Encryption in Prophecy

The “45th image” of 《Tui Bei Tu》 is cleverly encrypted and follows the “44th prophecy”, in a way that connects it back to the “43rd prophecy”. The 43rd image warns of “Frauds and deceivers”, while the 45th addresses “Mental illness”, specifically war mania and religious fanaticism. Sandwiched between these two is the “44th image”, which describes the "Sage", an enlightened individual. The arrangement itself is brilliant, as it portrays the Sage standing between deception and madness, symbolizing that taking a step too far in either direction leads to peril.

The image paints a clear picture: many people, in their pursuit of wisdom, attempt to cross the “Narrow bridge” symbolized by the Sage's path. However, most will fall into either deceit (Fraud) or madness (Fanaticism), highlighting the “Fine line” between enlightenment and delusion. This setup ------ placing the Sage between these extremes ------ is a “Masterstroke” of prophecy from the Tang Dynasty, showcasing how the ancient Chinese prophets foresaw even “Modern issues” of political manipulation and mental instability. They even foresaw the use of the term “China” as a national identity, long before modern states replaced dynastic names.

1) The Mystery of the Phrase "Wood, Fire, Metal, Water"

A central part of the "Encrypted prophecy" that has confounded interpreters is the phrase "Wood, Fire, Metal, Water, to cleanse this great shame". Many have tried to interpret this in terms of the traditional "Five Elements", noting the absence of "Earth". Some have linked this to land or territory, but the interpretation remains elusive.

Unlike many over-complicated analyses, where people "Over-analyze" or "Twist" meanings to fit their preconceived ideas, the authors of 《Tui Bei Tu》 were more direct. They didn't use unnecessary metaphors or convoluted wordplay. If something was meant to be known, it was presented clearly; if it wasn't, then the meaning was left unsaid.

The prophecy seems to warn of "Charlatans and false prophets" in contemporary society, particularly religious leaders who might claim they embody the qualities of the "44th image", the Sage. To guard against these impostors, the "45th image" strengthens the understanding of the "44th", showing that while many might claim they follow the path of the Sage, they are more likely to be frauds or delusional fanatics. The "45th image" also alludes to the "Unique theoretical framework" that the Sage brings to the world, likely centered on "Eastern wisdom and philosophy", offering an alternative to the false doctrines of both West and East.

2) Reinforcement from Other Prophecies

The 《Tui Bei Tu》 prophecy is further supported by other famous prophecies, including 《Qian Kun Wan Nian Ge》, 《Shao Bing Ge》, 《Ma Qian Ke》, 《Mei Hua Shi》, and 《Maya Prophecies》. These ancient texts also caution against "Charlatans" and warn of the "Misinterpretation" of future events. In this context, the "45th image" serves as a final safeguard, reminding followers that true wisdom and insight cannot be faked or hijacked by the masses who claim prophetic knowledge.

There are even astonishing details in other prophecies, such as 《Tie Guan Shu (铁冠数)》, also known as 《Tou Tian Xuan Ji (透天玄机)》, where it is said, "Born in the Meng family, lived in the Zhao family" This striking prediction delves into "Personal familial details", adding to the incredible foresight displayed by these ancient prophecies. The specificity of such predictions ----- down to surnames and living arrangements ------ serves as a testament to the "Remarkable accuracy" of these prophetic texts.

This layer of encryption within 《Tui Bei Tu》 is intended to protect the integrity of its message from the hands of impostors, while also serving as a guide for those truly seeking enlightenment.

2. Japanese hypothesis

Regarding the assumption that 《Tui Bei Tu》's 45th image refers to a war between China and Japan, where the Sun symbolizes Japan (Due to its flag and the title "Land of the Rising Sun"), a counter-analysis suggests that this interpretation may not be valid. Here are some key points:

1) Cultural Analysis

Japan's cultural foundation is deeply influenced by China, particularly during the Tang Dynasty. In many ways, Japan can be seen as an extension and preserver of ancient Chinese culture. Though Japan later adopted Western technology, it did not bring any major cultural shame to China. Instead, it is part of the "Sinosphere", upholding traditional Chinese values, especially those from the Tang period.

After World War II, Japan experienced rapid economic recovery and provided substantial economic aid to China, helping in its development. This aid was based on post-war reconciliation rather than aimed at humiliating China. Therefore, from a cultural or intellectual perspective, Japan did not cause China any lasting disgrace.

2) Counter-Evidence in War

If we consider whether Japan brought "National disgrace" to China through war, two major historical events are often mentioned: the Boxer Rebellion (Involving the Eight-Nation Alliance) and the Second Sino-Japanese War. However:

- The “Boxer Rebellion” involved multiple nations, not just Japan.
- The “Second Sino-Japanese War”, while brutal, did not end with China's permanent humiliation. Japan invaded Nanjing and caused tremendous suffering, but it did not fully defeat the Chinese government. Eventually, China fought back, and Japan surrendered at the end of World War II, with the loss of millions of Japanese lives. China's revenge was achieved through Japan's surrender, meaning there was no unresolved "Disgrace".

Similarly, Japan's “Pearl Harbor” attack on the U.S. temporarily humiliated America by sinking several warships, but the U.S. eventually retaliated with atomic bombs, killing hundreds of thousands of Japanese citizens. This too ended in revenge, without leaving an unaddressed sense of national disgrace for the U.S.

Thus, in terms of culture and war, Japan does not owe China any unrepented humiliation. Instead, Japan has reflected on its war wounds and aided China's reconstruction post-war, acting with a sense of reconciliation.

3) The Improbability of Future War

A future war between China and Japan is highly unlikely. Japan is culturally more conservative and traditional than China. Its companies, many centuries-old, continue to maintain the ancient Tang Dynasty culture, while respecting a feudal emperor system (Though its government adopts Western-style parliamentary democracy). Japan has also mastered Western technology, whereas China has remained aligned with the Soviet-style system, losing some of its own cultural direction. Despite the abolition of the emperor, China's governance retains elements of a bureaucratic, feudal system.

In some areas, China is now seen as less advanced than Japan, Korea, and Taiwan. South Korea maintains Song Dynasty cultural traditions similar to Japan, and Taiwan has inherited the Republic of China's culture ------ both regions being part of the broader Sinosphere. According to predictions, the future will be marked by "Nine Nations in Spring", suggesting a peaceful coexistence between mainland China and its neighboring countries.

If China were to attempt to avenge its past defeats by launching a war and aiming to capture Tokyo, it would be highly improbable and could lead to an even more devastating loss for China ------ especially if the U.S. were to intervene. Therefore, it is entirely unlikely that 《Tui Bei Tu》 's 45th image refers to Japan.

3. Slander and Verification

There are numerous so-called "Bloggers" online who, after exhausting their mental efforts and still failing to decipher 《Tui Bei Tu》, resort to slandering the text. They claim that prophets can make mistakes, or even suggest that the sequence of 《Tui Bei Tu》 has been tampered with by various rulers over the ages. It's as if the authors of 《Tui Bei Tu》 are obligated to write their prophecies according to the expectations of these modern interpreters. When the predictions don't align with their analysis, they immediately conclude that the sequence of the prophecies is wrong or that the prophet made errors.

History is like a mirror. These contemporary "Bloggers" claim to be so good at deciphering 《Tui Bei Tu》, but why haven't they written their own prophecies? It's one thing to predict a thousand years ahead, but how many of them can even accurately predict events for the coming years? As of now, it seems that the most well-known modern prophets are all foreigners, like Russia's Boriska and India's Abhigya Anand. Why is there no Chinese prophet among them?

Going further, it seems that 《Tui Bei Tu》 didn't use particularly intricate encryption when predicting past dynasties. People could easily guess which significant historical figure the prophecy referred to. So why is it that by the time we get to the modern era, particularly the 43rd, 44th, and 45th images, the prophecies are suddenly layered with encryption?

The reason is mainly that the 44th image refers to an ordinary person ------- a civilian theorist who is indifferent to fame and fortune, does not recruit followers, and does not seek to profit. The authors of 《Tui Bei Tu》 knew that by this era, many "Experts" would have already deciphered all previous prophecies with 100% accuracy. They would then start to backtrack and fabricate future predictions. Because of the rampant fabrications, it became hard to distinguish between true and false interpretations. Therefore, the authors added multiple layers of encryption, ensuring that the majority of the so-called "Bloggers" online could not decipher the true meaning. There is only one correct interpretation. For instance, many people claim that the 43rd image is about the unification of Taiwan or that the 45th image is about a war with Japan --- these are undoubtedly false interpretations. All these "Masters" are deceiving with their explanations. If so many people could all get the interpretation right, then what would be the purpose of encryption? Even if all people in the world tried to decipher it at the same time, they still wouldn't succeed.

Next, we must look to history for validation. The verification is simple: there is no war between China, Japan, and Taiwan. Therefore, all the fabricated and erroneous interpretations can be dismissed.

(Original writing from January 2022, for academic discussion, shared in "Blue Mountain Poetry Pavilion.)

Fig.C21-8 Book《Tui Bei Tu》

Appendix 3: The 46th Image of 《Tui Bei Tu》, A Prophecy of the Fate of Russia and China

Abstract: The Russia-Ukraine war serves as the trigger for Russia's devastating defeat, leading to the collapse of the Communist ideology's origin. Eastern European countries undergo transformations, which in turn influence the major political changes that will occur in China.

----

1. The Trigger of the 46th Image

Here, I will provide further explanation on the cause of the 46th image. Previously, in the analysis of the 46th image, it was believed that the events would soon occur in China, but the specific cause was unclear. There needed to be a trigger, and now, with the outbreak of the Russia-Ukraine war, it has become clear. The trigger for the 46th image is the second half of the 45th image, which concerns the Russia-Ukraine war.

Earlier predictions mentioned 10 major global disasters, of which the following have already occurred:

1) Earthquakes (Globally),
2) Tsunamis (Southeast Asia and Japan),
3) Nuclear contamination (Japan),
4) Forest fires (Globally),
5) Locust plagues (Africa),
6) Volcanic eruptions (Globally),
7) Floods (Asia and Europe),
8) Extreme heat and cold weather (Globally).

These events gradually seem like they are being orchestrated, as if controlled, such as the 9) pandemic (Globally).

What, then, is the 10th disaster?

Initially, it was believed that the Gods would simultaneously strike down the world's major religious leaders overnight, similar to the biblical plague in Egypt that killed the firstborn. However, based on current developments, it appears that the Gods do not intend to extinguish all four major religions at once. Instead, they will first eliminate one ------ specifically, the modern religion of "Marxism". God inspired Putin through dreams to start a war, which will lead to the direct destruction of the source of Marxism, as predicted in the second half of the 45th image. Following this, in the 47th image, global religions will be eradicated. Thus, the 10th disaster is war, specifically referring to the Russia-Ukraine war.

In the 45th image, it is shown that the four major Western religions, driven by madness, initiated wars, deceived the masses, and slaughtered people. Throughout history, three ancient religious institutions instigated many wars, but in modern times, the culprit is the autocratic religious state, with Putin as the war criminal. Russia is the birthplace of modern Marxism, with Marx as its founder. From Russia, Marxism spread, leading to the creation of Marxist followers and "Pastors" (Though these terms are no longer used in the same way today).

This clarifies the 45th image: the first half discusses how the four major religions will be unified by an Eastern theoretical system, while the second half presents an example, in which one modern religion is stopped, or at least “Will no longer dare to claim supremacy; its military power is exhausted, and its fate is sealed”.

Russia, as the leader of many Eastern European countries and so-called friendly nations, is the source and leader of the Marxist religion. It has long claimed to be the "Leader" or "Dominant force", with another layer of meaning referring to the "Bear" (As Russia is often symbolized as the "Polar bear"). However, after the Russia-Ukraine war, Russia's "Military power is exhausted, and its fate is sealed".

The Russia-Ukraine war began on February 24, 2022 (If you sum the digits of the date: 20 + 22 + 2 + 24 = 68. Similarly, if you add the dates of the beginnings of World War I and World War II, the sums also equal 68), which suggests that this is already the third world war. Russia and its allies (Some of whom send troops, like Belarus and Chechnya; others offer support, like North Korea and Iran) form a loose coalition against Ukraine, NATO, and the UK-US alliance. This is reminiscent of World War II, where the world fought against Germany, Italy, and Japan. It is also a war between "Democratic parliamentary systems" and "Feudal county systems," or as some describe it, a war between "Democracy" and "Dictatorship". The nations supporting the US and UK are democratic parliamentary systems, while those supporting Russia are feudal or religious autocratic states, like Iran and North Korea.

This third world war, like the previous two, began in the European "Powder keg", and its endpoint has been foretold by the Tang Dynasty prophet, who called it the "Fire Fate" period. It is expected to end around 2024-2027, known as the Fire Era. At that time, "World unity" will be achieved, meaning that the democratic parliamentary systems will prevail, and global consensus will be reached. The end of Marxism's source is another form of the "Fate is sealed" prophecy, as feudal systems have recently merged with religious systems. For example, the autocracy of emperors and theocracy of religious leaders are closely aligned.

2. Major Events in China as Foretold by the 46th Image

The prophecy about China in the 46th image is particularly intriguing. China will neither attack Taiwan or Japan, nor directly confront the US and UK. Instead, after the world embraces "Democratic parliamentary systems", China will experience internal strife. This is expected to occur during the "Fire Fate" period (Year 2024 - 2027) or sometime thereafter. More precisely, the Russia-Ukraine war serves as the catalyst for the major changes that will take place in China, as predicted in the 46th image.

In modern times, China has been quite a peculiar country. It was drawn into the Korean War without fully understanding the situation, leading to the needless deaths of many soldiers. Now, it finds itself involved in the Russia-Ukraine war, and it's unclear what the Chinese leadership is thinking. China seems to have been brainwashed by Western Marxism and is using its own propaganda to further mislead its people. From the day China cast its vote against removing Russia from the United Nations, it became entangled in this divinely orchestrated third world war.

China has historically been relatively backward and poor. It was only after Deng Xiaoping's three major political maneuvers and his efforts to strengthen ties with the US over the last 40 years that China became prosperous. However, neighboring countries like North Korea and Russia have continuously dragged China down. Is China destined to return to the closed-off and isolated state of 40 years ago?

The timeline of events predicted by the prophecy is as follows:

- 41st Image: 1949-1977, lasting 28 years
- 42nd Image: 1978-1989, lasting 11 years

- 43rd Image: 1990-2012, lasting 22 years (In the midst of a 30-year period)
- 44th Image: 2013-2021, lasting 8 years
- 45th Image: 2022, the defeat of Russia and the collapse of the Western Marxist church
- 46th Image: Significant internal changes in China, likely within 2-5 years after the previous image
- 47th Image: The downfall of the remaining three major Western religious institutions, occurring approximately 5-20 years later

In summary, the Russia-Ukraine war has accelerated the global acceptance of the "Democratic parliamentary system". Within the next 20 years, this system will dominate the world, gaining the recognition of most people. However, the four major Western religious institutions will perish, with one falling within 2-5 years and the remaining three within 5-20 years.

Meanwhile, the Eastern universal Law and the theory of Galactic Civilization will take a leading role in shaping the world. This is the interpretation of the short-term prophecy. Though the "Democratic parliamentary system" will gain temporary supremacy, regional wars will not cease immediately. The subsequent images of 《Tui Bei Tu》 ----- from the 48th to the 59th images ---- will be analyzed step by step as they continue to unfold.

The long-term prophecy remains unchanged: eventually, all nations will be unified under a "Unified republican system", and racial distinctions ---- red, yellow, black, and white ---- will blur, bringing harmony across all regions. This global integration aligns with the prophecies about the arrival of the Galactic Civilization. We will continue to observe the developments.

(Original article from April. 2022)

Five. Postscript

The Book of Wisdom Education

Abstract: Every celestial body in the universe, or every star system with intelligent beings, will have individuals who write similar books as wisdom education texts. These works serve to strengthen the spiritual faith of Earth's current inhabitants, establish a common belief system for all intelligent life in the universe, and spread universal spiritual truths. The aim is to reform the educational system on Earth, rebuild moral values, and integrate life sciences, natural sciences, and social sciences ---- similar to the revelations seen in crop circles.

For thousands of years, religious scriptures have preached kindness, righteousness, and morality. Yet, despite these teachings, prisons have multiplied, and more people are treated like animals in confinement ----especially political prisoners, who are often the product of dictators and religious autocrats.

Rulers portray themselves as dragons and phoenixes, heavenly beings whose words are law, while religious authorities elevate their leaders to the status of deities. They preach basic human values like goodness, righteousness, and morality, portraying these simple ethical concepts as universal laws worthy of worship. At the same time, those who criticize these rulers and religious institutions are often harshly controlled, labeled as rebels disrupting order and harmony, and charged with fabricated crimes.

While the ruling class views the people as troublesome and lacking goodness ----- justifying the use of military force, police, and prisons ----- the people, in turn, see the government as corrupt and hypocritical, demanding revolution to overthrow them. However, many revolutions merely replace old governments with new autocratic or theocratic regimes, leading to continued oppression and idolization. The root cause is a lack of understanding of the universal laws and an overreliance on rigid dogma.

Moral teachings like kindness and righteousness might have had some use in the past during times of primitive, slave, or feudal systems when people were ignorant and uncivilized. Even today, in countries ruled by theocratic, feudal, or authoritarian regimes, these teachings may hold some relevance. However, for future generations, these concepts will become obsolete.

In the future, there will be no need for prisons, as people will inherently understand truth and goodness. The focus will shift toward elevating the collective knowledge of humanity, aligning with the higher intelligence of beings throughout the universe. People will turn to the wisdom of Galactic civilizations for guidance, standing at the center of the universe to observe and comprehend everything that happens across the cosmos.

The books we write today will not require organized religions, parties, or rituals for dissemination. There will be no need to preach the same moral teachings that have been repeated for thousands of years, as the universal laws are already imprinted on every person's brain before birth. Even if one denies these laws, they are still inherently bound by them.

The "Universal Law" embodies the principles of unity across all religions, equality among all beings, compassion, harmony, and the pursuit of exploration and development.

- "Unity of all religions" is akin to every star system, like the Sun, being part of a larger galaxy, like the Milky Way.
- "Equality of all beings" means that everyone, with their unique brain patterns, believes in the same truth.
- "Compassion and harmony" reflect the peaceful coexistence of all individual elements, like each strand of hair on a head.
- "Exploration and development" represent the outward expansion of knowledge, rather than adhering to rigid dogma.

In this vision of the future, humanity will embrace the wisdom of the universe, transcending dogma and advancing toward a deeper understanding of life, science, and the cosmos.

1. Three of the most controversial historical figures are discussed here:

1) Jesus was a famous religious figure, an ordinary righteous man who knew something about prophecy and claimed to be the Son of God. He was able to gather crowds, and the church he created only amassed wealth after his death, causing the believing and unbelieving disciples to split into two factions. The believers further claimed that he was born of a virgin and had supernatural powers; the unbelievers claimed that he was hanged and was only human. The two factions argued for thousands of years, which in turn led to many cults and countless wars. Did he bring peace to the world? Or war? Extremely controversial!!!

2) Marx was a famous philosopher who advocated revolution, eradicating the old system and creating a new one. The church he created turned into a party, just amassing power, and in the process of the development of the party church, just killing people, and led to many cults, causing disasters to the world. His so-called socialism and communism only create poverty and class conflicts, and further dictatorship, corruption and despotism. Did he bring wealth to the world? Or poverty? Extremely controversial!!!

3) Einstein was a famous scientist with a high IQ, and his theories made atomic energy possible, which is supposedly beneficial to mankind, such as industry and power generation. But late in his life he pushed scientists to turn to weapons and persuaded the US government to build nuclear bombs. The first atomic bomb was dropped on Japan, killing 200,000 people, 80% of whom were women and children. Did he steer scientific research toward weapons? Or nature exploration? Extremely controversial!!!

2. Comparison with Chinese Civilization

1) In Chinese history, so-called religious figures like Confucius of Confucianism and Laozi of Daoism never gathered large crowds or developed many followers. They did not claim to be Gods or engage in widespread worship, nor did they organize churches or scam people for money. (However, emperors often claimed to be the Son of Heaven and deities.) As a result, there were few religious wars.

2) Chinese philosophers never spoke of revolution or deception for power but emphasized unity. Unity does not require killing, while revolution involves killing and seizing power. Therefore, China has always been a civilization focused on unity, whether in language, ethnicity, or territory.

3) Chinese scientists invented gunpowder long ago, but they never promoted it to rulers or continued researching it to develop large-scale killing weapons. Instead, they used gunpowder in festival celebrations, so the invention of gunpowder by Chinese scientists never caused any deaths.

This book lays the foundation for unifying religion, philosophy, and science. If followed, the world can achieve peace. However, some refer to it as a book of judgment, a judgment on all things and people on this planet. I believe it is not a judgment on ordinary people, as people are judged daily by government laws and fines.

3. The advanced always judge the backward

From a historical perspective, the advanced always judge the backward: Viviparity species judge Egg-laying species, Democratic systems judge Feudal systems, and Galactic civilizations judge Stellar civilizations. If these books are to be seen as judgment books, then the Galactic civilization judges the Stellar civilization based on "Heaven", "Earth", and "Man".

1) "Judging Heaven" means judging the false churches that claim to represent "Heaven". Their doctrines violate the laws of the universe. False churches promote worship, deifying their leaders, calling them Saints and Kings, dividing believers into sects, and producing a few chaotic scriptures. They recite and chant them without understanding, creating divisive symbols for each sect and inciting hatred and war between churches.

False churches often copy everything the religious leader says, and many leaders are illiterate, with disciples writing on their behalf. Mistakes are blamed on disciples, yet these writings are treated as unchangeable doctrine. Anyone who criticizes them is labeled an enemy of the church or an enemy of the faith, often punished with extreme measures. This was widespread in the Middle Ages, where they killed civilians, philosophers, and scientists. In modern times, the labels have changed to terms like counter-revolutionary, anti-faith, or anti-ideology.

2) "Judging Earth" means judging false rulers who manage the "Earth". Their governance violates the laws of the universe. When slavery should be replaced by feudalism, they stick to slavery. When democracy is needed, they choose dictatorship or feudalism. They control propaganda, abuse laws, build brutal armies and police forces, use the people's taxes for corruption, and suppress public dissent.

False rulers, or dictators, usually believe the nation belongs to them, the laws are their creations, and no one can judge them. Strong weapons and armies are their private parties' military forces. Due to internal conflicts and disunity, the United Nations can do little about dictators. However, the laws of the universe can judge them, which is called violating the "Heavenly Way". In history, almost all rulers have been judged. Good rulers are praised, like Lincoln, the father of democracy. Bad rulers are either killed by the people or forever nailed to the pillar of shame in history, like Hitler and Saddam Hussein.

3) "Judging Man" means judging the false scientists who study "Man", not ordinary people. False scientists often create large-scale killing weapons like biological, chemical, and nuclear weapons. In dictatorial states, false scientists provide pseudo-technology to rulers, dismiss supernatural human abilities as pseudoscience, recklessly exploit natural resources like oil and gas fields, and build dams that destroy the environment. Engineers who invented machine guns, nuclear, chemical, and biological weapons killed millions in the world wars. There are also pseudo-sociologists who deceive the people according to the ruler's ideas.

The evil combination of false churches controlling thought, false rulers funding operations, false scientists providing technology, and false sociologists controlling propaganda formed the structure of Hitler's government. Together, they had massive destructive power. False churches controlled minds, false rulers provided money, false scientists developed technology, and false sociologists controlled propaganda. Once they wage war, they can destroy all of humanity.

In every society with humans, there are people writing similar books, serving as books of wisdom and education. These books aim to improve the universal spiritual beliefs of the people on this planet, establish a shared belief system for all intelligent life in the universe, and spread the spirit of the cosmos. These books advocate for reforming the education system on this planet, rebuilding morality, and integrating life sciences, natural sciences, and social sciences, just like the messages revealed by crop circles.

4. Finally summarize the significance of the foundation of this book:

1) Eastern Galactic Civilization: innovative theoretical foundation of the seven-colored golden book (Future China is great again)

2) Galactic Atlantis continent civilization: promote into Australia new continent civilization (Australia more great)

3) Galactic Pyramid Civilization: display monuments labeled as Egyptian pyramids + Mayan pyramids + Australian red monoliths (Egyptian, Mayan and Australian civilizations become even greater)

4) Galactic Natural Law Foundations: Taoism + Confucianism + Legalism (Converted into Freedom + Democracy + Rule of Law) (Insisting that they made Europe and America greater)

5. The uplifting significance of this book:

1) Galactic Civilization Enhancement Beliefs: Christianity + Islam + Buddhism (Emphasize righteousness + truth + goodness) (Suggest to keep the useful parts and discard believers, organizations and parties)

If perfect religious books: 《Bible》 + 《Koran》 + 《Buddhist scriptures》 (Expanding the interpretation and deduction of the three Western scriptures)

2) Galactic civilization to improve the philosophy: Innovative Philosophy Universal Law (”.” , “1”, “0”)

E.g., perfecting the foundation of classical books: 《I Ching》 + 《Tao Te Ching》 + 《Tui Bei Tu》 (Expanding the interpretation and deduction of the three oriental scriptures)

3) Galactic civilization to enhance the state system: the Primitive Zen ceding system, the Slave enfeoffment system, the Feudal county system, the Democratic parliamentary system and the Unified republican system (Ultimately establish a Unified republican system)

4) Galactic civilization enhancement education: Primary school + Secondary school + University + Super university + Ultimate university (Unified religion, unified philosophy, unified science around theoretical research)

5) Galactic Civilization Enhancement System Science: “Natural Science” (Mathematics, Physics, Chemistry ......); “Social Science” (Politics, Economics, Psychology ......); “Life Science” (Zoology, Botany, Astronomy ......)

6) Galactic civilization establishes new disciplines: Gravitational Waves + Electromagnetic Waves + Life Wisdom Waves (Expanded Natural Interpretation and Extrapolation)

7) Galactic civilizations promote engineering: “Intelligence Technology” (Human Brain Intelligence + Human Intelligence + Artificial Creative Intelligence ......); “Space Technology” (Calculators + Materials + Rockets ......); “Communication Technology” (Light Wave Technology + Infrared Wave Technology + Ultraviolet Wave Technology ......).

6. From spatial extrapolation:

1) The Stellar civilization's beliefs and education are spread by means of oviparous organisms, reproducing large numbers of believers and students every year like bees, amassing vast amounts of money to build worship hive buildings and schools, and spreading its educational venues all over the globe. It prints educational materials and propaganda in large quantities to raise funds and money.

Such education will lead to Examination machine, the division of nations, the disorganization of beliefs and frequent wars. So the state can only control the spread, strengthen the army, suppress the people and slaughter the authors.

2) The Galactic civilization spreads its beliefs and education by means of fetal organisms, reproducing just a few every year like advanced animals, and educating in three fixed places around the globe: Egypt, Maya and Australia. It is inspired by new philosophies, propagates civilization and treats money like dirt.

This education has led to global unity, belief in the splendor and wisdom of life. So the country is advanced, opens up to all propaganda, abolishes the military, awakens the people, and encourages peace.

7. Looking at the time projection:

The year 2012 is the turning point in time, marking the rise of Galactic civilization and the fall of Stellar civilization, confirming the Mayan and 《Tui Bei Tu》 prophecies.

(End)

www.ingramcontent.com/pod-product-compliance
Lightning Source LLC
Chambersburg PA
CBHW071621230426
43669CB00012B/2029
* 9 7 8 1 7 6 3 5 4 8 0 7 7 *